A WORD OF THANKS

The present generation of Harvard men, and the generations to come, will always be grateful to the many alumni who gave their time and effort to the Program for Harvard College. This book is given to you as a continuing reminder of the College and a token of her appreciation for your share in the Program's success.

Nathan M. Pusey

President

Cambridge, May 15, 1960

THE

Harvard

Book

Selections from Three Centuries

EDITED BY

William Bentinck-Smith

Harvard University Press

Cambridge, Massachusetts

1960

© *Copyright, 1953, by the President and Fellows of Harvard College*

Program Edition

Typography by Burton J Jones

Library of Congress Catalog Card Number 53-11123

Printed in the United States of America

PREFACE

THERE comes a time in the life of almost every Harvard man when he suddenly awakens to the fascination of Harvard. Very likely it may be the moment when he sees the line of alumni marching to Commencement, or some other academic ceremony, as Emerson saw them at the Centennial and noted in his *Journal*

> Cambridge at any time is full of ghosts; but on that day the anointed eye saw the crowd of spirits that mingled with the procession in the vacant spaces, year by year, as the classes proceeded; and then the far longer train of ghosts that followed the company, of the men that wore before us the college honors and the laurels of the State — the long wind ing train reaching back into eternity. . .

Emerson's observation — something which the visitor, Rupert Brooke, also noticed — is an eerie moment, when the Harvard man becomes briefly a part of history in a way which is curiously elusive and hard to describe. It is a rare experience and yet it occurs over and over in different individuals.

In a similar mood many Harvard men have thought that somewhere and sometime a Harvard anthology should be put together. There have been Harvard anthologies before — the collections of stories and poems from the *Harvard Advocate* are examples — but none which sample material from the three centuries of Harvard history. That the task has now been carried out can be blamed upon three of my good Harvard friends who made the original suggestion and did the urging — Thomas J. Wilson, Director of the Harvard University Press, David McCord, Executive Secretary of the Harvard Fund Council, and William M. Pinkerton, Director of the Harvard University News Office.

It struck the editor in the beginning that the project should not be just an anthology of writing, related or unrelated to Harvard, by Harvard men; nor should it be simply writing about Harvard by anyone; but that the field should be limited in general to Harvard men (students or alumni) or Harvard teachers, writing about Harvard subjects — an essence of "Harvard literature" as I have tried to indicate in the introductory essay on "Writing Like a Harvard Man."

So much has been written about the first American college that it was almost a physical necessity from the beginning to put some limitations on the field. Yet Harvard has not suffered thereby. This method has served as a more intimate and subtle way of illustrating the historical and intellectual growth of Harvard as well as showing something of what Harvard has meant to its great and near-great sons and something of what it has meant to its teachers and students. Every educational institution is, after all, merely a refinement of the ancient combination of teacher, student, and log. The reader, therefore, should not expect to find in this volume much educational detail in the form of descriptive passages about courses and professional teaching methods. The book is intended to amuse, to stimulate the interest, to reflect something of the spirit of Harvard in its three centuries and more of existence.

After testing a chronological arrangement, the present form was decided upon where a simple collection of prose and a few poetical samples are arranged in approximate chronological order under headings suggesting some of the aspects of Harvard life. To facilitate the pleasure of reading, antique spelling and punctuation have, in most cases, been modernized.

The editorial task has been a most enjoyable process of self-education and a previously unimagined revelation of the vast amount of material available on the subject. Through the medium of his several volumes on Harvard, my constant mentor has been the Tercentennial Historian, Samuel Eliot Morison. No one investigating a Harvard subject can fail to be amazed at his sure and skillful pioneering, and anyone writing about Harvard owes him a tremendous debt. Without the assurance of Professor Morison's volumes an editor would be foolhardy indeed to essay the field.

First among those who have aided me in the search over the past four years has been Marjory Perry Johnson, whose cheerful, patient, and competent assistance has materially shortened a long job of research.

I must acknowledge with gratitude the courteous and unstinting aid of Dr. Clifford K. Shipton, Custodian of the Harvard University Archives, of Kimball C. Elkins, Senior Assistant, and present and former members of the Archives staff, including C. Wesley Drew, Anne Ewing Zettek, Mary M. Meehan, Charles Stoddard, and Elaine Trehub.

I owe thanks to my colleagues of the *Harvard Alumni Bulletin*, Henry M. Mahon, Norman A. Hall, Jane E. Howard, Barbara Gibbins Duffy, Nancy Shaw Esty, and Natica Bates. But especially do I owe much to David W. Bailey, Secretary to the Harvard Corporation, and to G. W. Cottrell, Editor in the Harvard University Library, for invaluable criticism at strategic moments in the development of this volume.

I must thank Frederick L. Gwynn, Assistant Professor of English at Pennsylvania State College and formerly head tutor of Adams House, for his thoughts and practical additions in the critical early stages; and

George A. Weller of the *Chicago Daily News* for two long sessions of talk about his Harvard novel, *Not to Eat, Not for Love.*

Friendly discussion with that well-known expert, Hamilton Vaughan Bail, whose interest in Harvardiana has already produced an invaluable scholarly volume, *Views of Harvard,* has helped immeasurably in clarifying my thoughts and has added several important items to my own list of Harvard fiction. My friend and classmate, Dr. I. B. Cohen, Associate Professor of the History of Science and of General Education, has helped greatly with his questions and proposals. Finally I must thank Marion L. Hawkes of the Harvard University Press for her patient and industrious supervision of the preparation of the manuscript for the printer.

CREDITS AND ACKNOWLEDGMENTS

The Trustees of the Adams Manuscript Trust for permission to make use of the typescript entitled "Extracts from the diaries of John Quincy Adams, 1787, and his son, Charles Francis Adams, 1825, relating to Harvard College from 1786 to 1880," selected and transcribed by Henry Adams and William G. Roelker (entry for Thursday 16th July [1857], pp. 45–48).

Mr. Edward C. Aswell, literary administrator of the Estate of Thomas Wolfe, for the quotation from the Wolfe notebooks, first published in the *Harvard Alumni Bulletin,* November 22, 1947 (p. 214).

Barnes & Noble, Inc., for excerpts from the *Journal of Jasper Danckaerts, 1679–1680,* edited by Bartlett Burleigh James and J. Franklin Jameson. Copyright 1913, 1941, Barnes & Noble, Inc., reprinted 1952.

The Boston Herald Traveler Corporation for Walter Prichard Eaton's "Here's to the Harvard Accent" and Lucius Beebe's "Notes on a Dry Generation," two articles printed in the Harvard Tercentenary supplement of the *Boston Herald,* September 13, 1936 (pp. 22 and 23).

Mr. Samuel Chamberlain and the Harvard University Press for permission to use excerpts from Donald Moffat's introduction to *Fair Harvard,* Cambridge, 1948 (pp. 5–10).

Mr. Carey J. Chamberlin, Secretary of the Harvard College Class of 1913, for the quotation from the biographical sketch of Richard C. Evarts, published in the 25th Anniversary Report of the Class.

University of Chicago Press for the brief quotation from "The American College in Fiction" by Richard C. Boys, first published in *College English,* April 1946 (pp. 379–387).

Colonial Society of Massachusetts for various quotations from the publications of the Society, in particular from Volume XIV (p. 193), for the text of Thomas Shepard's letter to his son, and from Volume XXXI (pp. 327 *et seq.*), for selections from the College laws and customs.

Constable and Company for the brief quotation from *Unforgotten Years* by Logan Pearsall Smith, London, 1938 (p. 115).

Mr. Laurence Curtis, Secretary of the Harvard College Class of 1916, for the quotation from the biographical sketch of Robert Nathan appearing in the 25th Anniversary Report of the Class.

Mr. John Dos Passos for the brief quotation from *Nineteen Nineteen* in his trilogy *U.S.A.*, published by Harcourt, Brace and Company, New York, 1933 ("Harvard stood for the broad A. . .") and for the first chapter of his novel *Streets of Night*, George H. Doran Co., New York, 1923 (pp. 9–30).

E. P. Dutton and Company for permission to use "Dr. Parkman Takes a Walk" (chapter 10, pp. 207–227), from *The Proper Bostonians*, by Cleveland Amory, New York, 1947.

Rinehart & Company, Inc., for the use of a brief quotation from Norman Hapgood's *The Changing Years*, "The phrase most used in our time to describe the college. . ." (p. 74).

Harcourt, Brace and Company for the excerpt "That Outer Whiter World of Harvard," from *Dusk of Dawn: An Essay Toward An Autobiography of a Race Concept* (pp. 34–40), by W. E. Burghardt Du Bois, New York, 1940.

Harper & Brothers for the quotation beginning "All my memories of the four years were happy ones. . ." from Thomas William Lamont's *My Boyhood in a Parsonage; Some Brief Sketches of American Life Towards the Close of the Last Century*, New York, 1946 (pp. 187–188), and for the quotation beginning "Students at Harvard. . ." taken from the *Journals of Francis Parkman*, edited by Mason Wade, New York, 1947 (I, 256).

Harvard Bulletin, Inc., proprietors of the copyright of the *Harvard Graduates' Magazine*, for numerous quotations from comments and reviews, but particularly "The Graduate's Window" [by Bernard De Voto] from the March 1932 issue (p. 298); "The True Harvard" by William James, September 1903 (pp. 6–8); "Harvard on the Eve of the Revolution," selections from the diary of Samuel Chandler by Sarah E. Mulliken, March and June, 1902; and for "Reunion" by Edward Weeks, a portion of "The Graduate's Window" in the issue of September 1933 (pp. 47–50).

Harvard Bulletin, Inc. for many and various excerpts from the *Harvard Alumni Bulletin*, particularly "The Social Future of the Harvard Man," by John P. Marquand, July 10, 1948 (pp. 776–779); "Harvard's Past" by Samuel Eliot Morison, November 22, 1935, pp. 265–274; "The Lights Come On," an unsigned editorial by David McCord, and various quotations from the Charles Garden sequence of David McCord, as well as the excerpt "Enter A Former Naval Person," taken from the news columns (pp. 11–15) of the issue of September 18, 1943; the couplet from "Maxus in Caelo" which originally appeared in The College Pump, June 20, 1942 (p. 517); "The Sophocles Myth," by Charles Loring Jackson, March 15, 1923 (pp. 716–720); "To Copeland at Eighty," by Arthur Calvert Smith, April 26, 1940 (pp. 897–898); "Emerson Hall Revisited," by Jacob Loewenberg, January 29, 1949 (pp. 348–351); Frederick West Holland's undergraduate diary for the years 1827 and 1828, first published in the September 29, October 6, and October 13 issues in 1927; Bishop Lawrence's account of Phi Beta Kappa Day in 1871 from the issue of December 14, 1940 (pp. 343–345); extracts from the undergraduate diary of James Woodbury Boyden, September 24, 1949 (pp. 6 and 30); "The Education of Epes Todd" by Frederick L. Gwynn, February 12, 1949 (pp. 388–391); "The Alumnus" by Willard L. Sperry, April 26, 1947 (pp. 587–590); Alan Gregg's "Forty Years After," originally published anonymously in the issue of April 7, 1951 (pp. 546–548); "Harvard As Seen by a Harvard Man," by LeBaron Russell Briggs, December 18, 1912 (pp. 208–217).

The *Harvard Crimson* for the brief quotation from William I. Nichols' article "Habits, Customs, and Manners at Harvard," published in the booklet "The History and Traditions of Harvard College," Cambridge, 1928 (pp. 68–69).

The *Harvard Lampoon* for numerous references and quotations and especially the excerpts from *Rollo's Journey to Cambridge*, originally published in 1880, and for the selection from *Alice's Adventures in Cambridge*, by R. C. Evarts, Cambridge, 1913 (pp. 7–15).

President and Fellows of Harvard College and the Harvard University Press for numerous quotations from *Three Centuries of Harvard*, Cambridge, 1936, *The Founding of Harvard College*, Cambridge, 1935, and *Harvard College in the Seventeenth Century*, Cambridge, 1936; for quotations from the addresses of A. Lawrence Lowell, printed in President Lowell's *At War with Academic Traditions in America*, Cambridge, 1934; for the brief quotation from "Handbook for English A," Harvard University, 1948; for quotations from William G. Land's *Thomas Hill*, Cambridge, 1933; for the description of President Lowell by Theodore Pearson, published in Henry Aaron Yeomans' biography, *Abbott Lawrence Lowell, 1856–1943*, Cambridge, 1948 (pp. 369–370); for the selection from *On Writing the Biography of a Modest Man*, by Rollo Walter Brown, Cambridge, 1935 (later published as one of the sketches in Mr. Brown's *Harvard Yard in the Golden Age*, A. A. Wyn, New York, 1948); for the quotations from the undergraduate letters of Edwin Arlington Robinson to Harry de Forest Smith, 1890–1905, published in *Untriangulated Stars*, edited by Denham Sutcliffe, Cambridge, 1947 (pp. 18 and 38–48); for the selections from *Charleston Goes to Harvard, The Diary of a Harvard Student of 1831*, edited by Arthur H. Cole, Cambridge, 1940 (pp. 87–93); and for the excerpt from the diary of Maria Sophia Quincy, included in *The Articulate Sisters*, edited by M. A. DeWolfe Howe, Cambridge, 1946 (pp. 176–189).

President and Fellows of Harvard College for the use of manuscript materials in the Harvard University Archives — Eliphalet Pearson's "Journal of Disorders," 1788; Thomas Hill's letters to his family and the typescript of an address about Louis Agassiz, included among the Hill papers; Richard Waldron's "Admittatur"; Oliver Wendell Holmes's letters from 1828 to 1830, now in the Houghton Library; and the selections from the official letter books of Presidents Quincy, Sparks, Felton, and Hill.

Hispanic Society of America for permission to translate into English a portion of the Spanish text (pp. 121–123) of *The Diary of Francisco de Miranda. Tour of the United States, 1783–1784*, edited with an introduction and notes by William Spence Robertson, Ph.D., Professor of History, University of Illinois (New York, 1928). Copyright, 1928, by the Hispanic Society. Translation by James E. Duffy, Ph.D.

Houghton Mifflin Company for selections from *The Heart of Emerson's Journals*, edited by Bliss Perry, Boston, 1926 (pp. 10 and 103); for quotations from Bliss Perry's autobiography *And Gladly Teach*, Boston, 1935 (pp. 232–233 and 253–254); for the selection "What a Day for Our Race!" from *Charles W. Eliot* by Henry James, Boston and New York, 1930 (pp. 80–84); for the quotation from *Bret Harte, Argonaut and Exile* by George R. Stewart, Jr., Boston and New York, 1931 (p. 201).

Mr. Horace Howard Furness Jayne and the Houghton Mifflin Company for quotation of the letter describing President Walker's inauguration from *The Letters of Horace Howard Furness*, edited by H. H. F. J., Boston and New York, 1922 (pp. 16–19).

Little, Brown and Company and the Atlantic Monthly Press for the use of "Jane Toppan's Case," taken from pp. 79–85 of *The Happy Profession* by Ellery Sedgwick, Boston, 1946; Little, Brown and Company for "Mr. Hilliard Tells All" (chapter II, pp. 15–28) in *H. M. Pulham, Esquire* by John Phillips Marquand, Boston, 1941.

Mr. Malcolm J. Logan, Secretary of the Harvard College Class of 1915, for the quotation from the biographical sketch of John P. Marquand, which appeared in the 25th Anniversary Report of the Class.

The Macmillan Company for the use of a portion of *Philosophy 4* by Owen Wister (pp. 45–95), New York, 1903. Copyright 1901, 1903, 1931, The Macmillan Company.

The Manchester Guardian and Alistair Cooke for Mr. Cooke's account of the Harvard-Yale cricket match, which was published in the May 21, 1951 issue of the *Guardian* (p. 5).

The Massachusetts Historical Society for selections from *The Education of Henry Adams*, Houghton Mifflin Company, Boston and New York, 1918 (the first part of chapter IV, pp. 54–55); for the biography of Joseph Mayhew from *Sibley's Harvard Graduates: Biographical Sketches of Those Who Attended Harvard College* (Volume VIII, 1723–1730, pp. 730–734), compiled by Clifford K. Shipton; and David Sewall's account of his journey to Portsmouth, New Hampshire and return, with Tutor Henry Flynt in the year 1754, which was printed in the Proceedings of the Society, First Series (Volume XVI, 1878–1879, pp. 5–11) and edited by Charles Deane.

Mr. Robert Nathan for permission to use portions of the second chapter of *Peter Kindred*, Duffield & Co., New York, 1919 (pp. 21–28).

The *New Republic* for John Reed's "Almost Thirty" in the issue of April 29, 1936 (pp. 332–333).

The *New York Times* for the quotation from "Inquiry Into College Humor," by R. C. Lewis, *New York Times Magazine*, January 4, 1948, p. 10.

Charles Scribner's Sons for the quotation "I want to go to Princeton. . ." from F. Scott Fitzgerald's *This Side of Paradise*, New York, 1920 (p. 27); for a portion of the chapter "The Harvard Yard" from George Santayana's *Persons and Places, The Background of My Life*, New York, 1944 (pp. 186–202); for chapter VII (pp. 89–93) from *Of Time and the River* by Thomas Wolfe, New York, 1935; for the excerpt from "American Pleasures," chapter VIII (pp. 326–332), from Paul Bourget's *Outre-Mer: Impressions of America*, New York, 1895; and for the use of chapter IV, "Boston and Harvard," from Rupert Brooke's *Letters from America*, New York, 1916.

Mr. Lee Simonson for the excerpt from his autobiography *Part of a Lifetime, Drawings and Designs, 1919–1940*, Duell, Sloan & Pearce, New York, 1943 (pp. 6–9).

Mr. George Weller for the quotation beginning "Generalizing about Harvard. . ." on p. 109, and for the chapter "eleven o'clock in November" taken from his novel *Not to Eat, Not for Love* (pp. 47–52), published by Harrison Smith and Robert Haas, New York, 1933.

Whittlesey House for the brief quotation from *The United States*, edited by Doré Ogrizek, New York, 1950 (pp. 121–122).

In 1875 two members of the Class of 1874 published a mammoth two-volume work designed for the library table, containing contributions of general and historical interest on the subject of Harvard. It is to that lavish example of printing and illustration and to its editors, F. O. Vaille and H. A. Clarke, that the present volume owes part of its title.

William Bentinck-Smith

15 August 1953

CONTENTS

III

TROUBLE UNDER THE ELMS

IV

"YOU CAN TELL A HARVARD MAN . . ."

V

SPORTS AND SPORTING MEN

VI

HER SOLITARY SONS

VII
THESE FESTIVAL RITES

VIII
THE ALUMNI

IX

SOME VISITORS FROM AFAR

INTRODUCTION

WRITING LIKE A HARVARD MAN

THERE is apparently some doubt in various professorial and editorial minds whether Harvard men know how to write — especially, perhaps, when they write about Harvard. The doubt has been accentuated by the development of dictating machinery and the seemingly constant supply of the supposedly inept who were forced year after year into Harvard's required freshman course in English composition. Wherever the uncertainty developed, it was certainly given its most helpful boost two decades ago by an editorial which appeared in the *Harvard Graduates' Magazine*, then in the charge of Bernard De-Voto. Now Mr. DeVoto is a man who practices forthrightness, among other virtues, and he let loose a salvo on the subject of Harvard writing which has seldom, if ever, been equaled.

"Writing like a Harvard man" is, happily, a restricted and occasional pathology. It derives from a resolution to be elegantly correct, to avoid the crassness of plain statement, to decorate one's pages with the ornaments of learning, and to be, above all, pompous, long-winded, and drowsy. The style is based on the once admired art of oratory but owes something to the formal inscriptions of public buildings. It has been most nearly epidemic in the reports of Harvard officials, too few of whom have cared to learn from the distinguished English of Mr. Eliot and Mr. Lowell. The books of one kind of Harvard man will show it till history ends. . . How far it has infected the literature of America outside the law only the monograph can determine, but many a page of fiction and biography must have turned rancid in imitation of Harvard elegance.

You may know this style by its genteel inversions and balances. "He was a man just and patient, honorable and fastidious, courteous in manner, inflexible in action, in leadership preëminent, in counsel unexcelled." That is writing like a Harvard man. You may know it by its parade of classical terms: "he entered the agora" for "he went to the legislature." You may know it by its unwillingness to use short words when long ones can be found. A subscriber writes, "Your pusillanimity impels me to request that my name be incontinently removed from your rolls"; he means, "Your stuff is awful — cancel my subscription." You may know it by its phobia of plain speech, its "valiant" for brave, its "decease" for death, its "purchase" for buy, its "imbibe" for drink, its "veritable" for real, its "asseverate" for say, its "donation" for gift; by the timidity of its qualifying "perhaps" and "it may be" and "so to speak"; by its sounding

latinisms, its "evokes" and "evinces" and "educes," its "epistolary,"
"contumacity," "extemporaneously," "negotiation," and so on. It is a style
forever dressed in spats — forever going to a wedding (that is to say,
"nuptials") or a funeral ("obsequies"). At its best it has in decay a leisure
and correctness that the Eighteenth Century, to which it thinks itself
related, had in health. At its worst it is death in prose.

Still, it is a style. That is, its effects are produced deliberately. The
man who is "writing like a Harvard man" has a terrifying purpose, but
at least he knows how to accomplish it. He knows which words will produce the effect he desires, and he uses them with full awareness of what
they say. And that is something.

Mr. DeVoto's impatient prejudice against "writing like a Harvard
man" is probably excusable in an editor weary with a particularly long
run of uninspiring contributions. Fortunately, before even beginning, he
allows Harvard men the loophole of "a restricted and occasional pathology" in practicing the devastating art. For whether or not Harvard men,
as a tribe, can really write — in the sense of constructing for their ideas
a sound literary framework — they have been putting pen to paper (or
paper to platen) with fierce determination since the day before Nathaniel
Eaton wisely decided not to keep a diary. (He was the rascal, you will
remember, whose accounts and disciplinary methods gave the founding
fathers so much trouble.)

No small part of the literary activities of Harvard men has been devoted to the subject of Harvard itself. It is in this narrower area that a
true yardstick can be found with which to measure the abilities of one
Harvard man against another. It should in fact offer the perfect gauge
for a case study of Harvard writing, for writing about his College has
long been the avocation and prerogative of the Harvard man. "Generalizing about Harvard," remarked the English A instructor in George Weller's *Not to Eat, Not for Love*, "is a great Harvard vice. You began doing
it before you came here and the habit had you. You came to Harvard to
find out why you had been so possessed. You will wallow in it four more
years and still you won't know the answer."

Yes, Harvard men write — some with their left hands, some with their
right hands, or with the stenographic aid of a dark-eyed intelligent secretary — and they love to reach broad conclusions about Harvard with the
feeling of membership that implies the privilege of self-criticism. But
for those who spread the comfortable creed that Harvard men write
better than other mortals, there will be others sure that they don't; just
as there are some people convinced that all Harvard men are short-haired
Bostonians who speak with a broad A, while others are equally certain
that all Harvard men are long-haired left-wingers who sport Phi Beta
Kappa keys.

It is more nearly the truth that Harvard men are no different than

any other men, except they happen to have gone to Harvard and instinctively resent the attempt to type them as this or that. One trouble, of
course, is that Harvard is big and old and rich and just a bit smug about
its tradition of freedom; and of course, it's a delightful temptation to
jibe at the members of a community who seem to have worked out a
pretty good system of life for themselves and are rather pleased with the
results on the whole.

The really important difference between Harvard men and other men
is that the former went to Harvard and the latter did not. Like it or not,
any entering Harvard freshman is subject to what might be called collegiate predestination. It does not matter that every Harvard generation
is made up of several thousand individuals. The Harvard man is bound
to be thought something that he probably is not and that handicap should
have some subconscious effect on his writing.

Take these examples of what non-Harvard sources say about Harvard:

Item first. – A selection from *This Side of Paradise* (1920) by F. Scott
Fitzgerald in which Harvard is seen through the boyish eyes of Amory
Blaine, conversing with his father confessor, Monsignor Darcy.

> "I want to go to Princeton," said Amory. "I don't know why, but I
> think of all Harvard men as sissies like I used to be, and all Yale men as
> wearing big blue sweaters and smoking pipes."
> Monsignor chuckled.
> "I'm one, you know."
> "Oh, you're different – I think of Princeton as being lazy and good-
> looking and aristocratic – you know, like a spring day. Harvard seems
> sort of indoors – "
> "And Yale is November, crisp and energetic," finished Monsignor.
> "That's it."

Item second. – The perpetual Harvard joke, a type of American college humor recognized among the ten most prevalent jokes in an analysis
of the subject by R. C. Lewis, himself a Harvard man, which appeared
in 1948 in the *New York Times Magazine*.

> Son of Harvard father: "Mamma, is it the rapid vibration of mole-
> cules in the extremity of the slipper which induces the slight tingling
> sensation noticeable after punitive measures of a corporal nature have
> been resorted to?"

Item third. – A passage from *The United States* (1950), an illustrated
guide, edited by Doré Ogrizek and written by eight apparently non-
Harvard men and women.

> Yale is the butt of most of Harvard's jokes. "He's no gentleman, he's
> a Yale man" – is a favorite sally. Yale is also Harvard's greatest competi-

tor scholastically and in wealth and in the number of famous men it produces.

The Yale man type as opposed to the Harvard youth type is more rugged and lusty, more athletic, freer in speech and thought and action than his more intellectual neighbor.

A Yale man, if he has been a Whiffenpoof (a society for the encouragement of conviviality) might burst into song in a public place with complete confidence that it was a good thing to do. His Harvard brother might conceivably sing too, but never with the same abandon and confidence.

This sort of sneak attack is deeply resented by the Harvard man. Why should he allow himself to be typed as a "character" any more than as a writer? Witness the reaction of John P. Marquand when a Marine captain affectionately said of him: "You really wouldn't be a son of a bitch at all if you weren't a Harvard man."

It did not appear to occur to him for a moment that I might still have been what I was if I had gone to Dartmouth or Cornell. I like to think he meant that I speak with a broad A, and obviously many people feel that all Harvard graduates should. But a few experiences such as these . . . have taught me one great truth. If you have ever been to Harvard, you will never be allowed to forget it.

Actually I have found that I can get on very well with most people until they discover this error in my past. Then there is a slight pause in the conversation, a lifting of the eyebrows, an exchange of meaning glances, and someone always says, "You never told us you were a Harvard man." It is time then to select some new and learned subject of conversation, and ever after things are never quite the same. Something more is expected. A mental picture has arisen, and an iron curtain has descended. Yes, for some reason, in the hard outer world through which we have all struggled, there is a fixed belief that a Harvard man is more studious, more conservative, more easily shocked than other men. He loves to quote Ralph Waldo Emerson. He is different from other American boys. Now what have we all done — or have any of us done anything — to have earned this reputation?

Harvard graduates, as I have known them, do not discuss classics in their leisure hours, or consistently vote Republican. Instead they come from divergent backgrounds and react in startlingly different manners, both socially and politically. A Harvard man now lies buried in the precincts of the Kremlin. Another was the founder of the New Deal, and several are still economic royalists, in spite of everything. There are devout Catholics, pagans, and atheists in the ranks of Harvard men. There are Harvard Frenchmen, Germans, Chinese, and Siamese. There are some very intellectually brilliant Harvard men and a great many more very dumb ones, and yet the belief still persists that we have all been poured into a mold, and, collectively, we are a part of American folklore.

No, Harvard men are really not different from other men except for the varying degrees of pride they feel in having attended Harvard. "To me Harvard is the glory of New England and of America," declared the grand old Dean Briggs, adding generously, "yet I can see how a Yale man may love Yale as I love Harvard." This is, of course, the ultimate in Harvard breadth of view and generosity to a worthy rival.

Mr. Marquand's reaction is suggestive of a peculiar quality in Harvard men and their writing. Only the Harvard caste have the precious privilege of commenting upon the flaws in Alma Mater. When outsiders attack, the answer is defense. Indeed it is a temptation not to pose a universal theorem about the Harvard character from a discovery which Epes Todd made in *Not to Eat, Not for Love*. Epes found in his freshman year that Harvard's football play is fundamentally defensive in nature. In broader terms every blow at Harvard seems directed toward the heart of each son of Harvard. What answer is there but defense? Only the Harvard man, therefore, has the right to criticize Harvard, and this he does with a will — but only because he sets a high standard for his University. As Dean Briggs once wrote:

> Even loyal alumni seem at times to dwell on the flaws they see or think they see in their Alma Mater, rather than on her eternal greatness and beauty; and thus Harvard men get the reputation for cynicism. The College teaches every man to think for himself and to say what he thinks. It rarely occurs to a Harvard man that there may be a reason for concealing faults in his University; and often the very intensity of his love makes him feel the more keenly any failure of Harvard to reach perfection.

The avocation of self-criticism — an inalienable Harvard right — explains why the Harvard man is so often found wearing a hair shirt in public. If outsiders take the hair shirt to mean Harvard's inherent evil and ultimate collapse, the Harvard man does not; for him it is a perfectly natural garment to be worn over and over and, when thoroughly soiled, to be laundered in the nearest public lavabo. "I was amazed at the annihilating frankness with which Harvard men discussed the personalities and policies of their Alma Mater," Bliss Perry (in *And Gladly Teach*) recalled of his years of instruction.

> Indifference was surely not a characteristic of the alumni. If they disliked some fact or tendency pertaining to Harvard, they never hesitated in public or private to express their views. Astonished as I was at first by this broad latitude of criticism, I came gradually to see that it was one of the priceless traditions of a freedom-loving university.

These random reflections on some peculiarities of the Harvard character will perhaps make more understandable two strong motivating forces in Harvard writing — a wish to assess things fairly (the General Education Report called this "discrimination among values") and the development of a highly individual quality. Harvard indifference as an escape mechanism may once have been popular with a small and sophisticated group of undergraduates — and in a sense perhaps it still is; but otherwise it is a complete misnomer. As Norman Hapgood has remembered in *The Changing Years* (1930),

> The phrase most used in our time to describe the college was "Harvard indifference," and it was most inaccurate. To Harvard's glory, be it conceded, the effective part of her was more indifferent than some colleges to mob interests, to victories on the field, to classmates merely as such, to social elections that were badges of popularity en masse. To intellectual interests she was the opposite of indifferent, though it is true she questioned all things. . . In our college, as in the first university we seem to know, which was led by Socrates in the market place, the purpose of the students was inquiry into life.

The dislike for personal labels, for mere "belonging," for obscuring one's individuality, is a natural result of the Harvard precept about the academic components — "every tub must stand on its own bottom." Harvard indifference does not necessarily mean the desire common to Harvard men "to lead their own lives in decent privacy," as William I. Nichols, now editor of *This Week*, wrote in 1928 while he was still a part of the Harvard scene. This sort of remark makes the hackles of any Harvard man rise, for he is by instinct and education neither intellectual nor social isolationist. The Commencement orator for the Harvard Class of 1950, Melvin L. Zurier, came much closer to the target:

> We at Harvard pride ourselves on our indifference. It is indeed the hallmark of our entire education — or at least that is what many of us would have you believe. But Harvard indifference is really, I believe, the expression of a form of individualism, and a refusal to accept values on first appearance. As such, it is healthy, even if often misunderstood by the more thin-skinned among us, or misinterpreted by the Colonel McCormicks. . . Today, more than ever, we need individualism; and if indifference is a peculiarly Harvard conception of this, then hurrah for indifference!

The right to his hair shirt, if not in decent privacy then unashamedly in public, cannot be denied our Harvard man; for as Donald Moffat has said, "Every day is crisis day at Harvard, and on few of them, be it said to her credit, has she failed to take the line leading up and on." Did not Mr. George return to Harvard after many years and point out to Rollo that the inscription " 'wickedly placed upon University Hall' . . . still read in faint black capitals . . . 'The University is going to Hell' "?

The Harvard man may feel less comfortable with pen or pencil than his counterpart elsewhere — who is to tell? — but there is a deadly earnestness in the way he goes about the task of taking Harvard apart and putting it together again in a more beautiful and effective form. He has been doing it since the days of Dunster. And he is still doing it as the age of

Conant comes to a close. Recently, judging from the number of architectural criticisms in the *Harvard Alumni Bulletin*, he is almost literally putting Harvard together again, brick by brick. But if it were not that subject, the point in question might just as well be the form of the war memorial, or the future of the economics department, or the efficiency of the football ticket office, or the proper version of the 78th Psalm as sung at Commencement. Do Harvard men write? They certainly do. Once in a while, too, they may take themselves just a little seriously in their rendezvous with history and educational preëminence. These various gestures in the direction of pen and pencil should be kept carefully in mind before one impetuously samples the springs of Harvard literature.

Contemporary critics bemoan the low level of "college writing" — and, of course, they are right, even though the criticism is usually directed at the lack of first-class fiction with a college background. Writing about college life suffers most because it is done usually by the young or the old; but there is no lack of it, at least so far as Harvard is concerned. No one who has browsed in Harvard's remarkable archives or simply thumbed the pages of such local publications as the *Harvard Graduates' Magazine* or the *Harvard Alumni Bulletin* (which together span more than sixty years and more than fifteen college generations) can fail to be impressed by the immense amount of material which has been written about the first of American colleges.

If there are riches to be found in college literature, surely they can be revealed in Harvard's lode. It is probably no exaggeration to state that about no other American college has so much been written, and probably few universities in the world — save Cambridge and Oxford — could exceed Harvard in sheer quantity. Quality, however, is another matter. Harvard has had its Ella Wheeler Wilcoxes as well as its Shelleys, its Weemses as well as its Trevelyans. What should give Harvard men great comfort (again that self-analysis!) is that, considering the source, the level is surprisingly high. It should be, of course — since an institution of higher learning is supposed to show its members how to use their native tongue; and in view of Harvard's vaunted tradition of encouraging independent thinking as well, it is not surprising to find that the first two sentences of the handbook used successfully for many years in freshman English offers the following injunction:

A student's grade in English A depends upon his ability and progress in the use of written English and upon his proficiency in reading and class discussion which should contribute to his development as a writer. The instructors must therefore be certain that every paper submitted for credit in the course is the student's own work.

Even at the freshman level, writing like a Harvard man is to be a highly individual craft! Alas, it has not always been so, however. Harvard men have been writing about Harvard since the founding, with wisdom, skill, and affection — and then, like Harvard men in Mr. DeVoto's sense. In the realm of Harvard literature there are spiritual peaks as well as pathological valleys. There is, it must be admitted, much sameness and mediocrity in the scenery too, but the landscape as a whole looks impressively well from the heights and furnishes us a really remarkable view of the growth of a complex social body within the framework of American life.

Harvard's literary heritage is a reflection of the national conscience and its progress to maturity. In the first 150 years Harvard men were inclined to be men of few words — or men with the word of God to interpret — busy with the task of building a nation. Those who did write exhibited not literary skill so much as the cramped penmanship characteristic of a time unfamiliar with the Palmer method or the chancery hand; and even the Harvard presidents — perhaps especially they — were hindered by the necessity for showing off their knowledge of three tongues, without which they might not have been thought learned.

Is it any wonder that the honest prose of *New England's First Fruits,* so Biblical in style, should be one of the great masterpieces in Harvard literature; or that Henry Dunster's simple and moving appeal to his religious opponents should stand head and shoulders above the routine correspondence and official acts of other Harvard leaders? Early Harvard writing exhibits primary concern for the spiritual welfare of the students and reflects relatively little of the physical and intellectual side of Harvard life. Except for a reconstruction of the fragments so ably carried out by the master of Harvard historians, Samuel Eliot Morison, we must depend as a first source on the pompous *Magnalia* of Cotton Mather, the snatches of the official records, and on admonitory letters like that of the Reverend Thomas Shepard, Jr. to his son. The college laws tell much, but we might wish for more in the record like the distasteful confession of Mistress Eaton, who by stretching a point may be admitted to the realm of Harvard literature, since she was the wife of Harvard's first "master."

Instead we must be content with Mather's biographical history and his learned puns and wish that Harvard had had a Bradford or a Winthrop to celebrate its early years. We have to wait for the writers of the late eighteenth century to set aside their commonplace books and take up their diaries to tell us more about Harvard and its students than immediately meets the eye in the first hundred years of Harvard history.

That the Harvard man was capable of graphic and delightful writing in an earlier day can be guessed by the occasional masterpiece which has been preserved — David Sewall's lively account of his trip to Portsmouth, New Hampshire in 1754 with Tutor Henry Flynt, for example. How many of such human documents came from Harvard pens is anyone's guess. These are flashes of brightness and humor and grace in some of the com-

monplace books and isolated entries in the journals. But in general the
impression is that Harvard students were encouraged to show another
side to the public eye — a habit which was inclined to influence their adult
literary lives.

The last half of the eighteenth century was a period of plot, war, revolution, and unsettled conditions. For Harvard it was a time of tragedy,
too, for on the eve of American independence, Harvard suffered the
irreparable loss of the college library in the burning of Harvard Hall. This
disaster seems historically symbolic today of the hard times faced by the
little college during the critical years of the young republic.

By 1820, however, the Harvard fields could be said to be producing
a regular and satisfying literary harvest. It was the fashion to keep a
journal, and the number of such documents which have been preserved
is impressive. Letter-writing was the thing to do, and receiving mail was
just as popular. The students were attacking the administration and the
administration the students, usually over such simple subjects as the
proper diet for growing boys. Flights of poetic fancy were lavished on
Commencement and other festival days, and the would-be man of letters
tested his abilities in the meetings of the Institute or the Hasty Pudding.
Publications like the *Harvard Lyceum, Harvardiana,* the *Harvard Reg-
ister,* or the *Harvard Magazine* served not so much as the vehicle for
student opinion about college life as an instrument for focusing student
literary attention on subjects outside the Harvard world.

The local literature of the early nineteenth century is full of celebra-
tory verse in the style of Southey or critical trials in imitation of the
Edinburgh Review. Perhaps this was the golden age of writing like a
Harvard man in the DeVoto sense of the phrase! It has certainly never
been surpassed for artificiality and naïve pomposity. Harvard literature
of the time was full of ups and downs. On the credit side, however, were
geniuses like Lowell and Holmes, whose student letters — especially
those of Holmes — show precocity and skill far beyond the power of the
modern undergraduate, a fact all the more remarkable when one considers that Lowell entered college at fifteen and Holmes at sixteen.
They were the shining examples — and all the more shining because, in
contrast with their predecessors, their chief literary preoccupation was
not with their immortal souls or with their undergraduate philosophical
theories as to the nature of the universe. Harvard prose began to come
of age at the time of Lowell and Holmes.

It was not until well into the nineteenth century, however, that the
Harvard man really turned his hand to Harvard as a subject of literary
worth. Where their elders had once been more concerned with the religious principles instilled in Harvard youth, now both young and old took
their turn at depicting Harvard life — Harvard remembered, as it was

in the twenties and thirties during the days of Edward Everett Hale, Josiah Quincy, Jr., and Andrew Preston Peabody; or Harvard seen through undergraduate eyes like those of Horace Howard Furness and Thomas Hill. This too was the age when Oliver Wendell Holmes, that laureate of Harvard laureates, began the series of commemorative poems with which for forty years he greeted every class reunion and nearly all significant Harvard celebrations. In this period appeared also the first Harvard novel written by a Harvard man (*Fair Harvard*, published anonymously in 1869 by William Tucker Washburn) and the first full-length work of reminiscence (*Memories of Youth and Manhood*, by Sidney Willard, 1855).

If the Harvard literature that evolved as the product of these earnest efforts had any fault, it was that it was the work of immaturity or of senescence. Frequently too the Harvard man became so serious in his effort to portray the Harvard he loved that much of the serious work of the time fails to give the present-day reader much of a real-life picture of Harvard. And many of the attempts at humor seem laboriously juvenile to contemporary eyes.

It is as true of Harvard letters as in most directions of human endeavor that the simple and the human approach, wherever possible, has the most meaning to successive generations of men. Harvard poets provide positive argument to support this broad contention. In his maturity James Russell Lowell wrote a noble Harvard Commemoration Ode (1865) and spoke majestically of

> . . . that stern device
> The sponsors chose that round thy cradle stood
> In the dim, unventured wood,
> The *Veritas* that lurks beneath
> The letter's unprolific sheath. . .

And Holmes himself celebrated the 250th anniversary by declaring of Harvard's founder

> Here, here, his lasting monument is found,
> Where every spot is consecrated ground!

In our own time Hermann Hagedorn asked "What of the Light, Harvard?" and received approving applause from the Tercentenary throng. Edwin Arlington Robinson unfurled his fledgling wings and sang of

> the deathless lore
> That haunts old Avon's classic shore . . .
> In Harvard 5.

These are random samples of the noble verse for the noble occasion, of the undergraduate poet testing his verse forms. It is hardly strange that

these fragments are not what stand out in any review of Harvard poetry
— judged, that is, on both the skill of the poet and his universality in
treating the Harvard scene. Instead it is the mock epic, "The Rebelliad,"
the master work by Augustus Peirce, of the Class of 1820, who commem-
orated an almost forgotten food riot in the college commons. It is the witty
Dr. Holmes using his sharp humorous sense to good effect in "Parson
Turell's Legacy," telling the story of the "President's old arm-chair" in
the spirit of the wonderful "one-hoss shay"

> God bless you, Gentlemen! Learn to give
> Money to colleges while you live.
> Don't be silly and think you'll try
> To bother the colleges, when you die,
> With codicil this, and codicil that,
> That Knowledge may starve while Law grows fat;
> For there never was pitcher that wouldn't spill,
> And there's always a flaw in a donkey's will

It is also sparkling bits like the little anonymous undergraduate tribute
"To Bridget, My Goody" (traditional name for the college bedmaker)
which will continue to be appreciated throughout Harvard history:

> Here lieth the body
> Of Bridget my goody.
> In life she swept my room;
> But Death, who sweeps all things,
> Both great things and small things,
> Came along one day with his great wide broom,
> And swept her away to the silent tomb:
> So no longer she'll dust off my mantel-shelf;
> For Death has compelled her to dust off, herself.

The Eliots, Mackayes, Bynners, Cummingses, and Hillyers have gone on
to great achievements, but this does not mean that they should necessarily outrank in Harvard literature the less complicated lyricists. The noble
sentiments belong to the alumni multitudes crowding the Yard on days
of academic celebration. The human, the delightful, the everyday, belong
especially to Harvard letters — David McCord's lines in his "Charles
Garden" sequence,

> The loveliest of autumn sports
> Is running miles in simple shorts. . .

or Edward L. Viets's refrain in affectionate tribute to that late purveyor
of second-hand "suitings," Max Keezer,

> Officially it's very nice in Heaven,
> Confidentially I'm missing Harvard Square. . .

or Laurence McKinney's touching tribute to "Kitty, Copey, and Bliss."
From generation to generation these fill the bill better than the "crepuscu-
lar approaches to Parnassus." Give us, as the *Harvard Graduates' Mag-*

azine implored more than forty years ago, more poems showing local color and illustrating the realities of Harvard experience and fewer poems of "billing-and-cooing (mostly imaginary)" and of "*Weltschmerz* (mostly pumped up)."

It is as true of other forms of Harvard writing as it is of poetry. The art of Harvard fiction, only three-quarters of a century old, is filled with horrid examples of the Harvard writer's overenthusiasm. Inspired by such splendid models as Master Tom Brown of Rugby and Mr. Verdant Green of Oxford, Harvard novelists and short-story writers tried to outdo each other in depicting the merry adventures of Harvard undergraduates, a privileged class of happy-go-lucky wastrels who managed somehow, by pluck or luck, to by-pass examinations, endure initiations, and survive all celebrations. At the end of the college road might be the cheering crowd, the victory over Yale, and the beautiful Boston girl. Fortunately for Harvard literature not many of them fell into that special school of college fiction made popular by the late Burt L. Standish (Gilbert Patten) who produced, without benefit of an education in New Haven, more than 200 novelettes about those amazing Yale brothers, Dick and Frank Merriwell.

But some of the Harvard books were bad indeed. Take *Guerndale* (1882), for example. It is hard to believe that the author was the same who helped create that satirical Harvard classic *Rollo's Journey to Cambridge* (1880). Frederic Jesup Stimson puts words in the mouths of some of his undergraduate characters which never before or since emanated from a Harvard man. Of a certain sunset one youth is made to remark, "It looks like an omelette *aux confitures* . . . When you reach the seventh heaven . . . I hope you will call the attention of the authorities up there to the bad taste of our American sunsets." In another spot Guerndale and a group of his pals decide to relax their minds with a little champagne and burgundy. "Let us get drunk with good taste," declares one of the company. "This is an aesthetic symposium, as becomes a cultured Harvard man and not, as is coarsely expressed in the . . . daily papers, a simple drunk." Anyone looking for the source of the Harvard myth had better examine *Guerndale*.

Happily *Guerndale* is a low point in Harvard writing. In the fiction field, Harvard can well be proud of two of the best books ever written about the American college scene. One is Charles Macomb Flandrau's *Harvard Episodes*, a volume of short stories, published in 1897. This book, though severely criticized at the time of its appearance, has stood the test of years remarkably well. The other notable example is George Weller's *Not to Eat, Not for Love* (1931) which comes closest to the ideal college novel described by Richard C. Boys in his study of "The American College in Fiction,"

The book we are looking for . . . must show us all kinds of students and all kinds of teachers, not just the malcontents, nor, on the other hand, the completely uncritical, satisfied individuals. Most of our college fiction has lacked this sense of proportion. Furthermore, most of this fiction reflects an uncompromising bitterness toward the system, which may explain why most of our fiction about college is satire, often amusing, often needed, but not telling the whole truth; no doubt those who are content with their lot do not write about it. Probably no one book will ever achieve an objective approach, nor do we ask for such conformity; but there is room for a good college novel which deals fairly and honestly with the subject, one which will capture the intricacies of college life. The appeal of such a book would be infinite. . .

Scanning the period between the publication dates of these books by Flandrau and Weller, it is somewhat remarkable that *Harvard Episodes* had so little influence upon the shape of Harvard fiction. Flandrau had attempted a rather broad condemnation of a certain section of Harvard life with which he felt out of sympathy; and Harvard defenders rose up loyally. What the public seemed to want at the time were the boyish, light-hearted tales for which the *Saturday Evening Post* was prepared to pay good money. Harold Everett Porter, writing under the pen name of Holworthy Hall, summed up the case in the introduction to his volume of Harvard tales, *Pepper* (1915):

This book [he said] . . . never was intended to be serious . . . I wrote it, not to turn the searchlight of publicity upon the university, but because an editor wanted some college stories and paid me a good price to write these. Don't think for a minute that they are designed to revolutionize the social system!

A few years earlier a reviewer in the *Harvard Advocate* had remarked that

For some unexplained reason the general public seems to find the college man fascinating. It takes a deep concern in all his affairs — his athletics, his literary and social attainments, his pranks and follies. Consequently college fiction is becoming a popular kind of literature. It finds many interested readers of two classes, — the curious general public, and the graduates and undergraduates of the colleges chronicled. These latter are the only ones to whom these tales with all their merit and popularity, are really intelligible. We of Harvard may enjoy stories about other colleges, we can appreciate only those about our own.

At the peak of the popularity of the college story the *Harvard Lampoon* offered in 1906 some sound advice to budding authors who yearned to write of campus life:

This is not a difficult kind of story to write, requiring merely imagination and a certain knack in producing atmosphere.
It is well to begin by spending at least half a day at the University,

jotting down the names of streets and buildings. You will depend on these for local color.

Make your characters extravagant, financially and otherwise.

Make them appear several times stretched in lounging robes before a blazing fire while the rain patters on the window panes — and at least once in the front row at the Tremont.

Make them drink frequently and variously, and smoke on every possible pretext.

Put a bull pup in each chapter and a Morris chair on every page.

Talk familiarly of the Regent, Gore Hall, and clubs.

Ring in a lot of humor of this pattern: "Ah, old boy, all rosy from your bath," said Pete, as his roommate entered, dressed in one slipper. "Well, I may look rosy, but I don't feel in the pink of condition," answered Winnie, meditatively lighting a cigarette.

Introduce a girl who is innocuous and one or two who are not.

Fill in with startling exploits in which the cops and proctors invariably get left, and label the gilded hash *Claverly Jones, The "Queen" at Radcliffe,* or *The "Discount" at the Coop.*

The book will sell; likewise be one.

And the *Harvard Advocate* in the same year described the Harvard man's fictional adventures as follows:

Our first glimpse of him is as he was in his undergraduate days — carrying the ball across the line in the fabled victory over Yale, while frenzied multitudes thundered forth his name, and far, far up in the stands, She stood silent, both hands pressed tightly to her heart. He was not thinking of the victory as he sat that night in a corner of the club — he had escaped the congratulations of his friends to retire to this solitary spot. So She had sent him no word — well, no matter, all women are false, and the world a vain thing — he will forget. With a hollow laugh he lights a cigarette, and boards the Subway to Park. What a scene of animation, what radiant scintillating colors, how white the tables, how beautiful the women, how cheerful the sound of the ice clinking against the sides of his tall glass! But all is dark to him; darker still, as the hackman helps him up to his princely apartments in Claverly.

This is the cheerful beginning of our hero's career. The following June he graduates in a blaze of glory, being president of his class, captain of all the teams, class orator, and other things too numerous to mention. It is on Class Day that we see him for the last time as an undergraduate. They are sitting at a window in Holworthy — he and She — the strains of the band float gently up to them — below, strings of bright lanterns swing to and fro in the light breeze, and as he gazes down at the lively scene, his eyes grow moist. Dear old Harvard, dear old college days! A soft hand steals into his — ah, She understands. . .

From here the *Advocate's* Harvard expert, Kenneth B. Townsend, takes the hero to Red Gulch, somewhere in the Great West; but, no matter, we can imagine the results.

Five years after the appearance of F. Scott Fitzgerald's *This Side of Paradise* (1920), a novel which concerned itself seriously with the sig-

nificance of a Princeton education, the *Harvard Alumni Bulletin* offered
a wise judgment on the college novel. Certainly it is as true today as when
it was written.

> The true enduring picture of the contemporary undergradute will
> probably never be written, chiefly because his life, like that of any nor-
> mal, average person is hopelessly dull. We must have spice. We must
> peer fearfully over the escarpments of license and liberty if we are to look
> at all upon the young gentlemen who walk in the sequestered vale of
> Academe.

Just to bring this judgment up to date, we can refer again to Bernard
DeVoto. The postwar era has brought forth such college fiction as *The
Spire* by Gerald Warner Brace, *Groves of Academe* by Mary McCarthy,
and *The Stones of the House* by Theodore Morrison (a Harvard man
who manages to avoid being too specific when he writes about college
life). All three can be recommended. That they have college backgrounds is fortuitous; as Mr. DeVoto tells his "Easy Chair" readers in
Harper's Magazine: "The college novel is going to get worse on the average, not better; college has replaced the war as the natural subject for
first novels, and the ads are going to be full of hurt sophomores and dis-
enchanted seniors."

The alumni rolls are studded with the names of those distinguished
in American letters who have attended Harvard University. Unfortunately relatively few of them have tried to write about Harvard, perhaps for the very reason which the *Bulletin* guessed would forever limit
the perspective of "the true, enduring picture." Yet the words of the few
who have written about their University are worth reading and re-
reading. Not only is the best of what they have said well written, but
taken as a whole it tells us a great deal about the history of America's
oldest college in a way never to be discovered by merely reading history.

In using the novel and the verse form to demonstrate certain characteristics of a Harvard literature, it is easy to overlook the major sources
of Harvard writing — autobiographies, essays, history, humor, and the
notable contributions published in the *Harvard Graduates' Magazine*, the
Harvard Alumni Bulletin, and other Harvard journals. Along these paths
Harvard is rich indeed. A study of Harvard literature would include
such letter writers as Norton, John Jay Chapman, or the Roosevelts;
here would be found also historians like Francis Parkman or Samuel Eliot
Morison. There are biographers, for example, Henry James and M. A.
DeWolfe Howe. There are writers of autobiography like Henry Adams
and George Santayana. There are essayists, among them Arthur Stanley
Pease or Donald Moffat. There are romanticists like Lucius Beebe and
purveyors of good stories like Cleveland Amory. There is a Harvard of
high comedy in John P. Marquand's Harry Pulham and a Harvard of

tragic loneliness in Thomas Wolfe's Eugene Gant. There is even a boy's Harvard and a Harvard of crime, a graduate student's Harvard, a Harvard of the summer school, and a Harvard of the Faculty.

In this rich treasury is a measure for writing like a Harvard man, and while we may regret that so many skilled Harvard writers did not try their hands at this special subject, we may also rejoice that so many real craftsmen did find the time and the inclination. In the enthusiasm of the discovery, however, it would be well not to overlook Mr. DeVoto's remarks on the "restricted and occasional pathology" of writing like a Harvard man. In strict confidence it is possible to reveal for nearly the first time that in almost the same proportion as Harvard men are no different from other men, so are Harvard writers really no better than any other writers. Bliss Perry, the Williams graduate and English professor who spent twenty-three teaching years at Harvard, put it most kindly in his autobiography when he said:

> there was a comfortable creed that the graduates of Harvard wrote better than the graduates of other colleges. I kept to myself the dreadful secret that in ten years of reading manuscript for the *Atlantic* I had never observed that Harvard men wrote any better than Yale men or Bowdoin men or men like Howells and Aldrich and John Burroughs who had never gone to college at all! It seemed to me that writing was a highly personal craft, to be perfected only after long practice, and that it made little difference where or how the practitioner learned the rudiments of his trade. Many years afterward, I admired Professor Grandgent's courage in declaring his fear that Harvard students "write rather poorly and speak worse."

Taking pen in hand as a Harvard man is a dangerous thing; the rule of thumb is that when you are good you are very very good and, when you are bad, you are no better than any other bad college writer anywhere.

I

WHAT IS THIS PLACE?

"Is that you,
John Harvard?"
I said to his statue.
"Aye — that's me," said John,
"and after you're gone."

DAVID MC CORD (1940)

Harvard was founded by dissenters. Before two generations had passed there was a general dissent from the first dissent. Heresy has long been in the air. We are proud of the freedom which has made this possible even when we most dislike some particular form of heresy we may encounter.

JAMES BRYANT CONANT (1936)

All my memories of the four years were happy ones: there was everything to remember, nothing to forget. And I think, as I left the Yard behind me, there were two feelings uppermost in my mind. The one was how humbling an experience four years at college was — to begin to have realization of the vast stores of learning and thought that had been made available to us; the wonderful minds and men at whose feet, so to speak, we had sat. . . The second emotion that kept coming back to me was the sense of freedom that the atmosphere of Harvard and the years we had spent in it had brought home to us.

THOMAS W. LAMONT (1946)

IN RESPECT OF THE COLLEGE
(1643)

The most important early statement of the aims of the founding fathers in establishing a college in New England was contained in the "promotion pamphlet," New England's First Fruits, and the section "In Respect of the College" is thought almost certainly to have been compiled with the help of Master Henry Dunster himself. That he was not the actual author is probable because of the complimentary references to Dunster in the text, which contained also an outline of the curriculum and a summary of the college laws.

AFTER GOD had carried us safe to New England, and we had builded our houses, provided necessaries for our livelihood, reared convenient places for God's worship, and settled the civil government, one of the next things we longed for and looked after was to advance learning and perpetuate it to posterity; dreading to leave an illiterate ministry to the churches, when our present ministers shall lie in the dust. And as we were thinking and consulting how to effect this great work, it pleased God to stir up the heart of one Mr. Harvard (a godly gentleman, and a lover of learning, there living amongst us) to give the one half of his estate (it being in all about £1700) towards the erecting of a college, and all his library; after him another gave £300; others after them cast in more, and the public hand of the State added the rest: the college was, by common consent, appointed to be at Cambridge (a place very pleasant and accommodate) and is called (according to the name of the first founder) Harvard College.

The edifice is very fair and comely within and without, having in it a spacious hall (where they daily meet at commons, lectures, exercises) and a large library with some books to it, the gifts of divers of our friends, their chambers and studies also fitted for, and possessed by the students, and all other rooms of office necessary and convenient, with all needful offices thereto belonging; and by the side of the college a fair grammar school, for the training up of young scholars, and fitting of them for academical learning, that still as they are judged ripe, they may be received into the college of this school: Master Corlet is the master, who hath very well approved himself for his abilities, dexterity and painfulness in teaching and education of the youth under him.

Over the college is Master Dunster placed, as president, a learned, conscionable and industrious man, who hath so trained up his pupils in the tongues and arts, and so seasoned them with the principles of divinity and Christianity, that we have to our great comfort (and in truth beyond our hopes) beheld their progress in learning and godliness also; the former of these hath appeared in their public declamations in Latin and Greek, and disputations logical and philosophical, which they have been wonted (besides their ordinary exercises in the college hall) in the audience of the magistrates, ministers, and other scholars, for the probation of their growth in learning, upon set days, constantly once every month to make and uphold. The latter hath been manifested in sundry of them, by the savoury breathings of their spirits in their godly conversation. Insomuch that we are confident, if these early blossoms may be cherished and warmed with the influence of the friends of learning, and lovers of this pious work, they will by the help of God, come to happy maturity in a short time.

Samuel Eliot Morison

JOHN HARVARD AND THE NOTE OF FREEDOM
(1636–1936)

Just as no anthology of American letters would be complete without a selection from the writings of Francis Parkman, so would no collection of Harvardiana be complete without a portion from the Tercentenary historian, Samuel Eliot Morison, whose sensitive interpretation of Harvard history is the best yet written. On the opening day of the Tercentenary Celebration — November 8, the Founder's birthday — Professor Morison read an essay which has never been equaled as an eloquent statement of the part Harvard has played "in the great stream of learning and enlightenment which sprang from antiquity and has pursued its course uninterruptedly during all the intervening centuries." Running through this historical treatment is one aspect of Harvard's tradition which most Harvard men, no matter how much they abhor the term "tradition," will defend to the last — the principle of liberty of the mind. The Harvard Alumni Bulletin commented on Professor Morison's essay: "During the greater part of its history Harvard was compelled to resist the interference of religion, as today it must resist the interference of political and economic creeds. There is always some orthodoxy whose adherents are afraid of thought, and against which a great university must guard its independence. Freedom does not mean heresy any more than it means orthodoxy, but it means that the honest love of truth, the discipline of science, and

*the accumulation of learning must be allowed to bring forth their own
fruits in their own time. It means that only by such a general grant of
freedom, scrupulously observed, can society profit by its universities.
Professor Morison has sounded the keynote of the Tercentenary Celebration: the reinvigoration of the soul of Harvard by the recollection of its
past and a rededication to its essential and abiding purposes."*

AUTUMN has crushed her vintage from the wine-press of the year. November has come, the days of family reunions and New England anniver-
saries. In November the Mayflower sighted Cape Cod, and the Compact
was signed; it is the month of Thanksgiving, the important football games,
and John Harvard's birthday. The *Old Farmer's Almanac* advises us to
observe November by taking in cabbage, casting up accounts, and filling
the cellar with good cider, "that wholesome and cheering liquor." So let
us pause, and take stock of the past, and for a moment forget about
Mussolini, Ethiopia, and our own politics. Let us take down from our
shelves Bradford's *History of Plimmoth Plantation* and turn to that noble
and prophetic passage where the Governor of the Pilgrim Fathers in his
old age summed up the history of his Colony:

"Thus out of small beginnings greater things have been produced by
His hand that made all things of nothing, and gives being to all things
that are; and as one small candle may light a thousand, so the light here
kindled hath shone to many; yea, in some sorte, to our whole Nation."

Another such light was kindled at Newtown in the Bay Colony in 1636.
But the spark that touched it off came from a lamp of learning first lighted
by the ancient Greeks, tended by the Church through the dark ages, blown
white and high in the medieval universities, and handed down to us in
direct line through Paris, Oxford, and Cambridge.

In the elder Cambridge across the seas another small beginning had
been made near the end of Queen Elizabeth's reign. Sir Walter Mild-
may, Chancellor of the Exchequer, founded and endowed a new college, to which he gave the Puritan name Emmanuel — God with us. Puri-
tanism was not in favor with Her Majesty, who, at her next meeting with
this aged public servant, burst out with:

"So, Sir Walter, I hear you have erected a Puritan foundation?"

"No, Madam," said he, "Far be it from me to countenance anything
contrary to your established laws; but I have set an acorn, which when
it becomes an oak, God alone knows what will be the fruit thereof."

One of the first fruits was Harvard College; and from that acorn,
planted in the new Cambridge, has grown a goodly oak, nigh three centuries old, whose own fruits in the arts and sciences, in law, medicine, and
letters, are spread through the length and breadth of this land.

John Harvard was one of the thirty-five graduates of Emmanuel Col-

lege who came to New England in the great Puritan migration. He settled at Charlestown and filled the pulpit on alternate Sabbaths. In the
summer of his arrival a committee composed largely of Cambridge alumni, appointed by the General Court of Massachusetts, were busying
themselves about a College, for which the Court had appropriated £400
in the autumn of 1636. In the "New Towne" they found a site that recalled their *Alma Mater* on the Cam. A spacious plain, "smooth as a bowling green," sloped to a quiet river winding among salt marshes to the
sea. The small village, New Town, was clustered near a good landing-
place; and Thomas Shepard, the minister, an Emmanuel man, was perhaps judged to be more effective than others as an inspirer of youth, because in college days he had been a rather wild youth himself. On the
north edge of the village stood Master Shepard's dwelling, and next it
another; behind them was a row of cow-yards where the people kept their
cattle at night behind palings, to protect them from prowling wolves and
Indians. The house next Shepard's and the cow-yard behind it were purchased by the committee; a master was engaged; and there the first
freshman class of the College, a dozen strong, was gathered in the early
summer of 1638; and the New Town was promptly renamed Cambridge.

Shortly after, perhaps on the opening day, John Harvard rode over
from Charlestown to look at the College. A well-to-do young man from
London's middle class, married but childless, he was touched by this
brave effort to reproduce in New England a Christian college like his
own Emmanuel; he decided to help it. But John had not long to live.
A "consumption," as the early chroniclers called it, had marked him down
as victim; and that autumn he died, in his thirty-first year. On his death-
bed John Harvard dictated a will that gave him an endless series of sons;
for to the College he left his library, and half his estate. And the General
Court at the next session "Ordered, that the colledge agreed upon formerly to bee built at Cambridg shalbee called Harvard Colledge."

Thus Harvard College was established *hic in silvestribus et incultis
locis,* on the edge of the wilderness, in a colony eight years old, number-
ing less than ten thousand people, who had barely secured the necessities
of existence; and with no help from any church, government, or individual in the Old World. No similar achievement can be found in colonial
history; and in the eight centuries of university annals, there have been
few nobler examples of courage in maintaining intellectual standards
amid hard material circumstances, than the founding and early history
of the Puritans' college by the Charles.

No university can pretend to be an end in itself. Universities are
founded and maintained in order to serve mankind; but the ideas prevalent in some communities regarding the services proper to universities

are, to say the least, peculiar; and if a university, to be popular, tries to be all things to all men, it is likely to become of slight value to anyone. Harvard has been singularly happy in having been permitted, even encouraged, to function in an atmosphere of freedom; to decide for herself what she shall contribute to learning; and how. She has never abused that freedom to her own advantage, or the community's prejudice. On the contrary, she has used the corporate autonomy with which the Commonwealth endowed her in 1650, and the wealth poured into her treasury, to pour forth ever greater services, on a constantly widening watershed.

It is not an easy matter to explain these services, or to defend learning to the unlearned. Most of what a university does cannot be measured by statistics, represented by graphs, weighed, or counted — or where it can be counted, as in Harlow Shapley's work on stellar galaxies, we cannot follow him much beyond the first hundred million light-years! The public can understand a university supporting teaching, or research in the natural and social sciences — provided historians forbear close inspection of idols' feet. But what of this ripe scholar, spending a lifetime editing and translating the works of a Greek dramatist a long time dead; of that modest man of science, working in his laboratory of cryptogamic botany on algae and fungi that even some of the botanists consider mildly obscene? How can we explain and defend the expenditure of money on these things? The answer is, we cannot; until the scholar is dead, or unless he becomes world-famous. Many of the state universities of this country, where professors are dependent for their daily bread on annual appropriations, have to do good by stealth, while maintaining shows in the way of extension lectures and football games, to get the votes and the money. Many things that members of a university write, do, and say, must be unpopular; for it is a university's business to be wiser, more liberal, and more hospitable to new ideas, *and more critical of them*, than the community. Badgering, bridling, and blindfolding the universities is cheap and popular, although the community hurts itself in the end more than it does the college. A professor with blinders on can see no farther than his feed-bag.

At the time of her foundation, Harvard was unique among the universities of the western world, in having no statutory oaths imposed on her teachers or students. The reason is clear: Harvard was founded by Puritans whose consciences had been troubled by the oaths to support the state religion that they had had to take at Oxford or Cambridge. In order to obtain a degree in an English university they had been forced to subscribe to principles that they abhorred; yet, as the lesser evil, they had taken the oaths and gone their way, as conscience dictated. Personal experience taught them the vanity of trying to control opinion by tests and oaths; and they made no such attempt here.

While the universities should lead, it is also true that no leader can afford to run too far ahead of his followers, or he becomes isolated and lost. Harvard has had plenty of experience of that during her three centuries of life. Henry Dunster, our first president, was pulled up short when he opposed infant baptism. The Governing Boards wished him to continue, regardless; but the General Court forced him to resign. A few years later there was another small but significant controversy. Someone more liberal than the majority wished to print on the College press a translation of that beautiful manual of Christian devotion, *The Imitation of Christ.* President Chauncy and his board of censors gave their consent, and the copy went to press. But when the General Court of Massachusetts got wind of it, they resolved that, whereas "there is now in the press reprinting a book entitled Imitations of Christ by Thomas a Kempis a Popish minister, wherein is conteyned some things that are unsafe for the people of this place . . . there shall be no further progress in that work." And the *Imitatio Christi* was not reprinted in Massachusetts — for some time. This taught the College authorities that their efforts to liberalize the community must be done quietly, almost imperceptibly, through a gradual process of education, and not by shocking departures from the Puritan canon. How well they succeeded may be seen in the Unitarian movement of the early nineteenth century.

President Mather once boasted of the "liberal manner of Philosophizing" at Harvard; but of liberal theology he would have none; and his attempt to incorporate an oath of orthodoxy in a new College charter was only foiled by the veto of a hearty Irish peer, Lord Bellomont, then Governor of Massachusetts. Oxford and Cambridge, less fortunate, had a stringent set of tests and oaths imposed on them by Charles II. The consequence was that the dissenters and Roman Catholics were excluded from the benefits of university education, and college tutors found that the safe way to hold their fellowships was to give up writing, or research; and both universities for a long period became contemptible as places of learning.

Another oath bill for Harvard was threatened in the 1740's, as a punishment for Harvard indifference toward the evangelical revival; but it failed to pass. As long as Massachusetts was a Royal Province, the Harvard Presidents were charged by the Royal Governor at their inauguration, to perform their duties "with loyalty to our Sovereign Lord, King George, and obedience to His Majesty's Laws." The last colonial President, Langdon, was installed in 1774. On a fine June morning the next year he might have been heard preaching rebellion against George III to the American army, just before it marched from Cambridge to Bunker Hill.

John Adams saw to it that Harvard University had a chapter to herself in the Massachusetts Constitution of 1780; but no oath of allegiance was required of the President or Professors. The Commonwealth was represented on the Board of Overseers until 1866; but never once, to my knowledge, did these official representatives of government use their positions to restrain or repress. Finally, in 1866, forty years after she had ceased to contribute to the support of the College, Massachusetts handed over the Board of Overseers to the Harvard alumni. On them now rests the responsibility of representing the community in the University constitution.

President Eliot's administration, coming in the greatest era of progress and liberalism, democracy, and optimism that America has ever known, was little troubled by problems of academic freedom. Commonwealth and University alike took it for granted that scholars and professors had complete liberty, within the limits of decency, to write, speak, and publish their minds. Free speech was regarded as an axiom of democracy, and the guardian of liberty.

But the Great War brought back that spirit of intolerance that Thomas Jefferson had hoped to bury forever. It took the form of demands for the dismissal of certain professors, either because they had the misfortune to be Germans, or because they spoke or wrote in a manner to alarm patriots or property-holders. And these demands came most sharply from some of our own alumni; from men who had benefited from the very freedom that they sought to restrain. It is the greatest glory of Mr. Lowell's administration that he maintained, in theory and in fact, this ancient principle of academic freedom, as an essential condition for the proper functioning of a university. In conferring upon him an honorary degree in 1934, his successor characterized Mr. Lowell as "our resolute captain who enlarged and deepened the life of this University, and preserved untainted the vitalizing spirit of liberty." And if Harvard and her sister universities are to serve the Great Republic in the future as they have in the past, they must be confirmed in their freedom to function as republics of learning.

Three centuries is a mere moment in human history; but a long era in the history of universities, over one-third of the time that has elapsed since groups of masters and scholars first organized as *universitates* in Bologna and Paris. As an institution for promoting the intellectual labors of mankind, the universities have had no rivals or competitors. Almost the whole of what we call civilization, certainly the nobler and more ideal aspects of it, have been wrought through the unselfish and devoted studies of their sons. In this noble pageant of learning, from the era of Gratian and St. Thomas to our own day, Harvard has worked up from a humble position in the rear ranks, to a place among the captains and the kings; and that place, God willing, she means to hold.

"Thus out of small beginnings greater things have been produced by His hand that made all things of nothing, and gives being to all things that are; and as one small candle may light a thousand, so the light here kindled hath shone to many; yea, in some sorte, to our whole Nation."

Samuel E. Morison, "Harvard's Past," *Harvard Alumni Bulletin*, November 22, 1935.

William James

THE TRUE HARVARD

(1903)

During the course of his distinguished teaching career, William James, M.D. 1869, LL.D. 1903, made many statements about his Alma Mater, including the offhand remark to his sister, shortly after his appointment as Professor of Philosophy, that "although I serve Harvard College to the best of my ability, I have no affection at all for the institution, and would gladly desert it for anything that offered better pay." Fortunately, he did not desert Harvard and he came to love and understand her better, as his address at the Harvard Commencement dinner in 1903 seems to indicate.

WE ARE glorifying ourselves today, and whenever the name of Harvard is emphatically uttered on such days, frantic cheers go up. There are days for affection, when pure sentiment and loyalty come rightly to the fore. But behind our mere animal feeling for old schoolmates and the Yard and the bell, and Memorial and the clubs and the river and the Soldier's Field, there must be something deeper and more rational. There ought at any rate to be some possible ground in reason for one's boiling over with joy that one is a son of Harvard, and was not, by some unspeakably horrible accident of birth, predestined to graduate at Yale or at Cornell.

Any college can foster club loyalty of that sort. The only rational ground for preëminent admiration of any single college would be its preëminent spiritual tone. But to be a college man in the mere clubhouse sense — I care not of what college — affords no guarantee of real superiority in spiritual tone.

The old notion that book learning can be a panacea for the vices of society lies pretty well shattered today. I say this in spite of certain utterances of the President of this University to the teachers last year. That sanguine-hearted man seemed then to think that if the schools would only do their duty better, social vice might cease. But vice will never cease. Every level of culture breeds its own peculiar brand of it as surely as one soil breeds sugar-cane, and another soil breeds cranberries. If we were asked that disagreeable question, "What are the bosom-vices of the level of culture which our land and day have reached?" we should be forced, I think, to give the still more disagreeable answer that they are swindling and adroitness, and the indulgence of swindling and adroitness, and cant, and sympathy with cant — natural fruits of that extraordinary idealization of "success" in the mere outward sense of "getting there," and getting there on as big a scale as we can, which characterizes our present generation. What was Reason given to man for, some satirist has said, except to enable him to invent reasons for what he wants to do. We might say the same of education. We see college graduates on every side of every public question. Some of Tammany's stanchest supporters are Harvard men. Harvard men defend our treatment of our Filipino allies as a masterpiece of policy and morals. Harvard men, as journalists, pride themselves on producing copy for any side that may enlist them. There is not a public abuse for which some Harvard advocate may not be found.

In the successful sense, then, in the worldly sense, in the club sense, to be a college man, even a Harvard man, affords no sure guarantee for anything but a more educated cleverness in the service of popular idols and vulgar ends. Is there no inner Harvard within the outer Harvard which means definitively more than this — for which the outside men who come here in such numbers, come? They come from the remotest outskirts of our country, without introductions, without school affiliations; special students, scientific students, graduate students, poor students of the College, who make their living as they go. They seldom or never darken the doors of the Pudding or the Porcellian; they hover in the background on days when the crimson color is most in evidence, but they nevertheless are intoxicated and exultant with the nourishment they find here; and their loyalty is deeper and subtler and more a matter of the inmost soul than the gregarious loyalty of the clubhouse pattern often is.

Indeed, there is such an inner spiritual Harvard; and the men I speak of, and for whom I speak today, are its true missionaries and carry its gospel into infidel parts. When they come to Harvard, it is not primarily because she is a club. It is because they have heard of her persistently atomistic constitution, of her tolerance of exceptionality and eccentricity, of her devotion to the principles of individual vocation and choice. It is because you cannot make single one-ideaed regiments of her classes. It is because she cherishes so many vital ideals, yet makes a scale of value among them; so that even her apparently incurable second-rateness (or only occasional first-rateness) in intercollegiate athletics comes from her seeing so well that sport is but sport, that victory over Yale is not the whole of the law and the prophets, and that a popgun is not the crack of doom.

The true Church was always the invisible Church. The true Harvard is the invisible Harvard in the souls of her more truth-seeking and independent and often very solitary sons. *Thoughts* are the precious seeds of which our universities should be the botanical gardens. Beware when God lets loose a thinker on the world — either Carlyle or Emerson said that — for all things then have to rearrange themselves. But the thinkers in their youth are almost always very lonely creatures. "Alone the great sun rises and alone spring the great streams." The university most worthy of rational admiration is that one in which your lonely thinker can feel himself least lonely, most positively furthered, and most richly fed. On an occasion like this it would be poor taste to draw comparisons between the colleges, and in their mere clubhouse quality they cannot differ widely: — all must be worthy of the loyalties and affections they arouse. But as a nursery for independent and lonely thinkers I do believe that Harvard still is in the van. Here they find the climate so propitious that they can be happy in their very solitude. The day when Harvard shall stamp a single hard and fast type of character upon her children, will be that of her downfall. Our undisciplinables are our proudest product. Let us agree together in hoping that the output of them will never cease.

This paper was originally delivered at the Harvard Commencement Dinner, June 24, 1903. It was first printed in the *Harvard Graduates' Magazine.*

Walter Prichard Eaton

HERE'S TO THE HARVARD ACCENT

(1936)

After twenty-five years of writing, newspaper work, and college teaching, Walter Prichard Eaton went to Yale in 1933 as a reluctant substitute for the late George Pierce Baker. Instead of a three-year stint at the most, he stayed to teach playwriting until the age of sixty-eight, became a full professor, and "had a very happy time." He is the author of nearly forty books, among them a series of juveniles.

GEORGE ADE once declared that his Alma Mater, Purdue, "gives you everything that Harvard does, except the pronunciation of *a* as in *father.*" George did not intend this remark to be complimentary to the university on the Charles, but as a matter of fact it is, for it points out one of the chief reasons for Harvard's greatness. Words, as Professor Kittredge has so often told us, are vastly important things. But the pronunciation of

words is vastly important, too. A way of pronouncing not only betrays
the speaker's regional origin, but carries with it most of the associative
ideas which belong to the region, and wakes them in the hearer. Regional
pronunciations are symbols of provincialism. They may be none the worse
for that; indeed they may often have a special charm on that account,
nor would we see them lost in the general uniformity of "correct" speech.
But they are provincialisms nonetheless.

Probably to Ade's ear (as to many others across the Continent) the
pronunciation of *a* as in *father* is also a provincialism, the provincialism
of Massachusetts Bay. Certainly he would not admit that because Boston
and Harvard employ it, it is therefore standard. But the fact remains that
for the best speakers of the language as a whole, on both sides of the
Atlantic, it is standard; it is the pronunciation which has brought the
music of Shakespeare most magically to our ears, whether spoken by
Edwin Booth or Ellen Terry or John Gielgud or Walter Hampden.
It is the pronunciation which has trumpeted the noblest prose in our
language from the loftiest pulpits, and without which even Isaiah loses
some of his rolling majesty. It is a kind of hall mark of oral dignity and
of English style; it is a syllabic sound around which cluster the associative
ideas of richest dignity and least provincial scope, least because they
embrace the whole confines of the language on both sides of the water.
Those associative ideas are so subtly and constantly playing upon any
sensitive man who spends four years at Harvard that whether he knows it
or not they color his life, and whether he can express it or not in words
they are much of what Harvard comes to mean to him.

So let him cling proudly to his broad *a*, and to his not always secret
belief that any other pronunciation is provincial. Let the Mid-West laff.
It is a prerogative of the young.

From the Harvard Tercentenary Supplement of the *Boston Herald*, September 13, 1936.

David McCord

THE LIGHTS COME ON
(1941)

*Emerson once wrote in his journal, "the sky is the daily bread of the
eyes," and David McCord has felt that those nine words have meant a
great deal to him over the years. They have stuck with him longer than
simply the moment when they suggested to him his early essay, "Cambridge Sky." Few Harvard men have written of their University with so*

*much affectionate perception and literary skill as the executive secretary
of the Harvard Fund Council and former editor of the* Harvard Alumni
Bulletin. *"By pure chance," he says, "vocation and avocation combined to
anchor me to Harvard. Though my list of natural regrets has enjoyed the
happy accretive growth of 25 years, I have never for a minute regretted
this. Harvard has given me everything: a living, a reasonably useful pen —
perfecto size — a catholic attitude toward art, and the winds of more doctrine than I can halfway handle." McCord has written nearly a score of
books, including* Oddly Enough, Stirabout, Notes on the Harvard Tercentenary, The Crows, Bay Window Ballads, About Boston, *and* A Star by
Day. *He has edited several anthologies, among them* What Cheer.

YOU NEVER KNOW just when, for there are not in all the buildings together filaments enough to make the Yard a brilliant place, even by any
city back-street standard. Murky Cambridge dusk — how damp, how
murky! — and then of a sudden you turn a corner and there is the familiar outdoor bracket beacon, like the carriage lamp of another age, brightening a segment of brick and showing a pool of amber on the rotting
snow beneath. Now half a dozen other lights are winking from the windows of Weld, Grays, and the rest. Back of tall pillars the curtain of
Widener slowly rises and inward illumination comes up as on a vast but
silent stage. A voice calls far across from the steps of Hollis. Figures
about the Yard grow shadowy and soft and moist. A match flares to a
cigarette. Evening becomes official, and the gloom is gradually filtered
everywhere with the innocent pin-points of sixty-cycle sunlight.

Down in the Basin, half the Harvard Bridge — the Boston half, perhaps — has already responded to the throwing of a giant switch. From
shore to center the dwindling silhouette is brilliant with little bulbs: an
accusing finger in the direction of Cambridge, warning her to forget
the budget and mounting taxes and turn on the juice of the other half.
This (in good time) the servants of the City Fathers will surely do.

Up the river sweep the beams and half-beams of homeward suburban
cars against the slower-moving glitter of inbound Boston traffic. The
Weeks Bridge, a pretty Georgian fragment thrown across the Charles,
and her less beautiful elder sister to the west, flank the batteries of increasing window light from the Houses and the Business School. It is
Monday evening — high table, that means, at Lowell House — and the
graceful Lowell tower emerges in the gloom, touched off by your modern
reflectors, cunningly concealed. Cambridge is a city of spires now, even
by night, and at other times there are three of them ablaze at once. In
the river, where the ice is going out in jigsaw-puzzle fragments, float the
images of phosphorous. A pretty sight, with spring so faintly stirring in
the night air: a moment of security, almost, in a world so pitifully insecure.

The lights of Harvard's Cambridge come on with a greater front and

a steadier shine than they did for our more somnolent ancestors. Even
the now old-fashioned arc of hotly sputtering carbon, still casting weird
tree-shadows on a wall in Plympton Street, has probably more candle-
power within one cracked globe than half the Yard could muster in the
rosy days of *The Rebelliad*. And what would the ancients say to the milk-
white Taj Mahal, the Good Gulf gas station on the site of dead Beck Hall,
the dreary?

Light has always been one of the first symbols of colleges and learning. Centuries and electrons have not changed us there. The point is that
at Harvard the lights *can* still come on — in fair weather or in rain, in a
time of free thinking, or of the soul's own darkness, when man shall save
his birthright only by a masterful resolve.

Harvard Alumni Bulletin, March 22, 1941.

Donald Moffat

ONE VIEW OF HARVARD

(1948)

*With true affection and the felicity of a master craftsman, Donald Moffat,
A.B. 1916, turned his hand to the introduction of Samuel Chamberlain's*
Fair Harvard *and brought forth a beautifully ordered essay on the char-
acter of Harvard, one of the best items in all Harvard literature. A writer
by trade, Moffat has published* A Villa in Brittany, The Mott Family in
France, *and* The Prejudices of Mr. Pennyfeather.

HERE AND THERE in the pages of Samuel Eliot Morison's *Three Centuries
of Harvard* occurs a phrase which might well have been taken for the
College motto, to stand beside the celebrated *Veritas*: "Harvard men
were divided in opinion."

In a present alumni army of some ninety thousand you will find,
where Harvard is concerned, no two elements agreeing on anything.
Among undergraduates the same law runs, and among the faculty too.
Harvard means conflict and conflict means passion and the only
sensible rule for identifying a Harvard man is to call him a minority of
one. United by a mystic loyalty which not only cements the family but
forms a useful shield to hold up against the world, Harvard is rent by
polite but fearful discord on every point worth mentioning from the

function of education to the function of the catch in rowing. There is no escaping this truth, which is called John's Law, after the founder. Historians are sharply divided on the question of John Harvard's right to the title of founder.

For if education may be defined in a word, that word is controversy. Where concord reigns, learning withers; where conflict rules, it flourishes. And the cumulative effect of three hundred years of conflict results — in the best, or Harvard, opinion — in a university three times as great as one which has been at it only one hundred years, and so on.

Harvard can point to no moment in her history and truthfully say, "Here we were in equilibrium." No college generation has known an armistice in the age-old war between the orthodox and the radical, the conservative and the progressive points of view towards current controversy among her student or faculty scholar-servants, whether it be academic, religious, political, social, or trivial. Every day is crisis day at Harvard, and on few of them, be it said to her credit, has she failed to take the line leading up and on.

She has been called godless from the beginning, a serious charge during her first two hundred years, when religious orthodoxy was the only passport to fair repute; and radical almost as long as godless. In fact, the dangerous radical at godless Harvard emerges as a stock figure in her history. Yet the important point is this: in all the long roster of Harvard heretics and rebels I find no instance of a student or teacher being disciplined purely because of his opinions. In this respect Harvard's tradition stands firm as a rock, the record is clear. Tomorrow's dissenters like yesterday's may be reviled by the press, the public, and the pulpit; they may be, as they have been, called atheist, imperialist, communist, or merely unAmerican: the College fathers will uphold their right to be heard. Of this we may be sure . . .

Four years are none too long: so many skins must be shed, so many new layers grown or grafted. If it be true that the first milestone on the road leading out of childhood is the discovery that your mother and father don't like spinach either, the next is perhaps the ability to tell an honest man from a scoundrel, and a third the precious lesson that because a thing is new, or because it is old, it is not therefore necessarily good: that the word "modern," fetish of youth and the advertising profession, is no more synonymous with "excellent" than the word "ancient." The knowledge that the integrity of the man who pushes the button is more important than the reliability of the machine the button starts is another item that hopeful but incredulous youth finds hard to accept, but must accept, if his education is to do him any good. The lesson of humility — hallmark of the truly great — can hardly be learned in four years; but a beginning can be made, a glimpse caught. The downy freshman looks at a classmate a little timidly, a little truculently, thinking "I'm just as good as you are!" Four years later he may have learned to change the emphasis, saying "You're just as good as I am." Simple humility is not easily won. But it is a step on the road to becoming a free man and an educated man, and may at last enable one to apply to himself the aphorism "that man is free who is conscious of himself as the law which he obeys."

Who is wise enough to swear that the air he breathes, the sound of echoing footsteps of generations of great men who have gone before, the impalpable influences which shape and form the spirit as well as the mind, do not play their part in these beginnings?

Since the vanished elms were planted in 1815 and the original paths laid out from building to building, door to door, a crisscross of new walks have appeared in the Yard, beaten out by the students' footsteps. Here and there are fences, some high, some low. But the short cuts are not fenced: the muddy or dusty tracks appear, then one fine morning the impatient undergraduate finds that official notice has courteously been taken of his trespasses, in the form of fresh gravel. A new dormitory, chapel, or library is built, a new star discovered, a great teacher is born, science pushes the mysterious curtain back another millimeter: presto! the new pathways appear. Harvard is too experienced to call them royal roads, wise enough to know that time is the precious factor which alone may prove their worth.

Fair Harvard, photographs by Samuel Chamberlain, with text by Donald Moffat (Cambridge: Harvard University Press, 1948).

Three Presidents

TOWARD A DEFINITION OF HARVARD
(1869–1950)

Many men, past and present, have sought to put into words something of the meaning of Harvard; but none should be more qualified to speak on the subject than Presidents Eliot, Lowell, and Conant. In the more than eighty years of expansion and consolidation represented by their administrations, Harvard grew from a small New England college into the great educational institution of today. Yet, despite Harvard's changing needs and vastly altered educational pattern, there is little essential difference to be found in the way these three Presidents interpret Harvard's mission. The following passages, culled from notable presidential statements, define in noble terms the spirit of a great university.

CHARLES W. ELIOT

THIS UNIVERSITY recognizes no real antagonism between literature and science, and consents to no such narrow alternatives as mathematics or classics, science or metaphysics. We would have them all, and at their best. To observe keenly, to reason soundly, and to imagine vividly are operations as essential as that of clear and forcible expression; and to develop one of these faculties, it is not necessary to repress and dwarf the others. A university is not closely concerned with the applications of knowledge, until its general education branches into professional. Poetry and philosophy and science do indeed conspire to promote the material welfare of mankind; but science no more than poetry finds its best warrant in its utility. Truth and right are above utility in all realms of thought and action. . .

The notion that education consists in the authoritative inculcation of what the teacher deems true may be logical and appropriate in a convent, or a seminary for priests, but it is intolerable in universities and public schools, from primary to professional. The worthy fruit of academic culture is an open mind, trained to careful thinking, instructed in the methods of philosophic investigation, acquainted in a general way with the accumulated thought of past generations, and penetrated with humility. It is thus that the university in our day serves Christ and the church. . .

Harvard College is sometimes reproached with being aristocratic. If by aristocracy be meant a stupid and pretentious caste, founded on wealth, and birth, and an affectation of European manners, no charge could be more preposterous: the College is intensely American in affection, and intensely democratic in temper. But there is an aristocracy to which the sons of Harvard have belonged, and, let us hope, will ever aspire to belong — the aristocracy which excels in manly sports, carries off the honors and prizes of the learned professions, and bears itself with distinction in all fields of intellectual labor and combat; the aristocracy which in peace stands firmest for the public honor and renown, and in war rides first into the murderous thickets.   (1869)

The brief history of modern civilization shows that in backward ages universities keep alive philosophy, and in progressive ages they lead the forward movement, guiding adventurous spirits to the best point of onward departure. They bring a portion of each successive generation to the confines of knowledge, to the very edge of the territory already conquered, and say to the eager youth: "Thus far came our fathers. Now press you on!" The hope of mankind depends on this incessant work of the philosophical pioneer, who may be years, or generations, or centuries in advance of the common march.

And universities are among the most permanent of human institutions. They outlast particular forms of government, and even the legal and industrial institutions in which they seem to be embedded. Harvard University already illustrates this transcendent vitality. . . (1886)

Universities have three principal, direct functions. In the first place, they teach; secondly, they accumulate great stores of acquired and systematized knowledge in the form of books and collections; thirdly, they investigate, or, in other words, they seek to push out a little beyond the present limits of knowledge, and learn, year after year, day after day, some new truth. They are teachers, storehouses, and searchers for truth.

(1891)

ABBOTT LAWRENCE LOWELL

THE INDIVIDUAL STUDENT ought clearly to be developed so far as possible, both in his strong and in his weak points, for the college ought to produce, not defective specialists, but men intellectually well rounded, of wide sympathies and unfettered judgment. At the same time they ought to be trained to hard and accurate thought, and this will not come merely by surveying the elementary principles of many subjects. It requires a mastery of something, acquired by continuous application. Every student ought to know in some subject what the ultimate sources of opinion are, and how they are handled by those who profess it. Only in this way is he likely to gain the solidity of thought that begets sound thinking. In short, he ought, so far as in him lies, to be both broad and profound. . .

Surely the essence of a liberal education consists in an attitude of mind, a familiarity with methods of thought, an ability to use information rather than in a memory stocked with facts, however valuable such a storehouse may be. . . The best type of liberal education in our complex modern world aims at producing men who know a little of everything and something well. . .

The university touches the community at many points, and as time goes on it ought to serve the public through ever increasing channels. But all its activities are more or less connected with, and most of them are based upon, the college. It is there that character ought to be shaped, that aspirations ought to be formed, that citizens ought to be trained, and scholarly tastes implanted. (1909)

The usefulness of a great university is by no means exhausted by its teaching. It has two functions, both so essential that neither can be said to be more important than the other. One is that of preserving and imparting the knowledge slowly acquired in the past, the other is that of adding to it. The question a university should ask is not whether an idea is old or new, but only whether it is true, and the universities have shown that there is no difficulty in combining the retention of what is good in the old with the strenuous search for new truth.   (1916)

The teaching by the professor in his classroom on the subjects within the scope of his chair ought to be absolutely free. He must teach the truth as he has found it and sees it. This is the primary condition of academic freedom, and any violation of it endangers intellectual progress. . . The gravest questions, and the strongest feelings, arise from action by a professor beyond his chosen field and outside of his classroom. Here he speaks only as a citizen. . . In spite, however, of the risk of injury to the institution, the objections to restraint upon what professors may say as citizens seem to me far greater than the harm done by leaving them free. . . It is not a question of academic freedom, but of personal liberty from constraint, yet it touches the dignity of the academic career. . . If a university or college censors what its professors may say, if it restrains them from uttering something that it does not approve, it thereby assumes responsibility for that which it permits them to say. This is logical and inevitable but it is a responsibility which an institution of learning would be very unwise in assuming. . .

Surely abuse of speech, abuse of authority and arbitrary restraint and friction would be reduced if men kept in mind the distinction between the privilege of academic freedom and the common right of personal liberty as a citizen, between what may properly be said in the classroom and what in public. But it must not be forgotten that all liberty and every privilege imply responsibilities. Professors should speak in public soberly and seriously, not for notoriety or self advertisement, under a deep sense of responsibility for the good name of the institution and the dignity of their profession. They should take care that they are understood to speak personally, not officially. When they so speak, and governing boards respect their freedom to express their sincere opinions as other citizens may do, there will be little danger that liberty of speech will be either misused or curtailed.   (1918)

We have believed that the problem of Harvard College is really a moral problem. We want men to think, and think seriously. We do not want them to think alike. That is an entirely different matter. We have stood, and we always shall stand, for absolute freedom of thought under any circumstances, both with our professors and with our students. We do not want them made in a pattern. We want them to think. In other words, if I may parody the motto of the University, what we desire here is not truth, but the search for truth.   (1933)

As wave after wave rolls landward from the ocean, breaks and fades away sighing down the shingle of the beach, so the generations of men follow one another, sometimes quietly, sometimes, after a storm, with noisy turbulence. But, whether we think upon the monotony or the violence in human history, two things are always new — youth and the quest for knowledge, and with these a university is concerned. So long as its interest in them is keen it can never grow old, though it count its age by centuries. The means it uses may vary with the times, but forever the end remains the same; and while some principles, based on man's nature, must endure, others, essential perhaps for the present, are doomed to pass away. . .   (1936)

JAMES BRYANT CONANT

ACCORDING to the account written nearly three hundred years ago, Harvard was founded "to advance learning and perpetuate it to posterity." We can all agree that these few admirable words still describe our aims, although the methods of advancing learning and the modes of perpetuating it have changed greatly in the course of three centuries. Our Puritan ancestors thought of education and theology as inseparably connected. It is hard for us to recapture their point of view; today, learning has become secular. Indeed, the universities are now the residuary legatees of many of the spiritual values which were guarded by the church three centuries ago. Our responsibilities are correspondingly increased and our ideals must be clearly defined. If future generations are to have that high regard for the achievements of the human mind which is essential to civilization, there must be a true reverence for learning in the community. It is not sufficient to train investigators and scholars, no matter how brilliant they may be; a large body of influential citizens must have a passionate interest in the growth of human knowledge. It is our ambition to inspire the undergraduates in Harvard College with an enthusiasm for creative scholarship and a respect for the accumulated intellectual treasures of the past. This is one way in which we today perpetuate learning to posterity.

Learning must be advanced as well as perpetuated. Indeed, in the last analysis it is only by advancing learning that it is possible to perpetuate it. When knowledge ceases to expand and develop, it becomes devitalized, degraded, and a matter of little importance to the present or future. The community loses interest, and the youth of the country responds to other challenges. Able young men enlist in an enterprise only if they are persuaded that they, too, may contribute by creative work. A zest for intellectual adventure should be the characteristic of every university. In the future as in the past, our teachers must be scholars who are extending the frontiers of knowledge in every direction. I hope there will never be a separation of our faculty into those who teach and those who carry on creative work. No line should be drawn between teaching and research. Our strength in the past has lain in the fact that the spirit of scholarship has pervaded our teaching and our scholars have seen the importance of perpetuating the ideals of scholarship as well as advancing knowledge in their own specialty.

A university is a group of men — a community of scholars and students — and here lies the real problem in regard to the future of all institutions of higher learning. Harvard's success will depend almost entirely on our ability to procure men of the highest caliber for our student body and for our faculty. . . Together with other institutions of higher learning, we are the trustees in whose hands lies the fate of the future of human knowledge. . .   (1934)

The primary concern of the University today should be what it always has been, to foster the search for truth; only secondarily should a university concern itself with the immediate applications of knowledge.
(1936)

If we attempt to sum up in one phrase the aim of higher education, we can do no better than to speak of "the search for truth. . ."
When the Puritans wrote *Veritas* upon the open books, they had in mind two paths by which truth could be obtained: one, Revelation as interpreted with the aid of human reason; the other, the advancement of knowledge and learning.   (1936)

The bedrock on which the scholarly activities of a university are founded is a charter of free inquiry; without this you may have an institution of advanced education, a technical school or a military college, for example, but you do not have a university. I am sure we are all agreed on that. There should be no barriers to an objective analysis of every phase of our national life. No compromise with this principle is possible even in days of an armed truce. The nation has a right to demand of its educational institutions that the teachers dealing with controversial subjects shall be fearless seekers of the truth and careful scholars rather than propagandists. But granted honesty, sincerity and ability there must be tolerance of a wide diversity of opinion.   (1948)

The old cliché that "education is what is left after all that has been learnt is forgotten" is worth repeating in any discussion of education. Through our departmental offerings we assist the student in learning many difficult skills ranging from the ability to handle mathematics or ancient and modern languages, to manipulation of both the concepts and the apparatus of the social and the natural sciences. By the same means we provide opportunities for absorbing a vast amount of knowledge. Along with the acquisition of knowledge and skills within an area comes the understanding and appreciation of an embryonic specialist, one who sees what the mastery of a field would mean. Even if twenty years later the student has forgotten nearly all that he learned through his field of concentration, he will know something of what it means to master a subject. On this point President Lowell used to insist repeatedly in expounding his philosophy of education.   (1950)

II

PEDAGOGUES AND PUPILS

The uses of adversity are beyond measure strange. As a professor, he regarded himself as a failure. Without false modesty he thought he knew what he meant. He had tried a great many experiments, and wholly succeeded in none. He had succumbed to the weight of the system. . . The only part of education that the professor thought a success was the students. He found them excellent company. Cast more or less in the same mould, without violent emotions or sentiment, and, except for the veneer of American habits, ignorant of all that man had ever thought or hoped, their minds burst open like flowers at the sunlight of a suggestion. They were quick to respond; plastic to a mould; and incapable of fatigue. Their faith in education was so full of pathos that one dared not ask them what they thought they could do with education when they got it.

HENRY ADAMS (1907)

I perceive that I got almost nothing of intellectual value from Harvard University. It was my fault, no doubt; if I had been a real student, I should have found genuine instruction. But, for all my assumption of superiority, the crudeness of my mind at the age of twenty wakens amazement in me.

LOGAN PEARSALL SMITH (1938)

Henry Dunster

CONSIDERATIONS

(1654)

Henry Dunster, the first and youngest of the long line of Harvard presi-
dents, at thirty-three took over the reins of the College after the infant
institution had been forced to close down for a year following the miser-
able regime of the Eatons. "Dunster's genius for organization was such,"
writes Samuel Eliot Morison, "that the curriculum, the forms, and the in-
stitutions established under his presidency long outlasted his time, and
even his century . . . and the Charter of 1650 that he obtained . . .
still serves as constitution of the modern University." Dunster's outspoken
conviction that only adult believers should be baptized resulted finally in
his resignation on October 24, 1654. Three weeks later he wrote with
"simple, touching pathos" to the General Court, begging leave to remain in
the President's house throughout the winter; his request was granted in
this case, although in other respects he was not treated with much con-
sideration, particularly as to his meager salary.

FIRST. The time of the year is unseasonable, being now very near the shortest day, and the depth of winter.

Second. The place unto which I go, is unknown to me and my family, and the ways and means of subsistence, to one of my talents and parts, or for the containing or conserving my goods, or dis- posing of my cattle, accustomed to my place of residence.

Third. The place from which I go, hath fire, fuel, and all provisions for man and beast, laid in for the winter. To remove some things will be to destroy them; to remove others, as books and household goods, to hazard them greatly. The house I have builded, upon very damageful conditions to myself, out of love for the College, taking country pay in lieu of bills of exchange on England, or the house would not have been built; and a considerable part of it was given me, at my request, out of respect to myself, albeit for the College.

Fourth. The persons, all besides myself, are women and children, on whom little help, now their minds lie under the actual stroke of affliction and grief. My wife is sick, and my youngest child extremely so, and hath been for months, so that we dare not carry him out of doors, yet much worse now than before. However, if a place be found, that may be comfortable for them, and reasonably answer the obstacles above mentioned, myself will willingly bow my neck to any yoke of personal denial, for I know for what and for whom, by grace, I suffer.

The whole transaction of this business is such, which in process of time, when all things come to mature consideration, may very probably create grief on all sides; yours subsequent, as mine antecedent. I am not the man you take me to be. Neither if you knew what, should, and why, can I persuade myself that you would act, as I am at least tempted to think you do. But our times are in God's hands, with whom all sides hope, by grace in Christ, to find favor, which shall be my prayer for you, as for myself,

Who am, honored Gentlemen, yours to serve,

Henry Dunster

Josiah Quincy, *The History of Harvard University* (Cambridge, 1840).

Cotton Mather

HARVARD FROM HOAR TO MATHER
(1702)

One of the most extraordinary personages in early Harvard history was Cotton Mather (1662–1728) whose prodigious learning and amazing energy were applied both to his ministry and to his voluminous writings. Disappointed twice in the expectation of becoming President of Harvard, he nevertheless left as his monument an early history of his alma mater in his greatest work, the Magnalia Christi Americana. *Until the histories of Peirce, Quincy, and Eliot, this was the standard general account of the early Harvard and despite its annoying pedantry and a humor strange to modern ears, it preserved much valuable information about the early years of the College. The following selection, with certain long-winded passages removed, gives the flavor of the famous book:*

AFTER the death of Mr. Chauncy . . . the Alma Mater Academia must look among her own sons to find a President for the rest of her children; and accordingly the Fellows of the College with the approbation of the Overseers, July 13, 1672, elected Mr. Leonard Hoar, unto that office; whereto, on the tenth of September following he was inaugurated.

This gentleman, after his education in Harvard College, travelled over into England, where he was not only a preacher of the Gospel in divers places, but also received from the University in Cambridge the degree of a Doctor of Physick. The doctor, upon some invitations relating to a settlement in the pastoral charge with the South Church at Boston, returned into New England; having first married a virtuous daughter of the Lord Lisle, a great example of piety and patience, who now crossed the Atlantic with him; and quickly after his arrival here, his invitation to preside over the college at Cambridge superseded those from the church in Boston. Were he considered either as a scholar or as a Christian, he was truly a worthy man; and he was generally reputed such, until happening, I can scarce tell how, to fall under the displeasure of some that made a figure in the neighborhood, the young men in the College took advantage therefrom to ruin his reputation as far as they were able. He then found the rectorship of a college to be as troublesome a thing as ever Antigonus did his robe . . . The young plants turned cud-weeds, and with great violations of the Fifth Commandment set themselves to travesty whatever he did and said, and aggravate everything in his behavior disagreeable to them, with a design to make him odious; and in a day of temptation, which was now upon them, several very good men did unhappily countenance the ungoverned youths in their ungovernableness. Things were at length driven to such a pass that the students deserted the College, and the doctor on March 15, 1675 resigned his presidentship. But the hard and ill usage which he met withal made so deep an impression upon his mind that his grief threw him into a consumption, whereof he died November 28 the winter following, in Boston, and he lies now interred at Braintree. . .

After the death of Dr. Hoar, the place of president *pro tempore* was put upon Mr. Urian Oakes, the excellent pastor of the church at Cambridge, who did so, and would no otherwise accept of the place; though the offer of a full settlement in the place was afterwards importunately made unto him. He did the services of a president even as he did all other services, faithfully, learnedly, indefatigably; and by a new choice of him thereunto, on February 2, 1679, was at last prevailed withal to take the full charge upon him. We all know that Britain knew nothing more famous than their ancient sect of Druids, the philosophers whose order, they say, was instituted by one Samothes, which is in English as much as to say, An Heavenly Man. . . Reader, let us now upon another account, behold the students of Harvard College as a rendezvous of happy Druids, under the influences of so rare a President; but alas! our joy must be short lived, for, on July 25, 1681, the stroke of a sudden death felled the tree.

> — Qui tantum inter Caput extulit Omnes,
> Quantum Lenta solent, inter Viburna Cypressi.

Mr. Oakes, thus being transplanted into the better world, the presidentship was immediately tendered unto Mr. Increase Mather; but his church
upon the application of the Overseers unto them, to dismiss him unto the
place where to he was now chosen, refusing to do it, he declined the
motion. Wherefore, on April 10, 1682, Mr. John Rogers was elected unto
that place, and on August 12, 1683, he was installed into it. This worthy
person was the son of the renowned Mr. Nathanael Rogers, the pastor to
the church of Ipswich, and he was himself a preacher at Ipswich until
his disposition for medicinal studies caused him to abate of his labors in
the pulpit. He was one of so sweet a temper that the title of *deliciae
humani generis* might have on that score been given him; and his real
piety set off with the accomplishments of a gentleman, as a gem set in
gold. In his presidentship, there fell out one thing particularly for which
the College has cause to remember him. It was his custom to be somewhat
long in his daily prayers (which our presidents used to make) with the
scholars in the college hall. But one day, without being able to give reason for it, he was not so long it may be by half as he used to be. Heaven
knew the reason! The scholars returning to their chambers found one
of them on fire, and the fire had proceeded so far that, if the devotions
had held three minutes longer, the College had been irrecoverably laid
in ashes, which now was happily preserved. But him also a premature
death, on July 2, 1684, the day after the Commencement, snatched away,
from a society that hoped for a much longer enjoyment of him, and
counted themselves under as black an eclipse as the sun did happen to
be at the hour of his expiration. . .

The College was now again by universal choice cast into the hands of
Mr. Increase Mather, who had already in other capacities been serving
of it; and he accordingly, without leaving either his house or his church at
Boston, made his continual visits to the College at Cambridge, managing
as well the weekly disputations as the annual Commencements, and in-
specting the whole affairs of the society; and by preaching often at Cambridge he made his visits yet more profitable unto them.

Reader, the interest and figure which the world knows this my parent
hath had in the ecclesiastical concerns of this country ever since his first
return from England in the twenty-second until his next return from England in the fifty-third year of his age makes it a difficult thing for me to
write the church history of the country. Should I insert everywhere the
relation which he hath had unto the public matters, it will be thought
by the envious that I had undertaken this work with an eye to such a
motto as the son of the memorable Prince of Orange took his device,
Patriaeque Patrique. Should I on the other side bury in utter silence all
the effects of that care and zeal wherewith he hath employed in his
peculiar opportunities with which the free grace of Heaven hath talented

him to do good unto the public, I must cut off some essentials of my story. I will however bowl nearer to the latter mark than the former, and if nobody blame Sir Henry Wotton for still mentioning his father with so much veneration as that best of men, my father, I hope I shall not be blamed for saying thus much: My father hath been desirous to do some good. Wherefore I will not only add in this place that when the Honorable Joseph Dudley, Esq., was by the King's Commission made President of the Territory of New England, this gentleman, among other expressions of his hearty desire to secure the prosperity of his mother whose breasts himself had sucked, continued the government of the College in the hands of Mr. Mather, and altered his title into that of a Rector. But, when wise persons apprehend that the constitution of men and things, which followed after the arrival of another governor, threatened all the churches with quick ruins, wherein the College could not but be comprehended, Mr. Mather did by their advice repair to Whitehall, where being remarkably favored by three crowned heads in successive and personal applications unto them, on the behalf of his distressed country, and having obtained several kindnesses for the College in particular, he returned into New England in the beginning of the year 1692, with a royal charter full of most ample privileges. By that royal charter under the seal of King William and Queen Mary, the country had its English and its Christian liberties as well as its titles to its lands (formerly contested) secured to it; and the Province being particularly enabled hereby to incorporate the College (which was the reason that he did not stay to solicit a particular charter for it); immediately upon his arrival, the General Assembly gratified his desire, in granting a charter to this University. Mr. Mather now reassuming the quality of president over the College, which in his absence had flourished for divers years under the prudent government of two tutors, Mr. John Leverett, and Mr. William Brattle, he does to this day continue his endeavors to keep alive that river, the streams whereof have made glad this City of God. . .

And now, I hope that the European churches of the faithful will cast an eye of some respect upon a little university in America, recommended by the character that has been thus given of it. Certainly they must be none but enemies to the Reformation, the sons of Edom (which the Jewish rabbins very truly tell us is the name of Rome in the Sacred Oracles) that shall say of such an university, Raze it! Raze it!

Cotton Mather, *Magnalia Christi Americana* (1702).

Clifford K. Shipton

THE NEPHEW OF UNCLE EXPERIENCE
(c. 1730)

The perils of a twentieth-century Pauline were as nothing to the torments suffered by the Tutors who kept a painful watch over the behavior of Harvard undergraduates in the seventeenth and eighteenth centuries. A familiar target for undergraduate pranks was Tutor Joseph Mayhew of the Class of 1730 who spent two postgraduate years in Cambridge and sixteen other years serving the College as disciplinarian, Tutor, and member of the Corporation. Because no detailed contemporary accounts exist, a reconstruction can be made only by compiling and editing the few scraps of isolated information which have been preserved through the forethought of antiquarians. Such scholarly detective work, combined with good writing, distinguishes Clifford K. Shipton's five volumes of Sibley's Harvard Graduates, *now our principal secondary source of information about the men who went to Harvard in the early days. Shipton resumed in 1930 the task which had come to a halt with the death of John Langdon Sibley (1804–1885), the indefatigable Harvard librarian and archivist, part of whose substantial estate was assigned to the Massachusetts Historical Society for the completion of the biographical studies begun in 1859. Mr. Sibley brought the records down to 1690; Mr. Shipton has continued them to 1730, and has also found time to serve as Custodian of the Harvard University Archives and as Librarian of the American Antiquarian Society. No collection of Harvardiana would be complete without an example of one of "Shipton's Lives."*

TUTOR JOSEPH MAYHEW was born on February 26, 1709/10, the eldest son of Deacon Simon and Ruth Mayhew of Chilmark. No member of this distinguished family had as yet been graduated at Harvard, and Simon, who was a farmer, might not have sent Joseph to college if Harvard had not in 1723 forced an honorary M.A. on Uncle Experience Mayhew in recognition of his work as a missionary to the Indians. At Cambridge, Joseph's career was marked by the unusual combination of the highest scholastic honors and a gnawing appetite which the regular issue of college commons could by no means satisfy. When he was a freshman, Thomas Hollis, who had no doubt heard of him from Uncle Experience, wrote to the college suggesting that he be awarded one of his rich scholarships, but the Corporation saw fit to ignore the donor's suggestion. It did, however, appoint him a monitor and award him the Hopkins prize for excellence in his studies. The prize consisted of copies of Cotton Mather's *Ratio Disciplinae* and *Manuductio.*

After he had taken his first degree, Mayhew was awarded a Hopkins fellowship, but he did not qualify by residing in Cambridge and performing academic exercises. At least a part of the year he spent keeping the Roxbury school. On February 22, 1730/1, he was offered a Boyle fellowship of £20 "provided his Father first give Bond for refunding the Said Sum to the College in Case his Son should live, & decline the Indian Service, or should not be imployed statedly in the said Service within the Space of five years." He did not, however, resume residence at the college until after he had taken his M.A. in 1733, on which occasion he presented a negative answer to the *Quaestio*, "An Damnati puniantur, ob Peccata in Inferno commissa?" About this time he was nominated to the Society for Promoting the Gospel in New England and Parts Adjacent to be a missionary to the Nantucket Indians, but in February 1733/4, he again took up residence at the college.

After another year at Cambridge, Mayhew was appointed by one of the Boston endowments to preach to the little congregation of Indians and Whites on Block Island. . . After a year on Block Island he returned to Cambridge where he was again awarded a Hopkins fellowship. In August 1737, he left the college, but in May 1738 he returned, and the following spring he was awarded Flynt and Gibbs fellowships to enable him to meet the bills which he had accumulated.

It was then the practice to choose the tutors from among recent graduates, but in August 1739 the Corporation departed from it to elect Mayhew. The Overseers stood upon their right to investigate his religious principles:

> Mr Joseph Mayhew having been Chosen by the Corporation a Tutor for three years he was now presented to the Overseers for their acceptance — and such of the Gentlemen of the Corporation as are present having Signified that the Corporation had Examined him as to his religious principles The Question was put Whether the Gentlemen of the Corporation here present be desired to give Some account of the said Examination and it passed in the affirmative and an account thereof was given accordingly and then the Overseers voted their Acceptance of Mr Joseph Mayhew as a tutor.

The worst that could be said of Mayhew's religious views was that he did not favor revivals, an attitude which he later demonstrated by subscribing for the *Seasonable Thoughts* of Charles Chauncy (A.B. 1721). He also subscribed for the *Chronological History* of Thomas Prince (A.B. 1707), which was at that day the mark of an intellectual. There is no reason to question the statement of a contemporary that he was "a man of superior abilities and learning."

Why any man of his age would want to be a tutor is a puzzle. In the years which followed his appointment he grew accustomed to being

greeted in the yard with "Contemptuous Noise & Hallowing" and to being
subjected to "Heinous Insults." He was defied by drunken students and
his orders were resisted with physical violence. Logs were rolled down
the stairs by his study door, his door knob was broken off, and his cellar
was broken open and his beer and brandy stolen. He fought back, and
when his window was broken by a stone he detected and apprehended
the culprit by calculating the arc of the missile. He also had to contend
with Overseers like Lieutenant Governor Andrew Oliver (A.B. 1724) who
had no hesitation about using their influence in behalf of any boy of good
family who was detected in such crimes.

Once when Mayhew ordered a Freshman to go to aid a sick upper-
classman, Tutor Nathan Prince (A.B. 1718) interfered. To expose Prince,
Mayhew insisted on a Faculty hearing:

> Mr. Mayhew bro't a complaint that he had been ill treated by Winslow
> a Senior Sophister, viz by his detaining a Freshman from him. On which
> Mr. Prince (said Winslows Tutor) told Mr. Mayhew, He thought it im-
> proper to bring so trifling an Affair before the President & Tutors but that
> if Mr Mayhew would consent he doubted not, They might make up that
> Affair amicably between themselves, which the President consented to,
> but when Mr Mayhew insisted upon its being consider'd then, Mr. Prince
> Said he had urgent Business & couldnt tarry; Mr Mayhew repeating his
> desires of a present Consideration, The President told Mr Prince that if
> Mr Mayhew insisted upon the Affair, He would proceed then to consider
> it, Mr Prince again repeating the Necessity of his going away, mov'd off
> abruptly, while Mr Mayhew was still declaring his desires to have the
> Affair then consider'd.

After other encounters of the sort, Prince came to the considered conclusion, publicly announced, that Mayhew was "a Rascall & a Rascally
Fellow."

When Prince finally drank himself out of the college in 1742, it was
Mayhew who succeeded him as a Fellow of the Corporation. He served
this body on committees to audit the accounts, to visit and report on the
college farms, to inspect the library, and to make a college inventory. The
Corporation supported him in matters of discipline, and with some degree
of regret accepted his resignation on July 24, 1755. The reason for his
action was apparently the recent death of his father.

Mayhew settled on the family farm on Martha's Vineyard where he
remained in quiet obscurity until the tremors of the approaching Revolution shook even that remote corner of the Province. . . Mayhew was still
active in civil affairs when death overtook him on March 31, 1782. He
was unmarried.

Clifford K. Shipton, *Sibley's Harvard Graduates*, VIII (1726–1730). Massachusetts Historical Society (Boston, 1951).

David Sewall

FATHER FLYNT'S JOURNEY TO PORTSMOUTH (1754)

It is regrettable that time has partly obliterated from the record the full personality of Tutor Henry Flynt (1676–1760), whose academic ministrations to Harvard men spanned nearly six decades, beginning shortly after his graduation, and continuing until his death at the age of eighty-four. Occasional flashes in the records have revealed him to us, this stalwart son of Harvard who served fifty-five years as Tutor, sixty years as Fellow, forty-six years as Secretary to the Board of Overseers, and one year, after the death of Wadsworth, as Acting President. In the spring of his final year as Tutor the venerable Flynt decided to make a trip to Portsmouth, New Hampshire, and engaged as his driver a member of the junior class, David Sewall. The nineteen-year-old undergradute recorded the events of the journey like a true Boswell, and for years his manuscript account was preserved among the papers of his classmate, John Adams. Aside from this first-hand portrait, there are few such human characterizations of this re- markable personage. The Latin of Father Flynt's tombstone proclaims him "a man of sound learning, of acute and discriminating intellect; firm but moderate, steadfast in opinion, but without obstinacy; zealous and faith- ful in the discharge of his various duties."

IN THE MONTH of June, 1754, after the Senior Sophisters, agreeable to the usage of Harvard College in those times, had left off attending and recit- ing to their tutor, and were making the necessary arrangements for grad- uating in July then next, the time of commencement, Henry Flynt, the senior tutor of the institution, who had then the care and instruction of the senior class of undergraduates, sent for me to his chamber, in the old Harvard Hall, on Saturday afternoon, and told me he intended to take a journey to Portsmouth, N. H.; and, being informed that I was an excellent driver of a chair, he wished to know if I would wait upon him in that situation, and return home for a few days. I replied, the proposi- tion was to me new and unexpected, and I wished for a little time to consider of it. He replied "Aye, prithee, there is no time for considera- tion: I am going next Monday morning." I paused about a minute, and then replied that I would wait upon him in the journey.

I afterwards learned that he had applied to T. Atkinson, a student from Portsmouth, who had declined, and who had recommended me as a skilful and careful driver of a chair. In those days a single horse and chair, without a top was the usual mode of conveyance. A covered chair, then called a calash, was very seldom used.

After my consenting to attend Mr. Flynt, he says, "Go to the President (Holyoke), and give my sarvice to him, and desire him to give leave for you to return home," that I might attend him in his proposed journey. I accordingly went, and obtained leave of absence, and was then directed to go to Mr. Stedman's, and procure a horse and chair for him to go the journey.

On Monday, after breakfast, I went with the horse (which was a pacing mare) and chair to the college yard, from whence we proceeded on the journey across the common, and up the Menotomy Road, until we came to the cross road, passing near the Powder House to Medford, and from thence through Malden to Lynn. The first stop we made was at the noted public-house kept in that day by landlord Newall, where we oated the horse; and, as it was a warm forenoon, Mr. Flynt had a nip of milk punch; after which Mr. Flynt took from a leather purse (of considerable bulk, filled with small silver change) a small piece of money, and gave me to discharge the reckoning, with this injunction: "Be careful, and take the right change." Which being done, we proceeded through Salem plain to Danvers, by the country seat of King Hooper (so called) of Marblehead, through Ipswich, and a little before sunset we reached the dwelling of the Rev. Mr. Jewett of Rowley; where we called, and Mr. Flynt acquainted him he meant to tarry there that night. We were cordially entertained, and at bed-time we were introduced to a chamber where was only one bed; upon getting into which, says Mr. Flynt to me, "You will be keeping well to your own side" (an injunction I had no disposition to disobey). The next day, Tuesday, we passed through Newbury, over Merrimack River, at the ferry called Salisbury Ferry. He conversed freely and sociably on many topics (a thing then unusual for a tutor with an undergraduate), and, among other things, that he had lately sold a farm to cousin Quincy, for £500 or thereabouts; but, as he had no present need of the money, he had taken his security for the purchase sum, payable at a future period on interest.

Mr. Flynt intended to call and dine with Parson Cotton of Old Hampton; and, as we came to the road that led from the post-road to Cotton's house, we met the parson and his wife walking on foot. Upon which Mr. Flynt informed Mr. Cotton that he intended to have called and taken dinner with him; but, as he found he was going from home, he would pass on and dine at a public-house. Upon which, says Mr. Cotton, "We are going to dine, upon an invitation, with Doctor Weeks, one of my parishioners; and Mr. Gookin and his wife, of North Hill, are likewise invited to dine there; and I have no doubt you will be as welcome as any of us; and, besides, the Doctor has a son who he intends shall enter college next commencement; and I will with pleasure introduce you to Doctor Weeks." After pausing a small space, Mr. Flynt agreed to go, provided Parson Cotton would pass on before us, [and] make the necessary explanation to show that we were not interlopers. Upon which Mr. Cotton and wife passed on before us, and I halted the chair, and moved on slowly behind them (about 100 rods) to Dr. Weeks's; and Mr. Cotton introduced us to him, where we were cordially received and hospitably entertained. After dinner, while Mr. Flynt was enjoying his pipe, the wife of Dr. Weeks introduced her young child, about a month old, and the twins of Parson Gookin's wife, infants of about the same age, under some expectation of his blessing by bestowing something on the mother of the twins (as was supposed), although no mention of that expectation was made in my hearing; but it produced no effect of the kind.

After dinner, we passed through North Hampton to Greenland; and, after coming to a small rise of the road, hills on the north of Piscataqua River appearing in view, a conversation passed between us respecting one of them, which he said was Frost Hill. I said it was Agamenticus, a large hill in York. We differed in opinion, and each of us adhered to his own ideas of the subject. During this conversation, while we were descending gradually at a moderate pace, and at a small distance, and in full view of Clark's Tavern, the ground being a little sandy, but free from stones or obstructions of any kind, the horse somehow stumbled, in so sudden a manner, the boot of the chair being loose on Mr. Flynt's side, threw Mr. Flynt headlong from the carriage into the road; and the stoppage being so sudden, had not the boot been fastened on my side, I might probably have been thrown out likewise. The horse sprang up quick, and with some difficulty I so guided the chair as to prevent the wheel passing over him; when I halted and jumped out, being apprehensive from the manner in which the old gentleman was thrown out that it must have broken his neck. Several persons at the tavern noticed the occurrence, and immediately came to assist Mr. Flynt; and, after rising, found him able to walk to the house; and, after washing his face and head with some water, found the skin rubbed off his forehead in two or three places, — to which a young lady, a sister of William Parker, Jr., who had come out from Portsmouth with him and some others that afternoon, applied some pieces of court plaster. After which we had among us two or three single bowls of lemon punch, made pretty sweet, with which we refreshed ourselves, and became very cheerful. The gentlemen were John Wendell, William Parker, Jr., and Nathaniel Treadwell, a young gentleman who was paying suit to Miss Parker. Mr. Flynt observed he felt very well, notwithstanding his fall from the chair; and, if he had not disfigured himself, he did not value it. He would not say the fault was in the driver; but he rather thought he was looking too much on those hills. John Wendell was just upon the point of marrying to a Miss

Wentworth; and he [Flynt] was asked if he had come at this time to attend the wedding. He replied he had not made the journey with that intent; but, if it happened while he was at Portsmouth, he should have no objection of attending it.

I was directed to pay for one bowl of the punch, and the oats our horse had received, after which we proceeded on toward Portsmouth; Mr. Treadwell and Miss Parker preceded us in an open chair. William Parker was going on to Kensington, where he was employed in keeping school; and J. Wendell returned on horseback to Portsmouth. The punch we had partaken of was pretty well charged with good old spirit, and Father Flynt was very pleasant and sociable. About a mile distant from the town, there is a road that turns off at right angles (called the Creek Road) into town, into which Mr. Treadwell and Miss Parker (who afterward married Captain Adams) entered with their chair. Upon which Mr. Flynt turned his face to me, and said, "Aye, prithee, I do not understand their motions; but the Scripture says, 'The way of a man with a maid is very mysterious.'"

The time and manner of this observation was such that, in order to suppress my risible faculties, the water fell in several drops from my eyes. We passed on the usual road to Portsmouth, to the dwelling-house of Thomas Wibird, — a respectable merchant, a bachelor, who kept house with several domestics. There I tarried on Tuesday night, and slept again in the same bed with Mr. Flynt. The next day, being Wednesday, after receiving directions at what day of the succeeding week he should commence the journey back to Cambridge, I passed the ferry, and walked on foot to York, and tarried there until the time assigned for my return, when I came again to Portsmouth.

We left the town, and, passing through Greenland, North Hampton, Hampton Old Town to Hampton Falls, stopped at Mr. Whipple's, the minister of the place, where Mr. Flynt intended to dine. But it so happened that dinner was over, and Mr. Whipple had gone out to visit a parishioner; but Madame Whipple was at home, and very social and pleasant, and immediately had the table laid, and a loin of roasted veal, that was in a manner whole, placed on it, upon which we made an agreeable meal. After dinner, Mr. Flynt was accommodated with a pipe; and, while enjoying it, Mrs. Whipple accosted him thus: "Mr. Gookin, the worthy clergyman of North Hill, has but a small parish and a small salary, but a considerable family; and his wife has lately had twins." — "Aye, that is no fault of mine," says Mr. Flynt. — "Very true, sir; but so it is." And, as he was a bachelor, and a gentleman of handsome property, she desired he would give her something for Mr. Gookin; and she would be the bearer of it, and faithfully deliver it to him. To which he replied, "I don't know that we bachelors are under an obligation to maintain other folks' children." To this she assented; but it was an act of charity she now requested for a worthy person, and from him who was a gentleman of opulence, and who, she hoped, would now not neglect bestowing it. "Madam, I am from home, on a journey, and it is an unseasonable time." She was very sensible of this; but a gentleman of his property did not usually travel without more money than was necessary to pay the immediate expenses of the journey, and she hoped he could spare something on this occasion. After some pause, he took from his pocket a silver dollar, and gave her, saying it was the only WHOLE DOLLAR he had about him. Upon which Mrs. Whipple thanked him, and engaged she would faithfully soon deliver it to Mr. Gookin; adding, it was but a short time to commencement, when it was probable Mr. Gookin would attend, and she hoped this was but an earnest of a larger donation he would then bestow upon Mr. Gookin. Father Flynt upon this replied, "Insatiable woman, I am almost sorry I have given you any thing."

Soon after which we pursued our journey, and, riding over the sandy road to the ferry, the easy motion of the chair lulled the old gentleman into a sleep for some time; upon which I carefully attended the boot of the chair, to prevent his being thrown from the carriage a second time, in case of the stumbling of the horse. We passed on through Newbury and Rowley, without calling upon the minister of either of the places, and reached Ipswich toward evening; when we stopped at the dwelling of Mr. Rogers, the clergyman of the old parish, who seemed much pleased with the visit, and introduced his wife (who, I understood, was a daughter of President Leverett); when Mr. Flynt accosted the lady, "Madam, I must buss you," and gave her a hearty kiss.

We enjoyed a social evening; and, upon his being asked some questions about the scholars, related the following anecdote: "One morning my class were reciting, and stood quite round me, and one or two rather at my back, where was a table on which lay a keg of wine I had the day before bought at Boston; and one of the blades took up the keg, and drank out of the bung. A looking-glass was right before me, so that I could plainly see what was doing behind me. I thought I would not disturb him while drinking; but, as soon as he had done, I turned round, and told him he ought to have had the manners to have drank to somebody." And this was all the reprimand made on the occasion.

We again slept in the same bed, together. In the morning I arose before him, and he slept on until breakfast-time, when I went upstairs to acquaint him of it. We had toast and tea. He was interrogated by Mrs. Rogers whether he would have the tea strong or weak, that she might accommodate it to his liking. He replied, he liked it strong of the tea, strong of the sugar, and strong of the cream; and it was regulated accordingly.

Breakfast being over, we departed, and passed through the hamlet now called Hamilton, to Beverly, and a ferry (where a toll-bridge is now erected), into Salem, and stopped at the home of Mr. Browne, an opulent merchant of the place, where we dined. This Mr. Browne was related to my classmate, William Browne; and, from the conversation which passed during dinner, I found he was a great genealogist. After dinner was over, we proceeded on our way, without any other remarkable occurrence, until we reached Cambridge, and finished the journey.

David Sewall's Account of His Journey to Portsmouth, N. H. with Tutor Henry Flynt in the Year 1754, Charles Deane, ed. Proceedings of the Massachusetts Historical Society, First Series (Vol. XVI, 1878–1879).

Andrew Preston Peabody

OLD POP

(c. 1830)

Few Harvard teachers of the first half of the nineteenth century were better known to the students at our little New England college than "Old Pop" (John Snelling Popkin, A.B. 1792). Professor Popkin was teacher of Greek and college disciplinarian in a time when Harvard was little other than a boarding school. This pleasant sketch of a remarkable man was written by Andrew Preston Peabody (1811–1893), himself one of the most admirable of Harvard servants, who was connected with the College as student and teacher, off and on, for some three score years, beginning with his entrance as a junior at the age of thirteen. He was Plummer Professor of Christian Morals and Preacher to the University (1860–1881); on two occasions he was acting President; he edited the North American Review *(1852–1863); he wrote a half-dozen books, largely on religious and ethical subjects, and published two volumes about Harvard —* Graduates Whom I Have Known *and* Harvard Reminiscences. *It is from the latter that this excerpt comes.*

DR. POPKIN was a bachelor, and for many years led a very lonely life. It was said that he had in his early days been strongly attached to a lady whose affections were bestowed elsewhere; and it is certain that when she died, in his old age, he sent for a carriage, and attended her funeral, though he had not been a wonted visitor at her house, nor, indeed, in any house. Till near the close of his professorship he lived in a college-room, for most of the time in the second story of Holworthy. He at first boarded in the college commons: but, finding the dining-hall too noisy and tumultuous, he after a little while took his meals in his own room; the venerable Goody Morse cooking his food, bringing it to him at the regular college hours, and in various ways taking the most assiduous care for his com-fort. Shortly before he resigned his office, a widowed sister and two orphan nieces of his came to Cambridge; and he established himself as the head of their family, in the old Wigglesworth house, which stood next to the president's house in Harvard Street. He afterward built a house on the North Avenue, adjacent to a house then recently built by his classmate and lifelong friend, Dr. Hedge. The two ex-professors used to hold the most pleasant intercourse on their several sides of the dividing fence, but neither ever entered the other's house; as Dr. Popkin, while the kindest of men, and social in his way, neither made nor invited visits.

Dr. Popkin was undoubtedly the best Greek scholar of his time; and there is a mine of recondite learning stowed away in his edition of the Gloucester Greek Grammar, and in the notes in the American edition of Dalzel's "Collectanea Graeca Majora" signed "P," and generally, with his characteristic modesty, pointed with an interrogation-mark, though no one was better entitled than he to employ the affirmative form of state-ment. I can hardly say that he gave instruction in the recitation-room, though he muttered in what seemed a breathlessly rapid soliloquy a great deal that would probably have been instructive, could it have been heard and understood. The criterion of a good recitation with him was not grammatical knowledge, but the accuracy and elegance with which the Greek was rendered into English. He had at the same time a singularly delicate ear for the detection of a rendering which was not the student's own; and, though he seemed to see very little, if a printed translation was brought in, he was not unlikely to discover and confiscate it. In like manner he accumulated a little library of interlined "Majoras," which had been made with assiduous care, transmitted from class to class, and held at a high price in the college market. But the students who cared little for the Greek language or literature could appear reasonably well at very small cost. He commonly called up the members of a division in alphabetical order, and one could always determine within a few lines the passage which he would have to construe. Once in a great while, however, Dr. Popkin would spread consternation by striking midway in the seats; but those who on such occasions utterly failed, felt entire security for many subsequent days. Those of us who really studied our whole lessons had a wearisome task. There was no Greek-English lexicon obtainable. Our chief dependence was on the often inadequate Latin definitions of Schrevelius, and we were not sufficiently good Latin scholars not to need the mediation of a Latin dictionary between the Greek and the English. There were in my class two or three copies of the more copious lexicon of Hedericus; and round one of these half a dozen of us would sit, each with his Schrevelius, depending, when he failed us, upon the fuller supply of Latin meanings in the larger vocabulary. Under such difficulties, the actual amount of Greek scholarship fell far short of the estimate which it had in the professor's generous credulity.

Dr. Popkin would have had a majestic presence, had he so chosen. He was tall, with a massive frame, with a broad and lofty brow, and with features indicative of superior mental power. But shyness and solitude gave him an aspect and manners more eccentric than can easily be imagined in these days, when, under the assimilating influence of modern habits, idiosyncrasies have faded out, and every man means and aims to look like every other. His dress, indeed, was, in an historical sense, that of a gentleman; but his tailor must have been the last survivor of an else long extinct race. He never walked. His gait was always what is termed a dog-trot, slightly accelerated as he approached its terminus. He jerked out his words as if they were forced from him by a nervous spasm, and closed every utterance with a sound that seemed like a muscular movement of suction. In his recitation-room he sat by a table rather than behind it, and grasped his right leg, generally with both hands, lifting it as if he were making attempts to shoulder it, and more nearly accomplishing that feat daily than an ordinary gymnast would after a year's special training. As chairman of the parietal government, he regarded it as his official duty to preserve order in the college yard: but he was the frequent cause of disorder; for nothing so amused the students as to see him in full chase after an offender, or dancing round a bonfire: while it was well understood that as a detective he was almost always at fault.

Oddities were then not rare, and excited less surprise and animadversion than they would now. The students held him in reverence, and at the same time liked him. His were the only windows of parietal officers that were never broken. Personal insult or outrage to him would have been resented by those who took the greatest delight in indirect methods of annoying him. Once, indeed, when he was groping on the floor in quest of smothered fire, in a room that had been shattered by an explosion of gunpowder, a bucket of water was thrown on him by a youth, whose summary expulsion was the only case of the kind that I then knew in which the judgment of the students was in entire harmony with that of the Faculty. As may be supposed, he was not without a nickname, which he accepted as a matter of course from the students; but hearing it on one occasion from a young man of dapper, jaunty, unacademic aspect, he said to a friend who was standing with him, "What right has that man to call me 'Old Pop'? He was never a member of Harvard College."

Dr. Popkin's only luxury was the very moderate use of tobacco. Every noon and every evening, Sundays excepted, he trotted to an apothecary's shop, laid down two cents, then the price for what would now cost five times as much, and carried to his room a single Spanish cigar. Of course, though the shop was open, he would not go to it on Sunday; and he would not duplicate his Saturday's purchase, lest he might be tempted to duplicate his Saturday evening's indulgence. A friend who often visited him on Sunday evening always took with him two cigars, one of which the doctor gratefully accepted.

Dr. Popkin took his turn in officiating at the daily college prayers, and his peculiarities of manner were almost always merged in the sacred dignity and the profound solemnity with which he conducted the service. While in his own soul it was evidently the utterance of sincere devotion, and not mere routine, there were certain phrases, scriptural for the most part, that recurred so often as to attach themselves indelibly to my memory of him. Thus, among his ascriptions of gratitude, he seldom failed to offer thanks for "wine that maketh glad the heart of man, and oil [*ile*, as he pronounced it] to make his face to shine, and bread which strengtheneth man's heart," — wine having not yet fallen under the ban of even the Society for the Suppression of Intemperance, of which he must have been a member, as were the president and most of the Faculty. In the chapel service Dr. Popkin was apt to falter and hesitate, and even to sink into an unconscious bathos, when there was any thing unusual in the occasion, especially at the close or the beginning of a term, when he in vain attempted to embody the homegoing or the re-assembling of the students in the stately phraseology which he was wont to employ. He seldom preached in the chapel; but on the rare occasions on which he supplied the president's place, he plainly showed that the pulpit was the fitting fulcrum for his life-power. He was a heedful listener to sermons, and a wise and discriminating critic. Some of us younger college officers sat with him on Sundays in the chapel gallery, and descended the stairs at his side, to hear what he had to say about the sermon; though we never knew whether he was talking to himself or to us, as he made his comments *sotto voce*. Once, when a minister from a neighboring town had been preaching on the choice between Baal and Jehovah, offered to the people of Israel by Elijah, Dr. Popkin indicated the strange, but actual omission of the preacher, by saying, "If we are going to choose Baal, I see no need of being in such a hurry about it."

Dr. Popkin resigned his office in 1833. With his inexpensive habits, he had acquired a competent provision for his remaining years. He lived till 1852, retired from the outside world, still reading the Greek poets; but most of all loving the Bible, studying the New Testament in the original, and, while a good Hebraist, preferring the Old Testament in the Septuagint version. While never entirely in gearing with the machinery of this world's life, no man ever lived in more genuine fellow-citizenship with those whose blessed company he joined in dying.

Andrew Preston Peabody, *Harvard Reminiscences* (Boston, 1888).

Presidential Tact

FOUR LETTERS FROM FOUR PRESIDENTS
(1829–1862)

Harvard Presidents have unhappily not always been noted for their tactful and blameless handling of great decisions. Forthright Quincy stirred up a disagreeable mixture of undergraduate pottage with his too strict treatment of the undergraduates. A century later aristocratic Lowell was widely criticized for his racial policy in rooming assignments. Fortunately Harvard Presidents have sometimes shown remarkable diplomacy and determination, as the following group of four communications demonstrates. None of these letters (culled from the Presidential letter books) has ever before been published; and the one from President Sparks is, of course, the answer to the action taken on April 23, 1849, to which Longfellow referred cryptically in his diary: "We have had at Faculty meeting an application from a young lady to enter College as a regular student."

PAINFUL FACTS COMPEL ME TO WRITE PLAINLY

Cambridge, July 30, 1829.

My dear Sir

You are apprised that circumstances have placed me at the head of Harvard University. I did not know until very recently that a son of yours was a member of it, — and the facts which have brought it to my knowledge are of that painful character which I would willingly conceal from you, did not duty compel me to write plainly, and without keeping back any of the truth. — During the last six or eight months such a series of depredations have been committed on property of the college, in its different public rooms, & buildings, that the Government were satisfied that access was had by means of false keys. —

In the same manner there was reason to believe that the public Arsenal, had been opened, and hand grenades, or shells, & powder pilfered. —

Although the last articles were not traced into the College, there was little doubt that the same person or persons who had been engaged in depredations in the college rooms were concerned in taking the public property; — and notice to that effect was given to the Adjutant General, that he might take measures for their detection and its preservation. —

Some time in May last, a set of carpenters who were working on the President's House, & who had their tools secured in a chest in the stable of that house, had their chest forced, and tools of various descriptions to the value of near fifty dollars taken away together with the key of the chest. —

The circumstances were of so gross & atrocious a kind, that they had no suspicion that it could have been done by any scholar, they accordingly ordered advertisements to be made offering a reward for the detection of the thief, — and actually took search warrants against houses suspected in the vicinity.

The loss was to the persons suffering under it very heavy, they being journeymen, and almost all they were worth vested in tools. — About a month afterwards however, a considerable number of the tools much abused, were found concealed in the garret of Massachusetts, which satisfied every one that the injury must have been done by some scholar, probably an inmate of that College. — No suspicion however attached to any one until yesterday, when I was called upon by the College carpenters, requesting that I would accompany them to the room occupied by your son, (I think Number 18, or 19) Massachusetts. — They informed me that being engaged in making the usual repairs of the rooms of scholars, always done in vacations, and having occasion to move a small table in your son's room they were satisfied by the rattling, that something not usual in college drawers, was contained in it. —

They had accordingly found a key that would open the lock, and in the drawers discovered a great number of false keys, suited to various locks, which however they would not touch until I had been called. — I went to the room, and found as they had stated in a table drawer, containing one or more letters to your son, & his receipted quarter bill, forty five keys, of which I took possession, and which on trial & inspection have been found to open almost all the public rooms in the College. Among the keys was that of the Carpenter's Chest, — broken open at the stable of the President's House, — before mentioned, and on farther search some of the tools taken from the Chest were found concealed in your son's room, and also various articles the property of the College. — A hole also was cut through the floor of his study, — into the cellar, and a sort of trap-door adjusted to it. — The Carpenters' key to tools have been identified beyond all manner of question. —

It is not for me to dwell in writing to you, on the nature of this evidence. — It is of that character, & the depredations have affected so many persons, that if your son return here, he will probably be subjected to a judicial process. — The usual college refuge of round denial, in such cases cannot I apprehend be resorted to with any success, and whatever should be the result of a judicial investigation, the disgrace which will attach to him must be such, that it is impossible his connexion with the College could longer be permitted. —

On this point however, I write after no consultation with any one, *not as the Head of the University*, but as a friend to a friend, on a subject of a very delicate and critical nature. —

If you ask me what I advise you to do, I am compelled to say, that were I placed under the same circumstances, I should by settling with the parties injured, preclude all possibility of farther publicity. — I should take my son immediately from the University, and under a most rigorous *surveillance.* —

It gives me great pain to be necessitated to communicate facts so distressing to a parent. — But there is no alternative. — I ought to add perhaps that on an inspection of the scale of merit of his class, I find he stands the lowest of any students now members of the University, & his continuance cannot probably be of any advantage to him, even should it be permitted. —

Respectfully yrs.,

Josiah Quincy.

Note [by Eliza Susan Quincy, the President's daughter]:

"Some months after the date of this letter, workmen repairing Harvard Hall, found under the floor of the Library, between it & the ceiling of the room beneath; — hand grenades, charged with powder, & a train of powder laid to them. —"

A SOLITARY FEMALE AT HARVARD?

Harvard University,
Cambridge, April 25th, 1849.

Miss Sarah Pellet,

Your letter, making inquiry whether you could be admitted into this University upon presenting the proper credentials of character and scholarship, was duly received. I am not aware that any law exists touching this point, and, as it is a novel case, it would be decided by a vote of the Corporation.

As the institution was founded, however, for the education of young men, all its departments arranged for that purpose only, and its rules, regulations, internal organization, discipline, and system of teaching designed for that end, I should doubt whether a solitary female, mingling as she must do promiscuously with so large a number of the other sex, would find her situation either agreeable or advantageous. Indeed, I should be unwilling to advise any one to make such an experiment, and upon reflection I believe you will be convinced of its inexpediency.

It may be a misfortune, that an enlightened public opinion has not led to the establishment of Colleges of the higher order for the education of females, and the time may come when their claims will be more justly valued, and when a wider intelligence and a more liberal spirit will provide for this deficiency.

Very respectfully yours,
Jared Sparks.

MR. FISKE OPENLY AVOWS HIMSELF AN INFIDEL

Mrs. Stoughton
New York

Cambridge, Oct. 16, 1861

Dear Madame.

It is with great regret that I have to inform you that your son, John Fiske, of the Junior Class, has incurred a public admonition by misconduct at the Episcopal Church. The particular acts complained of by the officers of the church were neglecting to conform to the customary modes of worship, and on two occasions, reading a secular book, which he had taken with him, during the service. These repeated marks of his contempt for the Episcopal service, and for the religious feelings of those among whom he had chosen to worship, exhausted the patience of the officers of the Church, and he was reported to the Faculty. Our laws require the attendance of every student at Church; but all are allowed to attend the church in which they are brought up, or which they prefer from "conscientious motives." Your son last year attended the College Chapel. He changed to the Episcopal Church, permission having been granted on your written request. Under these circumstances, the misconduct reported against him caused me great surprise: for he is a studious young man, and, so far as I know, of good moral character. I sent for him to ask an explanation. He very frankly admitted the facts charged against him, and added that he was not a Christian, i.e. a believer in Christianity. He further added in answer to a question of mine, that he had changed from the Chapel to the Church, from no conscientious motive, but in order to have a "pleasanter time."

We never attempt to control the religious opinions of young men. But I consider it a great and lamentable misfortune to a young man, when, in the conceit of superior wisdom, he openly avows himself an infidel. He has neither studied, nor reflected, nor experienced enough to make such an avowal anything more than a foolish, shallow, and whimsical affectation of superiority. I respect the doubts of a studious and enquiring mind, and would always treat such doubt with tenderness. But I have no such respect for open and positive denial by a youth in his teens, of truths held sacred by the wisest, most learned and best men, and I hold acts of insolent disrespect to the public rites and observances of a Christian Church, to be no common outrage. Your son's good character in general, and his faithful attention to his studies induced the Faculty to limit the censure to a public admonition. I have only to add, that while we claim no right to interfere with the private opinions of any student, we should feel it our duty to request the removal of any one who should undertake to undermine the faith of his associates. I hope you will caution your son upon this point, for any attempt to spread the mischievous opinions which he fancies he has established in his own mind, would lead to an instant communication to his guardian to take him away.

> Yours with much respect,
> C. C. Felton, President.

AN ADMONITION FOR MR. LINCOLN

Hon. Abraham Lincoln,
President of the United States,
Washington, D. C.

> Cambridge, Mass. Dec. 9, 1862.

Dear Sir

The Faculty last evening voted "that Lincoln, Junior, be publicly admonished for smoking in Harvard Square after being privately admonished for the same offence." The word *"publicly"* simply makes it my duty to inform you of the admonition, and I trust, Sir, that you will impress upon him the necessity not only of attention to matters of decorum, but of giving heed to the private admonitions of his instructors.

> Very respectfully yours,
> Thomas Hill,
> President of Harvard College

Harvard University Archives.

Thomas Hill

A COLLECTING TRIP WITH LOUIS AGASSIZ
(1848)

In the stimulating Harvard community of the mid-nineteenth century few names shone so brightly as that of Louis Agassiz. The foreign visitor who quickly sought out Longfellow, Lowell, Holmes, or Emerson, just as quickly went to call on the great and popular Swiss naturalist who had

*awakened so many Americans of his time to a love and knowledge of
science. Agassiz was a member of the Faculty for twenty-six years and he
established the Museum of Comparative Zoölogy, which has since been
supported by the copper fortune of the Agassiz family. The following description of an expedition with Professor Agassiz was written by Thomas
Hill, later President of Harvard. Hill reveals in this sympathetic sketch his
friendship for Agassiz and his feeling for the unity of God and nature
which characterized his gentle approach to life — the same qualities which
made him a good teacher and a thoughtful educator; but a relatively
poor administrator and neither an entirely successful nor a happy
President.*

WHEN Mr. Samuel Felton was superintendent of the Fitchburg Railroad
he used to take a party of friends, once or twice a year, to observe the
progress in building the Cheshire, and afterward the Sullivan Road. One
of the most delightful of these excursions was the last; when the line of
rail had been extended up the valley of the Ammonoosuc, as far as Littleton, New Hampshire. The party included his two brothers, Mr. Cornelius
Conway Felton, afterwards President of Harvard College; and Mr. John
B. Felton who afterwards died in California; Professor Arnold Guyot,
author of "Earth and Man," who died, a few years ago, at Princeton, New
Jersey; Professor Peirce; Agassiz; his son, Alexander Agassiz, then a boy
just arrived from Europe, and not knowing a word of English; and
myself.

I was surprised, during the journey, to find that Agassiz knew the
plants along the road as well as I did. I never knew him make any mistake
in naming a wild plant, but once; and then it was a mere slip of the
tongue, calling a Lespedeza a Hedysarum. His early intimacy with the
great botanists Braun and Schimper had given him a far better knowledge
of vegetable physiology, and of the classification of plants, and of the
names of species, than I have sometimes found in so-called Professor of
the Chair of Botany in colleges.

We started on this expedition in an accommodation train which had
picked up one man at Charlestown, two or three others at Cambridge,
and myself at Waltham. But at the end of the first twenty-five miles, all
got out at South Acton and waited for an express train. While thus waiting
we all utilized the time in hunting for specimens of animal life, for Agassiz.
His son Alexander had a gauze net at the end of a pole with which to
catch butterflies. Agassiz seeing a fine specimen on the wing called to the
boy to come and catch it. "Alexe! Vite! Beau Papillon" a few moments
after Mr. Samuel Felton turned over a log on the ground, and seeing a
fine black beetle under it, repeated the cry, "Alexe! Vite! Beau Papillon."
The boy ran up and seeing that his fine butterfly was a black beetle, burst
into such a merry laugh, that none of us, not even Mr. Felton himself,

could resist joining; and "Beau Papillon" became the watch-word of our party.

From Littleton we took stages for Franconia Notch. There was but one other passenger in the coach, an exceedingly solemn-looking man, and very silent. He was apparently shocked by the levity and gayety of our party; who, although on science bent, all had a cheerful mind. When we came to the foot of a long hill, we all got out and walked, except Professor Cornelius Felton who remained on the seat with the driver. As we were turning over stones and sticks, for hidden reptiles or insects; looking on the under side of leaves to discover butterflies, or snails; rapping the bushes, to start little moths, and occasionally shouting one to another "Beau Papillon"; the driver asked Professor Felton who these men were, that were with him. He replied "they are a set of naturalists, from an institution near Boston."

Our zoological pursuits retarded our movements up the hill so much that the coach had got far ahead of us, and our van was led by the solemn man, who had not taken any part in our performances. As we drew near the top of the hill, however, a remarkably beautiful butterfly went in front of him. The flush of his boyhood seemed instantly to return. He took off his hat, and made a sweep for it; and as the butterfly easily eluded him, he made a second and a third; growing more and more eager, till, at length, as the butterfly rose and soared over a high clump of bushes, our solemn man leaped into the air, made his last frantic swoop, and screamed, at the top of his voice, "Beau Papillon." At that moment, the stage in the opposite direction met ours, at the top of the hill. The drivers paused a moment to exchange salutations, and the other said to ours, "Why! You've a strange freight down there. Who are they?" Our driver, leaning toward him, said in a confidential whisper, "They are a set of naturals from that insane asylum near Boston. Their keeper just told me so."

The next day, Peirce and Agassiz were walking on the shores of Echo Lake. Agassiz saw a peculiar species of dragonfly, which he thought new, or at least rare. He had with him the muslin net on the pole, and set himself to work to catch them. Presently Peirce saw one and, in his eagerness to call Agassiz to it, gave it the name with which he had been familiar in his boyhood. "Here Agassiz, here's one of those Devil's Needles." As Agassiz came up, Peirce turned, following the insect with his eye, and saw that the solemn man had been within hearing and was looking shocked at this semi-profanity. "Sir," said he solemnly to Peirce, "can you tell me the proper botanical designation of that insect?" The delicious absurdity of the botanical name of an insect made "Botanical Designation" remain with us, ever since, a synonym for the proper name of anything in either of the kingdoms.

I cannot tell the delight which the friendship of Agassiz gave to me in more serious hours. His own conscientious fidelity to duty and the resulting approval of his conscience lay among foundations of his perennial cheerfulness and hope. But deeper than this was his religious faith in God, on which his faith in special endowment and special obligation was based. Certain scientific men have spoken of that faith in God as a weakness; inherited by Agassiz from six generations of pious Huguenot ancestry. But a man who has sustained a searching examination in Plato's philosophy, studied in the original Greek; a man who has thoroughly studied the metaphysics of Germany as far down as Hegel; and who has acomplished results in zoölogical and geological inquiry which, on the lowest estimate that can be made of them, must be acknowledged to be of the very highest magnitude and importance, is not a man to be pitied for his intellectual weakness. If weakness is to be charged upon any one, in these premises, it would seem as likely that it is weakness of intellect which fails to recognize the demonstrative force of the inductive reasoning by which Agassiz shows that there is no intelligent understanding of the animal creation, unless that creation is intelligible, i.e. in the product of intellect.

Louis Agassiz and Joseph Henry were two of the largest and broadest minds, in all directions, that I have ever chanced to meet; they were both men of indefatigable scientific industry; and both men who accomplished exceedingly high results, each in his own department; and they agreed in regarding every scientific investigation, wisely conducted, as an intelligent questioning of the Creator; so that scientific discoveries they regarded as his intelligible answers. Agassiz's adoption of Theism in preference to either Atheism, Agnosticism or Pantheism, was the result of profound original thought, and original investigation; during which he distinctly saw, and weighed, all the considerations which have ever been brought against his conclusions; weighed them and found them wanting. He once mentioned to me half a dozen of the very strongest arguments, which have been recently brought forward by the advocates of evolution, through natural selection, and assured me that he had distinctly seen, and distinctly weighed them, and rejected them, ten or fifteen years before the publication of Darwin's "Origin of Species"; and, of course, before the publication of those arguments by which others have attempted to supplement Darwin's reasoning.

Agassiz's views, on the origin of species, have often been misunderstood, and caricatured, by enthusiastic advocates of Darwin's views. Yet as the matter lay in Agassiz's own mind it seems to me that his positions were absolutely impregnable. He thought that the origin of species in their diversity, and the origin of life on this planet, were problems not within the present range of human knowledge; and that we must, for the present, rest content with studying the plan, order and connection of the universe, as a revelation of the Divine Thought. It was to him an axiomatic truth, that Science has dignity and value only when it is regarded as a recognition and exposition of the *intellectual* harmonies of the universe; that is, as an interpretation of God's thought. With this strong, clear sight of the fundamental truth in theology; there was joined a purity of heart, and a warmth of emotion, which naturally led him to a devout frame of mind. He shrunk from any display of such sacred feelings. He was repelled from those who make a boast of their piety; but he always reverenced and loved the truly devout. I never was acquainted with a man who seemed to me of purer, more temperate, self-restrained, charitable and loving character; or one who more perfectly fulfilled the royal laws of loving God with all the heart, and loving his neighbor as himself. The attachment of his friends to him was founded incomparably more upon their love of his genial, affectionate, modest, truthful, character; than upon their admiration of his transcendent abilities and marvelous accomplishments. . .

In his twenty-second year, February 14th, 1829, Agassiz wrote to his father; and among other things said, "Here is my aim. I wish it may be said of Louis Agassiz that he was the first naturalist of his time, a good citizen, and a good son; beloved of those who knew him. I feel within myself the strength of a whole generation to work toward this end; and I will reach it if the means are not wanting." These remarkable words of the young man were most remarkably fulfilled in every particular for more than thirty years before his too early death. Before a will thus consecrated to a noble aim, consecrated to the search for truth, to the service of men, to the perfection of his own character, obstacles vanished. That will was *equivalent* to the strength of a whole generation. This sentence of the young student, read in the light of his subsequent scientific achievements, and of the personal love and veneration in which his name is held, on both sides of the Atlantic, seems almost like prophetic inspiration. He was a man who, always and everywhere, not only commanded high respect, but drew men toward him in warm affection. When in an assembly of scholars, July, 1858, he announced his intention of remaining permanently in this country, and added: "I am no longer a European," a vast assembly rose, by a sudden impulse, to their feet; and greeted the announcement with joyous and repeated cheering.

Harvard University Archives.

John T. Wheelwright and Frederic J. Stimson

HOW ROLLO CAME TO BE EXAMINED

(1880)

Rollo's Journey to Cambridge was written by two of the editors of the Harvard Lampoon and first appeared in its pages in 1879–80. Since then it has gone through several editions, the latest of which appeared in 1926. Rollo is a Harvard classic. Of course, Rollo is dated today and probably would not seem funny to those who do not know Harvard, but it is a nice satire on the dangers which face a young innocent in an evil place such as Harvard. Yes, Rollo Holiday met an unhappy fate as the result of his trip to Cambridge with his Uncle George. The legend on his tombstone read:

ROLLO

Died Suddenly June 27th, 1879
"Those whom the gods love die hung"

[PRINCIPAL PERSONS OF THE STORY]

Rollo — *Fifteen years of age.*
Mr. and Mrs. Holiday — *Rollo's father and mother.*
Thanny — *Rollo's younger brother.*
Jane *or* Jinny — *Rollo's cousin, adopted by Mr. and Mrs. Holiday.*
Mr. George — *A young gentleman, Rollo's uncle.*

It was a bright June morning at about half past five. Rollo and Thanny were at play in the back yard. They had an half an hour back locked little Jinny, Rollo's cousin, in the wood-shed, and had been throwing empty tomato-cans and apple-cores through the window. Jinny had not been pleased at it, but, as Thanny said, Jinny was a girl.

Now, Thanny, who was a very ingenious boy, was cutting a willow stick into whistles with Mr. Holiday's razors, while Rollo, several years his senior, was smoking a paper cigarette which he had found in his Uncle George's pocket. Mr. George smoked for a cruel nervous disease, and therefore his smoking was no precedent for a boy to follow. Rollo knew this well, and therefore felt a little guilty when he heard Mr. George's voice over the fence.

"Rollo," said Mr. George.

"Yes," answered Rollo, hiding his cigarette behind his back.

"What are you about, Rollo?" asked Mr. George.

"About fifteen," answered Rollo.

"What!" inquired Mr. George, sharply, who was always very peremptory and decisive, though always just in his treatment of Rollo.

"Bunch! Uncle George," was Rollo's reply.

"Rollo," said Mr. George, waiving the repartee, "What are you going to do to-day?"

"To try to be good; Jonas has promised to make me a jack-a-lantern in the shed after tea, if I am a good boy all day."

"I have something far better for you to do to-day, Rollo," rejoined Mr. George.

Rollo was very much pleased, for Mr. George was a very thoughtful man, who had his nephew's interest very much at heart; so Rollo clambered briskly over the fence and went into the house.

He put on his cloth cap with a leather visor and a silken tassel, and brushed his green spencer; when his toilet * was made, he ran down into the "settin' room," where Mr. George was reading the Encyclopaedia.

Mr. George was reading this work through, and had advanced as far as Abyssinia.

"Uncle George," cried Rollo, "I am sorry to disturb you!"

"You are very polite, Rollo. See, I put a mark in my book that I may know where I left off. If I did not do so, I should have to begin over again. I once got as far as Xerxes, and, neglecting to put in the mark, was compelled to go back to Aaron."

It was very kind and thoughtful for Mr. George to tell Rollo this.

"What is your plan for to-day?" asked Rollo.

"I am going to drive with you, Jonas, and Thanny to Cambridge. I had intended to take Jinny with me, but she is in the wood-shed and I have no authority to take her out."

"What are we to do there?" asked Rollo.

"You are to be examined for College, Rollo. You will be examined in twenty required subjects and five optional ones all at once."

"But," interrupted Rollo, "I have travelled so much that I have never been to school, and have never studied!"

"That may or may not be unfortunate," was Mr. George's reply. "As I understand it, an examination is to find out what you do not know rather than what you do. If, as you say, you know nothing, you must see the necessity of your being examined."

Rollo was convinced by the argument, and was glad when he heard the sound of wheels on the carriage road, and saw Jonas flicking a fly from old Dapple's flank.

"Come, Rollo," said Mr. George, putting on his dress-coat and patent-leather shoes, "I am prepared to go . . ."

---

* Toilet is a French word. It means dressing yourself so as to look as spruce as possible, using little or no soap and water.

"One of the greatest benefits of a course at Harvard, Rollo," said Uncle George, as they descended the steps, "is that derived from viewing the noble architectural specimens which are all around you."

Rollo had seen many beautiful things, both in his journey to Cambridge on that morning and in his European travels, but he had never seen anything which impressed him so much as the spacious building which Mr. George pointed out to him. It was built in the perpendicular style of architecture, its lines were straight, its roof slated, and it had many windows in it, which gave upon the green.

"What is it used for?" asked Rollo.

"It is called Thayer's Hall; and as, from its size, Mr. Thayer would not require it all for his residence, I suppose that some of the scholars live here also."

"I want to know!" said Rollo. "Perhaps I shall live here next year, Uncle George."

"Whether you do or not depends upon yourself, my boy. Jonas and Thanny have not appeared yet. Can it be that they are in trouble? I must look after them, and after information as to your examinations. For, although the Dean was a frank-spoken and affable gentleman, I did not get from his remarks a clear idea of the requirements for admission. Therefore I leave you to look around here by yourself. You will undoubtedly commit many blunders; but that is your own look-out. In no event must you look for help from me."

Saying this, Mr. George walked off across a path leading to a gate. Rollo watched him go across the street and finally disappear. . .

"Rollo," said his uncle, ". . . It is high time for you to go to your examination. Jonas will show you the way."

Jonas took a large box under his arm, and they walked along together.

"Did you ever go to college, Jonas?" said Rollo.

"Yes," said Jonas. "I went to the Bussey Institute. In fact, I may say, Le Bussey Institute, c'est moi."

"Don't you wish you could go now?"

"Yes," said Jonas, "I think I should like it better than you will."

"Better than I?" said Rollo, looking up with surprise; "why, I like it very much indeed."

"You haven't tried it yet," said Jonas.

"O, but I know I shall like it."

"They all like it the first day; but afterwards they find a great many things which they do not like very well."

"What things?" asked Rollo.

"Why, sometimes you will get to playing poker after tea, and when prayertime comes before breakfast you will not want to go. Then your studies will be hard sometimes, and the Dean will not be nice to you. And perhaps they will not elect you into the St. Paul's."

Rollo felt somewhat disappointed at hearing such an account of the business of going to college from Jonas. He had expected that it was to be all pleasure, and he could not help thinking that Jonas must be mistaken about it. However, he said nothing, but walked along slowly and silently.

"Please to tell me what have you in the box, Jonas," asked Rollo.

"O, that I call my examination apparatus," answered Jonas.

"An examination apparatus?" cried Rollo.

"An examination apparatus," answered Jonas.

Jonas set the box upon the ground and opened the lid, which was fastened with two hinges and a hook. Rollo saw therein many strange things.

"This," said Jonas, taking up a bundle of cigarette papers, "contains all Latin and Greek Grammar, Chinese I, Fine Arts III, Ancient and Modern Geography, Calisthenics, Andrew's Latin Lexicon, and Quackenbos's History of the United States. And this is a preparation for producing a sudden and violent nose-bleed. This is a certificate of good moral character, signed by the Superintendent of Police and the Treasurer of the Howard Athenaeum. This bank-note is counterfeit. On the back — which is blank — is written in invisible ink all irregular verbs, the equations of eccentric curves, and the obscure and disputed points in American history."

"But suppose they ask me the regular verbs?" said Rollo.

"They will not," said Jonas. "They only wish you to know the exceptions, because they prove the rules."

"But suppose they see me with the bank-note — "

"They will only think you are endowing the proctor: and a percentage of all bribes goes to the fund for pensioning good and faithful servants."

John T. Wheelwright and Frederic J. Stimson, *Rollo's Journey to Cambridge* (Boston, 1880).

George Santayana

THE HARVARD YARD
(1882–1912)

George Santayana once described Harvard as a place where "much generous intellectual sincerity went with such spiritual penury and moral confusion as to offer nothing but a lottery ticket or a chance at the grab-bag to the orphan mind." Despite this disparagement, the Spanish-born Santayana remembered with tenderness and he in turn is remembered with reverence. After graduating from Harvard in 1886, he took two years of graduate study at Berlin. He came back to Cambridge at the age of twenty-six as an instructor in philosophy, and during twenty-two years of teaching rose to the rank of full professor. He resigned in 1912 and until his death in 1952 lived a meditative life in Europe, his last years as the guest of a convent just outside Rome. Aside from his philosophical writings, the chief of which is The Life of Reason, *Santayana is known as a poet and has published a three-volume autobiography* (Persons and Places, The Middle Span, *and* My Host the World) *as well as a "novel in the form of a memoir,"* The Last Puritan.

IF FORTUNE had been unkind to me in respect to my times — except that for the intellectual epicure the 1890's were enjoyable — in respect to places fortune has been most friendly, setting me down not in any one center, where things supposed to be important or exciting were happening, but in various quiet places from which cross-vistas opened into the world. Of these places the most familiar to me, after Avila, was the Harvard Yard. I lived there for eleven years, first as an undergraduate, later as an instructor and proctor. No place, no rooms, no mode of living could have been more suitable for a poor student and a free student, such as I was and as I wished to be. My first room, on the ground floor in the northeast corner of Hollis, was one of the cheapest to be had in Cambridge: the rent was forty-four dollars a year. I had put it first for that reason on my list of rooms, and I got my first choice. It was so cheap because it had no bedroom, no water, and no heating; also the ground floor seems to have been thought less desirable, perhaps because the cellar below might increase the cold or the dampness. I don't think I was ever cold there in a way to disturb me or affect my health. I kept the hard-coal fire banked and burning all night, except from Saturday to Monday, when I slept at my mother's at Roxbury. An undergraduate's room in any case is not a good place for study, unless it be at night, under pressure of some special task. At other times, there are constant interruptions, or temptations to interrupt oneself: recitations, lectures, meals, walks, meetings, and sports. I soon found the Library the best place to work in. It was not crowded; a particular alcove where there were philosophical books at hand, and foreign periodicals, soon became my regular place for reading. I could take my own books and notebooks there if necessary; but for the most part I browsed; and although my memory is not specific, and I hardly know what I read, except that I never missed *La Revue des Deux Mondes*, I don't think my time was wasted. A great deal stuck to me, without my knowing its source, and my mind became accustomed to large horizons and to cultivated judgments.

As to my lodging, I had to make up my sofa bed at night before getting into it; in the morning I left the bedding to be aired, and the "goody," whose services were included in the rent, put it away when she came to dust or to sweep. I also had to fetch my coal and water from the cellar, or the water in summer from the College pump that stood directly in front of my door. This was economy on my part, as I might have paid the janitor to do it for me; perhaps also to black my boots, which I always did myself, as I had done it at home. But my life was a miracle of economy. I had an allowance from my mother of $750 a year to cover all expenses. Tuition absorbed, $150; rent, $44; board at Memorial Hall, with a reduction for absence during the week-end, about $200; which left less than one dollar a day for clothes, books, fares, subscriptions, amusements, and pocket money. Sometimes, but very rarely, I received a money-prize or a money-present; I had no protection or encouragement from rich relations or persons of influence. The Sturgises were no longer affluent, and as yet they hardly knew of my existence. Later, when their natural generosity could (and did) express itself, it did so in other ways, because I was already independent and needed no help. Yet on my less than one dollar a day I managed to dress decently, to belong to minor societies like the Institute, the Pudding, and the O.K., where the fees were moderate, to buy all necessary books, and even, in my Junior year, to stay at rich people's houses, and to travel. Robert had given me his old evening clothes, which fitted me well enough: otherwise the rich people's houses could not have been visited. . .

Life in the Yard for me, during my second period of residence there, 1890–1896, had a different quality. I hadn't a horse or a valet, but could count on enough pocket-money, a varied circle of friends, clubs, and ladies' society in Boston and Cambridge, and the foreglow and afterglow of holidays spent in Europe. The first year, when I had only one foot in the stirrup and was not yet in the saddle as a Harvard teacher, I lived in Thayer; graceless quarters and the insecure stammering beginnings of a lecturer. The only thing I remember is the acquaintance I then made with my next-door neighbor, Fletcher, who was afterwards a professor of Comparative Literature and made a translation of the *Divina Commedia*. He was also a football player; and I remember one day when I was violently sick at my stomach — my digestion in those days being imperfect — he thought to help me by holding my head (a common illusion among helpful people) and his grasp was like a ring of iron. He was a very good fellow, with a richer nature than most philologists, and firm morals. We had long talks and discovered common tastes in literature and the arts; but he didn't remain at Harvard, and I lost sight of him. Even if he had been at hand, we should hardly have seen each other often: there were things in us fundamentally inaccessible to one another. Besides, though I became a professor myself, I never had a real friend who was a professor. Is it jealousy, as among women, and a secret un-willingness to be wholly pleased? Or is it the consciousness that a pro-fessor or a woman has to be partly a sham; whence a mixture of contempt and pity for such a poor victim of necessity? In Fletcher, and in the nobler professors, the shamming is not an effect of the profession, but rather, as in inspired clergymen, the profession is an effect of an innate passion for shamming. Nobody feels that passion more than I have felt it in poetry and in religion; but I never felt it in academic society or academic philos-ophy, and I gave up being a professor as soon as I could.

The next year I again had my pick of rooms in the Yard, securing No. 7 Stoughton, in the southeast corner of the first floor, where I stayed for six winters. Here there was a bedroom, and my coal and water were brought up for me by the janitor; on the other hand I often made my own breakfast — tea, boiled eggs, and biscuits — and always my tea in the afternoon, for I had now lived in England and learned the comforts of a bachelor in lodgings. Only — what would not have happened in Eng-land — I washed my own dishes and ordered my tea, eggs, milk and sugar from the grocers: domestic cares that pleased me, and that preserved my nice china — a present from Howard Cushing — during all those years. There was a round bathtub under my cot, and my sister's crucifix on the wall above it: only cold water, but the contents of the kettle boiling on the hearth served to take off the chill. I had also acquired a taste for fresh air, and my window was always a little open.

One day a new goody left the bathtub full of slops, explaining that she hadn't known what to do with it; it was the only bathtub in her entry. I had myself taken only recently to a daily sponge bath. When I was an undergraduate few ever took a bath in Cambridge; those who lodged in private houses might share one bathroom between them, and those who went to the Gymnasium might have a shower bath after exer-cise; but your pure "grind" never bathed, and I only when I went home for the week-end. In Little's Block I believe there was a bathroom on each floor; but Beck was the only luxurious dormitory where each room had its private bathroom. Habits, however, were rapidly changing. Vio-lent exercise and fiercely contested sports were in the ascendant among the athletes; this involved baths, but not luxury. Yet luxury was in the ascendant too; and the polite ideal of one man one bathroom, and hot water always hot, was beginning to disguise luxury under the decent names of privacy and health. . . .

Hollis and Stoughton were twin red-brick buildings of the eighteenth century, solid, simple, symmetrical and not unpleasing. No effort had been made by the builders towards picturesqueness or novelty; they knew what decent lodgings for scholars were, and that there was true economy in building them well. The rectangular wooden window frames divided into many squares, flush with the walls, and painted white, served for a modest and even gay decoration. There was a classic cornice, and the windows immediately under it were square instead of oblong and suggested metopes, while the slope of the roof also was that of a temple, though without pediments at the ends. On the whole, it was the architecture of sturdy poverty, looking through thrift in the direction of wealth. It well matched the learning of early New England, traditionally staunch and narrow, yet also thrifty and tending to positivism; a learning destined as it widened to be undermined and to become, like the architecture, flimsy and rich. It had been founded on accurate Latin and a spellbound constant reading of the Bible: but in the Harvard of my day we had heard a little of everything, and nobody really knew his Latin or knew his Bible. You might say that the professor of Hebrew did know his Bible, and the professors of Latin their Latin. No doubt, in the sense that they could write technical articles on the little points of controversy at the moment among philologists; but neither Latin nor the Bible flowed through them and made their spiritual lives; they were not vehicles for anything great. They were grains in a quicksand, agents and patients in an anonymous moral migration that had not yet written its classics.

In both these old buildings I occupied corner rooms, ample, low, originally lighted by four windows, with window seats in the thickness of the wall, which a cushion could make comfortable for reading. Between the side windows the deep chimney stack projected far into the room, and no doubt at first showed its rough or glazed bricks, as the low ceiling probably showed its great beams. But an "improvement" had spoiled the dignity of these chambers. The rage for "closets" invaded America, why I am not antiquary enough to know. Was it that wardrobes and chests, with or without drawers, had become too heavy and cumbrous for an unsettled population? Or was it that a feminine demand for a seemly "bed-sitting room" had insisted on a place of hiding for one's belongings? Anyhow, in 19 Hollis both the side windows had been hidden by oblique partitions, going from the edges of the chimney stack to the front and back walls and enclosing the desired closets, not large enough for a bed, but capable of containing a washstand, trunks, and garments hanging on pegs. Luckily in 7 Stoughton this operation had mutilated only one angle, and left me one pleasant side window open to the South, and affording a glimpse of Holden Chapel and the vista then open over the grass towards Cambridge Common.

Yet it was the outlook to the east, from both rooms, that was most characteristic. The old elms in the Yard were then in all their glory, and in summer formed a grove of green giants, with arching and drooping branches, that swung like garlands in the breeze. This type of elm, though graceful and lofty, has a frail air, like tall young women in consumption.

The foliage is nowhere thick, too many thin ribs and sinews are visible: and this transparency was unfortunate in the Harvard Yard, where the full charm depended on not seeing the background. In winter the place was ungainly and forlorn, and not only to the eye. The uneven undrained ground would be flooded with rain and half-melted dirty snow one day, and another day strewn with foul ashes over the icy pavements. This was a theme for unending grumbling and old jokes; but we were young and presumably possessed snow-boots called "arctics" or thick fisherman's boots warranted watertight. Anyhow we survived; and as bad going for pedestrians is made inevitable during winter and spring by the New England climate, the Yard was not much worse in this respect than the surrounding places.

Holworthy in my day was still nominally the "Seniors' Paradise," but not in reality: in reality those who could afford it lived in private houses, in Little's Block, or in Beck. Holworthy preserved, as it has sometimes recovered, only the charm of tradition. The two bedrooms to each study favored the pleasant custom of chumming; but as yet Holworthy had no baths, not even shower baths, and no central heating. Modern improvements seem to me in almost everything to be a blessing. Electricity, vacuum cleaning, and ladies' kitchens render life simpler and more decent; but central heating, in banishing fireplaces, except as an occasional luxury or affectation, has helped to destroy the charm of home. I don't mean merely the ancient and rustic sanctity of the hearth; I mean also the home-comforts of the modern bachelor. An obligatory fire was a useful and blessed thing. In northern climates it made the poetry of indoor life. Round it you sat, into it you looked, by it you read, in it you made a holocaust of impertinent letters and rejected poems. On the hob your kettle simmered, and the little leaping flames cheered your heart and ventilated your den. Your fire absolved you from half your dependence on restaurants, cafés, and servants; it also had the moralizing function of giving you a duty in life from which any distraction brought instant punishment, and taught you the feminine virtues of nurse, cook, and Vestal virgin. Sometimes, I confess, these cares became annoying; the fire kept you company, but like all company it sometimes interrupted better things. At its best, a wood fire is the most glorious; but unless the logs are of baronial dimensions, it dies down too quickly, the reader or the writer is never at peace; while a hard-coal fire (which also sometimes goes out) sleeps like a prisoner behind its iron bars, without the liveliness of varied flames. The ideal fire is soft coal, such as I had in England and also in America when I chose; like true beauty in woman, it combines brilliancy with lastingness. I congratulate myself that in the Harvard Yard I was never heated invisibly and willy-nilly by public prescription, but always by my own cheerful fire, that made solitude genial and brought many a genial friend who loved cheerfulness to sit by it with me, not rejecting in addition a drink and a little poetry; no tedious epic, but perhaps one of Shakespeare's sonnets or an ode of Keats, something fit to inspire conversation and not to replace it.

The quality of the Harvard Yard, both in its architecture and its manners, was then distinctly Bohemian: not of the Parisian description, since no *petite amie* or *grande amie* was in evidence, but of the red-brick lodging, tavern and stable-yard Bohemia of Dickens and Thackeray; yet being in a college, the arts and the intellect were not absent from it altogether. . .

Richard C. Evarts

EXAMINATION FOR ALICE

(1913)

One cannot read Alice's Adventures in Cambridge, *by Richard Conover Evarts, A.B. 1913, without asking what else this gifted humorist wrote; for his Alice must rank high among the many parodies of Lewis Carroll's little girl. The answer is nothing — at least for publication. Evarts has been a Boston lawyer and has lived in Cambridge since graduation. He has been active in Cambridge politics and was for many years City Solicitor. "Harvard is all right, I guess," he remarked in the 25th anniversary report of his College Class. "The Harvard Law School gave me an excellent training. It was my own fault if Harvard College didn't too. I sometimes think the denizens of Harvard, and probably of every other college too, are liable to consider themselves too élite and of a different race from the ordinary unregenerate people who make up the rest of the world, and they're not."*

ALICE was just about to enter one of the tempting little shops with purple socks and ties in the window, when she saw the White Rabbit hurrying across a mud puddle. She ran after him, and caught him just as he reached a curbstone.

"Please — " she began.

But the White Rabbit did not even turn his head.

"No, I haven't any pennies," he said.

"But I wanted to know — " said Alice.

"Oh, it's you, is it?" the White Rabbit said, turning round and blowing a huge cloud of smoke from his pipe into Alice's face. "Well, come on."

"Where?" asked Alice.

"To the Infection Meeting, of course," said the White Rabbit, starting off at a rapid pace.

"But I don't want to be infected," Alice said, as she ran after him, "I've had the mumps once, and the measles, and ever so many other things."

"Ah! But you haven't had probation yet," said the White Rabbit, "and you'll catch it sure if you don't go to your Infection Meetings. I'm a Sophomore and I ought to know. Come on."

"Who will give it to me?" asked Alice, feeling a little alarmed.

"The Queen, of course. Come on."

Alice didn't like being ordered about in this way, but she followed the White Rabbit, who led her to a room filled with animals of all kinds sitting on benches. At one end of the room was a platform where a large frog sat behind a desk. He was a very young-looking frog, Alice thought, but he looked so severe that she sat down quietly beside the White Rabbit.

The frog, after looking more severe than ever, suddenly began to write very fast on a blackboard behind him. Alice tried to make out what he was writing, but it seemed to be chiefly nonsense. It ran something like this:

"If, other things being equal, the level of prices should rise, and thus falling create a demand and supply with, and as which, would you consider this a division of labor? If so, when, and in what capacity? If not, why not, and under what circumstances?"

As soon as he had finished, all the other animals produced paper from nowhere in particular, and began to scribble as fast as they could. Alice noticed that the Lizard, who was sitting in the front row, was the only one who wrote anything original. All the others copied from his paper, and crowded round him so closely that Alice was afraid the poor little creature would be smothered. Meanwhile the frog looked at the ceiling. "He couldn't look anywhere else, poor thing," thought Alice; "his eyes are in the top of his head."

About two seconds had passed when the frog called out "Time!" and began to gather up the papers. When he had collected them all, he took them to his desk and began to mark them. He marked the first one A, the second one B, and so on down to F, when he began over again with A. All this time he kept his eyes tight shut. "So he will be sure to be impartial," the White Rabbit explained to Alice.

After the marking was finished, the frog handed the papers back to their owners. The White Rabbit, who had written nothing at all, had a large A on his paper. The Lizard, however, had an F marked on his.

"A," said the White Rabbit to Alice, "means that I wrote an excellent paper."

"But you wrote nothing," objected Alice.

"Nothing succeeds like success," said the White Rabbit, and hurried away, leaving Alice a little puzzled.

Meanwhile all the animals except the frog had disappeared.

"Would you mind telling me," began Alice, feeling that there ought to be some conversation, "why you — "

"Certainly not," said the frog, handing her a book. "I think you will find this a very able exposition of the subject."

Alice opened the book, and finding it to be poetry, she read the first piece through.

JABBERWOCKY

'T was taussig, and the bushnell hart
　　Did byron hurlbut in the rand,
All barrett was the wendell (Bart.)
　　And the charles t. cope-*land*.

Beware the Münsterberg, my son!
　　'T will read your mind — you bet it can!
Beware the Grandgent bird, and shun
　　The frisky Merriman.

He took his bursar sword in hand:
　　Long time his neilson foe he sought —
So rested he by the bernbaum tree,
　　And stood awhile in thought.

And as in coolidge thought he stood,
　　The Münsterberg, with eyes of flame,
Came spalding through the perry wood,
　　And babbit as it came!

One, two! One, two! And through and through
　　The bursar blade went snicker-snack!
He left it dead, and with its head
　　He santayanad back.

And hast thou slain the Münsterberg?
　　Come to my arms, my bierwirth boy!
O Kittredge day! Allard! Bôcher!
　　He schofield in his joy.

'T was taussig, and the bushnell hart
　　Did byron hurlbut in the rand,
All barrett was the wendell (Bart.)
　　And the charles t. cope-*land*.

"It's very interesting," said Alice, after she had finished, "but I don't *quite* understand it."

"You will absorb it after awhile," said the frog, as he got up and walked away, "if you have the faculty."

Richard Conover Evarts, *Alice's Adventures in Cambridge* (*Harvard Lampoon*, 1913). Illustrations by E. L. Barron. Copyright, 1913, by the Harvard Lampoon.

Charles Loring Jackson

THE SOPHOCLES MYTH
(1923)

It could be said that Charles Loring Jackson (1847–1935) served under four presidents of Harvard, for he was appointed instructor before the resignation of President Thomas Hill, and he was Erving Professor of Chemistry Emeritus during the first years of the Conant administration. One of the early investigators in the field of organic chemistry, Professor Jackson was known during his lifetime to hundreds of Harvard students. His memories of that unusual Harvard professor, Evangelinus Apostolides Sophocles, himself a member of the Faculty for forty-one years, are those of both student and academic colleague.

OF ALL the striking figures that have appeared in Harvard College, Professor Sophocles is undoubtedly the most picturesque; for his head was that of a Jupiter Tonans, and, although mounted on a short stocky body, it made him wonderfully impressive and even a little terrifying, when he rolled his great fierce eyes and threw out a question in his deep resonant voice; but behind this apparent fierceness lurked a genial humorist full of affectionate kindliness for his friends, and overflowing with delightful stories, which were caught up and repeated eagerly, until at the time of his death a real Sophocles myth had grown up around him.

With the dying out of the last generation that knew him personally these stories are vanishing, and, as I have been urged repeatedly to do what I can to preserve them, I have written the best that I remember, and am publishing them in spite of great misgivings, because they depended for much of their effect on his strange personality and especially on the racy quaintness of his speech both in its unusual idioms and rich foreign pronunciation, the greater part of which must be lost in the written word.

He was born in the Vale of Tempe, and, it would appear from the following stories, in the midst of a very primitive race:

"When I was a little boy, all the people of my village were frightened nearly out of their wits by some lights that they did see every night moving about in the churchyard. They did think the lights must be vampires, and so every night the whole population did collect in the largest house in the village and stayed there till broad daylight, as they were afraid to be alone in the dark.

"After some time the bravest among the young men did go out to investigate, and did find the lights were carried by men stealing grapes in the vineyard beyond the churchyard."

The next story was published by Professor Palmer in the *Atlantic Monthly* some years ago. I have also met with another version differing from this only in the names. I quote from memory:

"My father was proistos of Philippopolis. One night he was sitting in his house a short distance outside the town, when two men came in.

" 'What do you want?' Said my father.

" 'We have come to keell you.' Said the men.

" 'Who sent you?' Said my father.

" 'Constantinos.' Said the men. Constantinos was my father's political adversary.

" 'How much will Constantinos give you to keell me?' Asked my father.

" 'Seventy-five cents.' Said the men.

" 'I will give you a dollar to keell Constantinos.'

"My father left Philippopolis that night, but he came back in five years. Such things were forgotten quickly in Greece."

Their neighbors were, it seems, even more primitive:

"The Thracians are a rough people. When they have a great feast, one of the guests does get up on a stool with a sharp sword in his hand, fixes around his neck a halter from a beam above, and then does kick away the stool, and try to cut the rope, before he is hanged; and, if he does not succeed, they let him keek, till he is dead. They are a rough people."

And here is another story about some of his more remote neighbors:

"In Wallachia, when the shepherds dine, they sit in a great ring about a big iron pot, and do have only one spoon. The first does take a mouthful of the soup, and does pass the spoon to the next and he does take another mouthful, and so it goes on. At first the spoon moves slowly, but soon it goes faster and faster, until at last you can hardly see it.

"One day, when thirty shepherds were eating their soup in this way, a wolf came along, and did steal a sheep, and the whole thirty did have their mouths full, so that they could not cry out, and the wolf did get away with the sheep."

I have never heard why he left his native valley, or any details about his education except that it is said one of his teachers used to call him Sophocles, and he liked the name so much that he added it to his own — Evangelinus Apostolides. Apparently names did not soar above patronymics in his village.

I think it not improbable that he was educated in Egypt. At any rate he lived there for many years, but of his stories about it I can recall only one:

"They do talk about the plagues of Egypt, but they were there before Moses, and have been there ever since. Take the flies. They are still a plague. You will see a veiled woman making bread (if she is oogly, she is very closely veiled), and in her hand she will have a flyflap, and every few seconds she will swish it through the dough, but it is no use. There will always be flies in the bread. It is wise to try to think they are currants."

At a later date he became a novice in the monastery on Mount Sinai; and he told me that while there he found his faith was not sufficiently strong and consulted his superior about it, who advised him to go to the top of Mount Sinai, where the miraculously preserved body of Saint Katharine would banish all his doubts. Then he gave me a remarkable version of the legend of Saint Katharine, of which unfortunately I can remember only a few scraps:

"After Saint Katharine had been thrown into prison, the emperor did send twelve learned men to her, and they did argue with her the whole night, and in the morning they did go to the emperor and say:

" 'She has converted us. We are Chreestians.'

"And he did cut their heads off."

"Then he did send twelve other men still more learned than the first, and they did argue with Saint Katharine the whole night, and in the morning they did go to the emperor and say:

" 'She has converted us. We are Chreestians.'

"And he did cut their heads off."

"Then he did send to her the empress and his daughter, the princess, and they did argue with her the whole night, and in the morning they did go to the emperor and say:

" 'She has converted us. We are Chreestians."

"And he did cut their heads off."

I can remember nothing of his account of her martyrdom, I am sorry to say.

"After Saint Katharine was dead, her body was carried by four angels to the top of Mount Sinai, where it did turn to stone, and it is there to this day.

"Well! I did go up the mountain."

"And did you see the body?"

"Yes. I did see the body."

I, nearly springing out of my chair with excitement:

"What did it look like?"

"O! Joost a heap of stones."

I am inclined to connect this story with the fact that soon after we hear of him in America, where, I believe, he taught Greek for a time at Yale, but in a year or two came to Harvard, and stayed there from the early fifties till his death in the eighties, at first as tutor, and afterward as "Professor of Ancient, Modern, and Patristic Greek."

All this time he lived in the first entry of Holworthy Hall, and did his own cooking — most of it presumably in the second bedroom, which soon became known as the mysterious bedroom, since he positively refused to let anyone go into it. Many attempts were made to solve the mystery; the most promising was once, when Mr. Sophocles invited a caller to stay to luncheon, and began bringing things for the meal out of the bedroom, the visitor, recognizing the chance of a lifetime, sprang to his feet and said:

"Let me help you, Mr. Sophocles."

But he, blocking the doorway, answered in a voice like muffled thunder:

"No! There be dark mysteries in here."

One of my friends was so fortunate as to see something of his house-keeping, for once, meeting him in the College Yard, Mr. Sophocles put his mouth close to my friend's ear and asked in a sepulchral but resonant whisper:

"Do you like caviare?"

"Yes. I am not the general of whom Shakespeare spoke."

"Then come and take tea with me tomorrow. We will have some Samian wine also. You know what Byron says: 'Fill high the bowl with Samian wine.'"

The next evening the visitor found the table set with the caviare, a loaf of bread, some butter, and in the middle the "bowl of Samian wine." Mr. Sophocles sat by, whittling plates and spoons out of a shingle. The bread was toasted and spread with the caviare (of which the visitor got his fill for the first time in his life); and then, when the feast was over, the plates and spoons were thrown into the fire — a method of avoiding washing dishes that I would recommend to young housekeepers.

At this time he took snuff in large quantities continually — the only person I ever saw who indulged in this habit. I cannot say it increased his personal tidyness.

I first met him taking tea at the Botanic Garden, when I was about eight years old. Even then I was immensely struck with his appearance — especially by the incongruity between his head like a heroic Greek statue and his short, stout, stubby body, and I was quite as much surprised at seeing him from time to time during the meal take a bunch of keys out of his pocket and rattle it under the table.

After that I saw him often, as he frequently dined at the Botanic Garden with my aunt, who always made a point of treating him to baked beans, or some other dish that he especially liked, but could not manage in his room.

He took a great fancy to my brother and me, as he was very fond of children; and one evening, when he came to call at the Garden and my brother happened to be lying asleep on the porch, he stooped down and kissed him remarking:

"It is hard to keess with such a big beard as mine."

Then for some years I saw little of him; so that it was not until we were on the Parietal Board together that I became intimate with him once more.

Even after years of service on the Board his ideas of the undergraduate remained peculiar. One evening, when there was some noise in the Yard, I suggested that we should go out and see what was the matter, but he answered:

"I would not go. Those fellows would keell you as soon as not."

For many years he taught required Greek, but in my day gave only advanced electives, and, as science and German exhausted my three (!) electives, to my great regret I was unable to take a course with him, and cannot speak from personal experience in regard to his teaching, but he certainly resented its technical details, as he used to announce an examination by saying:

"Gentlemen! We must have an examination to *avoid* the law."

And on one occasion, when a proctor reported a man for cheating in his examination, his only comment was:

"It make no matter. I nevare look at his book anyway."

I have the following story on the highest authority —

In one of his recitations he asked:

"Pratt. Where did Homer see lions?"

"Not prepared. Sir."

"Landon. Where did Homer see lions?"

Landon (the first scholar in the class): "Not prepared. Sir."

"Nason. Where did Homer see lions?"

Nason was a very low scholar, and to make a laugh answered:

"In Barnum's circus. Sir."

"Right! You are right! He did see them in the collections of the kings."

And down went an 8 (the highest mark) for Nason, said to be the first that had ever come to him; and more than that afterward he got an 8 at every recitation, no matter how he recited (I tell the tale, as it was told me).

Years later the man I have called Nason made his will, and left to Harvard College the largest bequest ever received from a graduate up to that time. I have often wondered whether his pleasant remembrance of "old Sophy" had anything to do with this. It is possible.

The following story may be a garbled descendant of the last, or quite as probably refers to a different incident:

In one of his recitations he asked:

"How did the lions get into the Peloponnesus?"

The first man answered:

"Walked in. Sir."

"Wrong. The next."

"They were brought in a ship."

"Wrong. The next."

"Brought in a chariot."

Then the wildest guesses were in order — railroad trains, steamboats, even balloons were suggested with the same result, until at last he said:

"There nevare were any lions in the Peloponnesus."

One year on Class Day some young ladies told a student that they wished to meet Professor Sophocles, and, when he asked if he might introduce them, the answer was:

"I have no objection. Bring them along."

Accordingly the first one was brought up:

"Miss Smith, Professor Sophocles."

"Ah! Meess Smeeth. It ees a very fine day. That ees sufficient. The next."

And so on through the whole line.

He was a very distinguished scholar. His Greek Grammar was in common use in my day, but his great work was a "Dictionary of Patristic Greek" to which most of his time in Cambridge was devoted. I have been told that he was the first, or at least one of the first authorities in the world on this subject. I remember once, when I was an undergraduate, seeing in his room a bookcase extending nearly the whole length of the wall, which I looked at with positive awe, when told it was the dictionary.

A few years later he said to a friend that he was very anxious to go to an important meeting at a distance from Cambridge, but could not do so, because it would take him away from town over night.

"What harm would there be in that?" Asked his friend.

"I must stay to guard that box from burglars."

"Why! What is there in the box?"

"The materials for my dictionary."

He evidently had a high opinion of the culture of the Cambridge burglar.

When the dictionary was ready to come out, Professor Theophilus Parsons (who had been connected with the publishing business) in the kindness of his heart made arrangements for its publication, but Sophocles did not take it at all kindly, saying:

"I do not like Professor Parsons's offeecious inter-meddling."

And for some time kept out of his way. At last it happened that Parsons saw Sophocles reading in the University Bookstore, came up behind him and, slapping him on the back, shouted:

"Hullo Sophocles! What have you been doing with yourself these last thousand years?"

Sophocles rolled his great fierce eyes up at him, answered:

"Minding my own beezeness!"

And plunged fathoms deep into his book again.

In the last years of his life he took up keeping hens in a chickenhouse, which his friend Miss Fay allowed him to build beside her house — now the Fay House of Radcliffe College. Here he passed many happy hours among his pets; and it is said that he gave names to all of them and that the right fowl would come, when it was called. Also that he never could bear to have one of them killed, so that they all died, I was going to say, in their beds; but he did not carry this feeling so far as to refuse to eat the eggs. All of this is confirmed by the fact that he gave one of my cousins a gamecock with a long pedigree, named Demosthenes, I believe, on condition it should not be killed.

The fact that he kept hens is the only foundation for the ridiculous story that he kept them in the mysterious bedroom.

When in the late sixties some members of my family were going to Egypt, one of them called on Mr. Sophocles to ask for advice:

"Mr. Sophocles I am going to Egypt."

"Ah! You are going to Egypt. You will go to Cairo?" (I have often tried without success to catch the strange twist of the tongue with which he rolled out this name). "Yes. We shall certainly go to Cairo."

"You will go to the Armenian Monastery?"

"I should be very glad to go to the Armenian Monastery."

"You will meet my onkel."

"I shall be delighted to meet your uncle Mr. Sophocles."

"He will cheat you."

Harvard Alumni Bulletin, March 15, 1923.

Theodore Pearson

PRESIDENT LOWELL BUILDS HIS HARVARD
(1925)

One spring day in his senior year, when the seniors still lived in the College Yard, Theodore Pearson glanced through his study window and saw President Lowell on an inspection tour of the new freshman dormitories rising to cloister the older buildings from the noise of Harvard Square. His description of the scene comes from Dean Yeomans' life of President Lowell.

I WAS LOOKING out of my window in Hollis yesterday afternoon at the piles of dirt, the outhouses, and the concrete forms, when round the corner a small brown spaniel came into the enclosure. He was followed, at a respectful distance, by President Lowell, and he, in turn, by Professor

Yeomans. While the President was still on the path in front of Holden Chapel he was his usual self — the downcast head, the gloomy stoop of the shoulders, the plodding stride, and the inconsequential cane — but when he came in sight of the construction work, his aspect changed. His head became erect, his shoulders were thrown back, his pace was quickened, and his cane — here was the greatest difference — became the baton of a field marshal.

I was viewing the proceedings through a closed window, but the vigor of the pantomime told more clearly than words the subject of their conversation. President Lowell was expounding the system of paths within the quadrangle; the cane became positively voluble. It pointed, swept, darted, flourished, even commanded. It laid down gravel walks, covered the ground with green sod, planted shrubs . . . and perhaps a few "Keep off the Grass" signs. It spoke great volumes about its owner; it whispered that here, amid the lime barrels and the scaffolding, he daily found his happiness. Away from current cudgelings of press and alumni — albeit face to face with one of their favorite targets — the President dreamed and planned the Harvard that is to come.

Yet all this dumb-show was not really a conversation, but a monologue; Professor Yeomans had no cane, and was further gagged by having to carry an overcoat. He could do no more than tag along in polite acquiescence as the President stalked from one vantage point to the next. Only the spaniel took part in the comment; his tail was eloquent of approval. He clambered up the mounds of dirt, inspected the tool sheds, sniffed approbation at the lime barrels, and expressed satisfaction with odd corners of the lot. In fact, he continued his waddling appraisement some time after President Lowell had resumed his downcast carriage and reverted to the world of now.

Henry Aaron Yeomans, *Abbott Lawrence Lowell, 1856–1943* (Cambridge: Harvard University Press, 1948).

Rollo Walter Brown

THE OLD DEAN

(1934)

No Harvard teacher or administrator was more beloved or better known by Harvard men during his lifetime than Le Baron Russell Briggs (1855–1934), Dean of Harvard College. He was the ideal teacher, a man of compassionate interest in his fellow men, a kindly administrator whose modest and delightful personality endeared him to thousands in the "golden age" of the Harvard Yard. Among Dean Briggs's graduate stu-

dents near the beginning of the century was Rollo Walter Brown whose admiration led him to write "the biography of a modest man" and to enjoy thirty years of close friendship with Dean Briggs. Mr. Brown is a well-known writer and lecturer known especially for his book The Creative Spirit, *but he has also written many articles about Harvard and Harvard men; a novel,* The Hillikin, *about a hard-working undergraduate; an autobiography,* The Hills Are Strong; *and* Harvard Yard in the Golden Age, *a collection of sketches of Faculty personalities.*

IN THE EIGHT years of his life after the book was published, I saw more of him than before. He was busy much of the time as a member of committees of the Board of Overseers at Harvard, and he was active in many other groups that concerned themselves with semipublic enterprises. Yet he had greater freedom in using his time than he had ever before enjoyed. He had entered into an agreement with one of the large publishing houses to write his memoirs, but when he came face to face with the actual writing, he asked to be released from the agreement. "I saw," he explained to me one day in rejoicing over the still greater freedom that he hoped he was now to have, "that if I wrote those memoirs and did not conceal a part of the truth, I was going to cause pain to people whom I would not hurt for anything in the world — and get myself into a hornets' nest in the bargain. So I think I'll just concentrate on baseball for the rest of my life, and let it go at that."

He usually had supplies of tickets from the Boston Major League Clubs — he never got through explaining that while they were given to him he had not begged them — and he was always looking for somebody who could go to games with him. He liked to be there ahead of time. "It is never quite a whole game for me, you know," he always explained if he feared I might be late, "unless I can see the attendants make the white lines of the batter's box before play begins." Since my writing day is over rather early, it came to pass that we went much together — as often as two or three times a week. At seventy-seven he was the best-informed fan I have known. Constantly he set sports correspondents and baseball managers straight on college and league scores and players of ten, twenty, thirty, and forty years ago.

In his inside coat pocket he carried a leather case that served as a depositary for unusual scores. But it served also as a depositary for anecdotes from *Punch*, new poems that he liked, clippings about former students, photographs of his grandchildren, lists of groceries that he was to order, or take home with him, ideas that he thought worth jotting down. I never did see him get all the way through the contents of that case, and only on a few occasions did I ever see him find what he was looking for. But he invariably found something else that was interesting, something that started a train of stories, memories, observations. He did not repeat the same story to the same person after the manner of some old men. But he was always afraid that he might be doing so, and was constantly prefacing new stories with, "Did I ever tell you . . ." "Did I ever tell you how President Eliot said to me: 'No, don't say he is "low-down"; just say "less sensitive" '?" Or, "Have I ever said to you before . . ."

And on the subway train, in Fenway Park, at Soldiers Field, on Larz Anderson Bridge while we rested our elbows upon the coping and watched the crews on the river, his active mind was busy with all sorts of interesting oddments that he had remembered or thought upon. He was so free from guile that it never occurred to him to speak in veiled statements. With wholly untrammeled honesty he discussed men in public life — he remembered the grades they had made in college — he characterized colleagues, he commented upon changing conceptions of culture, he reflected upon new social practices. Sometimes he was caustic, as when he told me of a nationally known editor who bought an article from him and then "lifted" a certain section of it and published it as a part of one of his own signed editorials. "Of course, it was *his* after he bought it!" Sometimes he was distressed by the ethics of men in whom he had had confidence, as when he discussed a vice president of the United States who had proved in a magazine article that the Radcliffe undergraduates were a bolshevik lot, by showing that a debating team representing them had one evening argued for the closed shop, and by withholding the equally important information that another team representing them had on the same evening argued for the open shop. "I never can believe he wrote that article himself," the Dean declared. "He must have hired somebody to do it for him and then signed it without knowing what was in it. But let me see, that explanation would not help matters much, would it?" He made an effort to smile, as though he were trying to conceal the hurt of some great, inclusive soreness of body. "I'm afraid the terrors of the closed shop will remain as nothing compared with the terrors of the closed mind." Sometimes he became extremely grave and talked with the nervous, fading voice that troubled him much when he spoke in public. But more often he was swept by irrepressible humor and made his commentaries with invigorating saltiness. Once when the Harvard football team was having an unusually poor season, some players on their way to practice in a strikingly luxurious automobile nearly ran us down as they made the short trip from the north side of the Charles to Soldiers Field. "Perhaps I'm old-fashioned," the Dean observed as we walked on, "but I sometimes wonder" — and his voice became crackling and merry — "if Harvard may ever hope to win games unless we somehow find players who are equal to getting from one end of the Larz Anderson Bridge to the other under their own steam." On another occasion, while we stood by the Charles

and surveyed the Graduate School of Business Administration, dazzling
in its newness and much white paint, he remarked as a sly smile flitted
across his closely checked pink face, "It reminds me of the Spotless Town
in the old advertisement for Sapolio."

There were, to be sure, all sorts of occasions when baseball was not
responsible for our being together. Often I met him along lower Brattle
Street late in the afternoon when he was on his way home with a green
bookbag full of provisions, and he half leaned, half hung like a grotesque
question mark against the brick front of a grocery store and told me the
latest anecdote he had liked — of the British lady, for instance, who had
said, after heavy storms in the English Channel, "Just think, my dear, for
two days the Continent has been completely isolated!" When he was shut
in for several weeks of observation before he was taken to the hospital
for an operation that his friends feared might not be successful, I sometimes sat with him in the bright room upstairs, while he lounged on the
wide bed and read to me from the book of charades that he was writing.
He seemed to be much more concerned over the way the charades were
coming out than over any possible outcome of his period under observation. When finally it was decided that he must go to the hospital, he pro-
tested that they must hold off a little until he had finished the last of the
charades. "I promised Pottinger that he was to have the manuscript, and
he must have it." And after the operation — which turned out to have been
unnecessary — just as before, he remained my final court of appeal whenever I was finishing a manuscript, or was reading proofs and had to
contend with editors who believed the subjunctive mood ought to be
eliminated from the English language. After he had tried a sentence out
on himself — he had become eye-minded through a lifetime of theme
reading and had to look at whatever he put to the test — he would relive
a little of his experience as a teacher by digging from the leather case
in his pocket, or from his memory, every sort of interesting specimen of
idiomatic English, from Dryden's "He was a man stepped into years, and
of great prudence" down to the instance he had just found in some recent
volume written by a former student.

Yet through all this greater intimacy that grew from what I could not
fail to see — and with a certain regret — was a habit of looking on me less
as a youth and more as a near-contemporary, I never discovered in him
anything that would lead me to revise my earlier interpretation of his
life — save in this: the closer I came to him, the more genuine I found him.
The high level on which he lived was his natural level. The irrepressible
inclination to see the ridiculous in so many things was his natural appreciation of the vast chasm between what men pretend and what they achieve.
The glow of good will which shone in his face was the natural expression

of his own great humility and his own great beneficence. With Miguel de Unamuno he cried out through everything he did: "Warmth, warmth, more warmth! For men die of cold and not of darkness; it is not the night but the frost that kills."

This fundamental warmth of spirit infused every other quality of his character. No matter how his fellow beings chanced to come in contact with him, they discovered in him very soon something that was friendly to life. Colleagues said, "Yes, he's one of the fellows Briggs helped through college." Professors at Yale said, with the least trace of pleasure in their skepticism, "But do you think the Harvard of today produces men with the sympathies of Dean Briggs?" Harvard students far from home said, "We were feeling low last night and went over and spent an hour with the Dean — and his cat Joshua." Radcliffe graduates said, "We wouldn't for the world have had him a nice, sleek, impervious president in a morning coat." Policemen on the lower Brattle Street beat said, "And don't you suppose we could tell you about one or two ourselves that he kept from going plumb to hell?" The Irish housemaid who had long been with the family said, "And once in the country when he was taking me to ten-thirty Mass, and the door of the old machine came open a dozen times, he slammed it hard and said, 'Confound it!' And said I, 'Oh, Mr. Briggs! Now I've learned what I've been wanting to know all these years: you are no angel!' And then for days after, when he was in the house he'd say softly but so that I'd be sure to hear him, 'Well, confound it!' And I'd say, 'Oh, try to patch things up if you want to, but I don't believe you can ever get forgiven for anything as grievous as that!' " And Harvard men of all ages below fifty or sixty said when they saw him trudging along in front of the baseball stands with his big yellow blanket on his arm, "Why, there's the old Dean!" Then they gathered round him in such numbers that the policeman had to ask them — in the least obtrusive manner he could invent — not to block the way behind the catcher's net, and the Dean was unable to get to his accustomed seat along the third-base line until the first or second man at bat was out.

It was this warmth of spirit which resulted in such vast accumulations of renown and affection that to many he seems more like a legend than a man who took his departure only one morning in 1934. "He is not real!" "Men like that do not exist!" "He is too good to be true!" "He is somebody's creation!" And now that I never meet him in Harvard Square or in the Yard — though in some ineradicable way I am constantly expecting to do so — I sometimes wonder myself: Is it possible that I once walked in the full light of day in this matter-of-fact, turbulent world with such a man as that?

Rollo Walter Brown, *On Writing the Biography of a Modest Man* (Harvard University Press, 1935).

Arthur Calvert Smith

TO COPELAND AT EIGHTY
BY A LIFELONG PUPIL
(1940)

"Great is the teacher beyond scholarship and published books," remarked the Harvard Alumni Bulletin *on the occasion of Charles Townsend Copeland's eightieth birthday. ". . . When, in the fall of 1932, Copey moved from the Yard to an apartment five flights above Concord Avenue — to better food and swifter ventilation — newspapers carried the sad intelligence that the light in Hollis had gone out. A lot of occasions and strange and happy interludes were suddenly re-remembered; names and faces filled the October dusk, for Hollis 15 was first of all a room of names and faces. These belonged to students like Alan Seeger, John Reed, T. S. Eliot, Heywood Broun, Maxwell Perkins, Oliver La Farge, Robert Benchley, Donald Moffat, Frederick L. Allen, Conrad Aiken, Walter Lippmann, Brooks Atkinson, and Walter D. Edmonds. They belonged to visitors, old friends, who one at a time made memorable for lucky, tongue-tied undergraduates an evening of superlative talk. These would be Bishop Dallas, Mrs. Fiske, John Barrymore, Henry Rideout, Mark A. DeWolfe Howe, H. M. Tomlinson, Henry van Dyke, Christopher Morley, Waldo Peirce, Walter de la Mare, Alexander Woollcott, Stephen Benét, and more." Arthur Calvert Smith, 1914, the pupil who paid the following tribute to the Boylston Professor of Rhetoric and Oratory, was for five critical years secretary and executive assistant to President Conant, Secretary to the Corporation and to the Board of Overseers, and Associate Editor of the* Harvard Alumni Bulletin.

COPELAND is eighty. One hears, as on a current radio program, the rhythmic tramp of feet. Many men lifting them up, many men putting them down again. Young men coming in the Dexter Gate, presumably to grow in wisdom; young men leaving by the same gate, presumably the better to serve their country and their kind; young men, not so young men, older men, returning by all gates through the years for a day or an hour, and going back to the world once more.

Where the effect comes from on the radio is easy to understand. Any studio will show you the gadget. It consists of a series of blocks suspended by strings. Manipulate the strings and the blocks drop against a board with the progressive grinding crunch of armies in paved streets. But in the case of a man or an institution, the sources are less simple to determine. There isn't any gadget. There aren't any blocks. There aren't any visible strings. There is nothing you can see. There is only a confusion of intangibles falling in a special pattern.

Considerations of personality and tradition are among these intangibles. Things of the mind. Things of the heart. A superb feeling for the spoken and the written word — for style. A clear view of the realities behind style — the life that forms the matter of literature, as style the manner. A marvelous capacity for communicating this understanding. A voice to make it ring above coughing humans and clacking steam pipes. And the infinite capacity of the supreme teacher — the capacity for asking, not in the beaten way of pedagogy, but with the challenge of him who drank the hemlock, "Gentlemen . . . what make you at Elsinore?"

The wherefores cannot be disentangled, diagramed, and laid out as in an anatomical problem. One is only aware of results. One only knows there are always men passing Hollis, and that under the windows, like French units before the gates of Clos Veugeot, they are halting and presenting arms.

Literature may have been Copeland's subject — literature and composition. But the purpose was something more than this. Back of literature is life. And under the elms of a late-Victorian and post-War Athens he moved, a small, unbearded, disturbing, modern Socrates in mustard-colored suit. Annoying, buzzing, stinging, prodding, encouraging, cajoling, enticing, half-pushing, half-dragging young men up the painful slope of knowledge. Up from the academic shades, up above the timberline, until they caught glimpses of the kingdoms of the world. No such superficially glittering realms, let it be said, as those called up by the tempter in the Wilderness. But the world as it is, composed of men as they are — the mean and the noble, holding the vision, losing the vision, fighting, sweating, loving, hating, and dying together.

From these pilgrimages came friends. They were of all kinds, like the inhabitants of the world he showed them. They took the ordeal conscientiously and he helped them. They rebelled and he loved them. They were drawn from the rich, the well-placed, the assured, and the prominent. They were drawn equally from the poor, the humble, the frightened, and the lost. They have never forgotten.

It seems only a week of yesterdays ago, he was pushing his deliberate, determined way across the Yard to classes. No further in the past then that his spectacled countenance glowered over rostrum desks, berating young men in words as mordant as Flaubert ever wrote. No longer ago Husband, Biggers, Rideout, Reed, Broun, and a host of others living and departed, were seated on the floor of Hollis 15, joining talk of the legendary Booth and the young Barrymore, of Mrs. Fiske and Marshall Newell, of textile strikes at Lawrence, Sacco and Vanzetti, the first and second Balkan Wars. It seems only a week gone by that *Lampy* was immortalizing the humble sponge:

See the funny, porous thing,
Hanging by a bit of string,
Ever there from fall to spring,
Decorating Hollis Hall.

Copey, Copey, don't you remember
Where you left it last December
Or have you become a member,
Of the never wash at all?

It does not seem even a week ago that young men were dining in Boston restaurants at his behest with Isabella Gardner, with John Sargent, with others of the great of the time. Not even a week ago that covers of the cot in Hollis 11, known as the "hero's couch," were turned down to all comers in the uniform of the services — that letters were flowing in from all sectors of the fighting front to form the unique collection now in possession of the Harvard Club of New York.

It seems less than a week ago that one of these young men, fortunate enough to return, clad in resplendent un-regulation uniform after the fashion of soldiers gone diplomatic, found the master in a traditional Harvard windsor by the stoop of Hollis, tipped back against the bricks, eyes shaded by an ancient pliable straw, reading the *Transcript*. He glanced out from under the straw with annoyance. Neither did the front legs of the chair come down, nor was the *Transcript* lowered. The greeting was perfunctory, but the accent was plainer than words.

"We are not impressed. Take off those trappings. The war is over. The glory has departed. This is peace."

Being taught by Copeland did not end with graduation. Nor was it always soothing to the self-esteem. No one having experienced them has ever forgotten the groaning and "ho-hum"-ing and incidental expeditions to other rooms while themes were being read.

In the little red brick schoolhouse where he learned his letters, there was no slovenly unpunctuality, no Boeotian swinish ignorance — that, too, is common knowledge. And who has forgotten the fate of the hapless Munn (not the present head of the English Department, we understand) who came late to class and banged collapsible seats en route to his own?

On the fulcrum of one elbow, the Professor rose stratospherically above his desk.

"Er-ah-ugh-um, what is your name?" he wrung forth in a final agony of exasperation.

"Munn, sir," came the reply.

"Sic transit gloria Mun-di. Leave this course never to return."

But of course Munn, and all the other banished, returned, if they really wanted to.

"Down East" has always been home to Copeland. There the beautifully clean plain rigorous lines of northern hills look across the St. Croix to Canada. There a few miles down-river the first group of European settlers to winter on the New England seaboard — the party of Monts and Champlain — spent the terrible months of 1604–1605, which only half their number survived. He was brought up to uncompromised realities. He has never forgotten them. Young men who came under his tutelage were not allowed to forget them either.

No illusions of sentimentality, no Damon and Pythian tradition sustain his genius for friendship. Behind those Confucian goggles winnows a rugged and a critical mind. The genius lies in the tempering — quick, native perceptions, shrewd sympathy, and the endless understanding that comes from a warm heart.

At eighty, Charles Townsend Copeland, A.B., Litt.D., Boylston Professor of Rhetoric and Oratory, *Emeritus*, has the right to pride. By many home fires and on distant continents the glasses are raised. Conversationalist without peer; reader extraordinary; teacher in a great tradition, without benefit of Xanthippes; from his name, like the eternal snowplume of Everest, trail the affectionate memories of friends.

Harvard Alumni Bulletin, April 26, 1940.

Jacob Loewenberg

EMERSON HALL REVISITED

(1948)

When Jacob Loewenberg, Professor of Philosophy at the University of California, came back to Cambridge in 1947–48 as Visiting Lecturer in Philosophy, he found himself teaching in Emerson Hall in the very rooms where he had listened forty years before to "the great masters — Palmer, James, Royce, Münsterberg, Santayana, et al." He wrote to the Secretary of his College Class: "These men who belonged to the 'golden age' of the Department of Philosophy . . . are not dead. The influence they exerted by their independent and constructive thinking is still a dominating force. . ." A graduate of the College in 1908, Professor Loewenberg also took the A.M. degree in 1909 and the Ph.D. in 1911. He has been teaching at Berkeley since 1915 and is the author of an edition of Royce's Lectures on Modern Idealism, a volume of Fugitive Essays, *and a text of selections from Hegel.*

THERE ARE many advantages in growing older. One is freedom to gratify with impunity a sense of humor. Another is freedom to indulge in reminiscences. After the lapse of so many years, the temptation to recall with natural piety the Harvard philosophers of the past is irresistible. For these philosophers shaped my mind and influenced my point of view.

Emerson Hall is the intellectual home of my youth, and in revisiting it I feel as if I were walking into a hallowed place, hallowed by unseen but living spirits. The great teachers who belonged to a sort of "golden age" of American philosophy are not dead: Their inspirations and aspirations, though forgotten by some, have not been completely ignored or neglected by all our contemporaries. There are of course modern rebels against philosophy in the grand manner (such as was taught here in my student days, its roots deep in tradition yet wide and broad in speculative sweep), but their rebellion strikes me as too *enragé* and extravagant, often without focus or direction or aim. Analysis and criticism, when not directly related to the "thick" and varied content of human experience, are in danger of becoming merely verbal, that is, concerned with words as signs or symbols, and with sentences having such words for their constituents.

The semantic method is important, and I am far from belittling it, but if carried to great lengths, esoterically and zealously, the risk is great that the depth and wealth of philosophic ideas will be lost sight of or will become so simplified and attenuated as to be virtually meaningless. And what is worse, our modern analysts and semanticists and positivists may be led by their passion for clarity to identify the principal task of philosophy with their favorite method of utterance, method thus ceasing to be ancillary to subject matter and acquiring instead the position of an autonomous discipline, universal in its quest, the quest for the method of method, the meaning of meaning, the language of language.

This is not the place to raise controversial issues. I have noted elsewhere that exclusive preoccupation with methodology, initially governed by the spirit of criticism, may end in dogmatism, taking the form of *methodolatry*, the worship of a single method, which breeds one phobia or another, the chief being ontophobia, the fear of metaphysics. The old masters, who taught at Harvard in my day, subordinated technology to fecundity of reflection, reflection about first and last things in life and the world, requiring not only analysis but synopsis, not only refinement of locution but creative thought.

To this old-fashioned view, if it be old-fashioned, I am not ashamed to confess that I still adhere. I have brought it back to Harvard where originally it received its inception and cultivation. The courses I [have given] here all show traces of what I learned from James and Perry, from Palmer and Santayana, from Münsterberg and Royce. It was my privilege to enjoy close associations with some of these men, and especially with Palmer and Santayana and Royce.

To Palmer and Santayana I owe my interest in literature, for its own sake as well as for the philosophic content it may be made to elicit. And to Santayana in particular I am beholden for the conviction that philosophic discourse need not be carried on in the bloodless categories of certain schools; philosophic diction may even be musical without forfeiting either lucidity or cogency. Imagery and eloquence have their place in a human philosophy which aspires also to be humane. There is after all no virtue in being artless. Those who disparage metaphor and rhetoric, affecting a jejune or graceless style, probably do so because of scruple either of method or doctrine. But there is no necessary connection between obscurity and euphony of expression. Palmer and Santayana, in different ways and from different standpoints, taught me never to be afraid of the felicitous and pregnant phrase — but to be master and not the slave of it.

What Josiah Royce taught me, who resorted to a passionate eloquence of his own, would take too long to recount. For with Royce my relations were peculiarly personal and intimate. I shall single out but one of the many ways in which he influenced my thinking and teaching. What I have in mind is his tolerance.

Royce proclaimed the truth volubly enough, but he always retained a genial indulgence of opinions opposed to his own. How was it that so staunch a believer could have harbored such a tolerant soul? His tolerance was not that of the sceptic, for whom one belief is as uncertain as another; his was the tolerance of the catholic mind eager to assimilate the insights vouchsafed to others. His doctrine was such as to permit him to include within its ample embrace the most antagonistic views. But his penchant for synthesis, which prompted him to justify as partial or fragmentary aspects of truth whatever ideas struggled for expression, explains only one side of his tolerant spirit.

Apart from doctrinal considerations, his vocation as teacher, a vocation in which his conscience was engaged, laid upon him the obligation to inculcate in his pupils freedom of thought and independence of belief. Acquiescence in his ideas, merely because they were his, he did not countenance. He welcomed vigorous opposition, for what he valued in his students was not docility but power.

He took delight in the exercise of dialectic, and thrusts aimed at his arguments, if serious and well-directed, gave him much satisfaction, not only because he rejoiced in parrying them, but also because he enjoyed the logical prowess and skill of his opponents. A dissenter himself in matters his reason could not commend, he sincerely respected those who dissented from him. And for those who were disposed to accept his teaching uncritically he had a feeling bordering on disdain.

I remember how on one occasion he humorously reproved me for too docile a conformity to his views. He was my examiner in metaphysics for the doctor's degree. The day before I was to be examined he called me to his study and suggested that, to enable him to test my acumen, I prepare a detailed table of contents for a systematic treatise I might perhaps be inclined to write at some future time. Well, I was no Aristotle, and even the young Stagirite might have required more than twenty-four hours for the planning of a work on metaphysics. It was natural, anxious as I was to pass the examination, that I should have freely availed myself of the ideas derived from my teacher. The safest thing, I foolishly thought, was to play the role of disciple. And, as it happened, I was then not altogether averse to the doctrine Royce had been maintaining.

At the appointed hour I presented the fatal document. For an interminable time he tormented me with questions, acting as a sort of devil's advocate for positions hostile to his own. I stoutly held my ground by reproducing faithfully his favorite arguments which I knew by heart. When it was all over, he looked at me quizzically, and a merry smile tempered his evident disappointment.

"Well," he said, "I do not know what to say about your examination. You know too much about Royce and not enough about metaphysics. I wonder if, instead of the Ph.D., you should not receive the degree of R.D. You are certainly qualified to hold the title 'Doctor of Royce.'"

I recall another occasion when Royce lauded a student for a trenchant attack upon his doctrine. For some years, as his assistant, it fell to my lot to read and appraise the essays written in connection with his course on metaphysics, known as "Philosophy G." His procedure was to let me select for his personal perusal and comment some of the essays worthy of his attention. Some papers, which frankly puzzled me, especially those with a slant towards the occult, he would interpret for my benefit, reading into them out of the goodness of his heart ideas and motives of which their authors were blissfully unconscious. Towards painstaking work, however obscure or mediocre, his attitude was charitable; he took seriously what import he could divine or find there. No earnest mind, though ungifted or confused, went from him discouraged. But he relished superior performance, and upon such performance, no matter how odd in method or result, he would lavish high praise.

One day I consulted him about a paper which contained a devastating criticism of his philosophy expressed in what seemed to me too light a vein. Comparing Royce's Absolute to a "purple cow," the writer contrasted its apotheosis with the worship of the "golden calf," and he candidly preferred the latter as being more useful in its greater promise of "cash-value."

The criticism was not without substance and it certainly had style, but somehow I did not like the "purple cow." I questioned the propriety of the image and I asked Royce whether I should not return the paper with the comment that it was too frivolous.

"I don't think you understand the man," was Royce's reply after reading the essay with ill-concealed pleasure. "He has wit, imagination, and understanding. How James would have liked his style! Give him an 'A,' and compliment him on his originality. I shall myself have something to say about his brilliant criticism in the course of my next lecture."

I shall never forget that lecture. He devoted it entirely to an analysis of the young man's ideas, and with his inimitable humor he expatiated on the far-reaching metaphysical implications the contrasted images entailed. To his class this was a welcome interlude; for what abstract exposition failed to impart, the "purple cow" and the "golden calf" made wonderfully luminous.

I could mention dozens of incidents to illustrate Royce's method of teaching. It was a method altogether free from proselytism. His tolerance and considerateness were almost excessive. He was not one of those who felt called upon to exorcise error to insure the triumph of truth. So robust was his faith in truth that he looked for the foundation of it in the very existence of error. He was willing to let the truth take care of itself. He did not think that to honor truth we must ruthlessly abolish differences of opinion. Fear of assailants of one's belief, he seemed to feel, was a dubious compliment to its truth; if true, no attack could damage it. And so he perpetually courted criticism on the part of his pupils and colleagues.

Very characteristic is an incident related by Professor Palmer. Once when Royce was to be absent for six weeks to lecture at Aberdeen, he asked Palmer to take charge of his advanced course.

"I told him," writes Palmer, "that there might be an objection to my doing so in that I dissented from everything he had been saying. He said he was aware of this and for that reason he had asked me. He thought my coming would enrich the course. I took it and devoted myself to pulling up all the plants which Royce had carefully set out. When he came home he ordered a thesis on the entire work of the half-year, and he told me it was the best thesis he had ever received."

Palmer recalls also how Royce and James, intimate friends but philosophic opponents, once combined in a course on metaphysics, Royce occupying the first half-year, and James exposing the fallacies of idealism during the second.

Cultivation of the critical spirit as belonging to the very essence of creative philosophy — this was what all of Royce's colleagues aimed at. It was exhilarating if bewildering to hear of their polemics and mutual respect. In such atmosphere it was impossible not to delight in the free play of ideas. And no one contributed to its zest more fully than Royce. It was his habit, for instance, to invite to one of his seminars scholars from different departments who would discourse broadly on their respective fields of research.

One year, as I remember, his visitors included a geologist, an archaeologist, a historian, a philologist, a chemist, a bio-chemist, a psychiatrist; each of them expounded some theme relevant to his special corner of knowledge, dwelling particularly upon a crucial experiment or problem illustrative of the inductive method. The discussion which ensued consisted for the most part in an amicable altercation between Royce and his guests, the students picking up whatever crumbs of learning they could.

I can still see Royce sitting at the head of the table in Emerson C, a large notebook in front of him, in which he would record minutely the visitor's discourse and his replies to questions. It was a thrilling experience to watch the encounter of critical minds and to participate in a free trade of ideas. The trade was indeed a flourishing one, for Royce appropriated from the many scholars valuable material for interpretation and synthesis, and the scholars in their turn learned to appreciate the importance and relevance of philosophy. Some of them would return to the seminar year after year. And as for the students, the vistas gained into unsuspected worlds of knowledge loosened their dogmatism and deepened their understanding.

The method in Royce's case was well adapted to the content of his teaching. He exemplified in his person an uncommon consistency of theory and practice. His life was a superb illustration of his philosophy. His attitude towards his pupils and colleagues was a concrete expression of his ethics of loyalty. His devotion to the ideal of truth did not preclude perfect courtesy on his part in dealing with the devoted labors of those who radically disagreed with him. He honored unselfish devotion in whatever form it chanced to express itself. For in such devotion lay for him the secret of the good life. The values and virtues of the good life he derived from principles designed to justify the heterogeneous objects of men's rational allegiance. And these principles, to the formulation and defense of which he dedicated his efforts, governed unswervingly his daily conduct. What Royce preached he practiced. He walked by the light which his heart kindled and his mind sustained.

Although I have traveled very far from some of Royce's cherished beliefs, the influence his intellectual tolerance exerted upon my mind still dominates, after all these years, my thoughts and perspectives. I must of course walk by my own light; and if I find such light luminous, I am never tempted to mistake it for a divine revelation; consequently, it does not occur to me to impugn as dark what other philosophers declare to be the sources of their illumination.

There are now current everywhere too many expressions of dogmatism and authoritarianism, and in certain circles the Roycean conception of loyalty would be considered obsolescent, demanding as it does critical *and* sympathetic attention to the diversity of human beliefs. Yet what Royce emphasized belongs to the very essence of democracy. Democracy like charity, begins at home; if democratic or tolerant hospitality of ideas and persuasions opposed to our own does not take root within the private precincts of our minds, it can take root nowhere else.

Harvard Alumni Bulletin, January 29, 1949.

III

TROUBLE UNDER THE ELMS

When I was asked to come to this university, I supposed I was to be at the head of the largest and most famous institution of learning in America. I have been disappointed. I find myself the sub-master of an ill-disciplined school.

EDWARD EVERETT (1847)

While these labors were in progress, I was becoming, of course, better acquainted with the history and character of the graduates. Several instances of strange experience in childhood, of brave struggles to obtain an education, of virtue and heroism under temptations of wealth and worldly honors, awakened hearty sympathy and admiration. Notwithstanding short-comings, and cases of iniquity which may have escaped punishment, I was convinced that the worth and influence of the graduates as a body had not been properly appreciated. More than two centuries have passed since the College was established, yet I found but one graduate who had been executed as a malefactor, and he was the victim of the witchcraft delusion; and but one who had been sent to a State penitentiary, and this was for passing counterfeit money. . .

JOHN LANGDON SIBLEY (1873)

Mistress Eaton

I OWN THE SHAME AND CONFESS MY SIN
(1639)

Complaints about the cooking have been characteristic since the estab-
lishment of the College. The Harvard epic — "The Rebelliad" (1819) —
was inspired by one of the many food riots in the College commons, but
the first and nastiest complaint about Harvard food occurred in the second
academic year of the College's existence. When the first master, Nathaniel
Eaton, was haled into court for beating his assistant with a walnut tree
cudgel, it was an occasion for a general ventilation of grievances against
Eaton for the severity of his discipline, and against his wife for the quality
of food and drink she served her boarders in the Peyntree House. As a
result, the Eatons lost their jobs and have gone down in Harvard history
as a pair of rogues. Here is Mrs. Eaton's apologia for her "loathesome
catering," one of the few documents recording the unpleasantnesses of
the College's first years:

FOR THEIR BREAKFAST, that it was not so well ordered, the flour not
so fine as it might, nor so well boiled or stirred, at all times that
it was so, it was my sin of neglect, and want of that care that
ought to have been in one that the Lord had intrusted with such
a work. Concerning their beef, that was allowed them, as they affirm,
which, I confess, had been my duty to have seen they should have had
it, and continued to have had it, because it was my husband's command;
but truly I must confess, to my shame, I cannot remember that ever
they had it, nor that ever it was taken from them. And that they had not
so good or so much provision in my husband's absence as presence, I
conceive it was, because he would call sometimes for butter or cheese,
when I conceived there was no need of it; yet, forasmuch as the scholars
did otherways apprehend, I desire to see the evil that was in the carriage
of that as well as in the other, and to take shame to myself for it. And
that they sent down for more, when they had not enough, and the maid
should answer, if they had not, they should not, I must confess, that I
have denied them cheese, when they have sent for it, and it have been
in the house; for which I shall humbly beg pardon of them, and own

the shame, and confess my sin. And for such provoking words, which my servants have given, I cannot own them, but am sorry any such should be given in my house. And for bad fish, that they had it brought to table, I am sorry there was that cause of offence given them. I acknowledge my sin in it. And for their mackerel, brought to them with their guts in them, and goat's dung in their hasty pudding, it's utterly unknown to me; but I am much ashamed it should be in the family, and not prevented by myself or servants, and I humbly acknowledge my negligence in it. And that they made their beds at any time, were my straits never so great, I am sorry they were ever put to it. For the Moor his lying in Sam. Hough's sheet and pillow-bier, it hath a truth in it: he did so one time, and it gave Sam. Hough just cause of offence; and that it was not prevented by my care and watchfulness, I desire [to] take the shame and sorrow for it. And that they eat the Moor's crusts, and the swine and they had share and share alike, and the Moor to have beer, and they denied it, and if they had not enough, for my maid to answer, they should not, I am an utter stranger to these things, and know not the least footsteps for them so to charge me; and if my servants were guilty of such miscarriages, had the boarders complained of it unto myself, I should have thought it my sin, if I had not sharply reproved my servants, and endeavored reform. And for bread made of heated, sour meal, although I know of but once that it was so, since I kept house, yet John Wilson affirms it was twice; and I am truly sorry, that any of it was spent amongst them. For beer and bread, that it was denied them by me betwixt meals, truly I do not remember, that ever I did deny it unto them; and John Wilson will affirm, that, generally, the bread and beer was free for the boarders to go unto. And that money was demanded of them for washing the linen, it's true it was propounded to them, but never imposed upon them. And for their pudding being given the last day of the week without butter or suet, and that I said, it was miln of Manchester in Old England, it's true that I did say so, and am sorry, they had any cause of offence given them by having it so. And for their wanting beer, betwixt brewings, a week or half a week together, I am sorry that it was so at any time, and should tremble to have it so, were it in my hands to do again.

Samuel E. Morison, *The Founding of Harvard College* (Harvard University Press, 1935).

Edward Holyoke

THE BURNING OF HARVARD HALL
(1764)

"The opening of the year 1764," wrote Josiah Quincy in his history, "had been distinguished by the completion of Hollis Hall, under the patronage of the legislature; but the bright sky, which thus dawned on Harvard, was early obscured by the heaviest cloud that ever burst on the head of our Alma Mater." In the midst of the bitter and snowy night of January 24, Harvard Hall, the oldest and most valuable college building, was burned to the ground. With it were destroyed the 5000-volume College library, the scientific equipment of the Apparatus Chamber, and other treasures accumulated since the early years of Harvard history. This account of the conflagration was prepared for the newspapers by President Holyoke himself, who though seventy-five years of age at the time had been present to direct the fire fighting. The President spent much of the remaining five and a half years of his life repairing the damage (the new Harvard Hall was completed in 1766) and arousing the sympathy and interest of friends of Harvard in replacing books and equipment.

LAST NIGHT Harvard College suffered the most ruinous loss it ever met with since its foundation. In the middle of a very tempestuous night, a severe cold storm of snow, attended with high wind, we were awaked by the alarm of fire. Harvard Hall, the only one of our ancient buildings which still remained, and the repository of our most valuable treasures, the public library and philosophical apparatus, was seen in flames. As it was a time of vacation, in which the students were all dispersed, not a single person was left in any of the Colleges, except two or three in that part of Massachusetts most distant from Harvard, where the fire could not be perceived till the whole surrounding air began to be illuminated by it. When it was discovered from the town, it had risen to a degree of violence that defied all opposition. It is conjectured to have begun in a beam under the hearth in the library, where a fire had been kept for the use of the General Court, now residing and sitting here, by reason of the small-pox at Boston: from thence it burst out into the library. The books easily submitted to the fury of the flame, which with a rapid and irresistible progress made its way into the Apparatus Chamber, and spread through the whole building. In a very short time, this venerable monument of the piety of our ancestors was turned into a heap of ruins. The other Colleges, Stoughton Hall and Massachusetts Hall, were in the utmost hazard of sharing the same fate. The wind driving the flaming cinders directly upon their roofs, they blazed out several times in different places; nor could they have been saved by all the help the town could afford, had it not been for the assistance of the gentlemen of the General Court, among whom his Excellency the Governor was very active; who, notwithstanding the extreme rigor of the season, exerted themselves in supplying the town engine with water, which they were obliged to fetch at last from a distance, two of the College pumps being then rendered useless. Even the new and beautiful Hollis Hall, though it was on the windward side, hardly escaped. It stood so near to Harvard, that the flames actually seized it, and, if they had not been immediately suppressed, must have carried it.

But by the blessing of God on the vigorous efforts of the assistants, the ruin was confined to Harvard Hall; and there, besides the destruction of the private property of those who had chambers in it, the public loss is very great, perhaps irreparable. The Library and the Apparatus, which for many years had been growing, and were now judged to be the best furnished in America, are annihilated.

Josiah Quincy, *The History of Harvard University* (Cambridge, 1840).

Samuel Chandler

A COLLEGE TRAGEDY

(1773)

Sam Chandler, the Gloucester minister's son, studied at Harvard during the exciting days before the outbreak of the Revolution. A favorite of his father, Sam was more attracted by music and magic than he was by such mundane subjects as spelling. Still, he kept a journal until just before his graduation in 1775, and from it is reprinted an account of an unhappy student accident. Chandler served on seacoast defense in the war, married a sea captain's daughter, and led the life of a teacher of mathematics until his death in 1786.

THURSDAY July 1. This forenoon at half after ten I saw Lovel Padock & Winslow a going through the east entry in Massachusetts in order to go in a swimming. I was in company with Hendley. We moved to go with them but by some cause or other did not. I got excused from reciting at eleven of clock. About ten minutes after the bell tolled, news came to the College Yard that Padock was drowned. Being struck with the news I ran down to the river where I imagined they went in, a place above the bridge near a creek, a place they commonly called the brick works, a place where there was no bank but descended gradually from high water to low, the tide running very strong which makes it very dangerous for those who can't swim. When I came to the place I find they have just got him out of the water. They were all but ———— at swimming and Padock and Lovel going off deep, Padock was suddenly carried off by the tide where it was over his head. He catched hold of Lovel and pulled him under water once or twice but Lovel disengaged himself and got clear, leaving Padock to drive from this world to the world of immortality. They gave without doubt all the assistance they were capable of with safety. There was an old man named Huse — a crazy part of a man — who being within sight ran for assistance, but never called to any man till he got to the College when the scholars flocked down in multitudes. I hear likewise that there was a man a raking hay on the meadow who came part of the way and seeing him a sinking returned to raking saying that he could not swim. It is my opinion that he might have saved him easy with his rake if he had gone for he was then within a few yards of the shore. The scholars soon got a diving to find him. Parker, a boy belonging to Welsh the painter, first felt him. Bliss first brought him off the bottom, and Peele who saved his life yesterday first brought him out of the water, when he was soon brought on shore, rolled and rubbed with salt etc. . . . He was supposed to be under water near half an hour before they found him. They brought him ashore about half after eleven, tried all experiments such as rolling him, rubbing with salt, pouring spirits down his throat, blowing into his mouth with bellows etc. They tried to bleed him but could find no vein. There was not a quart of water in him which made the doctors think he was frighted into a fit. They worked on him at the side of the bank till near twelve when they carried him to Welsh's the painters where they wrapped him up in ashes and continued rubbing and applying hot cloths. Dr. Lord who came from Boston accidentally made out to bleed him in the jugular vein. He bled very freely but no life appeared. After dinner I went down again to see him when he was quite stiff and cold. His father got there a little after one but could not see him. The whole College and even all the town seem much affected as he was the prettiest and likeliest youth in his class about fifteen years of age. He was kept the afternoon wrapped up in salt all but his head. I continue with him likewise numbers of other scholars the chief of the afternoon. At night he was carried to Mr. Sewal's and put in a warm bed. The news was sent to his father about twelve and before one it was spread all about Boston, likewise all the other neighboring towns. At four we do not recite neither do I attend prayers.

Friday 2. This morning in at declaiming there was a sort of funeral oration offered by Maynard. At about ten of the clock the corpse was carried down in Welsh's boat to Boston, it being put in a coffin. After dinner

I walk to Boston. Have some time at my sister's. I go about the wharves to inquire for an opportunity to send a letter to my father by my mother's desire as she has a mind to go home next week. I go to Bethune's store and drink punch with him there when finding Paston I spend some time very agreeable with him as he is going away next week for Philadelphia College. I walk by Major Padock's and incline to go in. I lay at my sister's at night.

Saturday 3. In the morning I rose early and got up to Cambridge before breakfast so as to wait. Mr. Wadsworth has got leave for the freshmen to wear black gowns and square hats at the funeral today. After dinner Hendley rode up in his father's chaise and carried me down to Charlestown. I go over the ferry and stay some time at my sister's when I go up to the factory in a room which is provided for the scholars where young Padock's picture is hung up for them to see. I go to see the button makers etc. in the factory. The freshmen several of them have walked about the town with their black gowns on, the inhabitants not knowing what it meant nor who they were. Gay, Gove, two Leverits, Lovel & Winslow were chosen bearers but afterwards Peele was chosen bearer in the room of Gay. They proceeded from Major Padock's about five of clock when the bells tolled, even the grammar school bell. The freshmen went in procession in their dress, then followed the corpse, then the mourners which were very numerous, then the governors of the college, then the scholars, and then followed a very numerous retinue of the inhabitants. The streets were crowded with spectators. They went down Prison Lane up School Street and into the Middle Burying Place where he was interred in a tomb where there was no other coffin. Near the Bridewell opposite his own house, when coming into the Burying Yard the freshmen opened to the right and left till the students had all passed through then waited upon the Major to his house, then to the factory, and then home. Numbers of the freshmen walked over the ferry with their gowns on. Seemed very grand in general. Thatcher sent a piece to Salem for the print, another he left at Edes & Gils and upon his returning back to give an account of the funeral found Mr. Eliot reading of it who did not very much approve of it. I drank coffee at my sister's. Went to Mr. Hendley's and rode up with Zech. I tried at Charlestown to get my watch but in vain. It has been a very warm day. I believe the proceedings in Boston were agreeable in general.

Monday 10. This morning very early the President and Tutors go out a fishing.

Harvard Graduates' Magazine (March and June 1902).

Eliphalet Pearson

JOURNAL OF DISORDERS
(1788)

The great Eliphalet — "big name, big frame, big voice and beetling brow" — came to Harvard in 1786 as Hancock Professor of Hebrew after a period of service as first principal of Phillips Academy, Andover, Massachusetts. Those were the days when the "stiff and unbending" President Willard's conduct of affairs encouraged disorder and disrespect among the students. From 1788 until 1797 Professor Pearson kept a "journal of disorders" in which the most lengthy and frequent entries occurred during December 1788 and January 1789. Pearson was elected a Fellow of Harvard College in 1800 and, after the death of Willard in 1804, acted for more than a year as President. When Harvard began a swing toward Unitarianism, Pearson resigned (1806) and went back to Andover, where he founded the Andover Theological Seminary.

DEC. 4 [1788]. Exhibition A.M. before the immediate government. — P.M. A large collection at the chamber of Vose & Whitwell. Present, the occupants, Fay, 2 Sullivans, Trapier, Walker, Welles, Withers, & two strangers. A disorderly, riotous noise called up Mr. Webber who desired them to be still. Immediately upon his leaving them, the noise became more violent, which occasioned his return. He then ordered all to their chambers; but none withdrew. He then ordered them individually & by name. The two Sullivans declined going, & James said he would go, when he pleased. — After this the two Sullivans conducted improperly towards Mr. Smith, & disobeyed a positive order of Mr. James. —

Dec. 5. A snow ball was thrown at Mr. Webber, while he was in the desk at evening prayers.

Upon complaint, a meeting was called 6 Dec. And, upon pleading, as others had done before, that he was intoxicated, Sullivan 2d was admitted to a public confession; which was exhibited at a meeting 8 Dec. At which meeting the government had a talk with Sullivan 1.

Dec. 9. The President read the confession of Sullivan 2; but there was such a scraping, especially in the junior class, that he could not be heard. He commanded silence, but to no purpose. Disorders coming out of chapel. Also in the hall at breakfast the same morning. Bisket, tea cups, saucers, & a *knife* thrown at the tutors. At evening prayers the lights were all extinguished by powder & lead, except 2 or 3. Upon this a general laugh among the juniors. — From this day to 13 Dec. disorders continued in hall & Chapel, such as scraping, whispering &c. Lights were blown out one morning, & two evenings, the last time by Howard, as it is said, many scholars being present. — The disorders by this time had spread, in a degree, among the Sophomores and Freshmen.

Dec. 12. After prayers Sullivan 1 called a class meeting, in order to prevent disorders in the chapel among the juniors. After which there was less disorder in the chapel for several days. Many of the chapel windows also were broken.

N.B. On the evening of the 5 Dec. all the Sophomores, except Ward, were collected at Bayley's chamber in a disorderly manner, from which they were ordered to their chambers by Mr. James. Upon this they went to the chamber of King & Whitney; from which they sallied out, & ran thro' the entries of Massachusetts in a noisy and tumultuous manner. Three were caught by Mr. Abbot, viz. Ellery, Derby, & Hodge. Between 8 & 9 o'clock, same evening, Mr. Abbot had 6 squares of his study window broken. All the tutors' windows were also broken the same week Sullivan's confession was read.

Dec. 15. More disorders at my public lecture, than I ever knew before. The bible, cloth, candles, & branches, I found laid in confusion upon the seat of the desk. During lecture several pebbles were snapped, certain gutteral sounds were made on each side [of] the chapel, beside some whistling.

Dec. 16. Still greater disorders at Dr. Wigglesworth's public lecture. As he was passing up the alley, two volleys of stones, one from each side, were thrown at him, or just before him. Upon this the Doctor turned about & addressed the scholars. After which he proceeded; but, before he reached the pew, another volley of stones was discharged from the north side of the alley. During the first prayer there were disorders; after which the Doctor again addressed them more largely, & particularly cautioned them against disorders; but, notwithstanding this, they continued thro' the lecture; such as sending stones, making gutteral noises, whistling &c. — While the Doctr. & two tutors were walking down the alley, a stone was sent into the chapel thro' a window, the glass of which was driven against one of the gentlemen.

Dec. 20. The government were called together.

Dec. 22. Government met again, & voted that Bowman & Howard be removed from College for 6 months, & that Ellery be degraded to the bottom of his class.

Dec. 24. Dr. Howard took away his son.

Dec. 25. Ellery's sentence of degradation was read in the chapel. Upon which, instead of taking his place as ordered, Ellery withdrew several steps, & then turned about, & told the President that "he should leave a society, the government of which is actuated by *malice*, & whose decisions are founded in prejudice," or to this effect. — That evening, a few minutes before 11, a stone, weighing 8 lbs. 11 oz., was thrown into Dr. Wigglesworth's sleeping room. — Previously to this, the same evening, there had been a very great noise, principally, as was said, at Rice's chamber, & partly at Thacher's.

Dec. 26. In the evening there was a firing of pistols between 8 & 11. This evening there was a collection at Rice's chambers till just after 12, without noise. After separating, candles were lighted at the chambers of Hodge, Harris & Phelps, King & Whitney.

Dec. 27. Bowman went off. — That night, between 1 & 2, two persons, in a violent & noisy manner ran up the stairs of the east entry in Massachusetts, & went into Rice's or Thacher's chamber.

Dec. 30. In the evening, about 10 o'clock, Messrs. Smith & Abbot caught a riotous company, which had been driving thro' town in a noisy & violent manner, some of which appeared to be very drunk.

Dec. 31. The government voted to accept Ellery's confession, which the next morning he read in the chapel.

Jan. 1 [1789]. Mr. Smith & Abbot took up the conduct of the rioters. In the evening Mr. Smith prayed. Several coppers were thrown at him, while in prayers, as was supposed by juniors on the north side of the chapel. — After which Mr. Smith sent down the punishments of the rioters, viz, Trapier 5/ for noise in town, 1/6 for not going to chamber when ordered, & 1/6 for intoxication; Welles 5/ for noise, 3/ for not going to chamber, when repeatedly ordered, & 1/6 for intoxication; Callender 5/ for noise, Hubbard Do., Thacher Do., Tilton Do., Withers Do. & Wragg Do.

Jan. 2. Mumbling noise & whispering at morning prayers, chiefly among the juniors on the north. Bible taken away at evening prayers.

Jan. 3. Bible taken away at morning prayers & concealed at evening prayers. In the evening, which was Saturday eveng., there was a large collection at Withers's room, which sallied out in a noisy manner, one of which, viz, Whitwell, was caught by Mr. Crosby in a cellar.

Jan. 4. Bible concealed at eveng. prayers, & several squares of glass found broken in the window of the desk.

Jan. 5. Government met A.M., & Dr. Waterhouse requested in writing that Rice, Harris, Phelps, Whitney, & Thacher, might be examined relative to the charge, brought against Ellery, of his throwing stones in the College yard. Meeting continued thro' the day.

Jan. 6. Met by adjournment at 9 o'clock, & at 4 P.M. determined that nothing asserted by the above named persons invalidated the direct evidence against Ellery.

Jan. 7. Vacation commenced.

Augustus Peirce

OVERTURE TO THE RIOT

(1818)

The great epic of Harvard history, "The Rebelliad," commemorating a food riot in the College commons, was written "principally in the recitation room" and delivered in July 1819 before the College Engine Club. The author, Augustus Peirce, of the Class of 1820 (founders of the famous "Med. Fac."), was then only seventeen, but his comic and poetic senses were highly developed. Peirce's method of composition was a daily stint undertaken immediately after he had completed his own recitation. After many months of such installment invention, the work was completed. It was in such demand that his classmates made their own personal hand-written copies, which were widely circulated. (Such a manuscript, copied off by a Bowdoin student, was recently offered for sale by a dealer in rare books.) The original manuscript, however, was destroyed by Peirce's father, and the author had to reconstruct a large portion of his classic from memory. The first printed edition did not appear until 1842. Peirce studied medicine under Dr. George C. Shattuck of Boston, practiced in Tyngsboro, Massachusetts, and died in 1849.

PROLOGUE. OH! IN HARVARD!

Parody on Hohenlinden

I.

AT Harvard, when the sun was low,
All bustling was the kitchen's glow,
And hot as tophet was the flow
    Of coffee, boiling rapidly.

II.

But Harvard saw another sight
When the bell rang at fall of night,
Commanding every appetite
    To snatch a supper hastily.

Everyone who ever attended Harvard should know that a goody (said to be a contraction of the word "Good-wife") is one of the College bedmakers, and the author of "The Rebelliad" specially identifies his Goody Muse as "Miss Morse, the daughter of her mother." Others of Peirce's allusions deserve a word of explanation. Lord Bibo was President Kirkland; Dr. Pop was John Snelling Popkin, Professor of Greek; Sikes was the Reverend Henry Ware, Professor of Divinity; Nathan was sophomore Robert W. Barnwell, later United States Senator from South Carolina; Abijah was "a freshman." Carolus McIntire was a local shoemaker who was given a spurious honorary degree by the Med. Fac. in 1823.

III.

By mess and table fast arrayed,
Each Freshman drew his eating blade,
And furious every jaw-bone played,
    Devouring Cooley's cookery.

IV.

Then shook the Halls with racket riven,
Then rushed each Soph to battle driven,
And louder than the bolts of heaven,
    Round smashed the brittle crockery.

V.

And louder yet that noise shall grow;
And fiercer yet that strife shall glow;
And hotter yet shall be the flow
    Of coffee, boiling rapidly.

VI.

'T is night, — but scarce had Dr. Pop
Put half his supper in his crop,
When Freshman fierce and furious Soph
    Shout in their savory canopy.

VII.

The combat deepens. On, ye brave,
And let the cooks the pieces save!
Wave, Goodies, all your besoms wave!
    Inspire their souls with chivalry.

VIII.

Ah! few shall part where many meet
With anything but blows to eat,
And every dish beneath their feet
    Shall be a supper's sepulchre.

THE REBELLIAD

Canto I

THE ARGUMENT

Invocation. — Battle between the Sophomores and Freshmen in Commons Hall. — Doctor Pop endeavors to obtain a suspension of arms; goes to Lord Bibo's study; makes a speech. — Sikes also pours forth a torrent of eloquence.

TIME: — *Two hours on Sunday evening.*

OLD Goody Muse! on thee I call,
Pro more, (as do poets all,)
To string thy fiddle, wax thy bow,
And scrape a ditty, jig, or so.
Now don't wax wrathy, but excuse
My calling you old Goody Muse;
Because "Old Goody" is a name
Applied to ev'ry College dame.
   Aloft in pendent dignity,
     Astride her magic broom,
   And wrapt in dazzling majesty,
     See! see! the Goody come!
Riding sublime on billowy air,
She tun'd her instrument with care;
And that her voice and fiddle might
In mingling harmony unite,
She blow'd her nose and cried, ahem!
To throw off maccaboy and phlegm:
Then, with slow melancholy, sung
How for a witch her ma' was hung;
And with a doleful aspect blunder'd
Through half a stanza of "old hundred."
   She ceas'd, her misty mantle shook,
And from her magic pocket took
A box — not such as that in story,
A gift from Jove to Miss Pandora;
From which went forth as many ills,
As from a box of Conway's pills;
No: it was fill'd with vulgar stuff,
Call'd maccaboy, or headache snuff.
   Her pocket held another thing,
Which ancient dames do sometimes squeeze,
   A bottle of New England sling,
Or any other kind you please;
   (For't does not signify a pin,
     Whether 't was brandy, rum, or gin;)

Which, ever and anon, she'd kiss
  With smacking fondness and delight;
Until her fancy, full of bliss,
  Was fir'd to sing of deeds of might.
Her viol she attun'd anew;
To lofty themes her fingers flew.
Hark! the melodious sounds have ris'n!
  The spirits of the tuneful nine
    Delay their dewy car,
In which they cleave the arch of Heav'n,
  On their celestial harps recline,
    And listen from afar;
While thus she sung: One Sunday night
The Sophs and Freshmen had a fight.
'T was when the beam that linger'd last
Its farewell ray on Harvard cast,
Or Sol, with night-cap on his head,
Was just a creeping into bed,
When Cookum told a boy to tell
Another boy to toll the bell,
To call the students to their tea.
As when a brood of pigs, who see
Their feeder with a pail of swill,
With which their maws they're wont to fill,
Do squeal and grunt, and grunt and squeal,
In expectation of a meal;
So they to commons did repair
And scramble, each one for his share:
When Nathan threw a piece of bread,
And hit Abijah on the head.
The wrathful Freshmen, in a trice,
Sent back another bigger slice;
Which, being butter'd pretty well,
Made greasy work where'er it fell.
And thus arose a fearful battle;
The coffee-cups and saucers rattle;
The bread-bowls fly at woful rate,
And break many a learned pate.
As when a troop of town-school boys
Fall out and make a plaguy noise,
On either side the boldest close,
And kick and cuff with furious blows;
While others, fearful of their bones,
Slink out of sight and fight with stones,

Although they now and then appear,
And rave heroic, curse and swear;
But, when the danger comes, quick flee
Behind a neighb'ring wall or tree;
Just so these learned sons of College
Did bruise their instruments of knowledge.
Regardless of their shins and pates,
The bravest seiz'd the butter plates,
And rushing headlong to the van,
Sustain'd the conflict — man to man.
There, in the thickest of the fight,
Did Nathan show such deeds of might,
As would have rais'd, in times of yore,
A statue o'er a tavern door;
And 'Bijah, fearless of his foes,
Help'd many to a bloody nose.
From right to left these heroes fly
Until they catch each other's eye.
As when two ram-cats, fierce for fight,
Do bristle up with vengeful spite,
And, as the combat dread they dare,
With caterwaulings rend the air;
So they, when each the other saw,
Their grinders grittingly did gnaw;
And grumly growl'd, with dire intent,
As at it terribly they went.
First each uprais'd his brawny fist,*
And aim'd a deadly blow, but — miss'd.
Then 'Bijah seiz'd a coffee-pot,
Surcharg'd with liquid boiling hot,
And hurl'd it with such matchless force,
As smash'd two pitchers in its course;
But Nathan dodg'd the mighty blow,†
And, turning quickly on his foe,
Repaid the visit with his foot,
Cas'd in a McIntirian ‡ boot.
Full drive it hit Abijah's bum
And keel'd him over; but his chum

* Est mihi fist-ula.
† — : ille ictum venientem a vertice velox
Prævidit, celerique elapsus corpore cessit. — *Æneid.* v. 444.
‡ Carolus McIntire, qui ocreas, quæ Galoches necessitatem *supersedent*, facit,
etc. Vid. Cat. Fac. Med.

Had wielded, in his just defence,
A bowl of vast circumference.
Ye Powers of Mud! no mortal tongue
Can tell how all the College rung,
How stars did shoot from eye to eye,
How suns and moons flew flashing by,
When Nathan's thick-bon'd jobbernowl
Did come in contact with the bowl!
The foeman, likewise, in the rear,
On both sides valiantly appear;
And fiercely brandishing on high
Their missiles, straightway let them fly;
Though some there were, oh! shame to say!
Who fled like cowards from the fray,
And slily sneak'd behind the door,
Where they might safely bawl and roar;
From whence they now and then did pop,
To throw a cup or tea-pot top. . . .
Go on, dear Goody! and recite
The direful mishaps of the fight.
Alas! how many on that eve,
O'er suppers lost, were doom'd to grieve!
What daylights pummell'd black and blue!
What noddles smear'd with goreless hue!
How dishes did *not* float in blood,
As Noah's Ark did in the flood!
What heroes fell to bite the bricks,*
O'erthrown by bowls! perchance by kicks!

* The floor of Commons Hall is made of bricks.

Cleveland Amory

DR. PARKMAN TAKES A WALK
(1849)

When Dr. George Parkman disappeared from sight one day in late November 1849, it caused a convulsion in Cambridge and Boston, the spasms
of which have even now hardly subsided. Edmund Pearson, A.B. 1902,
has called the Parkman case "America's Classic Murder," and no one has
reported the crime in so spirited and yet sympathetic a fashion as Cleveland Amory, A.B. 1939. A writer by profession, Amory is the author of
Home Town, *a novel, as well as* The Last Resorts *and* The Proper Bostonians, *from which the present chapter is an excerpt.*

TO THE STUDENT of American Society the year 1849 will always remain a red-letter one. In that year two events occurred at opposite ends of the country, both of which, in their own way, made social history. At one end, in Sutter's Creek, California, gold was discovered. At the other, in Boston, Massachusetts, Dr. George Parkman walked off the face of the earth.

The discovery of gold ushered in a new social era. It marked the first great rise of the Western *nouveau riche,* the beginning of that wonderful time when a gentleman arriving in San Francisco and offering a boy fifty cents to carry his suitcase could receive the reply, "Here's a dollar, man — carry it yourself," and when a poor Irish prospector suddenly striking it rich in a vein near Central City, Colorado, could fling down his pick and exclaim, "Thank God, now my wife can be a lady!"

Dr. Parkman's little walk did no such thing as this. It must be remembered, however, that it occurred some three thousand miles away. Boston is not Sutter's Creek or Central City or even San Francisco. There has never been a "new" social era in the Western sense in Boston's rock-ribbed Society, and it remains very doubtful if there ever will be one. The best that could be expected of any one event in Boston would be to shake up the old. Dr. Parkman's walk did this; it shook Boston Society to the very bottom of its First Family foundations. Viewed almost a hundred years later it thus seems, in its restricted way, almost as wonderful as the Gold Rush and not undeserving of the accidental fact that it happened, in the great march of social history, in exactly the same year.

The date was Friday, November 23rd. It was warm for a Boston November, and Dr. Parkman needed no overcoat as he left his Beacon Hill home at 8 Walnut Street. He wore in the fashion of the day a black morning coat, purple silk vest, dark trousers, a dark-figured black tie, and a black silk top hat. He had breakfasted as usual, and he left his home to head downtown toward the Merchants Bank on State Street. Dr. Parkman was quite a figure as he moved along. His high hat and angular physique made him seem far taller than his actual five feet nine and a half inches. He was sixty years old and his head was almost bald, but his hat hid this fact also. To all outward appearances he was remarkably well-preserved, his most striking feature being a conspicuously protruding chin. Boston Parkmans have been noted for their chins the way Boston Adamses are noted for their foreheads or Boston Saltonstalls are noted for their noses, and the chin of old Dr. Parkman was especially formidable. His lower jaw jutted out so far it had made the fitting of a

Taken from *The Proper Bostonians,* by Cleveland Amory, published by E. P. Dutton & Co., Inc., New York. Copyright, 1947, by Cleveland Amory.

set of false teeth for him a very difficult job. The dentist who had had that job had never forgotten it. He was proud of the china-white teeth he had installed. He had even kept the mold to prove to people that he, little Dr. Nathan Keep, had made the teeth of the great Dr. George Parkman.

Although he had studied to be a physician and received his degree Dr. Parkman had rarely practiced medicine in his life. He was a merchant at heart, one of Boston's wealthiest men, and he spent his time in the Boston manner keeping sharp account of his money — and a sharp eye on his debtors. He had many of the traits of character peculiar to the Proper Bostonian breed. He was shrewd and hard, but he was Boston-honest, Boston-direct and Boston-dependable. Like so many other First Family men before his time and after Dr. Parkman was not popular but he was highly respected. It was hard to like a man like Dr. Parkman because his manners were curt and he had a way of glaring at people that made them uncomfortable. Without liking him, however, it was possible to look up to him. People knew him as a great philanthropist and it was said he had given away a hundred thousand dollars in his time. The phrase "wholesale charity and retail penury" as descriptive of the Proper Bostonian breed had not yet come into the Boston lingo, though the day was coming when Dr. Parkman might be regarded as the very personification of it. Certainly he had given away large sums of money with wholesale generosity — even anonymously — yet with small sums, with money on a retail basis, he was penny-punctilious. "The same rule," a biographer records, "governed Dr. Parkman in settling an account involving the balance of a cent as in transactions of thousands of dollars."

Children in the Boston streets pointed out Dr. Parkman to other children. "There goes Dr. Parkman," they would say. People always seemed to point him out after he had passed them. There was no use speaking to Dr. Parkman before he went by. If you weren't his friend, Dr. George Shattuck, or his brother-in-law, Robert Gould Shaw, Esq., or a Cabot or a Lowell, or perhaps a man who owed him money — and then, as someone said, God help you — the doctor would ignore you. Dr. Parkman had no need to court favor from anybody. The Parkmans cut a sizeable chunk of Boston's social ice in 1849, and they still do today. Like other merchant-blooded First Families they were of course economically self-sufficient. They hadn't yet made much of an intellectual mark on their city, but a nephew of the doctor, Francis Parkman, had just published his first book and was on his way to becoming what Van Wyck Brooks has called "the climax and crown" of the Boston historical school. The Parkmans were in the Boston fashion well-connected by marriages. Dr. Parkman's sister's marriage with Robert Gould Shaw,

Boston's wealthiest merchant, was a typical First Family alliance. As for Dr. Parkman's own wealth, some idea of its extent may be gathered from the fact that his son, who never worked a day in his life, was able to leave a will which bequeathed, among other things, the sum of five million dollars for the care and improvement of the Boston Common.

On the morning of that Friday, November 23rd, Dr. Parkman was hurrying. He walked with the characteristic gait of the Proper Bostonian merchant — a gait still practiced by such notable present-day First Family footmen as Charles Francis Adams and Godfrey Lowell Cabot — measuring off distances with long, ground-consuming strides. Dr. Parkman always hurried. Once when riding a horse up Beacon Hill and unable to speed the animal to his satisfaction he had left the horse in the middle of the street and hurried ahead on foot. On that occasion he had been after money, a matter of debt collection.

This morning, too, Dr. Parkman was after money. He left the Merchants Bank and after making several other calls dropped into a grocery store at the corner of Blossom and Vine Streets. This stop, the only non-financial mission of his morning, was to buy a head of lettuce for his invalid sister. He left it in the store and said he would return for it on his way home. The time was half past one and Dr. Parkman presumably intended to be home at 2:30, then the fashionable hour for one's midday meal. Ten minutes later, at 1:40, Elias Fuller, a merchant standing outside his counting room at Fuller's Iron Foundry at the corner of Vine and North Grove Streets, observed Dr. Parkman passing him headed north on North Grove Street. Fuller was later to remember that the doctor seemed particularly annoyed about something and recalled that his cane beat a brisk tattoo on the pavement as he hurried along. What the merchant observed at 1:40 that day is of more than passing importance, for Elias Fuller was the last man who ever saw the doctor alive on the streets of Boston. Somewhere, last seen going north on North Grove Street, Dr. George Parkman walked off the face of the earth.

At 8 Walnut Street Mrs. Parkman, her daughter Harriet and Dr. Parkman's invalid sister sat down to their two-thirty dinner long after three o'clock. Their dinner was ruined and there was no lettuce, but Mrs. Parkman and the others did not mind. They were all worried about the master of the house. Dr. Parkman was not the sort of a man who was ever late for anything. Right after dinner they got in touch with Dr. Parkman's agent, Charles Kingsley. Kingsley was the man who looked after the doctor's business affairs, usually some time after the doctor had thoroughly looked after them himself. Almost at once Kingsley began to search for his employer. First Family men of the prominence of Dr. Parkman did not disappear in Boston — and they do not today — even for an afternoon. By night-fall Kingsley was ready to inform Robert

Gould Shaw. Shaw, acting with the customary dispatch of the Proper Bostonian merchant, went at once to Boston's City Marshal, Mr. Tukey. Marshal Tukey did of course what Shaw told him to do, which was to instigate an all-night search.

The next morning the merchant Shaw placed advertisements in all the papers and had 28,000 handbills distributed. The advertisements and the handbills announced a reward of $3,000 for his brother-in-law alive and $1,000 for his brother-in-law dead. The prices, considering the times, were sky-high but Shaw knew what he was doing in Yankee Boston. Before long virtually every able-bodied man, woman and child in the city was looking for Dr. Parkman. They beat the bushes and they combed the streets. Slum areas were ransacked. All suspicious characters, all persons with known criminal records, were rounded up and held for questioning. Strangers in Boston were given a summary one-two treatment. An Irishman, it is recorded, attempting to change a twenty-dollar bill, was brought in to the police headquarters apparently solely on the assumption that no son of Erin, in the Boston of 1849, had any business with a bill of this size in his possession.

Every one of Dr. Parkman's actions on the previous day, up to 1:40, were checked. At that time, on North Grove Street, the trail always ended. Police had to sift all manner of wild reports. One had the doctor "beguiled to East Cambridge and done in." Another had him riding in a hansom cab, his head covered with blood, being driven at "breakneck speed" over a Charles River bridge. Of the papers only the Boston *Transcript* seems to have kept its head. Its reporter managed to learn from a servant in the Parkman home that the doctor had received a caller at 9:30 Friday reminding him of a 1:30 appointment later in the day. The servant could not remember what the man looked like, but the *Transcript* printed the story in its Saturday night edition along with the reward advertisements. Most people took the caller to be some sort of front man who had appeared to lead Dr. Parkman to a dastardly death. By Monday foul play was so thoroughly suspected that the shrewd merchant Shaw saw no reason to mention a sum as high as $1,000 for the body. Three thousand dollars was still the price for Dr. Parkman alive but only "a suitable reward" was mentioned in Shaw's Monday handbills for Dr. Parkman dead. Monday's handbills also noted the possibility of amnesia but the theory of a First Family man's mind wandering to this extent was regarded as highly doubtful. Dr. Parkman, it was stated, was "perfectly well" when he left his house.

All that the Parkman case now needed to make it a complete panorama of Boston's First Family Society was the active entry of Harvard College into the picture. This occurred on Sunday morning in the person of a caller to the home of Rev. Francis Parkman, the missing doctor's brother, where the entire Family Parkman in all its ramifications had gathered. The caller was a man named John White Webster, Harvard graduate and professor of chemistry at the Harvard Medical School. He was a short squat man, fifty-six years old, who had a mass of unruly black hair and always wore thick spectacles. He had had a most distinguished career. He had studied at Guy's Hospital, London, back in 1815, where among his fellow students had been the poet John Keats. He was a member of the London Geological Society, the American Academy of Arts and Sciences, and during his twenty-five years as a Harvard professor had published numerous nationally noted scientific works. His wife, a Hickling and aunt of the soon-to-be-recognized historian William Hickling Prescott, was "well-connected" with several of Boston's First Families.

The Rev. Parkman was glad to see Professor Webster and ushered him toward the parlor expecting that his desire would be to offer sympathy to the assorted Parkmans there assembled. But Webster, it seemed, did not want to go into the parlor. Instead he spoke abruptly to the minister. "I have come to tell you," he said, "that I saw your brother at half past one o'clock on Friday." The minister was glad to have this report. Since Webster also told him he had been the caller at the Parkman home earlier that day it cleared up the mystery of the strange appointment as recorded in the *Transcript*. Webster explained he should have come sooner but had been so busy he had not seen the notices of Dr. Parkman's disappearance until the previous night. The minister was also satisfied with this. Webster further declared that, at the appointment shortly after 1:30 which took place in his laboratory at the Medical School, he had paid Dr. Parkman the sum of $483.64 which he had owed him. This, of course, explained why the doctor had last been seen by the merchant Fuller in such a cane-tattooing hurry. It had indeed been a matter of a debt collection.

When Professor Webster had left, Robert Gould Shaw was advised of his visit. Shaw was intimate enough in his brother-in-law's affairs to know that Webster had been owing Dr. Parkman money for some time. He did not, however, know the full extent of Webster's misery. Few men have ever suffered from the retail penury side of the Proper Bostonian character as acutely as John White Webster.

The professor received a salary from Harvard of $1,200 a year. This, augumented by income from extra lectures he was able to give, might have sufficed for the average Harvard professor in those days. But Webster was not the average. His wife, for all her connections with Boston's First Families, was still a socially aspirant woman, particularly for her two daughters of debutante age. Mrs. Webster and the Misses Webster entertained lavishly at their charming home in Cambridge.

Professor Webster went into debt. He borrowed money here and he borrowed money there. But mostly he borrowed from Dr. George Parkman.

Who better to borrow from? Dr. Parkman, man of wholesale charity, Proper Bostonian merchant philanthropist. He had given Harvard College the very ground on which at that time stood its Medical School. He had endowed the Parkman Chair of Anatomy, then being occupied by the great Dr. Oliver Wendell Holmes. He had himself been responsible for Webster's appointment as chemistry professor. There were no two ways about it. When Webster needed money the doctor was his obvious choice. As early as 1842 he had borrowed $400. He had then borrowed more. In 1847 he had borrowed from a group headed by Dr. Parkman the sum of $2000. For the latter he had been forced to give a mortgage on all his personal property. He knew he had little chance to pay the debt but he was banking on the generosity of the "good Dr. Parkman." A year later, in 1848, he even went to Dr. Parkman's brother-in-law, the merchant Shaw, and prevailed upon him to buy a mineral collection for $1,200. This was most unfortunate. The mineral collection, like the rest of Webster's property, in hock to Dr. Parkman and his group, was not Webster's to sell. By so doing he had made the doctor guilty of that cardinal sin of Yankeeism — the sin of being shown up as an easy mark. No longer was there for Webster any "good Dr. Parkman." "From that moment onward," says author Stewart Holbrook, "poor Professor Webster knew what it was like to have a Yankee bloodhound on his trail. His creditor was a punctilious man who paid his own obligations when due and he expected the same of everybody else, even a Harvard professor." *

Dr. Parkman dogged Professor Webster in the streets, outside his home, even to the classrooms. He would come in and take a front-row seat at Webster's lectures. He would not say anything; he would just sit and glare in that remarkable way of his. He wrote the professor notes, not just plain insulting notes but the awful, superior, skin-biting notes of the Yankee gentleman. He spoke sternly of legal processes. Meeting Webster he would never shout at him but instead address him in clipped Proper Bostonian accents. It was always the same question. When would the professor be "ready" for him?

Dr. Parkman even bearded Professor Webster in his den, in the inner recesses of the latter's laboratory at the Medical School. He had been there, in the professor's private back room — according to the janitor of the building — on Monday evening, November 19th, just four days before he had disappeared.

The janitor was a strange man, the grim New England village type, a small person with dark brooding eyes. His name was Ephraim Littlefield.

* "Murder at Harvard," by Stewart Holbrook, *The American Scholar*, 1945.

He watched with growing interest the goings-on around him. Following
Webster's call on Rev. Francis Parkman, which established the farthest
link yet on the trail of Dr. Parkman's walk, it had of course been necessary
to search the Medical School. Littlefield wanted this done thoroughly, as
thoroughly for example as they were dragging the Charles River outside.
He personally led the investigators to Webster's laboratory. Everything
was searched, all but the private back room and adjoining privy. One of
the party of investigators, which also included Dr. Parkman's agent
Kingsley, was a police officer named Derastus Clapp. Littlefield prevailed
upon this officer to go into the back room, but just as Clapp opened the
door Professor Webster solicitously called out for him to be careful.
There were dangerous articles in there, he said. "Very well, then," said
Officer Clapp, "I will not go in there and get blowed up." He backed out
again.

The whole search was carried on to the satisfaction of even Robert
Gould Shaw who, after all, knew at firsthand the story of Webster's
duplicity via the mineral collection. And who was the little janitor
Ephraim Littlefield to dispute the word of the great merchant Robert
Shaw? As each day went by the theory of murder was becoming more and
more generally accepted, but in a Boston Society eternally geared to the
mesh of a Harvard A.B. degree the idea of pinning a homicide on a Harvard man — and a professor at that — was heresy itself. One might as well
pry for the body of Dr. Parkman among the prayer cushions of the First
Family pews in Trinity Church.

But Littlefield was not, in the socially sacrosanct meaning of the
words, a "Harvard man." He was a Harvard janitor. Furthermore he was
stubborn. He wanted the Medical School searched again. When it was,
he was once more prodding the investigators to greater efforts. He told
them they should visit the cellar of the building, down in the section
where the Charles River water flowed in and carried off waste matter from
the dissecting rooms and privies above. The agent Kingsley took one
gentlemanly sniff from the head of the stairs and refused to accompany
the janitor and the other investigators any farther. The others, however,
went on. As they passed the wall under Webster's back room the janitor
volunteered the information that it was now the only place in the building
that hadn't been searched. Why not, the men wanted to know. The janitor
explained that to get there it would be necessary to dig through the wall.
The men had little stomach left for this sort of operation and soon rejoined
Kingsley upstairs.

Littlefield, however, had plenty of stomach. He determined to dig
into the wall himself. Whether he was by this time, Monday, already
suspicious of Professor Webster has never been made clear. He had, it is
true, heard the Webster-Parkman meeting of Monday night the week

before. He had distinctly overheard the doctor say to the professor in that ever-insinuating way, "Something, Sir, must be accomplished." Just yesterday, Sunday, he had seen Professor Webster enter the Medical School around noontime, apparently shortly after he had made his call on Rev. Francis Parkman. Webster had spoken to him and had acted "very queerly." Come to think of it, Littlefield brooded, Sunday was a queer day for the professor to be hanging around the School anyway. "Ephraim," writes Richard Dempewolff, one of the Parkman case's most avid devotees, "was one of those shrewd New England conclusion-jumpers who, unfortunately for the people they victimize, are usually right. By putting two and two together, Mr. Littlefield achieved a nice round dozen." *

The janitor's wife was a practical woman. She thought little of her husband's determination to search the filthy old place under the private rooms of the Harvard professor she had always regarded as a fine gentleman. Her husband would lose his job, that would be what would happen. Just you wait and see, Mr. Littlefield.

Mr. Littlefield deferred to Mrs. Littlefield and did wait — until Tuesday, five days after Dr. Parkman's disappearance. On Tuesday something extraordinary happened. At four o'clock in the afternoon he heard Professor Webster's bell jangle, a signal that the janitor was wanted. He went to Webster's laboratory. The professor asked him if he had bought his Thanksgiving turkey yet. Littlefield did not know what to say. He replied he had thought some about going out Thanksgiving.

"Here," said Webster, "go and get yourself one." With that he handed the janitor an order for a turkey at a near-by grocery store.

John White Webster had here made a fatal error. The call he had paid on Rev. Francis Parkman had been bad enough. It had aroused the searching of the Medical School and had brought Littlefield actively into the case. But as Webster later admitted he had been afraid that sooner or later someone would have found out about his 1:30 Friday rendezvous with Dr. Parkman and felt that his best chance lay in making a clean breast of it. For this action in regard to the janitor's Thanksgiving turkey, however, there could be no such defense. If he hoped to win the janitor over to "his side," then he was a poor judge of human nature indeed. Harvard Janitor Ephraim Littlefield had worked for Harvard Professor John Webster for seven years — curiously the same length of time Professor John Webster had been borrowing from Dr. Parkman — without ever receiving a present of any kind. And now, a Thanksgiving turkey. Even the deferentially dormant suspicions of Mrs. Littlefield were thoroughly aroused.

Janitor Littlefield had no chance to begin his labors Wednesday. Pro-

* *Famous Old New England Murders,* by Richard Dempewolff (Brattleboro, Vt.: Stephen Daye Press, 1942).

fessor Webster was in his laboratory most of the day. On Thanksgiving, however, while Mrs. Littlefield kept her eyes peeled for the professor or any other intruder, the janitor began the task of crow-barring his way through the solid brick wall below the back room. It was slow work and even though the Littlefields took time off to enjoy their dinner — the janitor had characteristically not passed up the opportunity to procure a nine-pound bird — it was soon obvious he could not get through the wall in one day. That evening the Littlefields took time off again. They went to a dance given by the Sons of Temperance Division of the Boston Odd Fellows. They stayed until four o'clock in the morning. "There were twenty dances," Littlefield afterwards recalled, "and I danced eighteen out of the twenty."

Late Friday afternoon, after Professor Webster had left for the day, Littlefield was at his digging again. This time he had taken the precaution of advising two of the School's First Family doctors, Doctors Bigelow and Jackson, of what he was doing. They were surprised but told him since he had started he might as well continue. But they were against his idea of informing the dean of the School, Dr. Holmes, of the matter. It would, they felt, disturb the dean unnecessarily.

Even a half-hearted First Family blessing has always counted for something in Boston, and Janitor Littlefield now went to work with renewed vigor. Again his wife stood watch. At five-thirty he broke through the fifth of the five courses of brick in the wall. "I held my light forward," he afterwards declared, "and the first thing which I saw was the pelvis of a man, and two parts of a leg . . . It was no place for these things."

It was not indeed. Within fifteen minutes Doctors Bigelow and Jackson were on the scene. Later Dr. Holmes himself would view the remains. Meanwhile of course there was the matter of a little trip out to the Webster home in Cambridge.

To that same police officer who had been so loath to get himself "blowed up" in Webster's back room fell the honor of making the business trip to Cambridge and arresting the Harvard professor. Once bitten, Derastus Clapp was twice shy. There would be no more monkeyshines, Harvard or no Harvard. He had his cab halt some distance from the Webster Home and approached on foot. Opening the outer gate he started up the walk just as Webster himself appeared on the steps of his house, apparently showing a visitor out. The professor attempted to duck back inside. Officer Clapp hailed him. "We are about to search the Medical School again," he called, moving forward rapidly as he spoke, "and we wish you to be present." Webster feigned the traditional Harvard indifference. It was a waste of time; the School had already been searched twice. Clapp laid a stern hand on his shoulder. Webster, escorted outward and suddenly noting two other men in the waiting cab, wanted to go back for his keys. Officer Clapp was not unaware of the drama of the moment. "Professor Webster," he said, "we have keys enough to unlock the whole of Harvard College."

Boston was in an uproar. Dr. Parkman had not walked off the face of the earth. He had been pushed off — and by the authoritative hands of a Harvard professor! Even the *Transcript*, calm when there was still a hope the Parkman case was merely a matter of disappearance, could restrain itself no longer. It threw its genteel caution to the winds. There were two exclamation marks after its headline, and its editor called on Shakespeare himself to sum up the situation:

> Since last evening, our whole population has been in a state of the greatest possible excitement in consequence of the astounding rumor that the body of Dr. Parkman has been discovered, and that Dr. John W. Webster, Professor of Chemistry in the Medical School of Harvard College, and a gentleman connected by marriage with some of our most distinguished families, has been arrested and imprisoned, on suspicion of being the murderer. Incredulity, then amazement, and then blank, unspeakable horror have been the emotions, which have agitated the public mind as the rumor has gone on, gathering countenance and confirmation. Never in the annals of crime in Massachusetts has such a sensation been produced.
>
> In the streets, in the market-place, at every turn, men greet each other with pale, eager looks and the inquiry, "Can it be true?" And then as the terrible reply, "the circumstances begin to gather weight against him," is wrung forth, the agitated listener can only vent his sickening sense of horror, in some expression as that of Hamlet, —
> "O, horrible! O, horrible! most horrible!"

There is irony in the fact that proud, staid Boston chose the time it did to provide American Society with the nineteenth century's outstanding social circus. Boston was at the height of its cultural attainments in 1849. In that year a scholarly but hardly earth-shaking book by a rather minor Boston author, *The History of Spanish Literature* by George Ticknor, was the world literary event of the year and the only book recommended by Lord Macaulay to Queen Victoria. Yet just three months later, on March 19, 1850, Boston put on a show which for pure social artistry Barnum himself would have had difficulty matching. The Boston courtroom had everything. It had one of Boston's greatest jurists, Judge Lemuel Shaw, on its bench; it had the only Harvard professor ever to be tried for murder, John White Webster, as its defendant; it had promised witnesses of national renown, from Dr. Oliver Wendell Holmes on down; and in the offing, so to speak, it had the shades of Dr. George Parkman, perhaps the most socially distinguished victim in the annals of American crime.

Nobody wanted to miss such a sight. Trains and stages from all parts of the East brought people to Boston. They wanted tickets. Everybody in Boston wanted tickets, too. Consequences of revolutionary proportions were feared if they could not be accommodated. Yet what to do? There was only a small gallery to spare, it having been decreed in typical Boston fashion that the main part of the courtroom would be reserved on an invitation basis. Finally, Field Marshal Tukey hit on the only possible solution, which was to effect a complete change of audience in the gallery every ten minutes during the proceedings. It took elaborate street barricades and doorway defenses to do the job, but in the eleven days of the trial, to that little gallery holding hardly more than a hundred souls, came a recorded total of sixty thousand persons. Considering that the constabulary of Boston assigned to the job numbered just fifteen men, this feat ranks as a monumental milestone in police annals.

From the suspense angle the trial, which has been called a landmark in the history of criminal law, must have been something of a disappointment. By the time it began, despite Webster's protestations of innocence, there was little doubt in the minds of most of the spectators as to the guilt of the professor. A few days after his arrest a skeleton measuring 70½ inches had finally been assembled from the grisly remains found lying about under the professor's back room, and while the sum total of this was an inch taller than Dr. Parkman had been in happier days, there had been no question in the minds of the coroner's jury, of Dr. Holmes, and of a lot of other people, but that Dr. Parkman it was. The case against the professor was one of circumstantial evidence of course. No one had seen Webster and Parkman together at the time of the murder; indeed, during the trial the time of the murder was never satisfactorily established. But the strongest Webster adherents had to admit that it was evidence of a very powerful nature, as Chief Justice Shaw could not fail to point out in his famous charge to the jury, an address which lawyers today still consider one of the greatest expositions of the nature and use of circumstantial evidence ever delivered.

There were a number of pro-Websterites. Harvard professor though he may have been, he was still the underdog, up against the almighty forces of Boston's First Families. Many of the Websterites had undoubtedly had experiences of their own on the score of Proper Bostonian retail penury and were ready to recognize that Dr. Parkman had been so importunate a creditor that he had quite possibly driven the little professor first to distraction and then to the deed. They went to Rufus Choate, Boston's great First Family lawyer, and asked him to undertake the defense. After reading up on the case Choate was apparently willing to do so on the condition that Webster would admit the killing and plead manslaughter. Another First Family lawyer, old Judge Fay, with whom the Webster family regularly played whist, thought a verdict of manslaughter could be reached.

But Webster would not plead guilty. From the beginning he had made his defense an all but impossible task. He talked when he shouldn't have talked and he kept quiet when, at least by the light of hindsight, he should have come clean. On his first trip to the jail he immediately asked the officers about the finding of the body. "Have they found the *whole* body?" he wanted to know. This while certainly a reasonable question in view of the wide area over which the remains were found was hardly the thing for a man in his position to be asking. Then, while vehemently protesting his innocence, he took a strychnine pill out of his waistcoat pocket and attempted to kill himself, an attempt which was foiled only by the fact that, though the dose was a large one, he was in such a nervous condition it failed to take fatal effect. At the trial Webster maintained through his lawyers that the body he was proved to be so vigorously dismembering during his spare moments in the week following November 23rd had been a Medical School cadaver brought to him for that purpose. This was sheer folly, and the prosecution had but to call upon the little dentist, Nathan Keep, to prove it so. Tooth by tooth, during what was called one of the "tumultuous moments" of the trial, Dr. Keep fitted the fragments of the false teeth found in Webster's furnace into the mold he still had in his possession. Charred as they were there could be no doubt they had once been the china-white teeth of Dr. Parkman.

The spectators were treated to other memorable scenes. The great Dr. Holmes testified twice, once for the State on the matter of the identity of the reconstructed skeleton and once for the defense as a character witness for the accused. Professor Webster's character witnesses were a howitzer battery of First Family notables, among them Doctors Bigelow and Jackson, a Codman and a Lovering, the New England historian John Gorham Palfrey and Nathaniel Bowditch, son of the famed mathematician — even Harvard's president Jared Sparks took the stand for his errant employee. All seemed to agree that Webster, if occasionally irritable, was basically a kindhearted man, and President Sparks was thoughtful enough to add one gratuitous comment. "Our professors," he said, "do not often commit murder."

Credit was due Webster for his ability as a cadaver carver. He had done the job on Dr. Parkman, it was established, with no more formidable instrument than a jackknife. A Dr. Woodbridge Strong was especially emphatic on this point. He had dissected a good many bodies in his time, he recalled, including a rush job on a decaying pirate, but never one with just a jackknife. Ephraim Littlefield was of course star witness for the prosecution. The indefatigable little janitor talked for one whole day on the witness stand, a total of eight hours, five hours in the morning before recess for lunch and three hours in the afternoon. Only once did he falter and that on the occasion when, under cross-examination with the defense making a valiant attempt to throw suspicion on him, he was asked if he played "gambling cards" with friends in Webster's back room. Four times the defense had to ask the question and four times Littlefield refused to answer. Finally, his New England conscience stung to the quick, he replied in exasperation, "If you ask me if I played cards there *last winter*, I can truthfully say I did not."

In those days prisoners were not allowed to testify, but on the last day of the trial Professor Webster was asked if he wanted to say anything. Against the advice of his counsel he rose and spoke for fifteen minutes. He spent most of those precious moments denying the accusation that he had written the various anonymous notes which had been turning up from time to time in the City Marshal's office ever since the disappearance of Dr. Parkman. One of these had been signed CIVIS and Webster's last sentence was a pathetic plea for CIVIS to come forward if he was in the courtroom. CIVIS did not, and at eight o'clock on the evening of March 30th the trial was over.

Even the jury seems to have been overcome with pity for the professor. Before filing out of the courtroom the foreman, pointing a trembling finger at Webster, asked: "Is that all? Is that the end? Can nothing further be said in defense of the man?" Three hours later the foreman and his cohorts were back, having spent, it is recorded, the first two hours and fifty-five minutes in prayer "to put off the sorrowful duty." When the verdict was delivered, "an awful and unbroken silence ensued, in which the Court, the jury, the clerk, and the spectators seemed to be absorbed in their own reflections."

Webster's hanging, by the neck and until he was dead, proceeded without untoward incident in the courtyard of Boston's Leverett Street jail just five months to the day after he had been declared guilty. Before that time, however, the professor made a complete confession. He stated that Dr. Parkman had come into his laboratory on that fatal Friday and that, when he had been unable to produce the money he owed, the doctor had shown him a sheaf of papers proving that he had been responsible for getting him his professorship. The doctor then added, "I got you into your office, Sir, and now I will get you out of it." This, said Webster, so infuriated him that he seized a stick of wood off his laboratory bench and struck Dr. Parkman one blow on the head. Death was instantaneous and Webster declared, "I saw nothing but the alternative of a successful removal and concealment of the body, on the one hand, and of infamy and destruction on the other." He then related his week-long attempt to dismember and burn the body. Even the clergyman who regularly visited Webster in his cell during his last days was not able to extract from the professor the admission that the crime had been premeditated. He had done it in that one frenzy of rage. "I am irritable and passionate," the clergyman quoted Webster as saying, "and Dr. Parkman was the most provoking of men."

The late Edmund Pearson, recognized authority on nonfictional homicide here and abroad, has called the Webster-Parkman case America's classic murder and the one which has lived longest in books of reminiscences. Certainly in Boston's First Family Society the aftermath of the case has been hardly less distinguished than its actual occurrence. To this day no Proper Bostonian grandfather autobiography is complete without some reference to the case. The Beacon Hill house at 8 Walnut Street from which Dr. Parkman started out on his walk that Friday morning almost a hundred years ago is still standing, and its present occupant, a prominent Boston lawyer, is still on occasion plagued by the never-say-die curious.

Among Boston Parkmans the effect was a profound one. For years certain members of the Family shrank from Society altogether, embarrassed as they were by the grievous result of Dr. Parkman's financial punctiliousness and all too aware of the sympathy extended Professor Webster in his budgetary plight. In the doctor's immediate family it is noteworthy that his widow headed the subscription list of a fund taken up to care for Webster's wife and children. Dr. Parkman's son, George Francis Parkman, was five years out of Harvard in 1849. He had been, in contrast to his father, a rather gay blade as a youth and at college had taken part in Hasty Pudding Club theatricals; at the time of the murder he was enjoying himself in Paris. He returned to Boston a marred man. He moved his mother and sister from 8 Walnut Street and took a house at 33 Beacon Street. From the latter house he buried his mother and aunt, and there he and his sister lived on as Boston Society's most distinguished recluses. His solitary existence never included even the solace of a job. Describing him as he appeared a full fifty years after the crime a biographer records:

> Past the chain of the bolted door on Beacon Street no strangers, save those who came on easily recognized business, were ever allowed to enter. Here George Francis Parkman and his sister Harriet, neither of whom ever married, practised the utmost frugality, the master of the house going himself to the market every day to purchase their meager provisions, and invariably paying cash for the simple supplies he brought home.
>
> The windows of his house looked out upon the Common but he did not frequent it . . . He always walked slowly and alone, in a stately way, and attracted attention by his distinguished though retiring appearance . . . In cool weather he wore a heavy coat of dark cloth and his shoulders and neck were closely wrapped with a wide scarf, the ends of which were tucked into his coat or under folds. He sheltered himself against the east winds of Boston just as he seemed, by his manner, to shelter his inmost self from contact with the ordinary affairs of men.*

* *Famous Families of Massachusetts,* by Mary Caroline Crawford (Boston: Little, Brown & Co., 1930).

Tremors of the Parkman earthquake continued to be felt by Boston Society often at times when they were least desired. Twenty years later, when Boston was privileged to play proud host to Charles Dickens, there was a particularly intense tremor. Dickens was asked which one of the city's historic landmarks he would like to visit first. "The room where Dr. Parkman was murdered," he replied, and there being no doubt he meant what he said, nothing remained for a wry-faced group of Boston's best but to shepherd the distinguished novelist out to the chemistry laboratory of the Harvard Medical School.

A Webster-Parkman story, vintage of 1880, is still told today by Boston's distinguished author and teacher, Bliss Perry. He recalls that for a meeting of New England college officers at Williamstown, Massachusetts, his mother had been asked to put up as a guest in her house Boston's First Family poet laureate, diplomat and first editor of the *Atlantic*, James Russell Lowell. Unfortunately Lowell was at that time teaching at Harvard and for all his other accomplishments Mrs. Perry would have none of him. He had to be quartered elsewhere.

"I could not sleep," Mrs. Perry said, "if one of those Harvard professors were in the house."

Ellery Sedgwick

JANE TOPPAN'S CASE

(1892)

Of the eight successive pilots of the Atlantic Monthly, *Ellery Sedgwick, said E. K. Rand in 1944, was "the quickest to catch the breeze" — a man who combined business ability with literary taste. During thirty years as editor, he built the modern Atlantic from a small, unprofitable, rather local magazine of 13,500 circulation into one of national importance with ten times that number of subscribers. "I have a great affection for Harvard College," he has written, "atavistic as well as personal . . . but I do not look back on my own four years with any touch of nostalgia. The decades at Harvard have multiplied its opportunities by geometric progression, but it is my feeling that the elixir cultural or perhaps spiritual which is the essence of the educated man has been diluted with the years. We have thrown off the prejudices of our fathers, not realizing that the heart of intelligent prejudice is conviction."*

THE MOST IMPORTANT fact for a parent to know about Harvard or any other college for that matter is never mentioned in the catalogues. College walls are not high enough to shut out the larger life which flows about them. Education aims at segregated experience, but experience like all nature abhors a vacuum, and the influences to which young men are subject are beyond calculation. As an odd instance of this I will tell of a curious incident which happened to me during my sophomore year. In bitter weather, after a late party, I had driven out from Boston in one of those ancient sleighs known, I know not why, as "booby-hutches." The characteristic of these eccentric conveyances was their discomfort. They were shrouded in leather curtains which flapped wildly in the wind and had an inanimate genius for intensifying drafts. After the heat of the dance, this particular booby-hutch did for me. I caught a heavy cold, pneumonia followed, and within a day or two both my lungs were seriously involved. Harvard had no hospital in those days, and there I was; my big room in Holworthy Hall heated by the coals of a single grate, with running water three floors below and two trained nurses to assist such chances of life as sick students had in those days.

Now as it happened the attack had caught me just as I was wrestling with a thesis on the character of Jonathan Swift, and turbulent incidents in the life of the ferocious Dean of St. Patrick's swam about me in my delirium. One of my nurses, distinguished by red hair and an angular figure, I called Vanessa. The other was to me the dearer Stella. She was a comfortable body, pink, plump, and motherly, and between us the happiest of domestic relations were soon established, in spite of my whirling head and the desperate pain in my left side. When I tried to throw myself out of the big picture over the bed which I took to be a window, it was Stella who made me all snug again. She it was who watched me with a nurse's intentness as I fixed my own gaze on a tobacco jar standing on the mantel across the room, and said aloud (as she afterwards reported), "I am too tired. That jar holds the elixir of life in it. All I have to do is to struggle up, walk five steps, and drain life from it. But I am too tired. The road back is rougher and longer than the way ahead." Then she bathed my hot forehead, whispered that she would bring that draught of life to me, gave me my medicine, and slipped me off to sleep. Stella's American name was Jane Toppan, and as the crisis passed, the bond between Jane and me grew strong. Some weeks after the crisis, Vanessa left, but Stella stayed to see me through my convalescence and many a confidence we exchanged during the long days and nights. We laughed together about how I had christened her my "Star," and I gave her a deal of instruction about the savage Dean and his inscrutable affections, and translated for her, whether correctly or not I can't remember, the famous inscription on his tomb: — *Ubi saeva indignatio ulterius cor lacerare nequit.*

Then we would fall into more personal discourse. She asked me about my ambitions, and in return would tell me of the satisfactions of her own

Ellery Sedgwick, *The Happy Profession* (Boston: Little, Brown & Co., 1946).

career, the passionate interest surrounding endless battles between life and death in the sick-room, and how it was in the nurse's lap that the destiny of the patient lay. As I grew stronger, I told her stories about the three: Clotho, Lachesis, and Atropos, who spin the thread, wind it, and cut it with the shears. She listened eagerly and explained in return how it was not the doctor but the nurse who held the shears and how she was ever conscious that the fate of a human being rested upon her. On Sunday evenings it had been her custom to go to church, but she hated to leave me and said it was better fun to settle me in an armchair at one side of the grate, while she threw on another scuttle, poked the red coals below, and made all ready for a good talk. When the time came for saying good-bye, we promised always to be friends.

For years I heard nothing of Jane Toppan, and then a strange history appeared in the newspapers. Jane Toppan had been arrested and charged with murder, not the indiscretion of a single homicide, but the massacre of thirty-one patients. Thirty-one only were proved victims but the doctors believed that the holocaust numbered nearly one hundred. After all, thirty-one is a sufficient number of indictments for murder. It seemed unnecessary to pursue the gruesome trail to the end. Many families preferred to let their sisters and brothers rest quiet in their graves and not to open the gates of speculation as to whether their deaths had been owing to natural causes. It seemed, and later evidence bore it out, that my Stella had a homicidal mania on an imperial scale. For three or four deaths she had been responsible before she undertook to weigh my own fate, and skipping occasional patients, as she mercifully skipped me, she put away the rest in a succession that grew more rapid with practice. Her method and the fascination of it gave me a tiny peephole into the deeper abnormalities. Jane would fight hard for a patient's life, but when victory seemed within her grasp and the doctor, confident that vitality was mounting, had left for the night, Jane would stand by the lonely pillow holding two vials in her hand. One contained morphia, one atropin. She would give a dose of morphia and, stooping over the bed, scrutinize the dilation of the patient's pupils as they expanded into a wide and vacant stare. Then with a dose of atropin she would watch the drama of the pupils as they narrowed further and further till they became pin points of light. To such treatment there was an inevitable end. The extraneous and unexpected symptoms would puzzle the physician. They seemed to transcend his experience, and it was not until a long line of patients collapsed, one after another, just as they seemed destined for physical salvation, that suspicion turned upon Jane.

And just at that unfortunate moment Jane did an imprudent thing. She had been the devoted nurse of two sisters. One had just died and Jane, like a decent body, went to the funeral. As the coffin was lowered into the grave, to the consternation of the bereaved family some one thought she heard Jane mutter: "It won't be long now before the other goes." Vague suspicion gathered about her but Jane was known as the best nurse in Cambridge and any definite imputation was too dreadful to be spoken aloud. It was only when four members of a single family in which Jane had been the competent nurse followed each other to the grave within the unreasonable interval of forty-one days that action was taken. Jane was questioned and arrested. A series of bodies were exhumed, stomachs were analyzed. Finally the whole terrifying story came to light. The nurse's mania was diagnosed. Her fifteen years in the assiduous practice of murder were reviewed by the court. She was convicted, sent to Bridgewater, and incarcerated in a hospital for the criminal insane, where I trust she found nurses competent and considerate as she. There, for thirty-five years, till at the ripe age of eighty-one her own time came, Jane Toppan revolved the story of the Three Fates.

Much that was interesting was said of Jane Toppan's career. I quote a pungent paragraph from the unpublished papers of Dr. Charles F. Folsom, Professor of Mental Diseases at Harvard.

"In the pleasure and excitement of crime," he wrote, "Jane Toppan seemed to find the criminal enjoyment of doing aesthetic work to which danger appeared to add zest."

But perhaps Jane's attitude toward life can but be summed up in words of her own, uttered during her trial. She had paused to recall the circumstances surrounding the murder of one of her particular cronies who had come all the way up from Cataumet on the Cape for a sociable visit. The women dined together. The dinner was prepared by Jane. The visitor was taken violently ill and a few days later returned to Cataumet in her coffin. Jane, who never failed a friend, had journeyed to the Cape for the funeral and thus described her sensations as a mourner: —

"When the people came down to Cataumet from Cambridge with Mrs. Davis's body and brought flowers and other emblems of sorrow, I wanted to say to them: 'You had better wait, for in a little while I shall have another funeral for you. If you will only wait, I will save you the trouble of going back and forth.'"

How much better they order these things abroad. Here was a champion of American murder without an equal, yet she was permitted to die in obscurity. Jack the Ripper in London, Bluebeard in Paris; how much had they accomplished? Jack the Ripper may have had half a dozen or perhaps a dozen killings to his credit; Bluebeard, eight or ten wives, yet their names are blazoned in the majestic history of crime. But this New England spinster who could have taught both of them their trade from the ground up has left no biographer behind. This simple tribute of mine is her unique reward.

What ought a boy to carry away from college? Facts are convenient but of little value compared with knowledge of how to read shutting out every avenue of consciousness except the single road which he is traveling; to understand just why two and two make four; to know a man when he sees one — all these are cheap at cost of three or four years. But there is something else, which if the student understands it, and few do, is a possession of great price. The boy has lived in a community free from the grosser iniquities of the world, a society of scholars to whom learning is its own ample return, a republic where the crown of olive is the unmaterial reward. And if the young graduate is wise as well as knowledgeable, his diploma will tell him that in all this world there is no such fun as learning to understand.

IV

"YOU CAN TELL A HARVARD MAN . . ."

And who was on the Catalogue
When college was begun?
Two nephews of the President,
And *the* Professor's son;
(They turned a little Indian by,
As brown as any bun;)
Lord! how the seniors knocked about
The freshman class of one!

OLIVER WENDELL HOLMES (1836)

Students of H[arvard] do not on all occasions appear much better than their less favored countrymen, either in point of gentlemanly and *distingué* appearance or in conversation.

FRANCIS PARKMAN (1844)

As I look back on my college days it strikes me that we were boys. Honest, energetic, square-trotting, manly boys, but still boys. The fault was not wholly ours; the apparent aim of the authorities was to keep us so.

ROBERT GRANT (1896)

A Series of Excerpts

KEEP THOU THE COLLEGE LAWS

(1655–1790)

One of contemporary Harvard's proudest boasts is that of its encouragement of students' personal responsibility — responsibility toward society and toward self-education. Despite the arguments over the parietal regulations, and other College requirements, there are today relatively few rules to hinder a student in his development as a person. In the early years it was a different story. The College laws were intended to confine students to the Yard and the College twenty-four hours a day; the students could not go to the nearby pub, join a military company, or be seen in the company of those who "lead an ungirt and dissolute life." President Dunster formed the first law code for the College in 1642 and thereafter "the laws, liberties, and orders of Harvard College" were required to be copied by all entering students "for the perpetual preservation and government." From 1790 onward they were regularly revised and printed in English.

EVERY undergraduate shall be called only by his surname unless he be the son of a nobleman, or a knight's eldest son or a fellow commoner. [1655]

All students shall be slow to speak, & eschew and (as much as in them lies) shall take care that others may avoid all swearing, lying, cursing, needless asseverations, foolish talking, scurrility, babbling, filthy speaking, chiding, strife, railing, reproaching, abusive jesting, uncomely noise, uncertain rumors, divulging secrets, & all manner of troublesome & offensive gestures, as being they who should shine before others in exemplary life. [1655]

No scholar shall go out of his chamber without coat, gown or cloak, & every one, every where shall wear modest & sober habit, without strange ruffianlike or new-fangled fashions, without all lavish dress, or excess of apparel whatsoever; nor shall any wear gold or silver, or such ornaments, except to whom upon just ground the president shall permit the same: neither shall it be lawful for any to wear long hair, locks or foretops, nor to use curling, crisping, parting or powdering their hair. [1655]

Candidates for admission into Harvard College, shall be examined by the President and two at least of the Tutors. No one shall be admitted, unless he can translate the Greek and Latin authors in common use, such as Tully, Virgil, The New-Testament, Xenophon &c understands the rules of grammar, can write Latin correctly, and hath a good moral character. [1767]

If any undergraduate shall lead an idle & dissipated life, after those in the government of the College shall have taken pains to reform him; or if he shall otherwise so offend against those rules and laws of the College, . . . they shall judge it most tending to the reformation of the delinquent (the honor of the College at the same time being secured) that he should, for a time, be taken from the College, and be put under the immediate inspection & instruction of some private gentleman in the country. [1767]

If any undergraduates shall be absent from, or carelessly perform their stated exercises with their respective tutors, or absent themselves from the private lectures of the professors, they shall be fined not exceeding two shillings; and if they do not speedily reform by such pecuniary mulcts, they shall be admonished, degraded, suspended, or rusticated, according as the nature and degree of the offence shall require. [1790]

To animate the students in the pursuit of literary merit and fame, and to excite in their breasts a noble spirit of emulation, there shall be annually a public examination, in the presence of a joint committee of the Corporation and Overseers, and such other gentlemen as may be inclined to attend it. [1790]

If any scholar shall associate with any person of dissolute morals, or, in the town of Cambridge, with one that is rusticated, or expelled, within three years after such rustication or expulsion, unless the rusticated person shall be restored within that space, he shall be fined not exceeding five shillings for the first offence; and if any Undergraduate shall persist therein, he shall be farther liable to admonition, degradation, suspension, or rustication, according to the circumstances of the offence. And if any undergraduate shall lead a life of dissipation, after those in the Government of the College shall have endeavored to reform him by admonition and the lesser punishments, he shall be degraded, suspended, or rusticated, as the degree of the offence may require. [1790]

If any scholar shall go into any tavern or victualling house in Cambridge, to eat and drink there, unless in the presence of his father or guardian, without leave from the President or one of the Tutors, he shall be fined not exceeding two shillings. [1790]

If any resident graduate shall play at cards or dice, after having been admonished by the President, he shall not be allowed to continue any longer at the College. [1790]

If any scholar or scholars, belonging to the College, shall be found guilty of making tumultuous or indecent noises, to the dishonour and disturbance of the College, or to the disturbance of the town or any of its inhabitants; or, without leave from the President, Professors and Tutors, shall make bonfires or illuminations, or play off fireworks, or be any way aiding or abetting of the same, every scholar, so offending, shall be liable to a fine not exceeding ten shillings, or to be publicly admonished, degraded, suspended, or rusticated, according to the degree and aggravation of the offence. [1790]

All the undergraduates shall be clothed in coats of blue gray, and with waistcoats and breeches of the same colour, or of a black, a nankeen, or an olive colour. The coats of the freshmen shall have plain buttonholes: The cuffs shall be without buttons. The coats of the sophomores shall have plain button holes like those of the freshmen; but the cuffs shall have buttons. The coats of the juniors shall have cheap frogs to the button holes, except the button holes of the cuffs. The coats of the seniors shall have frogs to the button holes of the cuffs. The buttons upon the coats of all the classes shall be as near the colour of the coats as they can be procured, or of a black colour. And no student shall appear, within the limits of the College, or town of Cambridge, in any other dress, than in the uniform belonging to his respective class, unless he shall have on a night gown, or such an outside garment, as may be necessary, over a coat: Except only, that the seniors and juniors are permitted to wear black gowns; and it is recommended that they appear in them on all public occasions: Nor shall any part of their garments be of silk; nor shall they wear gold or silver lace, cord or edging upon their hats, waistcoats, or any other parts of their clothing: And whosoever shall violate these regulations, shall be fined a sum not exceeding ten shillings for each offence.
[1790]

From "College Laws and Customs," *Publications of the Colonial Society of Massachusetts,* XXXI, and from the official printing of "The Laws of Harvard College" (Boston, 1790).

Thomas Shepard, Jr.

"THAT PRECIOUS TIME YOU NOW MISSPEND"
(1672)

*Two famous letters of advice to seventeenth-century Harvard students
have come down to us. One was from Leonard Hoar, A.B. 1650, to his
freshman nephew Josiah Flynt, and principally concerned matters of the
curriculum. The other was from Rev. Thomas Shepard, Jr., A.B. 1653, to
his son, Thomas, who graduated from Harvard in 1676. President Hoar's
letter was reproduced in full in Morison's* Harvard College in the Seventeenth Century. *The Shepard letter is less well known, although written
by one of the prominent Harvard graduates of the seventeenth century.
Thomas Shepard, Jr., was the son of the founder of the first permanent
church in Cambridge, an Overseer of the College, and a defender of the
principles of religious toleration. His son, according to Cotton Mather,
was "his Grandfather's and his Father's genuine Off-Spring" who came
"unto such Learning as gave him an Early Admission into the College, and
raised great Hopes in good Men concerning him." Unhappily he died in
1685, at the age of twenty-six, only eight years after his father's death,
and a brief ministerial career. Here is a portion of the father's "Paper of
Golden Instructions."*

REMEMBER that these are times and days of much light and knowledge
and that therefore you had as good be no scholar as not excel in knowledge and learning. Abhor therefore one hour of idleness as you would be
ashamed of one hour of drunkenness. Look that you lose not your precious
time by falling in with idle companions, or by growing weary of your
studies, or by love of any filthy lust; or by discouragement of heart that
you shall never attain to any excellency of knowledge, or by thinking too
well of your self, that you have got as much as is needful for you, when
you have got as much as your equals in the same year; no verily, the
Spirit of God will not communicate much to you in a way of idleness,
but will curse your soul, while this sin is nourished, which hath spoiled
so many hopeful youths in their first blossoming in the College. And therefore tho' I would not have you neglect seasons of recreation a little before
and after meals (and altho' I would not have you study late in the night
usually, yet look that you rise early and lose not your morning thoughts,
when your mind is most fresh, and fit for study) but be no wicked example all the day to any of your fellows in spending your time idly. And
do not content yourself to do as much as your tutor sets you about, but
know that you will never excel in learning, unless you do somewhat else
in private hours, wherein his care cannot reach you: and do not think

that idling away your time is no great sin, if so be you think you can hide it from the eyes of others: but consider that God, who always sees you, and observes how you spend your time, will be provoked for every hour of that precious time you now misspend, which you are like never to find the like to this in the College, all your life after.

Publications of the Colonial Society of Massachusetts, XIV (1913).

Richard Waldron

A FRESHMAN GUIDE

(1735)

One of the freshman's first duties in Harvard's early days was to procure a copy of the College laws. This document, signed by the President or one of the Fellows, was considered a certificate of admission. More than a score of these admittaturs *exist as examples of the laws of different periods, as early as 1683. Richard Waldron, who copied his on June 24, 1735 with his own immature hand and erratic orthography, was the son and namesake of the Secretary of the Province of New Hampshire, himself a graduate of Harvard (1712). Little is known about young Richard after his graduation in 1738. At the time he went into the wide world his father was engaged in a political life-and-death struggle which resulted in his removal from office. The younger Richard Waldron was lost at sea in 1745.*

1. No freshman shall wear his hat in the College yard except it rains, snows, or hails, or he be on horseback or hath both hands full.

2. No freshman shall wear his hat in his senior's chamber or in his own if his senior be there.

3. No freshman shall go by his senior, with out taking his hat off if it be on.

4. No freshman shall intrude into his senior's company.

5. No freshman shall laugh in his senior's face.

6. No freshman shall talk saucily to his senior or speak to him with his hat on.

7. No freshman shall ask his senior an impertinent question.

8. Freshmen are to take notice that a senior sophister can take a freshman from a sophomore, a middle bachelor from a junior sophister, a master from a senior sophister & a fellow from a master.

9. Freshmen are to find the rest of the scholars with bats, balls, and footballs.

10. Freshmen must pay three shillings apiece to the Butler to have their names set up in the Buttery.

11. No freshman shall loiter by the [way] when he is sent of an errand, but shall make haste and give a direct answer when he is asked who he is going [for], no freshman shall use lying or equivocation to escape going of an errand.

12. No freshman shall tell who [he] is going [for], except he be asked, nor for what except he be asked by a fellow.

13. No freshman shall go away when he hath been sent of an errand before he be dismissed which may be understood by saying it is well I thank you, you may go or the like.

14. When a freshman knocks at his senior's door he shall tell [his] name if asked who.

15. When anybody knocks at a freshman's door he shall not ask who is there, but shall immediately open the door.

16. No freshman shall lean at prayers but shall stand upright.

17. No freshman shall call his class mate by the name of freshman.

18. No freshman shall call up or down to or from his senior's chamber or his own.

19. No freshman shall call or throw any thing across the college yard.

20. No freshman shall mingo against the College wall or go into the fellows' cuzjohn.

21. Freshmen may wear their hats at dinner and supper except when they go to receive their commons of bread and beer.

22. Freshmen are so to carry themselves to their seniors in all respects so as to be in no wise saucy to them and whosoever of the freshmen shall break any of these customs shall be severely punished.

Harvard University Archives.

Frederic West Holland

A FRESHMAN HAZING
(1827)

"Be ready in fine to cut, to drink, to smoke, to swear, to haze, to dead [i.e. be unprepared to recite], to spree, — in one word, to be a sophomore," so runs an early nineteenth-century epigram. The plight of the green freshman was perilous indeed. Early in Harvard history he became errand boy and unpaid servant to the sophs and when he was not plagued with errands, he was plagued with tricks, some of them unusually disagreeable. The perils of being a freshman in 1827 were carefully recorded by Frederic West Holland, A.B. 1831, who later became a Unitarian clergyman. It did not take Holland and his friends long to discover that they were the victims of a series of labored jokes.

SEPTEMBER 1st 1827. I moved my goods & effects to Stoughton No. 4 & in the afternoon with my chum commenced housekeeping. But scarcely had the shades descended, when we were visited by a numerous company of Juniors, most of them my acquaintances, who smoked, talked, & laughed with us, and made a most tremendous noise. It was then after eight. In about ¼ of an hour, we were told some one wished to see us at No. 24 Stoughton. We went there; & were there admonished for disrespect, & a lesson of 5 pages of Grotius and 10 of Adams' Antiquities was set. The presiding personage was named Dr. Farmer; another one was named Mr. Van Bomb-shell; as I enter'd I mentioned to chum that I thought it was a hoax. The presiding personage was seated in an arm-chair at a table, a shade-lamp before him, around him were many persons seated without much order. After they had set the lesson, they dismissed me, but they kept my chum, & reproached him with lewdness and profane language; we could before hardly keep from laughing-out loud; when chum went out, he slammed the door after him like vengeance.

Well that concern having had enough of me, I returned to my room, and before my chum returned, I was summoned to appear before Tutor Lunt, the Proctor of our cntry.

I followed my conductor to the 3rd story, corner room, Stoughton, he entered and made a low bow, I did the same; he (Lunt) bade me step in, & asked me if there had not been a great noise in my room. I told him there had; he then asked me if I did not know that it was contrary to the Laws; I told him I had not yet recd a copy of the Laws; he replied that then it was partly excusable, but that it was contrary to law to have a noise after study hours in our rooms; & that, in addition, Saturday night was sacred, he then sent me for my chum; after waiting a few moments chum came in, I informed him of the circumstances, & then showed him the room, told him to make his bow and departed: on his return I found out that he was treated pretty much as I was: Lunt told him he was sorry to be obliged to note him the first night, etc., etc. Whilst chum was yet absent, the door suddenly opened and a mean soph threw at me a large winter squash; this formidable & destructive weapon bounced powerless upon the floor at about ¾ of a yard from me, & the assailants immediately fled. My chum returned; and by the time he was informed of the foregoing event, our window suddenly flew open and a heavy shower of pieces of punkins proceeded. We were rather startled, I confess, at this strange visitant: but in a few moments down came the Junior Sophisters again; the instruments of attack still reclined in various positions on the floor. We informed them that we had been called up before Proctor Lunt, and noted; and requested them to be as still as possible; but they on the contrary, thumped the squash against the walls, & and made an awful racket. They shortly retired, and in an hour afterwards we were summoned before the Proctor of our entry. We were again asked with regard to the noise, confessed, were reprimanded; and he concluded with saying, that he would represent our affair to the Government in as favourable a light as possible.

After we had returned, the visiting sophs entered our rooms; we stated our case & requested them to make as little noise as possible, they soon peaceably retired. And we having bought lots of books, & having broken lots of laws, retired to bed.

Harvard Alumni Bulletin, September 29, 1927.

Oliver Wendell Holmes

OF CAMBRIDGE AND FEMALE SOCIETY
(1828–1830)

In his time, there was surely no more enthusiastic son of Harvard than Oliver Wendell Holmes, who entered College in 1825 and kept up an active interest in the College and in his classmates until his death in 1894 at the age of eighty-five. Holmes was the perennial toastmaster, the ready versifier for the suitable occasion, and he kept up the pace through-out his life, despite a busy medical practice and his teaching duties as Parkman Professor of Anatomy and Physiology. No reunion of the famous class of 1829 was complete without a word from the good doctor, and it was an annual event after 1851. The written record of Holmes's days at Harvard is unfortunately meager, but it is freshened by his desultory though sparkling correspondence with a boyhood friend, Phineas Barnes, then a student at Bowdoin ("a fine rosy-faced boy, not quite so free of speech as myself, perhaps, but with qualities that promised a noble manhood"). This was one of the two or three friendships which lasted all the doctor's life. The letters from Harvard — now in the Harvard Library — span part of his College days, his year at the Law School, and his venture into medicine.

August 15, 1828

I SUPPOSE I must begin with an apology for not writing sooner. I have been away from home about a month, or I would not have been guilty of such neglect. Your letter was the first token of remembrance that I have received from any of my old Andover friends or acquaintance, saving certain catalogues of the different colleges, in which article I have kept up quite a brisk correspondence. . . With regard to myself I am determined that you shall not be so much in the dark. I shall therefore describe myself as circumstantially as I would a runaway thief or apprentice. I, then,

Oliver Wendell Holmes, Junior in Harvard University, am a plumeless biped of the height of exactly five feet three inches when standing in a pair of substantial boots made by Mr. Russell of this town, having eyes which I call blue, and hair which I do not know what to call, — in short, something such a looking kind of animal as I was at Andover, with the addition of some two or three inches to my stature. Secondly, with regard to my moral qualities, I am rather lazy than otherwise, and certainly do not study as hard as I ought to. I am not dissipated and I am not sedate, and when I last ascertained my college rank I stood in the humble situation of seventeenth scholar. You must excuse my egotism in saying all this about myself, but I wish to give you as good an idea as I can of your old friend, and I think now you may be able to form an idea of him from this. The class we belong to is rather a singular one, and I fear not much more united than yours. I am acquainted with a great many different fellows who do not speak to each other. Still I find pleasant companions and a few good friends among the jarring elements. . .

I am sorry you feel so sober for want of friends, but you need not be afraid that I shall think it silly in you to say so, for indeed I have had many such feelings myself. I have found new friends, but I have not forgotten my old ones, and I think I have had quite as pleasant walks within the solemn precincts of Andover as I have ever had amidst the classic shades of Cambridge. I should like to go over some of those places again in the same company. . .

October 23, 1828

It is Saturday afternoon — the wind is whistling around the old brick buildings, in one of which your humble servant is seated in the midst of literary disorder and philosophical negligence. . .

Wednesday . . . was our Exhibition; on the whole it was very poor; sometimes fellows will get high parts who cannot sustain them with credit. Our Exhibition days, however, are very pleasant; in defiance of, or rather evading, the injunctions of the government, we contrive to have what they call "festive entertainments" and we call "blows." A fine body of academic militia, denominated the "Harvard Washington Corps," parades before the ladies in the afternoon, and there is eating and drinking and smoking and making merry. . .

December 1828

I am going to answer part of the fifty questions, and I suspect I shall not have much room to ask anything in return. And so here I am, with your two last sheets before me, like a sheep about to be sheared, or a boy to be catechised.

Imprimis. . . "What do I do?" I read a little, study a little, smoke a little, and eat a good deal! "What do I think?" I think that's a deuced hard question. "What have I been doing these three years?" Why, I have been growing a little in body, and I hope in mind; I have been learning a little of almost everything, and a good deal of some things. . .

If you ever come to Boston you will, of course, come out to Cambridge. Our town has not much to boast of excepting the College. . . I have studied French and Italian, and some Spanish. We have been studying this year Astronomy, Good's *Book of Nature*, Brown's *Philosophy of the Mind*, and attended Dr. Ware's Lectures on the Scriptures. We have themes once a fortnight, forensics once a month, and declamation every week. . .

I will send you a catalogue of the officers and students, and one of the Medical Faculty. This will need some explanation. It is a mock society among the students, which meets twice a year in disguise, and, after admitting members from the junior class, distributes honorary degrees to distinguished men. The room where they meet is hung round with sheets and garnished with bones. They burn alcohol in their lamps, and examine very curiously and facetiously the candidates for admission. Every three years they publish a catalogue in exact imitation of the Triennial Catalogue published by the College. The degrees are given with all due solemnity to all the lions of the day. I thought it might afford you a little amusement, although it was not intended for wide circulation. Remember, it is only a private thing among the students. . .

September 1829

. . . I am settled once more at home in the midst of those miscellaneous articles which always cluster around me wherever I can do just as I please, — Blackstone and boots, law and lathe, Rawle and rasps, all intermingled in exquisite confusion. When you was here, I thought of going away to study my profession; but since Judge Story and Mr. Ashmun have come, the Law School is so flourishing that I thought it best to stay where I am. I have mislaid your last letter, and my not being able to find it has been one reason, in addition to my procrastinating disposition, why I have not written sooner. And now, young man, I have no more conception where you are, or how you are situated, than I have of the condition of the ear-tickler to his majesty the Emperor of China. I can imagine, however, that you are in some queer little outlandish Eastern town, with a meetinghouse the timbers of which bore acorns last autumn, that you live in the only painted house in the village, and that at this present time you are seated in magisterial dignity, holding the rod of empire over fourscore little vagabonds, who look up to you as the embodied essence of all earthly knowledge. I might go farther and fancy some houri of the forest welcoming you home from your daily labors with a kiss and a johnny-cake and all other sweet attentions that virgin solicitude can offer to the champion of education. Alas! I [fear] too much that, where you had fondly anticipated a blushing maiden of sixteen, you have a good-natured dowdy of forty, or an ill-natured walking polygon of fifty. You must write and tell me all about these things, if you have indeed persisted in your plan of school-keeping. As for Cambridge, nothing great has happened here, and even what seems great to us can have little interest for you. I will just tell you that the Law School has increased from one solitary individual to twenty-six. . .

January 13, 1830

. . . And now I suppose that you are brooding over your involuntary retirement, and thinking what a fine time I must have in this focus of literature and refinement. Nothing is easier than to make disadvantageous comparisons between ourselves and our neighbors. I will tell you honestly that I am sick at heart of this place and almost everything connected with it. I know not what the temple of the law may be to those who have entered it, but to me it seems very cold and cheerless about the threshold. And another thing too; I feel, what one of the most ill-begotten cubs that ever entered college when he was old enough to be a grandfather most feelingly lamented, "the want of female society." If there was a girl in the neighborhood whose blood ever rose above the freezing point, who ever dreamed of such a thing as opening her lips without having her father and her mother and all her little impish brothers and sisters for her audience, — nay if there was even a cherry-cheeked kitchen girl to romance with occasionally, it might possibly be endurable. Nothing but vinegar-faced old maids and drawing-room sentimentalists, — nothing that would do to write poetry to but the sylph of the confectioner's counter, and she — sweet little Fanny has left us to weep when we think of her departed smiles and her too fleeting icecreams. I do believe I never shall be contented till I get the undisputed mastery of a petticoat. . .

Harvard College Library

James Woodbury Boyden

EXAMINED FOR ENTRANCE

(1838)

When James Woodbury Boyden came down to Cambridge from Salem in late summer of 1838, the admission process was neither so simple nor so condensed as it is today. In this year of grace a candidate most likely picks a March day to race through a series of aptitude and "achievement" tests. Boyden came to Harvard after two years' teaching experience, and went through several long days of testing before he was adjudged fit for acceptance. After his college career, Boyden went on to Law School and later lived in Chicago.

Monday, August 27th 1838.

LAST NIGHT, I walked from Beverly to Salem, with Joseph and Charles, who carried my preparatory books. On arriving there, I went to Dr. Johnson's, who will carry me with his son [Samuel Johnson, 1842] to Cambridge for examination.

I was waked at three-o-clock by the Dr., and after drinking a cup of coffee, we all started in a carryall for Cambridge.

It was yet dark, the streets and houses were shrouded in the thick mantle of night, and all was silent and still, save the rattling of our carriage upon the stony pavements. A few stars would now and then show their dim faces in the heavens, but they were few and far between, for their light could not find a way through the clouded atmosphere.

Our course was over the Forest River road, & through Lynn; — when we reached the latter place, the sun had just risen and shone in all its splendor.

We reached Cambridge at 6¼ o'clock and carried our books to No. 13, Stoughton Hall, occupied by Edward B. Pearson [Peirson], who had kindly offered us the use of the room, during our examination. Thence we went to University Hall, were met at the door by President Quincy who took the certificates of good moral character and sent us in.

Entering a room to the right, we encountered old Dr. Ware, who took down our names and sent us to the Salem division, so called. In this room were fifty-seven young men, some standing, others sitting, in different postures — some full of dread and apprehension, half afraid to meet the eye of others, and shivering: — these are generally known as *Green-horns*. Some were full of confidence and bold, — full of self respect, — observing others, — laughing at the awkward or diffident, — all however were very orderly and quiet.

In a short time, each division was called, in order, into the two adjoining rooms, where we sat down at tables, upon which, were sheets of paper, ink-stands, quills and a printed copy of some English sentences, which we were required to translate into Latin and commit to paper, sign our names & then hand it to the Tutor who occupied the "highest seat in the synagogue."

But first, each member of the several divisions gave his name — age — month in which he was born — name of his parent (father) and of the instructor who sent him, all which were duly recorded by the Tutors.

We were now dismissed till 7½-o-clock, that the Faculty and Students might take breakfast. In the meantime, Johnson and myself returned to Pearson's [Peirson's] room, where I translated the seventeenth section of the fourth book, containing the plan of Caesar's Bridge over the Rhine, into Germany.

At the appointed hour, we took our dictionaries and grammars, proceeded to our seats in University Hall, and commenced writing the translation of the English sentences into Latin.

Our division, the fifth, had been seated a few minutes only, when we were called out and directed to go to Professor Felton's room, to be examined in Greek Prosody and Syntax. I was asked two questions, viz: — what cases do verbs of admiring — despising etc. govern? Ans. the Genitive and Dative; — what cases do verbs of commanding and abounding govern; Ans. Genitive, Dative or Accusative.

We resumed writing our translation, but shortly after were sent to Mr. Very, who examined us in the Etymology of the Greek Grammar. He asked me the formation of the first and second aorists active, and the synopsis of the verbs in -$\mu\iota$. At the expiration of two hours, we had finished our translations and were sent into the next room, where we were furnished with printed papers containing sentences to be translated into Greek.

Shortly after we were sent to Dr. Beck, who examined us in Latin Grammar. He asked me the several terminations of the futures in the different conjugations; together with the manner in which they are distinguished from each other. We then went down to the room and finished the Greek translation. A recess followed till eleven.

I saw Dr. Johnson, who had been looking for a room for his son: — he had found one in Divinity Hall, which he liked very much and which he engaged for Samuel. He told me that there was one more, which I had better endeavor to secure; we went down and examined the two and I thought I would like to have it, but concluded to wait till my father came up tomorrow.

At eleven, we resumed our seats, and remained till two. Our division was sent to Mr. Mason's room, where we were examined in scanning.

Besides asking us some of the rules, he required us to scan several lines each in Virgil, and to give the rules.

Then (two-o-clock) we were dismissed till four.

From University Hall, I went to the Tavern, and took dinner. The table was laid tolerably well for a common tavern — among the "multa bona," were roast beef, mutton boiled into a stew — potatoes, — onions — applesauce — and other delicacies. The second table was graced by a large plum-pudding, with sugar-sauce, followed by mince pies and water-melons. For this dinner, I paid fifty cents.

I then went to Peirson's room and talked over matters and things with Johnson till four.

At this hour, we adjourned to the University Hall. Here Mr. Peirce, Professor of Mathematics gave us some sums in Algebra. The first was to multiply $a + b$ by $a - b$. The second was a long sum in Division. The third was to raise $a + x$ to 5th power by Binomials. The fourth was to solve an equation & the fifth was to find the distance between two signals etc. etc. rather difficult.

When we had finished these sums, we were sent to Mr. Wheeler to be examined in Ancient and Modern Geography. Here one or two questions were asked me; the ancient names of Scotland and Ireland which I could not answer, all the others I knew very well.

We then went to another room, where we were examined in like manner, in Arithmetic. Eight sums were given us, in vulgar fractions, — Compound Subtraction-Decimals — Double rule of Three and Compound Interest. These occupied us till six, when we were dismissed. I eat no supper, but studied a few sections in Caesar and retired at nine in Pierson's room.

Tuesday, August 28th.

The ringing of the Bell in the church opposite the College Buildings, at twenty minutes past five, waked me.

After dressing, I studied a few of the sections in the beginning of each of the last five books in Caesar.

Johnson and myself then went to a refreshment room and bought two mince pies and two ounces of lozenges, whole cost being eighteen cents, being nine cents apiece.

Thence we returned to Peirson's room, and took breakfast, eating pies & drinking good, cold water from the pumps in the yard.

At half past seven, we went to University Hall; and found on our tables a Latin extract, printed, which we were required to translate into English and commit to writing, one hour and a half being allowed us.

A half an hour afterward, our division was sent to Professor Felton's room, and examined in Greek Poetry, translating and scanning. None of us failed here, and we were all in good spirits as we descended to the lower room.

When we had finished the Latin Exercises, we were dismissed till ten & told to go to the next room, on our return at eleven. Till this hour, I was in Peirson's room, looking over a few of the Rules in Greek Grammar.

On taking our seats, we found a printed copy of an extract from some Latin Poet, which we translated into English Prose. Then we were presented with a printed page from Xenophon, and when that was written, with some Greek verse, copies of which, Greek and English, I have preserved.

We were sent to Mr. Very, who examined us in Greek Prose, our division had no difficulty, either in translating, parsing or giving the roots and themes.

We went also to Dr. Beck, and were examined in Caesar, and made no mistakes or *bulls*.

Mr. Mason examined us in Virgil, taking us up in the sixth book, seven hundred and third line. At two we were dismissed and directed to come to the University Hall door at four-o-clock whence each division would be called, in order, to the Faculty, and would receive from them certificates of admission.

Harvard Alumni Bulletin, September 24, 1949.

Thomas Hill

THERE IS NOTHING BUT
MISCHIEF IN THEIR HEADS
(1839)

"My objections to Cambridge," wrote Thomas Hill, during the period when he was uncertain what college to attend, "are: its expenses are entirely beyond my means; its nearness to the sea shore I am afraid would injure my lungs . . . and its great and peculiar advantages are useless to me because my preparatory school studies have not been enough to enable me to enjoy them." Yet, Thomas Hill entered Harvard College at the age of twenty-one in 1839. His studious habits and his religious attitude made him a target for the unkind and the light-hearted members of his Class and the College; the early months of his freshman term were misery, but Hill made a mark for himself and he was regarded by Professor Benjamin Peirce as one of the ablest mathematicians to come under his tutelage. For many years a Unitarian clergyman, Hill became President of Antioch and was President of Harvard during the Civil War. The undergraduate letters to his family quoted here were written between August and December of Hill's first year in Cambridge.

Having become very near settled into College I thought I would begin another letter as no lessons have appointed, and thus I am at leisure. I suppose you would like to know where I am fixed. The room is on the north entry of Hollis Hall ground floor, south side west end. . . I board in Commons, where the table is very good indeed and victuals are furnished at cost. I wish they were more of them . . . It would please me better and cost them less. I suppose that many of the students however care nothing either for health or economy. There is nothing but mischief in their heads from morn till night. While I am writing some of the wise fools are amusing themselves by throwing shot into my open windows. I advised them not to waste their lead so, for it was silly to be so extravagant. They have now gone. Perhaps some of them may want the cost of the shot ere long, to buy a halter to hang themselves. I would however hope . . . better things of most of them. There is a scandalous degree of profanity and wine bibbing here, I don't care who says to the contrary. I've seen enough since I've been here to make me sick of the sight. I have a room mate from N. York city named Spear. As I have been in his company but an hour or two, I can tell you nothing of his character; but Phrenologicaly it is tolerable, rather much self conceit and obstinacy perhaps. . . On looking at my floor I find that it was gravel that was thrown in my windows. This is the first time I have been troubled I hope twill be the last, for as they saw I neither moved nor raised my eyes from the paper they will think I care nothing for them and thus leave me. . .

This evening at six we were called together for prayers and the freshmen had their places assigned. An old man who could hardly see even with his specs on officiated, and in a very feeling manner too. (Rev. Dr. Ware, father of H. W. Jr.) I do not know with whom I shall meet tomorrow to commemorate the love of the dying Saviour, but I trust it will be with brethren having their hearts filled with a sense of that love, and that we shall have a pleasant season together. . .

I was surprised on coming here to find that furniture of every kind must be purchased by the student, and I have well nigh spent my money in buying a four years stock of furniture consisting of hair mattress and pillow, sheets pillow cases and comfortables, bedstead, chairs, table, table cover, lamp, lampfiller, oil, broom, shovel and tongs, wash stand, bowl & ewer, etc. etc. I shall have no more necessity for money till after next vacation, when the term bill is due for this term . . .

The Freshman Class consists of 76 and is divided into three divisions; the first containing thirty seven or eight; the second twenty two or three, and the third sixteen. The divisions are made according to the scholarship and apparent talents of the scholars; the third division containing the best scholars and taking rather longer lessons than the second, and the second than the first. Our division recites in Livy (Latin historian) at 8, and in Herodotus (Greek historian) at 9. At two o'clock we recite in Geometry. Our lessons are pretty long and we spend a good deal of time in studying.

. . . One of our Tutors Robt Bartlett, has been two years in the Divinity School here, and is I believe now studying. He is a very kind man and has shown me marks of his good feelings. He says that the best condition to be in with respect to college is to be unknown & disregarded. The second best is to be hated by all hands. The worst is to be beloved and "popular." For if the whole class are hanging about you seeking assistance and counsel, or dragging you into sports & amusements, they waste your time and entirely prevent you from becoming any thing . . .

. . . I confess I did wrong in not telling you what my trouble was, but I did not know whether it was yet over and I wanted to tell you of it altogether. Some little brats had gone into a closet and opening the window were firing out of this dark hole at the windows in Kingmans room. My own windows had just been stoned in and I thought these fellows were firing at mine too, Kingmans room adjoining mine. We went outside, found out who were firing, and told a college officer who came and scared the chaps by scolding them. This immediately gave us the character of spies and the next night, I unguardedly going to bed with the door unlocked, some ruffians came in, dragged the mattress from under me and emptied several pails of water on me. I immediately ran yelling out of doors and when I waked up I was dancing on the frosty grass in the bright moonlight, dripping with water. I ran back to my room and it was 15 or 20 minutes before I could think what was the matter. A young man lost his life in this way a few years ago, the shock and the chill bringing on a cold which soon killed him. I was half sick under it for four or five days, trembling and jumping at even the creaking of my own shoes.

In addition to this I was hissed and laughed at, had bottles thrown out of the windows at me etc. etc. Our windows were broken almost every night and at last we moved to the 3d story of Mass. Here we were in peace till last Friday night, when two or 3 more lights were broken. On Sunday night they were fired at again. On Monday night they were fired at again, and I complained of the boys to the Faculty and on Tuesday morning 2 of them were expelled. From this I suppose fresh trouble will arise, but I will be better prepared to meet it if it comes now.

I should not have been injured if most infamous lies had not been previously circulated, which had already made me hated. For instance such stories as these were circulated by two whom I had previously offended; vis that I had boasted that I was going to become the first scholar; that I had said I was about to reform the University and bring it into a state of good order; that I had thrown my door open and prayed aloud when folks were passing; and a parcel more ridiculous tales; told out of sheer malice by these two boys.

. . . In College commons the board is $2.25 a week. The boys are very unruly, yelling, throwing bread at each other, and firing boiled potatoes round the room. The board is a great part of it hot wheat flour bread and milk which makes me suffer very much from costiveness. I grew so fat living at commons that even my friends laughed at me and I was ashamed of myself . . .

. . . I am sorry you are grieved on account of my college troubles. They do not trouble me any more; I mean the past transactions do not trouble me; nor are the students making any fresh trouble with fresh insult. Mr. Stebbins passed through just such an ordeal at Amherst, and so must every one who prefers his idea of duty to a slavish compliance with wicked customs. Every year however this necessity is diminished for these customs are broken up gradually and it is hoped that in a few years this system of college honor and discipline will be put to rest with the laws of duelling and war.

Harvard University Archives.

William Tucker Washburn

A MEETING OF THE MED. FAC.

(c. 1858)

When the "Medical Faculty" was outlawed as a secret student organization in 1905–06, the deeds and misdeeds of this reckless and mysterious group passed almost into oblivion. Founded in the early 1800's, the Med. Fac. was originally a society dedicated to relatively harmless undergraduate pranks, but it had many imitators and, when the hazing of freshmen became an accepted practice, some of the evening fun grew very rough indeed. We may assume the following description is a not-too-exaggerated account of the College in its adolescence. The scene is Harvard in the 1850's. The time is late in an autumn evening just after the freshman, Wentworth Saulsbury, hero of Fair Harvard, has left his friends in No. 1 Holworthy to return to his own lodgings. The author of this "story of American college life," William Tucker Washburn (1841–1916) of the Class of 1862, was a successful New York lawyer who published four novels and two volumes of poems in a busy lifetime. He has the distinction of having written the first Harvard novel. That he did not take his achievement too seriously is indicated in the preface where he remarks that, despite the adverse opinions of friends, "the author feels it to be a crime to keep his work longer from the Public."

"THAT'S THE FELLOW," whispered some one as Wentworth turned into Linden Street, and at the words, four men in masks sprang out upon him, from the doorway of the corner house. Saulsbury was no coward, but the darkness and the surprise for a moment unnerved him. He, however, struck one fair blow at the man just in front of him. The man stooped, the blow passed over his head, and the next moment Wentworth was seized around the waist, and thrown; two hands grasped his throat; his own were tied behind his back, his eyes bandaged, and his mouth gagged. Our hero exerted all his strength in a desperate struggle to gain his feet.

"How the child wriggles," muttered one of the masks, and gave Wentworth a blow with the flat of his hand, which made him writhe in a frenzy of rage.

"Lift him," now whispered one of the men, and Wentworth was placed in a vehicle which drove rapidly off.

He lay still, though burning with anger. "I'd give my life," he thought, "for one blow at that coward who struck me." They drove rapidly for several minutes, until at length the carriage stopped, and Wentworth was taken out, turned round half a dozen times, and led up a flight of stairs into a room.

"Mr. President, we have brought you the culprit," said one of the men who held Saulsbury.

"Remove the band," commanded a voice resembling the angry mew of a cat. The band was removed and our hero glanced around him not without a feeling of terror. The walls of the room in which he found himself were painted with revolting figures, representing the growth of Disease. In the rear a table was placed, on the centre of which rested a large Bible presented to Harvard by the pious youth of Yale College in expectation of a similar gift in return. Behind the Bible stood a box of medical instruments with a letter from the Emperor Nicholas. The front of the table discovered bunches of skeleton keys; a few delicate Freshman moustaches, with the names of their former possessors; rich folds of hairs marked, "the wig of Tutor Jones, captured Oct. 3rd, 185–;" and a billet with cords twisted around its handle.

The Bible itself sustained a punch bowl of singular shape, adorned with the motto, "Satano duce, nil desperandum," and two huge clubs, rough with letters and figures. The words "Hell Fire Club" on the larger of these would have recalled to the antiquary the deeds of iniquity by which that society had justified its name. Carved upon this sole memorial of a famous brotherhood were the initials of men distinguished in the law and ministry, who in their youth had furnished employment to the professions which in their advanced years had supported them. On the smaller club was the mysterious name, "Thundering Bolus." This weapon, in former times swung by the arm of the bravest Senior in the College, for many years struck dismay into the hearts of hostile villagers, trusting in their numbers.

Little desire, however, had our hero to examine these or the other objects of interest which the chamber held. His eyes were fastened on the scene before him. Directly in front of him sat a hideous monster, with horns projecting from his forehead, and his dress ablaze with flames. Next the Devil to the right, was a creature whose features were nearly eaten off by a cancer, while on the left leered a withered hag. Flanking these three stood a dozen wretches, each incarnating some malady.

Between Wentworth and the "Leeches and Doctors," for such was the title these horrors wore on their breasts, was a table covered with a sheet, on one end of which stood a small brazier with scalpels, pincers, and other instruments around it. Above, at the centre of the wall, before Wentworth, was hung a strip of black cloth, on which were written in scarlet six letters. The sight of these at once riveted our hero's eyes, drove a cold iron rod down his spine, and made him tremble with fear. These six letters were M E D.   F A C.

"Remove the gag," ordered the Devil, and Wentworth's tongue was set free.

"Where's that d—— coward who struck me?" he exclaimed. "I dare——"

"Burn the profane fellow! dissolve him, flay him, dissect him," and other suggestions interrupted his words.

"Gag the rebel!" screeched the Devil. "Delilah!" he added, "chasten the lawlessness of this young Samson."

At this, Wentworth was forced upon the table and the hag shuffled up to him, and slowly pulled from his head twenty-seven hairs and burnt them in the brazier.

"Remember," the Devil warned him, as the gag was again removed and Wentworth set on his feet, "that you are in the august presence of the Medical Faculty of Harvard University. You are charged," he continued solemnly, "with having spoken lightly of the godly society of the 'Med. Fac.' Is the accusation true?"

"I think you have done a great many mean acts," muttered Wentworth, losing all prudence in his anger.

"He blasphemes against the Med. Fac.!" shrieked a dozen voices, mingled with groans.

"Brother Plummer," commenced the Devil, "read the punishment decreed against one who offends against the majesty of the Med. Fac."

"Whoever," began a deep voice behind our hero, "shall speak evil against the Medical Faculty of Harvard University shall receive the punishment of air, fire, water, and earth, and the purification of assafœtida and brimstone." "Such are the words of holy writ," added the Devil. "Your own good compels us to punish you, with whatever pain to ourselves. Let the law be executed," he concluded, and waved his sceptre, at which sign each monster removed a leg or arm and brandished it over his head.

Wentworth was then blindfolded, led into the open air and placed in a blanket. Were we writing a romance, we should not allow our hero to be tossed in a blanket, but the spirit of truth, which rules all histories, compels us to set down the evil with the good.

"Are you ready?" cried one of the men, holding the blanket. "Now all together — one, two, three, toss!" and at the word our hero winged his way heavenward with such aid as ten stalwart devils could lend him.

Wentworth was now nearly exhausted with excitement and fatigue, yet he nerved himself to endure without flinching. Suddenly a device occurred to him. As he was descending from his third flight, feeling like Vulcan landing upon Lemnos he extended both his feet to the utmost. "Heavens!" cried one of his tormentors, "my head's broken," and Wentworth had the pleasure of feeling his heel strike a hard skull; this was, however, lessened at the same moment, by his falling heavily upon the ground.

"Let the punishment of fire be now inflicted," commanded the Devil, after Wentworth had been led back to his room. At this two bands, the ends of which were attached to hooks in the ceiling, were placed one round Wentworth's feet and the other round his chest. Again the boy broke out in execrations.

"Hush," whispered in his ear the voice of some one half relenting, "or they'll gag you," and with a sullen look of rage, Wentworth repressed his words.

The "Leeches and Doctors" then placed the brazier beneath him; some fluid was poured into it and lighted, and our hero swung to and fro over it several times, and then taken down.

"Let the punishment of water be inflicted," commanded the Devil. At this, Wentworth was placed in a coffin, and borne from the room. Soon he heard a noise as of the turning of a windlass, and felt himself sinking lower and lower. "What if the rope should break!" he thought, and derived little pleasure from the reflection. Suddenly the bottom of the coffin struck water, and Wentworth heard the men talking above him. "Pull him up!" "pull him up!" "No, bless him; give him a dowse; he nearly broke my head!" and the coffin sunk still lower. The water pours through the cracks: it covers the boy's ankle: it rises to his knee: the air grows dense: the water has reached his waist: his head seems bursting: his eyes start from their sockets; and with a cry of despair, he loses all remembrance.

"You oughtn't to have let him down so far." "Confound the fellow! Why doesn't he come to?" are the first words Wentworth hears on returning to consciousness, and at the same moment water is dashed in his face, and he feels some one chafing his hands.

The boy opens his eyes and looks languidly around him. "Where am I?" he asks, and shudders at the masks and figures.

"We've punished him enough." "There's game in the fellow." "We'll drive him home." Wentworth heard the men whisper to each other. A glass of brandy was then given him, his eyes were again bandaged, and he was placed in a carriage. After a drive of some minutes he was taken from the carriage and set upon the ground. He pulled off his bandage, and found himself by the familiar gate of Danforth's. Through this he passed, and groped his way to his room, where he was soon buried in sleep, not without strange dreams.

William Tucker Washburn, *Fair Harvard: A Story of American College Life* (New York, 1869).

Robert Nathan

PETER KINDRED'S FIRST DAYS

(1919)

Robert Nathan followed the steps of his Peter Kindred from Phillips Exeter Academy to Harvard, and Peter Kindred *became the first of his more than a score of books. In this early novel can be seen some of the characteristics of Nathan's later writing. An illusive, transitory thread slips through much of his work — a sense of place but not time. Whether his setting is Central Park or Truro near the "Cape end" — "There the old house, much loved, and cosily panelled, stands on its hill between the elms and the pine trees" — the poetry is there, and the fantasy, which have made Nathan one of the most appealing writers in contemporary American letters. Among his books are* One More Spring, Portrait of Jennie, Journey of Tapiola, But Gently Day, *and* Long After Summer.

IT SEEMED that Harvard had expected their coming, and when Peter registered, which he found to be a simple enough matter, no one told him that he had no right to do so, but a weary and patient man handed him a large pink card, and sent him in search of his faculty advisor. He was struck by the great number of such pink cards moving aimlessly about. Upper classmen carried different colors, and moved about more purposefully, much as the second year men had done at Exeter. Peter made his way to Warren House, and waited on his advisor, watching the small group of men about him curiously. There was an unkempt lad from some northern village, powerful, and mother fearing. There was a lean and wan-looking elderly man who clutched a couple of shabby books close to his coat, and asked questions of Peter humbly. There was a keen-faced youth in tweeds, who wore tremendous rimmed glasses which gave him an affable and owllike appearance, and an aristocratic-looking fellow with a delicately chiselled face, who carried himself delightfully, his shoulders back and his chin high, and whom the professor seemed very glad to see again. Peter thought he was very fine, and wondered who he was; he wished that he himself made so splendid an appearance, or that David did.

Men whose lives are given to the contemplation of letters and sciences, who do not spend their days bickering in the market place, but whose dens are chosen from among the choicest rooms in the house, dens that remain strewn and inviolate for years, attain a quiet and complacent dignity which creates a deeper impression upon the perplexed youth of our land than all the doughtiest and most profound lectures ever given. There is something about a serene and vigorous old age which constitutes a fairer promise of heaven than all the creeds and tenets of belief.

Peter's advisor was such a man, a stalwart and patriarchal figure, unhurried and resolute. Peter felt that he must know a vast deal, as indeed he did, but Peter did not give sufficient credit to the holy quiet of the man's den, and to the rows upon rows of friendly books between the ceiling and the floor. But, mind you, I would not advocate a den of that sort for any common man; he would do nothing in it at all.

For all his learning, the professor proved to be amazingly ignorant of the courses Peter had chosen to attend, and since there was therefore nothing to say one way or another about them, he signed Peter's card and dismissed him. Peter passed the Union with a warming sense of belonging finally to Harvard, and walked slowly down Massachusetts Avenue toward Harvard Square.

The street, with its small, well-appointed shops, hummed with the coming and going of students. They passed in groups or singly, alert, cheery, well-groomed men; and all with the same satisfied look on their faces. For a college is no more than an attitude toward life, and the kindly gentlemen of Oxford are as far removed from the contented moralists of Harvard, as the latter differ from the wistful youths of Yale, and the happy children of Princeton.

To Peter there was the same romance in the name Harvard as there had been in Exeter, and he was as mightily beguiled by the small but venerable Yard and the enchanted flavor of the halls, which, like old men before a fireside, seemed in their silence to be forever considering themselves.

At Holyoke Street he turned down toward Mount Auburn and climbed the creaking steps of No. 26. He had chosen a room in a ramshackle frame house at the edge of the gold coast, opposite the yellow walls of the Institute.

Below his windows the men passed down the street, through the gate, and into the Institute. Peter watched them with a deal of wonder and a stir of envy at first. For the Institute is the solid basis of Harvard clubdom. It goes through Harvard with a coarse comb, separating the wheat from the chaff; all men who are socially possible are Institute men. Among these the exclusive clubs move with finer combs in varying degrees, but, on the whole, a man at Harvard is an Institute man, or he is not.

Peter's room was two dilapidated flights up, but he found, to his surprise, that such a place was considered very fine at Harvard, much more desirable, indeed, than the new brick houses far removed from the coast, or the dormitories in the Yard. But that was characteristic of Harvard, to put up splendid draperies in a tumbled down room, and glory in the result. Peter had no splendid draperies, but David envied him his room and his two sunny windows facing the south. David had chosen a modern brick building not far from the Square, where he had his own bath to delight him, but no sun at all. He had installed a grand piano, and was making a desk of a soap box.

Peter's room, at first in its barrenness, had depressed that gentleman almost to despair, but as he began to unpack his furniture, he saw some possibility in it, and when at last his rug was down, he haled David over to view it. David was impressed, but left at once for his soap box and some intricate figuring he had been doing, whereby he hoped to discover some way of also buying a bed.

Peter's desk chair had not come, and to ask advice, he tapped on his neighbor's door. A voice roared for the son-of-a-gun to come in, and he stepped into a scene of such boundless confusion that he could do nothing but stare. At first glance it looked as though some truckman had moved the belongings of one room into another, and had dumped them all pell mell on top of each other. Clothes and books competed with sofa cushions and pictures for the seats of chairs, and overflowed onto the floor. Where there were no books, there were shoes, and occasional beer mugs. In the midst of this chaos stood a dark-browed, rugged man, puffing at a long calabash pipe.

"Oh," he said, "come right in. Excuse me. I thought you were a friend of mine." He swept the vista of the room with his arm. "Find a place to sit down, and make yourself at home. I'm not usually so upset, but our amiable goody forgot me to-day."

He sat down himself and regarded Peter curiously. Before him, Peter was shy and confused; he explained the reason for his visit, and asked him if he could suggest anything to do about the chair. The dark-browed man regarded the ceiling somberly, puffed at his pipe, and shook his head, but suggested at last that the chair would probably turn up some day, and that a desk chair was a small matter at best, and that if Peter needed one, he could let him have several to choose from. Peter thanked him, and somewhat encouraged, asked him how one might unearth the bursar and pay him the fabled ninety dollars. The man directed him to Dana [Dane] Hall, and Peter asked him how he would know what to do when he got there.

"Trust to the Lord," said the big man, and lost himself in reverie. Peter stammered a thanks, and returned to the tidy primness of his own room. The advice, for all its absurdity, was soothing and Peter's troubles fell away. He no longer felt responsible for his affair with the bursar.

That night both he and David went to the freshman reception at Brooks House, hoping for much, but doubting that anything would befall them. They were given little tags on which they wrote their names. These they tied diffidently in their buttonholes, where they dangled unnoticed for the rest of the evening. With a vast mob of shoving and perspiring men they were herded into a large room where they sat on the floor at first, but later stood in a vain effort to hear some part of the speeches. On a low platform tall heroes appeared, bowed, were tremendously applauded, spoke, waved their arms, grinned, bowed, and sat down in the din. Mr. Molmf presented Mr. Smith of the Grmmpump, who in turn presented Mr. Xmymst. Tommy Reilly, captain of the eleven, rose and received an ovation. Amid a dead silence, he started in.

"Well, fellows," he said. The applause was interminable. Through it he went on.

"Well, fellows, Percy Haughton here thinks we've got a pretty good team here this year, and I guess Yale will think so all right." Cheers, shrieks, whistles, and the prolonged stamping of feet. "Well, fellows, all I want to say is I want you fellows to stand back of the team and give us the right support and get some good, snappy cheering over this year when we go down to New Haven, and I guess we can leave the rest to Percy Haughton here." He bowed awkwardly and sat down, amid a bedlam. Peter and David fought their way to the door and emerged disheveled.

They walked back through the Yard together across the Autumn moonlight, under the looming, black shadows of the dormitories. Beyond the wall, a car jarred distantly around the curve of the street, and died away toward Boston. Occasional low voices reached them, and the twang of a mandolin. The sky was calm and luminous with stars, the light breeze redolent of earth. But Peter and David could find no words to gauge their thoughts, wherefore they left each other without discussing the event.

Again the greater freedom of the college aroused in Peter a sense of transformation, of gathering manhood, and for a while he, too, walked with his shoulders thrown back and his chin held high. Then lectures began, and he forgot everything in the rush to buy books, and the trouble of their expense. In the large classes he sat unnoticed, scribbling notes, and hearing for the first time new principles in unexplored fields of thought discussed and expounded. To each he reacted with a faint shock of appreciation, believing everything, his imagination powerfully exercised. David came with the same enthusiasm from his classes, and their discussions grew top heavy with the weight of their learning until they made no headway at all.

Robert Nathan, *Peter Kindred* (New York, 1919).

V

SPORTS AND SPORTING MEN

The passage of horse-cars to and from Boston, nearly, if not quite, a hundred times a day, has rendered it practically impossible for the Government of the College to prevent our young men from being exposed to all the temptations of the city.

THOMAS HILL (1864)

I was talking with Schuman the other day concerning Harvard when he made the remark that the whole damned institution ought to be wiped out. I can hardly agree with him, although I think myself that it is the root of a world of unlicensed deviltry; but for that matter, who can name a place of any considerable size that is not? The matter seems to me something like this: the college is there with its corps of instructors, and the student has his choice as to improving the opportunities placed before him or not. If a fellow goes there and spends all his time raising the devil, it does not seem exactly a fair thing to lay the whole burden of blame upon the college.

EDWIN ARLINGTON ROBINSON (1891)

After the severe intellectual labors of the day it is a not infrequent custom of the ingenuous youth of Harvard to refresh the weary mind with convivial ale, the social oyster, jolly songs, and conversation upon topics of less profundity than those that usually occupy the thoughts of young truthseekers.

FAIR HARVARD (1869)

Jacob Rhett Motte

A SOUTHERN SPORT AT HARVARD
(1831)

A delightfully complete record of the thoughts and emotions of a lively young southerner is contained in the diary of Jacob Rhett Motte of Charleston, South Carolina, who spent the Cambridge summer of 1831 alternately velocipeding and drinking soda water. Motte's comments are perhaps the best of the many journals preserved in the Harvard archives. Motte followed his Harvard course with study at the Medical College in South Carolina, served ten years in the Army Medical Corps (including the Seminole War), practiced medicine in Charleston, and died shortly after the close of the Civil War.

16th August. Tuesday. [1831]

GOT UP earlier than usual this morning — before breakfast bought two dozen crackers and some hot rolls, which, with a pound of fresh butter, were no insignificant additions to my larder; — while enjoying this delectable breakfast, a knock is heard at the door; the usual open sesame being given, in stalk Crafts and Gray, come by appointment to attend a furniture auction, at Mrs. Mellen's, in Cambridge. Saw nothing there worthy of a bid — some old bottles, of all shapes and sizes, and some old books, valuable only as antiquities. There was one very comfortable old-fashioned easy-chair, which I felt very much disposed to buy. We left them at it about 5 o'clock to go and take a bathe, after which I went for my velocipede, agreeing to meet the two fellows at the post-office; my velocipede I found painted a neat light blue; but not so light was the price. On my way to the post-office met brother, who had been waiting at my room for me an hour. He came out for a dagger I had in my possession, he being determined to walk the next day to Yarmouth, and therefore wished some defence. After drinking a glass of soda water, which he *admired* (yankeeism), we started for Boston, I on my horse. — Of course, I got to the bridge long before him, and amused myself by racing with the horses I met there until he came up. — Invited me to go on and drink tea at Mr. Loring's. — I called at

Mrs. Wolcott's, where Crafts and Gray staid. — Was threatened by a man, whom I frightened, by running on his heel, with a fine for riding on the side-walk — disregarded him. — Went to Mr. L. where I found a Miss Sullivan, in whose company I took a hot cup of tea to cool me, philosophically. — After tea, gratified this lady by exhibiting my rosinante to her. — expressed great satisfaction at my condescension and benignity. — In riding back to Cambridge, through a back street in Boston — Pleasant street — anything but pleasant to me at this time — was in rather an unpleasant predicament. A mob of boys attracted by my strange horse, soon collected around me, and if a rolling stone gathers no moss, I can test, that a rolling velocipede will certainly gather more spectators than is agreeable to a modest rider. On I went, and on went the mob, shouting and hollowing, until I could bear it no longer, but stopt, — they stopt too; I hollowed at them; they hollowed in return at me, when I found that safety lay in flight, and on reaching the wooden side-walk by the Common, on I flew leaving my persecutors some distance in the rear. When I got to Beacon street, I found myself alone, much to my heart's content; and never shall I be found in such a situation again, if I can help it. I reached Cambridge in about an hour, having stopt some time to converse with a sociably disposed chap, whom I fell in with in Port. He wished to appear a great connoisseur in velocipedes, having been on one for about 5 seconds once; he said he once had some intention of making one for himself, having frequently to go on errands to the Point, but he gave up the idea after a while. He must be a cute chap, and deserves to have a leather medal awarded to him, for his judicious scheme; however, he was a well spoken fellow, and quite the reverse of the Boston chaps, and deserves a medal for his civility if nothing else; at least I would have given him one at the time.

17th August. Wednesday.

That I might recover from the fatigues of my last night's violent exercise, slept until 9 o'clock — debated within myself whether to go to Boston or not — came to the determination about 11 to go — shaved — dressed, and started for Boston — got there at 12 o'clock — called for Crafts and Gray — went to 24 Collonade Row, where an auction of Mr. Price's furniture was held — bought nothing, but put on a connoisseur-like look, and tried all the wines that were sold. Went to my brother's house — not a living thing visible — house all shut up — got in by means of my key — attempted to make a dinner on a half loaf of mouldy bread which I found and some butter, which, by long soaking in water, and proximity to some antiquated lobster, was not the sweetest I ever tasted. I was wrong when I said not a living thing was visible, for a piece of cheese, which I found, was nothing but life — I carefully left it to its merry gambols. After sitting an hour to digest my dinner, I directed my course to the Athenaeum gallery of pictures . . . Saw little company there, but many pictures, a few of last year's exhibition, — not a very splendid collection, notwithstanding the premiums offered. The portrait of my father, which he mentioned in his letter as having sent on, not there — I suppose not arrived. Returned to my brother's house, intending to sleep there; on my way, bought a loaf of rye bread, and a muskmelon, for my supper. — Was taken for a robber in the house by Mr. Richardson and Francis Alger; they having entered the house to shut a window, which I had opened, not knowing me to be there, heard me moving upstairs, which they supposed to be made by a thief, who had broken in; immediately retreating, Mr. Richardson ran for help, while Francis remained outside the house to watch; he saw me at a window, and hailed, I answered, and the whole stood disclosed; Mr. R. brought two stout men to catch the thief, but was disappointed, I know not whether agreeably or not, on finding it was *only* unconscious me. One good consequence followed from this affair, — I got a light, by means of which I amused myself with a book — Mrs. Manley's novels — until near 12 o'clock; whereas, before, I was preparing to go to bed at 9 o'clock.

18th August. Thursday.

Rose at 7 — read a little — breakfasted on bread and butter, and muskmelon — in the midst of my breakfast, startled by a knock at the door — an invitation for brother to the English school examination, and afterwards to dinner. Having finished my breakfast, started to my appointment, at the Julian Hall; auction of New England society held there today. Saw one or two things I was much in want of, such as a table and a desk, or a gentleman's writing table; but the one thing needful was also wanting. Gray bought a bed and washstand; the former half moss half hair, for $3; the latter for $1.25. Saw J. Sargent. — Went home to dinner, on the remains of my breakfast. In the afternoon read. Walked out to Cambridge, through the Common, where the Portland Rifle Corps were encamped. They presented a strange appearance on guard with pikes. — A warm walk to Cambridge.

19th August. Friday.

The heat being very oppressive to-day, instead of going to Boston as I intended, remained at my room. — Succeeded admirably in amusing myself with John Shipp's memoirs, and cooling myself with soda water. — I ought certainly to be in a perfect state of health, if abstinence and exercise conduce to it; my diet is that of Byron, crackers and soda water; my exercise riding on the velocipede in the evening . . .

20th August. Saturday.

Still too warm to walk to Boston; — feel more like lying on the sofa with a novel, than trudging through the abominable Cambridge Port, that abomination of all that is sweet-scented. Read John Shipp the whole morning — dined on herrings and crackers, with a dessert of crackers and honey. After dinner, and after bathing read, and after reading rode, and after riding supped, and after supping rode again. This afternoon tried the road to West Cambridge on my velocipede; find it very hard, and accommodating to my horse, but not quite long enough in its accommodations. Attract quite as much attention as a modest man may desire, ladies stopping to look at me, and furl up their pretty mouths in still prettier smiles. Read after my return until near 1 o'clock, then to bed.

Arthur H. Cole, ed., *Charleston Goes to Harvard, The Diary of a Harvard Student of 1831* (Cambridge: Harvard University Press, 1940).

Charles W. Eliot

WHAT A DAY FOR OUR RACE!
(1858)

President Eliot, a graduate of 1853, was Assistant Professor of Mathematics and Chemistry at Harvard and found recreation in rowing on the Charles. To use the President's own words: "In the season of 1857 the Harvard eight-oared crew had been very badly defeated by a crew organized by the Union Boat Club of Boston; and the undergraduates were so much discouraged as to Harvard's prospects in rowing that it turned out to be impossible to get together even a six-oared crew for the season of 1858. I had graduated in 1853 and Mr. Agassiz in 1855. Thus it came about that I rowed in two regattas on the Charles River Basin. . . The crew ordered from St. John builders a new boat, which was the first shell-boat to appear on the Charles. It was short and broad compared with the shells of today, but it was much lighter in construction and much more ticklish than Harvard crews had been accustomed to. It had long outriggers, but no sliding seats and no coxswain. The bow oar used the rudder by means of a yoke which was close to his feet. In both these races the Harvard crew carried off the first prize, a purse of money . . ."

It was during the season of 1858 that crimson first was used as a Harvard color. President Eliot's account of the race is from two letters written to his fiancée, Ellen Peabody.

June 19 [1858]

Very Dear Ellen, — . . . What a day for our race! just perfect — clear and bright, not hot, no wind. If it is like this at 6 oclk tonight, those Irishmen will have to pull about as hard as they conveniently can in order to beat the Harvard. Crowninshield is going to row stroke, so I get my old oar — No. 3 — which I like better than any other. Everybody, as far as I have heard, thinks that the Harvard is to be beaten, and it certainly is very possible that she may be, but unless we meet with some accident, we shall make better time round the course than any American or Irish crew has ever made before, so that we shan't disgrace ourselves if we are beaten. I had rather win than not, but it is mighty little matter whether we beat or are beaten — rowing is not my profession, neither is it my love, — it is only recreation, fun, and health. I am going to remember your injunctions, and take the best possible care of myself, and row just as hard as I comfortably can, and not a bit harder. I have been rowing so much within three days that my fingers feel as stiff as any hodcarrier's, — hence certain eccentricities and irregularities in the form of my letters. I shall miss you this afternoon, *if* we win, — I had rather see you up in one of those windows, than see all the thousands of people that I suppose will be there. What do I care for them, and what don't I care for you! And I shall miss you tomorrow too — Sunday won't be Sunday without you. What a grind it was, bidding you good-bye in those cars, and letting you go off alone — I hope I shan't have to do that many times in our lives for I didn't relish it a bit — quite the contrary. Now I must stop, and when I go on that race will have been settled one way or the other.

Sunday morning 8½oclk.

Hurra! Hurra!! Hurra!!! We've beaten the entire crowd tremendously — and made the quickest time ever made round the course. 19 min. 22 sec. was our time; 21 min. 20 the time of the next boat; we therefore beat by 1 m. 58 s. which is a very large difference. Ellen, it was perfectly splendid — we had the sympathy of the entire crowd, and what a crowd it was! The moment we appeared, the people began to clap and hurrah — we looked "flash," I tell you — and rowed mighty prettily up by the houses and back to our place which was on the outside, next the Judges boat. Then we saw the men we were to row against — great stout Irishmen, with awful muscles — as Crowninshield said, his heart was right in his mouth — in a moment Shimmin said "ready" and the pistol was fired. At the first stroke, Crowninshield bent his rowlock, we were too nervous, the boat rocked and we did not get ahead of all the boats as we hoped to. I saw two green boats shooting ahead of us, and felt decidedly scared. The girls [his sisters] were up at Dr. Hooper's, they saw that we were not ahead, and thought it was all up with us. If you had been there you would have been frightened. But in a moment we got steady, and pulled with a will, and the boat slipped along like a beauty, — we began to gain. How nice I felt! we left all the Irish boats but two in the first half mile, those two kept up, one nearly even with us, the other a little behind. At the end of the first mile we were rowing first, and we saw that we had the best chance of winning. The larboard side was a little too strong for the starboard (here Cooke came in to congratulate me, so I had to stop writing, and walk into town, to hear Mr. Huntington preach at the King's Chapel, and to go to church with my family for the last time in our old pew) so that I did not have to work as hard as I could by any means, and had time to see that we were ahead and likely to come first to the turning stake. Just as we had completely turned and started on the return, the next boat came so near us that her bow nearly hit our stern; but that boat had only half turned and we had wholly turned and we stretched away from them before they could turn round, making a long gap between the two boats. In the next half mile the Irish boat next behind us began to pull up; Crowninshield saw it, and said "Come, fellows, she [is] gaining! Give way!" So we all put in together, and left that green boat behind, just like walking by a post, as Agassiz expressed it. Oh, wasn't it jolly! The boys say that Eliot was excited, and I know I felt mighty pleasant, not an idea of being tired. Goodwin heard a Sophomore giving an account of the matter on the steps of Hollis, and said Sophomore stated that "Eliot got tremendously excited," called Caspar Crowninshield, "Cas," and told him to "go it, my boy"; all of which is true in the main, I believe. In the last half mile the people shouted and clapped, and cheered tremendously, which was a very nice thing to hear, and made us pull all the harder and better — we came in in beautiful style, ever so far ahead of the next boat. What an ovation we had — the paddies behaved beautifully, — shook hands and owned up handsomely — Everybody seemed to be in a state of ecstasy; the Cambridge boys did not think that we should beat, so they were doubly glad, and made a great row about it in Boston, and afterwards at Cambridge.

Profs. Peirce, Agassiz, and Huntington were all in Boston to see the race, and came out to Cambridge in a state of exaltation. Huntington cheered and shouted to such an extent that he was as hoarse as a crow today.

There were many other circumstances which you would like to hear about, but I must take this letter to the post-office in five minutes or it will not reach you on Monday, as I hope it may, and if I say anything more about that race, I shan't have time to tell you how dearly I love you, how much more I should have enjoyed our victory, if you had been there to see, or how much I long to hear something from you. Tell me how you do, what you are enjoying and when you are coming home to

Your affectionate   CHARLES W. E.

I have got lots more to say and shall write again very soon.

Henry James, *Charles W. Eliot* (Boston and New York: Houghton Mifflin Company, 1930).

Mark Sibley Severance

THE CONTEST ON THE DELTA

(c. 1855)

Through the eyes of the lovely Miss Darby and her cousins the Barlows, from Jamaica Plain, we are treated to a descriptive account of the annual football match between the "sophs" and the "freshies" — a genteel free-for-all banned by the Faculty in 1860. Among the participants in the Olympian struggle are our hero, Tom Hammersmith, and his classmate, George Goldie. The episode occurs in Hammersmith: His Harvard Days, *a half-humorous account of student life by Mark Sibley Severance (1846–1931).* Hammersmith *sold widely, coming as it did on the heels of William Tucker Washburn's successful* Fair Harvard *(1869). Indeed, this episode is reminiscent of a similar scene in* Fair Harvard. *Both novels followed the literary pace of Cuthbert Bede who wrote about Oxford's notorious* Mr. Verdant Green.*

Most of Mr. Severance's life was spent in developing ranch land and in raising fruit in San Bernardino County, California.

THEY WERE so near now, that they could see the freshmen lying in groups under the trees towards the apex of the Delta. Several of their leaders were moving among them, apparently giving advice. If the young ladies had been still nearer, they would have seen several small freshmen sheepishly extracting cotton-wool and old handkerchiefs, and other such padding, from their boot-legs, and might have heard them chaffing each other on their ignorance of the game and the precise point of attack. But they were not near enough for that, or to see the blanched lips of many of the young fellows, for the first time in their lives brought into such an arena, and feeling that the coming struggle was big with Fate for them.

They could only pity the raw young fellows in a general way, and look about them at the faces that they knew, in carriages and elsewhere.

"Why, there's Miss Fayerweather! I thought she was in Newport," said Miss Barlow. "Who's that on horseback talking to her?"

"One of the Abbotts, I think," said her sister Madelon. "But, Ellen, as sure as you live, isn't that your father leaning against the post? In a line with that horrid red shawl — don't you see?"

"Red shawl? It certainly is. I thought he had some Latin papers to look over. But what's that noise?" asked Miss Darby.

"There they come!" shouted young Barlow, forgetting his awful self in the excitement. "Aren't they a jolly set of coves?"

As he speaks, a long procession comes in view. Can they be students, these tatterdemalions in old coats and older hats, in winged raggedness both, marching two by two past Holworthy, and singing at the top of their voices some popular college-song, — "We won't go home till morning," I think it was! They file out of the quadrangle, cross the street, and, entering the enclosure by an old gate long since vanished, take up their places by the two spreading trees which formerly stood guard near the broad end of the Delta.

It is all changed now: the noble Memorial Hall has been flung down into the middle of the Delta; and the noise of knives and forks in commons, the rounded periods of orators, and the festive music of commencements, have chased away the echoes of the games and contests of Hammersmith's day. Whether these two trees, the rendezvous in so many different sports of the early times, have given way before the eastern façade of Memorial Hall, I know not, in my exile; but they spread a welcome shade for the young cricketers and athletes of the days of which I write. And under them now our sophomores have collected, depositing their coats at their bases, and looking across at the band of freshmen.

The latter have risen, and are bunched near the middle of the Delta.

"Do you know many of the men?" said Miss Madelon, addressing Miss Darby. "What frights those sophs are!"

"Only my cousin George Goldie, a classmate of his named Hammersmith, and one or two others."

"Hammersmith! One of *the* Hammersmiths? Is he nice?"

"M — m — I hardly — There he is now, looking this way"; and, as Mr. Tom raised his cap to her, she said, "How do you do, Mr. Hammersmith?" in that bated whisper with which one addresses people rods away, feeling inexpressibly silly for it afterwards.

"Yes; and there's George going over towards the sophomores; and that big fellow has the ball. They're going to begin," she added. . .

The game goes whirling on. The ball is almost lost sight of for a while, as the leaders of both parties are engaged in single combat, and the rest await the issue.

Tom had met more than his match this time. When Goldie's signal came, he found himself near the fence, towards the quadrangle; and, turning to select his man, he ran plump into McGregor, a smallish but long-armed boating man, who immediately made for him, and put him on his defence. Poor Tom put in practice the few hints on counter and defence that Goldie had given him; but the science and long arms of the boating-man were too much for him. He received a shivering blow under the chin, staggered a moment, but came up with a good defence and clinched teeth. An old gentleman on the sidewalk leaned over the fence, and shook his cane deprecatingly, "Why, young men, you're fighting, you're fighting!" and young ladies looking on held their breath to see the way that Tom stood up under the blows, which were coming faster and more effectively as he began to lose his head more and more. He remembered afterward hearing the old gentleman's call, and vowing that he'd die game for the old man's edification, at any rate.

McGregor was not to be stopped longer by this stubborn freshman, however, and made a furious rush at him. Tom caught the blow on his right eye, and fell backward heavily just a second too soon; for Goldie, who had had a drawn battle with Miles not far away, spying Tom's plight, dashed towards him, and sent McGregor reeling in the opposite direction. The crowd now came tearing this way with the ball, and, before Tom and McGregor could rise, had rushed completely over them, leaving freshmen and sophomores piled about them and above them.

"All right?" asked Goldie, as he pulled Tom from under a wreck of freshmen.

"Y-e-s, I think so," said Tom, trying his jaw, and blinking with one eye, while he grinned through a dusty stratum.

"Follow me, then," returned Goldie, plunging like an old war-horse into the thickest of the fight; and, followed by Tom, he made his way as best he could towards the ball.

Heavens! Miles has it! He has passed the van of the freshmen, and is making with long strides for their goal. Will nobody stop him? But what is this?

From the freshmen's very rear a tall figure, in long, flapping coat, suddenly darts towards the rushing Miles as he is preparing to kick the ball over the goal. He falls upon the very kick, as it were, plucks the ball from him, and dashes forward, Miles striking at him in vain. He dodges men and blows alike; his men gather in his wake, but he presses on ahead of them all.

"Who is he?" "Is he a freshman?" "He's the devil!"

"By Jove, it's Breese," gasps Pinckney, — "the fellow that nearly broke my fist. Follow him — hurrah!" And the gallant Pinckney, almost gone with fatigue from his rapid work, — for he has been everywhere, — makes after him with the rest of the freshmen.

And Breese strides and rolls on through the crowd, as though he were himself india-rubber. Men dart out, and deal him blows; but he brushes them off with his long, sinewy arms. They trip him up; but he rolls over and over, and comes up hugging the ball as if it were a pet "principle," or he a kangaroo in flight. The fleetest runners make after him; but he only shows them his long coat-tails floating horizontally on the breeze.

"He's down!"

He surely is; and a mass of struggling men — Miles, Appleton, McGregor, Goldie, and many others — are fighting and falling about him. Nobody can see for the dust, and the crowd outside the Delta is filled with excitement; for it is the turning-point of the game, as everybody can see, and the apparition of the long-skirted one is a novelty in the learned neighborhood.

Nobody can see and nobody can tell who will emerge with the ball; but as the struggling and pushing go on, and a dozen men are rolling in the dust about Breese, he suddenly extracts himself from the mass, holding the ball, and rushes, with a solitary coat-tail now following him like an exclamation-point, for the sophomore goal. A few men are standing guard, expecting a rush; but, just before reaching them, he takes a drop-kick, and sends the ball flying far up into the apex of the Delta.

The freshmen cry, "Game, game!" and run up to congratulate Breese, who does not wait for them; but, vaulting the fence in an easy manner, makes his way through the carriages, and quietly walks towards the halls.

"Breese, Breese, come back!" his classmates shout; and Goldie, Pinckney, and others rush after him.

"For Heaven's sake, come back, man! Where are you going? You've saved our side, my dear fellow. Aren't you well?" asked Goldie.

"Perfectly so. I've had enough, that's all." And no amount of beseeching and complimenting could bring him back. He went off slowly to his rooms, as though returning from an afternoon constitutional: and the freshmen felt much like the Romans after the battle of the Lake Regillus and the disappearance of the two horsemen; or as the people of Hadley after the Indian fight, and their deliverance by the mysterious old man in white hair, supposed to be a regicide, who fought, and saved them, and vanished into the night.

The evening light is going fast, however; and Goldie is calling "Warners!" again; for the rubber comes now; and the freshmen will have ample time after this to discuss their curious victory.

We need hardly follow them through this last struggle. The game wavered and varied much as before, except that the freshmen had not the endurance of their opponents, and worked with less vim now. The encouragement of their victory, however, was almost a counterpoise for their fatigue; and they girded themselves for their work with grim determination.

Only those who have struggled in an up-hill, stubborn game like this for hours, who have felt that they had a furnace for lungs, and a scorching lime-kiln for a throat, but who have yet put all their remaining strength into the last desperate charges, can appreciate the condition in which both sides, and more especially the freshman, are playing this decisive rubber. It is a terrible strain on the heart and the lungs, and a test of the stoutest pluck.

Only one episode marks the grim monotony of the game now, which is played in almost complete silence.

The ball flies over the fence, and falls in the street, among a number of carriages drawn up near the Delta. Horses snort and prance; and a half-dozen men of both sides, who have gone over the fence like deer, dash in among them. McGregor has the ball; but a pair of high-stepping grays, from under whose feet he had pulled it, plunge and rear; and there is a cry of horror, as Pinckney, trying to avoid them, is knocked over, and lies motionless under the forward-wheels of the carriage. There is a rush for him; and while men of both sides swarm over the fence, and many too inquisitive strangers press around him, Goldie, the glorious, comes vaulting over the rails, and diving through the crowd.

"For God's sake, give him air, gentlemen!" he shouts, as he pushes them away, and lifts the flaccid form of his chum. "Pinck, Pinck! are you hurt? Where is it? — Some water, quick, some of you!" And somebody runs for the quadrangle.

Pinckney opens his eyes at length, draws a long breath, with wide-opened mouth, and puts his hand to his side. It was a cruel kick in the side, which had knocked the breath out of him for the moment, but has worked no permanent injury.

"Shall we stop the game?" asked Miles.

"No, no! — You can go on, can't you, Pinck?" said Goldie.

"I think so," answered Pinckney; and, straightening himself with an effort, he climbed the fence, and took his position; while the united classes and the crowds about the Delta joined in a mighty shout, and clapping of hands.

"Take your kick," called Goldie; and the sophomore kicked off. Pinckney started, as of old, in the direction of the ball, but doubled over as a sharp stitch in his muscles caught him. He walked to the side of the Delta, leaned wearily against a stone post, and saw, with a bitter, sickly feeling, in less than five minutes, the victorious sophomores driving the ball over the freshman goal.

Victory had settled with the sophomores, to be sure. But as the conquerors and their not unworthy opponents mingled, and walked towards the quadrangle, and the mass of spectators broke up and melted away, if you had been among them, you would have heard them declaring that such a well-fought game had never been, in the memory of the oldest graduate. Miles and Goldie, leaders and followers, were complimented on their brilliant play; and Tom felt that his cup was full when McGregor, who had knocked him down, caught him up as they were nearing the halls, and extended his hand frankly, saying, —

"How's the eye, Hammersmith? You're the toughest customer, for a novice, that I ever got hold of." And Tom opened a rather unhappy eye for proof, and became a fast friend of his generous antagonist, from that day on.

So the first rough initiation into his university life had come and gone; and Tom (who could call this his first initiation without tautology, for he was to have many more), in spite of pounding and bruises, weeping eye, and somewhat of disgust at the rather barbarous pastime, was glad that he had been through it, and felt more of a man than ever in his life before, as he walked to his room in the midst of these fellows, who could give and take such severe punishment without wincing.

Philosophers, and you, gentle readers, may smile; but such was the fact. I find in Tom's diary, under date of Monday, Sept. 19, 185–, the following entry: —

> Weather fine all day. Recitations not yet under way, except in Latin. Darby is a brick. Took little lesson in boxing in Goldie's room. Football match in evening; great crowd. Bowed to Miss Darby; had pretty girls with her. We won only one innings, — the second. Breese, queer fellow, ran clear through with ball. Fight with McGregor; knocked down; bad eye. Pinckney kicked by horse. "Bloody Monday" night; lots of hazing. [Here occurs a star, referring to a blank page at the end of his book, where he went for space to describe the hazing of that evening. We need not follow him now.] Feel more of a man to-night than ever in my life. Began a letter home.

Mark Sibley Severance, *Hammersmith: His Harvard Days* (1878).

Owen Wister

THE SEARCH FOR THE BIRD-IN-HAND
(1903)

If Harvard's good name had been threatened by the revelations of Flandrau's Harvard Episodes, *it was rescued from peril by the publication of a gay little volume,* Philosophy 4. *This tale recounted the adventures of Billy and Bertie, two of Harvard's gilded youth, who hired as a tutor a fellow student named Oscar and then proceeded to prove to the satisfaction of many that the best of a gentleman's education does not lie in books. To modern ears this has a jarring sound, but the story has long been one of the most popular in Harvard literature. To print only the latter half of this tale seems a little like coming in at the end of the picture, but we cannot have it all. The author, Owen Wister (1860–1938), was a member of the Class of 1882 at Harvard, a graduate of the Law School (1888), and an Overseer. Although he is best known for his novel* The Virginian *(1902), he also wrote* Red Men and White, Members of the Family, A Straight Deal, The Pentecost of Calamity, *and* Indispensable Information for Infants.

BILLY got up early. As he plunged into his cold bath he envied his room-mate, who could remain at rest indefinitely, while his own hard lot was

Owen Wister, *Philosophy 4: A Story of Harvard University*, copyright, 1901, 1903, 1931, by The Macmillan Company, New York, and used with their permission.

hurrying him to prayers and breakfast and Oscar's inexorable notes. He sighed once more as he looked at the beauty of the new morning and felt its air upon his cheeks. He and Bertie belonged to the same club-table, and they met there mournfully over the oatmeal. This very hour to-morrow would see them eating their last before the examination in Philosophy 4. And nothing pleasant was going to happen between, — nothing that they could dwell upon with the slightest satisfaction. Nor had their sleep entirely refreshed them. Their eyes were not quite right, and their hair, though it was brushed, showed fatigue of the nerves in a certain inclination to limpness and disorder.

> Epicharmos of Kos
> Was covered with moss,

remarked Billy.

> Thales and Zeno
> Were duffers at keno,

added Bertie.

In the hours of trial they would often express their education thus.

"Philosophers I have met," murmured Billy, with scorn. And they ate silently for some time.

"There's one thing that's valuable," said Bertie next. "When they spring those tricks on you about the flying arrow not moving, and all the rest, and prove it all right by logic, you learn what pure logic amounts to when it cuts loose from common sense. And Oscar thinks it's immense. We shocked him."

"He's found the Bird-in-Hand!" cried Billy, quite suddenly.

"Oscar?" said Bertie with an equal shout.

"No, John. John has. Came home last night and waked me up and told me." "Good for John," remarked Bertie, pensively.

Now, to the undergraduate mind of that day the Bird-in-Hand tavern was what the golden fleece used to be to the Greeks, — a sort of shining, remote, miraculous thing, difficult though not impossible to find, for which expeditions were fitted out. It was reported to be somewhere in the direction of Quincy, and in one respect it resembled a ghost: you never saw a man who had seen it himself; it was always his cousin, or his elder brother in '79. But for the successful explorer a dinner and wines were waiting at the Bird-in-Hand more delicious than anything outside of Paradise. You will realize, therefore, what a thing it was to have a room-mate who had attained. If Billy had not been so dog-tired last night, he would have sat up and made John tell him everything from beginning to end.

"Soft-shell crabs, broiled live lobster, salmon, grass-plover, dough-birds, and rum omelette," he was now reciting to Bertie.

"They say the rum there is old Jamaica brought in slave-ships," said Bertie, reverently.

"I've heard he has white port of 1820," said Billy; "and claret and champagne."

Bertie looked out of the window.

"This is the finest day there's been," said he. Then he looked at his watch. It was twenty-five minutes before Oscar. Then he looked Billy hard in the eye. "Have you any sand?" he inquired.

It was a challenge to Billy's manhood. "Sand!" he yelled, sitting up.

Both of them in an instant had left the table and bounded out of the house.

"I'll meet you at Pike's," said Billy to Bertie. "Make him give us the black gelding."

"Might as well bring our notes along," Bertie called after his rushing friend; "and get John to tell you the road."

To see their haste, as the two fled in opposite directions upon their errands, you would have supposed them under some crying call of obligation, or else to be escaping from justice.

Twenty minutes later they were seated behind the black gelding and bound on their journey in search of the Bird-in-Hand. Their notes in Philosophy 4 were stowed under the buggy-seat.

"Did Oscar see you?" Bertie inquired.

"Not he," cried Billy, joyously.

"Oscar will wonder," said Bertie; and he gave the black gelding a triumphant touch with the whip.

You see, it was Oscar that had made them run so; or, rather, it was Duty and Fate walking in Oscar's displeasing likeness. Nothing easier, nothing more reasonable, than to see the tutor and tell him they should not need him to-day. But that would have spoiled everything. They did not know it, but deep in their childlike hearts was a delicious sense that in thus unaccountably disappearing they had won a great game, had got away ahead of Duty and Fate. After all, it did bear some resemblance to an escape from justice.

Could he have known this, Oscar would have felt more superior than ever. Punctually at the hour agreed, ten o'clock, he rapped at Billy's door and stood waiting, his leather wallet of notes nipped safe between elbow and ribs. Then he knocked again. Then he tried the door, and as it was open, he walked deferentially into the sitting room. Sonorous snores came from one of the bedrooms. Oscar peered in and saw John; but he saw no Billy in the other bed. Then, always deferential, he sat down in the sitting room and watched a couple of prettily striped coats hanging in a half-open closet.

At that moment the black gelding was flirtatiously crossing the draw-bridge over the Charles on the Allston Road. The gelding knew the clank of those suspending chains and the slight unsteadiness of the meeting halves of the bridge as well as it knew oats. But it could not enjoy its own entirely premeditated surprise quite so much as Bertie and Billy were enjoying their entirely unpremeditated flight from Oscar. The wind rippled on the water; down at the boat-house Smith was helping some one embark in a single scull; they saw the green meadows toward Brighton; their foreheads felt cool and unvexed, and each new minute had the savor of fresh forbidden fruit.

"How do we go?" said Bertie.

"I forgot I had a bet with John until I had waked him," said Billy. "He bet me five last night I couldn't find it, and I took him. Of course, after that I had no right to ask him anything, and he thought I was funny. He said I couldn't find out if the landlady's hair was her own. I went him another five on that."

"How do you say we ought to go?" said Bertie, presently.

"Quincy, I'm sure."

They were now crossing the Albany tracks at Allston. "We're going to get there," said Bertie; and he turned the black gelding toward Brookline and Jamaica Plain.

The enchanting day surrounded them. The suburban houses, even the suburban street-cars, seemed part of one great universal plan of enjoyment. Pleasantness so radiated from the boys' faces and from their general appearance of clean white flannel trousers and soft clean shirts of pink and blue that a driver on a passing car leaned to look after them with a smile and a butcher hailed them with loud brotherhood from his cart. They turned a corner, and from a long way off came the sight of the tower of Memorial Hall. Plain above all intervening tenements and foliage it rose. Over there beneath its shadow were examinations and Oscar. It caught Billy's roving eye, and he nudged Bertie, pointing silently to it. "Ha, ha!" sang Bertie. And beneath his light whip the gelding sprang forward into its stride.

The clocks of Massachusetts struck eleven. Oscar rose doubtfully from his chair in Billy's study. Again he looked into Billy's bedroom and at the empty bed. Then he went for a moment and watched the still forcibly sleeping John. He turned his eyes this way and that, and after standing for a while moved quietly back to his chair and sat down with the leather wallet of notes on his lap, his knees together, and his unblacked shoes touching. In due time the clocks of Massachusetts struck noon.

In a meadow where a brown amber stream ran, lay Bertie and Billy on the grass. Their summer coats were off, their belts loosened. They watched with eyes half closed the long waterweeds moving gently as the current waved and twined them. The black gelding, brought along a farm road and through a gate, waited at its ease in the field beside a stone wall. Now and then it stretched and cropped a young leaf from a vine that grew over the wall, and now and then the warm wind brought down the fruit blossoms all over the meadow. They fell from the tree where Bertie and Billy lay, and the boys brushed them from their faces. Not very far away was Blue Hill, softly shining; and crows high up in the air came from it occasionally across here.

By one o'clock a change had come in Billy's room. Oscar during that hour had opened his satchel of philosophy upon his lap and read his notes attentively. Being almost word perfect in many parts of them, he now spent his unexpected leisure in acquiring accurately the language of still further paragraphs. "The sharp line of demarcation which Descartes drew between consciousness and the material world," whispered Oscar with satisfaction, and knew that if Descartes were on the examination paper he could start with this and go on for nearly twenty lines before he would have to use any words of his own. As he memorized, the chambermaid, who had come to do the bedrooms three times already and had gone away again, now returned and no longer restrained her indignation. "Get up, Mr. Blake!" she vociferated to the sleeping John; "you ought to be ashamed!" And she shook the bedstead. Thus John had come to rise and discover Oscar. The patient tutor explained himself as John listened in his pyjamas.

"Why, I'm sorry," said he, "but I don't believe they'll get back very soon."

"They have gone away?" asked Oscar,

"Ah — yes," returned the reticent John. "An unexpected matter of importance."

"But, my dear sir, those gentlemen know nothing! Philosophy 4 is tomorrow, and they know nothing."

"They'll have to stand it, then," said John, with a grin.

"And my time. I am waiting here. I am engaged to teach them. I have been waiting here since ten. They engaged me all day and this evening."

"I don't believe there's the slightest use in your waiting now, you know. They'll probably let you know when they come back."

"Probably! But they have engaged my time. The girl knows I was here ready at ten. I call you to witness that you found me waiting, ready at any time."

John in his pyjamas stared at Oscar. "Why, of course they'll pay you the whole thing," said he, coldly; "stay here if you prefer." And he went into the bathroom and closed the door.

The tutor stood awhile, holding his notes and turning his little eyes this way and that. His young days had been dedicated to getting the better of his neighbor, because otherwise his neighbor would get the better of him. Oscar had never suspected the existence of boys like John and Bertie and Billy. He stood holding his notes, and then, buckling them up once more, he left the room with evidently reluctant steps. It was at this time that the clocks struck one.

In their field among the soft new grass sat Bertie and Billy some ten yards apart, each with his back against an apple tree. Each had his notes and took his turn at questioning the other. Thus the names of the Greek philosophers with their dates and doctrines were shouted gayly in the meadow. The foreheads of the boys were damp to-day, as they had been last night, and their shirts were opened to the air; but it was the sun that made them hot now, and no lamp or gas; and already they looked twice as alive as they had looked at breakfast. There they sat, while their memories gripped the summarized list of facts essential, facts to be known accurately; the simple, solid, raw facts, which, should they happen to come on the examination paper, no skill could evade nor any imagination supply. But this study was no longer dry and dreadful to them: they had turned it to a sporting event. "What about Heracleitos?" Billy as catechist would put at Bertie. "Eternal flux," Bertie would correctly snap back at Billy. Or, if he got it mixed up, and replied, "Everything is water," which was the doctrine of another Greek, then Billy would credit himself with twenty-five cents on a piece of paper. Each ran a memorandum of this kind; and you can readily see how spirited a character metaphysics would assume under such conditions.

"I'm going in," said Bertie, suddenly, as Billy was crediting himself with a fifty-cent gain. "What's your score?"

"Two seventy-five, counting your break on Parmenides. It'll be cold."

"No, it won't. Well, I'm only a quarter behind you." And Bertie pulled off his shoes. Soon he splashed into the stream where the bend made a hole of some depth.

"Cold?" inquired Billy on the bank.

Bertie closed his eyes dreamily. "Delicious," said he, and sank luxuriously beneath the surface with slow strokes.

Billy had his clothes off in a moment, and, taking the plunge, screamed loudly. "You liar!" he yelled, as he came up. And he made for Bertie.

Delight rendered Bertie weak and helpless; he was caught and ducked; and after some vigorous wrestling both came out of the icy water.

"Now we've got no towels, you fool," said Billy.

"Use your notes," said Bertie, and he rolled in the grass. Then they chased each other round the apple trees, and the black gelding watched them by the wall, its ears well forward.

While they were dressing they discovered it was half-past one, and became instantly famished. "We should have brought lunch along," they told each other. But they forgot that no such thing as lunch could have induced them to delay their escape from Cambridge for a moment this morning. "What do you suppose Oscar is doing now?" Billy inquired of Bertie, as they led the black gelding back to the road; and Bertie laughed like an infant. "Gentlemen," said he, in Oscar's manner, "we now approach the multiplicity of the ego." The black gelding must have thought it had humorists to deal with this day.

Oscar, as a matter of fact, was eating his cheap lunch away over in Cambridge. There was cold mutton, and boiled potatoes with hard brown spots in them, and large pickled cucumbers; and the salt was damp and would not shake out through the holes in the top of the bottle. But Oscar ate two helps of everything with a good appetite, and between whiles looked at his notes, which lay open beside him on the table. At the stroke of two he was again knocking at his pupils' door. But no answer came. John had gone away somewhere for indefinite hours and the door was locked. So Oscar wrote: "Called, two P.M.," on a scrap of envelope, signed his name, and put it through the letter-slit. It crossed his mind to hunt other pupils for his vacant time, but he decided against this at once, and returned to his own room. Three o'clock found him back at the door, knocking scrupulously. The idea of performing his side of the contract, of tendering his goods and standing ready at all times to deliver them, was in his commercially mature mind. This time he had brought a neat piece of paper with him, and wrote upon it, "Called, three P.M.," and signed it as before, and departed to his room with a sense of fulfilled obligations.

Bertie and Billy had lunched at Mattapan quite happily on cold ham, cold pie, and doughnuts. Mattapan, not being accustomed to such lilies of the field, stared at their clothes and general glory, but observed that they could eat the native bill-of-fare as well as anybody. They found some good, cool beer, moreover, and spoke to several people of the Bird-in-Hand, and got several answers: for instance, that the Bird-in-Hand was at Hingham; that it was at Nantasket; that they had better inquire for it at South Braintree; that they had passed it a mile back; and that there was no such place. If you would gauge the intelligence of our population, inquire your way in a rural neighborhood. With these directions they took up their journey after an hour and a half, — a halt made chiefly for the benefit of the black gelding, whom they looked after as much as they did themselves. For a while they discussed club matters seriously, as both of them were officers of certain organizations, chosen so on account of their recognized executive gifts. These questions settled, they resumed the lighter theme of philosophy, and made it (as Billy observed) a near thing for the Causal law. But as they drove along, their minds left this topic on the abrupt discovery that the sun was getting down out of the sky, and they asked each other where they were and what they should do. They pulled up at some cross-roads and debated this with growing uneasiness. Behind them lay the way to Cambridge, — not very clear, to be sure; but you could always go where you had come from, Billy seemed to think. He asked, "How about Cambridge and a little Oscar to finish off with?" Bertie frowned. This would be failure. Was Billy willing to go back and face John the successful?

"It would only cost me five dollars," said Billy.

"Ten," Bertie corrected. He recalled to Billy the matter about the landlady's hair.

"By Jove, that's so!" cried Billy, brightening. It seemed conclusive. But he grew cloudy again the next moment. He was of opinion that one could go too far in a thing.

"Where's your sand?" said Bertie.

Billy made an unseemly rejoinder, but even in the making was visited by inspiration. He saw the whole thing as it really was. "By Jove!" said he, "we couldn't get back in time for dinner."

"There's my bonny boy!" said Bertie, with pride; and he touched up the black gelding. Uneasiness had left both of them. Cambridge was manifestly impossible; an error in judgment; food compelled them to seek the Bird-in-Hand. "We'll try Quincy, anyhow," Bertie said. Billy suggested that they inquire of people on the road. This provided a new sporting event: they could bet upon the answers. Now, the roads, not populous at noon, had grown solitary in the sweetness of the long twilight. Voices of birds there were; and little, black, quick brooks, full to the margin grass, shot under the roadway through low bridges. Through the web of young foliage the sky shone saffron, and frogs piped in the meadow swamps. No cart or carriage appeared, however, and the bets languished. Bertie, driving with one hand, was buttoning his coat with the other, when the black gelding leaped from the middle of the road to the turf and took to backing. The buggy reeled; but the driver was skilful, and fifteen seconds of whip and presence of mind brought it out smoothly. Then the cause of all this spoke to them from a gate.

"Come as near spillin' as you boys wanted, I guess," remarked the cause.

They looked, and saw him in huge white shirt-sleeves, shaking with joviality. "If you kep' at it long enough, you might a-most learn to drive

a horse," he continued, eying Bertie. This came as near direct praise as
the true son of our soil — Northern or Southern — often thinks well of.
Bertie was pleased, but made a modest observation, and "Are we near
the tavern?" he asked. "Bird-in-Hand!" the son of the soil echoed; and he
contemplated them from his gate. "That's me," he stated with compla-
cence. "Bill Diggs of the Bird-in-Hand has been me since April '65." His
massy hair had been yellow, his broad body must have weighed two
hundred and fifty pounds, his wide face was canny, red, and somewhat
clerical, resembling Henry Ward Beecher's.

"Trout," he said, pointing to a basket by the gate. "For your dinner."
Then he climbed heavily but skilfully down and picked up the basket
and a rod. "Folks round here say," said he, "that there ain't no more trout
up them meadows. They've been a-sayin' that since '74; and I've been
a-sayin' it myself, when judicious." Here he shook slightly and opened the
basket. "Twelve," he said. "Sixteen yesterday. Now you go along and turn
in the first right-hand turn, and I'll be up with you soon. Maybe you
might make room for the trout." Room for him as well, they assured
him; they were in luck to find him, they explained. "Well, I guess I'll
trust my neck with you," he said to Bertie, the skilful driver; " 'tain't five
minutes' risk." The buggy leaned, and its springs bent as he climbed in,
wedging his mature bulk between their slim shapes. The gelding looked
round the shaft at them. "Protestin', are you?" he said to it. "These light-
weight stoodents spile you!" So the gelding went on, expressing, however,
by every line of its body, a sense of outraged justice. The boys related
their difficult search, and learned that any mention of the name of Diggs
would have brought them straight. "Bill Diggs of the Bird-in-Hand was
my father, and my grandf'ther, and his father; and has been me sence I
come back from the war and took the business in '65. I'm not commonly
to be met out this late. About fifteen minutes earlier is my time for gettin'
back, unless I'm plannin' for a jamboree. But to-night I got to settin' and
watchin' that sunset, and listenin' to a darned red-winged blackbird, and
I guess Mrs. Diggs has decided to expect me somewheres about noon
to-morrow or Friday. Say, did Johnnie send you?" When he found that
John had in a measure been responsible for their journey, he filled with
gayety. "Oh, Johnnie's a bird!" said he. "He's that demure on first appearance. Walked in last evening and wanted dinner. Did he tell you
what he ate? Guess he left out what he drank. Yes, he's demure."

You might suppose that upon their landlord's safe and sober return
fifteen minutes late, instead of on the expected noon of Thursday or
Friday, their landlady would show signs of pleasure; but Mrs. Diggs
from the porch threw an uncordial eye at the three arriving in the buggy.
Here were two more like Johnnie of last night. She knew them by the

clothes they wore and by the confidential tones of her husband's voice as he chatted to them. He had been old enough to know better for twenty years. But for twenty years he had taken the same extreme joy in the company of Johnnies, and they were bad for his health. Her final proof that they belonged to this hated breed was when Mr. Diggs thumped the trout down on the porch, and after briefly remarking, "Half of 'em boiled, and half broiled with bacon," himself led away the gelding to the stable instead of intrusting it to his man Silas.

"You may set in the parlor," said Mrs. Diggs, and departed stiffly with the basket of trout.

"It's false," said Billy, at once.

Bertie did not grasp his thought.

"Her hair," said Billy. And certainly it was an unusual-looking arrangement.

Presently, as they sat near a parlor organ in the presence of earnest family portraits, Bertie made a new poem for Billy, —

> Said Aristotle unto Plato,
> "Have another sweet potato?"

And Billy responded, —

> Said Plato unto Aristotle,
> "Thank you, I prefer the bottle."

"In here, are you?" said their beaming host at the door. "Now, I think you'd find my department of the premises cosier, so to speak." He nudged Bertie. "Do you boys guess it's too early in the season for a silver-fizz?"

We must not wholly forget Oscar in Cambridge. During the afternoon he had not failed in his punctuality; two more neat witnesses to this lay on the door-mat beneath the letter-slit of Billy's room. And at the appointed hour after dinner a third joined them, making five. John found these cards when he came home to go to bed, and picked them up and stuck them ornamentally in Billy's looking-glass, as a greeting when Billy should return. The eight o'clock visit was the last that Oscar paid to the locked door. He remained through the evening in his own room, studious, contented, unventilated, indulging in his thick notes, and also in the thought of Billy's and Bertie's eleventh-hour scholarship. "Even with another day," he told himself, "those young men could not have got fifty per cent." In those times this was the passing mark. To-day I believe you get an A, or a B, or some other letter denoting your rank. In due time Oscar turned out his gas and got into his bed; and the clocks of Massachusetts struck midnight.

Mrs. Diggs of the Bird-in-Hand had retired at eleven, furious with rage, but firm in dignity in spite of a sudden misadventure. Her hair, being the subject of a sporting event, had remained steadily fixed in Billy's mind, — steadily fixed throughout an entertainment which began at an early hour to assume the features of a celebration. One silver-fizz before dinner is nothing; but dinner did not come at once, and the boys were thirsty. The hair of Mrs. Diggs had caught Billy's eye again immediately upon her entrance to inform them that the meal was ready; and whenever she reëntered with a new course from the kitchen, Billy's eye wandered back to it, although Mr. Diggs had become full of anecdotes about the Civil War. It was partly Grecian: a knot stood out behind to a considerable distance. But this was not the whole plan. From front to back ran a parting, clear and severe, and curls fell from this to the temples in a manner called, I believe, by the enlightened, *à l'Anne d'Autriche*. The color was gray, to be sure; but this propriety did not save the structure from Billy's increasing observation. As bottles came to stand on the table in greater numbers, the closer and the more solemnly did Billy continue to follow the movements of Mrs. Diggs. They would without doubt have noticed him and his foreboding gravity but for Mr. Diggs's experiences in the Civil War.

The repast was finished — so far as eating went. Mrs. Diggs with changeless dudgeon was removing and washing the dishes. At the revellers' elbows stood the 1820 port in its fine, fat, old, dingy bottle, going pretty fast. Mr. Diggs was nearing the end of Antietam. "That morning of the 18th, while McClellan was holdin' us squattin' and cussin'," he was saying to Bertie, when some sort of shuffling sound in the corner caught their attention. We can never know how it happened. Billy ought to know, but does not, and Mrs. Diggs allowed no subsequent reference to the casualty. But there she stood with her entire hair at right angles. The Grecian knot extended above her left ear, and her nose stuck through one set of Anne d'Autriche. Beside her Billy stood, solemn as a stone, yet with a sort of relief glazed upon his face.

Mr. Diggs sat straight up at the vision of his spouse. "Flouncing Florence!" was his exclamation. "Gee-whittaker, Mary, if you ain't the most unmitigated sight!" And wind then left him.

Mary's reply arrived in tones like a hornet stinging slowly and often. "Mr. Diggs, I have put up with many things, and am expecting to put up with many more. But you'd behave better if you consorted with gentlemen."

The door slammed and she was gone. Not a word to either of the boys, not even any notice of them. It was thorough, and silence consequently held them for a moment.

"He didn't mean anything," said Bertie, growing partially responsible.

"Didn't mean anything," repeated Billy, like a lesson.

"I'll take him and he'll apologize," Bertie pursued, walking over to Billy.

"He'll apologize," went Billy, like a cheerful piece of mechanism. Responsibility was still quite distant from him.

Mr. Diggs got his wind back. "Better not," he advised in something near a whisper. "Better not go after her. Her father was a fightin' preacher, and she's — well, begosh! she's a chip of the old pulpit." And he rolled his eye towards the door. Another door slammed somewhere above, and they gazed at each other, did Bertie and Mr. Diggs. Then Mr. Diggs, still gazing at Bertie, beckoned to him with a speaking eye and a crooked finger; and as he beckoned, Bertie approached like a conspirator and sat down close to him. "Begosh!" whispered Mr. Diggs. "Unmitigated." And at this he and Bertie laid their heads down on the table and rolled about in spasms.

Billy from his corner seemed to become aware of them. With his eye fixed upon them like a statue, he came across the room, and, sitting down near them with formal politeness, observed. "Was you ever to the battle of Antietam?" This sent them beyond the limit; and they rocked their heads on the table and wept as if they would expire.

Thus the three remained, during what space of time is not known: the two upon the table, convalescent with relapses, and Billy like a seated idol, unrelaxed at his vigil. The party was seen through the windows by Silas, coming from the stable to inquire if the gelding should not be harnessed. Silas leaned his face to the pane, and envy spoke plainly in it. "O my! O my!" he mentioned aloud to himself. So we have the whole household: Mrs. Diggs reposing scornfully in an upper chamber; all parts of the tavern darkened, save the one lighted room; the three inside that among their bottles, with the one outside looking covetously in at them; and the gelding stamping in the stable.

But Silas, since he could not share, was presently of opinion that this was enough for one sitting, and he tramped heavily upon the porch. This brought Bertie back to the world of reality, and word was given to fetch the gelding. The host was in no mood to part with them, and spoke of comfortable beds and breakfast as early as they liked; but Bertie had become entirely responsible. Billy was helped in, Silas was liberally thanked, and they drove away beneath the stars, leaving behind them golden opinions, and a host who decided not to disturb his helpmate by retiring to rest in their conjugal bed.

Bertie had forgotten, but the playful gelding had not. When they came abreast of that gate where Diggs of the Bird-in-Hand had met them at sunset, Bertie was only aware that a number of things had happened at once, and that he had stopped the horse after about twenty yards of battle. Pride filled him, but emptied away in the same instant, for a voice on the road behind him spoke inquiringly through the darkness.

"Did any one fall out?" said the voice. "Who fell out?"

"Billy!" shrieked Bertie, cold all over. "Billy, are you hurt?"

"Did Billy fall out?" said the voice, with plaintive cadence. "Poor Billy!"

"He can't be," muttered Bertie. "Are you?" he loudly repeated.

There was no answer; but steps came along the road as Bertie checked and pacified the gelding. Then Billy appeared by the wheel. "Poor Billy fell out," he said mildly. He held something up, which Bertie took. It had been Billy's straw hat, now a brimless fabric of ruin. Except for smirches and one inexpressible rent which dawn revealed to Bertie a little later, there were no further injuries, and Billy got in and took his seat quite competently.

Bertie drove the gelding with a firm hand after this. They passed through the cool of the unseen meadow swamps, and heard the sound of the hollow bridges as they crossed them, and now and then the gulp of some pouring brook. They went by the few lights of Mattapan, seeing from some points on their way the beacons of the harbor, and again the curving line of lamps that drew the outline of some village built upon a hill. Dawn showed them Jamaica Pond, smooth and breezeless, and encircled with green skeins of foliage, delicate and new. Here multitudinous birds were chirping their tiny, overwhelming chorus. When at length, across the flat suburban spaces, they again sighted Memorial tower, small in the distance, the sun was lighting it.

Confronted by this, thoughts of hitherto banished care, and of the morrow that was now to-day, and of Philosophy 4 coming in a very few hours, might naturally have arisen and darkened the end of their pleasant excursion. Not so, however. Memorial tower suggested another line of argument. It was Billy who spoke, as his eyes first rested upon that eminent pinnacle of Academe.

"Well, John owes me five dollars."

"Ten, you mean."

"Ten? How?"

"Why, her hair. And it was easily worth twenty."

Billy turned his head and looked suspiciously at Bertie. "What did I do?" he asked.

"Do! Don't you know?"

Billy in all truth did not.

"Phew!" went Bertie. "Well, I don't, either. Didn't see it. Saw the consequences, though. Don't you remember being ready to apologize? What do you remember, anyhow?"

Billy consulted his recollections with care: they seemed to break off at the champagne. That was early. Bertie was astonished. Did not Billy remember singing "Brace up and dress the Countess," and "A noble lord the Earl of Leicester"? He had sung them quite in his usual manner, conversing freely between whiles. In fact, to see and hear him, no one would have suspected — "It must have been that extra silver-fizz you took before dinner," said Bertie. "Yes," said Billy; "that's what it must have been." Bertie supplied the gap in his memory, — a matter of several hours, it seemed. During most of this time Billy had met the demands of each moment quite like his usual agreeable self — a sleep-walking state. It was only when the hair incident was reached that his conduct had noticeably crossed the line. He listened to all this with interest intense.

"John does owe me ten, I think," said he.

"I say so," declared Bertie. "When do you begin to remember again?"

"After I got in again at the gate. Why did I get out?"

"You fell out, man."

Billy was incredulous.

"You did. You tore your clothes wide open."

Billy, looking at his trousers, did not see it.

"Rise, and I'll show you," said Bertie.

"Goodness gracious!" said Billy.

Thus discoursing, they reached Harvard Square. Not your Harvard Square, gentle reader, that place populous with careless youths and careful maidens and reticent persons with books, but one of sleeping windows and clear, cool air and few sounds; a Harvard Square of emptiness and conspicuous sparrows and milk wagons and early street-car conductors in long coats going to their breakfast; and over all this the sweetness of the arching elms.

As the gelding turned down toward Pike's, the thin old church clock struck.

"Always sounds," said Billy, "like cambric tea."

"Cambridge tea," said Bertie.

"Walk close behind me," said Billy, as they came away from the livery stable. "Then they won't see the hole."

Bertie did so; but the hole was seen by the street-car conductors and the milkmen, and these sympathetic hearts smiled at the sight of the marching boys, and loved them without knowing any more of them than this. They reached their building and separated.

One hour later they met. Shaving and a cold bath and summer flannels, not only clean but beautiful, invested them with the radiant innocence of flowers. It was still too early for their regular breakfast, and they sat down to eggs and coffee at the Holly Tree.

"I waked John up," said Billy. "He is satisfied."

"Let's have another order," said Bertie. "These eggs are delicious." Each of them accordingly ate four eggs and drank two cups of coffee.

"Oscar called five times," said Billy; and he threw down those cards which Oscar had so neatly written.

"There's multiplicity of the ego for you!" said Bertie.

Now, inspiration is a strange thing, and less obedient even than love to the will of man. It will decline to come when you prepare for it with the loftiest intentions, and, lo! at an accidental word it will suddenly fill you, as at this moment it filled Billy.

"By gum!" said he, laying his fork down. "Multiplicity of the ego. Look here. I fall out of a buggy and ask —"

"By gum!" said Bertie, now also visited by inspiration.

"Don't you see?" said Billy.

"I see a whole lot more," said Bertie, with excitement. "I had to tell you about your singing." And the two burst into a flare of talk.

To hear such words as cognition, attention, retention, entity, and identity, freely mingled with such other words as silver-fizz and false hair, brought John, the egg-and-coffee man, as near surprise as his impregnable nature permitted. Thus they finished their large breakfast, and hastened to their notes for a last good bout at memorizing Epicharmos of Kos and his various brethren. The appointed hour found them crossing the college yard toward a door inside which Philosophy 4 awaited them: three hours of written examination! But they looked more roseate and healthy than most of the anxious band whose steps were converging to that same gate of judgment. Oscar, meeting them on the way, gave them his deferential "Good morning," and trusted that the gentlemen felt easy. Quite so, they told him, and bade him feel easy about his pay, for which they were, of course, responsible. Oscar wished them good luck and watched them go to their desks with his little eyes, smiling in his particular manner. Then he dismissed them from his mind, and sat with a faint remnant of his smile, fluently writing his perfectly accurate answer to the first question upon the examination paper.

Here is that paper. You will not be able to answer all the questions, probably, but you may be glad to know what such things are like.

Philosophy 4

1. Thales, Zeno, Parmenides, Heracleitos, Anaxagoras. State briefly the doctrine of each.

2. Phenomenon, noumenon. Discuss these terms. Name their modern descendants.

3. Thought=Being. Assuming this, state the difference, if any, between (1) memory and anticipation; (2) sleep and waking.

4. Democritus, Pythagoras, Bacon. State the relation between them. In what terms must the objective world ultimately be stated? Why?

5. Experience is the result of time and space being included in the nature of mind. Discuss this.

6. Nihil est in intellectu quod non prius fuerit in sensibus. Whose doctrine? Discuss it.

7. What is the inherent limitation in all ancient philosophy? Who first removed it?

8. Mind is expressed through what? Matter through what? Is speech the result or the cause of thought?

9. Discuss the nature of the ego.

10. According to Plato, Locke, Berkeley, where would the sweetness of a honeycomb reside? Where would its shape? its weight? Where do you think these properties reside?

Ten questions, and no Epicharmos of Kos. But no examination paper asks everything, and this one did ask a good deal. Bertie and Billy wrote the full time allotted, and found that they could have filled an hour more without coming to the end of their thoughts. Comparing notes at lunch, their information was discovered to have been lacking here and there. Nevertheless, it was no failure; their inner convictions were sure of fifty per cent at least, and this was all they asked of the gods. "I was ripping about the ego," said Bertie. "I was rather splendid myself," said Billy, "when I got going. And I gave him a huge steer about memory." After lunch both retired to their beds and fell into sweet oblivion until seven o'clock, when they rose and dined, and after playing a little poker went to bed again pretty early.

Some six mornings later, when the Professor returned their papers to them, their minds were washed almost as clear of Plato and Thales as were their bodies of yesterday's dust. The dates and doctrines, hastily memorized to rattle off upon the great occasion, lay only upon the surface of their minds, and after use they quickly evaporated. To their pleasure and most genuine astonishment, the Professor paid them high compliments. Bertie's discussion of the double personality had been the most intelligent which had come in from any of the class. The illustration of the intoxicated hack-driver who had fallen from his hack and inquired who it was that had fallen, and then had pitied himself, was, said the Professor, as original and perfect an illustration of our subjective-objectivity as he had met with in all his researches. And Billy's suggestions concerning the inherency of time and space in the mind the Professor had also found very striking and independent, particularly his reasoning based upon the well-known distortions of time and space which hashish and other drugs produce in us. This was the sort of thing which the Professor had wanted from his students: free comment and discussions, the *spirit* of the course, rather than any strict adherence to the letter. He had constructed his questions to elicit as much individual discussion as possible and had been somewhat disappointed in his hopes.

Yes, Bertie and Billy were astonished. But their astonishment did not
equal that of Oscar, who had answered many of the questions in the
Professor's own language. Oscar received seventy-five per cent for this
achievement — a good mark. But Billy's mark was eighty-six and Bertie's
ninety. "There is some mistake," said Oscar to them when they told him;
and he hastened to the Professor with his tale. "There is no mistake,"
said the Professor. Oscar smiled with increased deference. "But," he
urged, "I assure you, sir, those young men knew absolutely nothing. I
was their tutor, and they knew nothing at all. I taught them all their
information myself." "In that case," replied the Professor, not pleased with
Oscar's tale-bearing, "you must have given them more than you could
spare. Good morning."

Oscar never understood. But he graduated considerably higher than
Bertie and Billy, who were not able to discover many other courses so
favorable to "orriginal rresearch" as was Philosophy 4. That is twenty
years ago. To-day Bertie is treasurer of the New Amsterdam Trust Company, in Wall Street; Billy is superintendent of passenger traffic of the
New York and Chicago Air Line. Oscar is successful too. He has acquired
a lot of information. His smile is unchanged. He has published a careful
work entitled "The Minor Poets of Cinquecento," and he writes book
reviews for the *Evening Post*.

John Dos Passos

ADVENTURE AT NORUMBEGA

(1923)

This episode at the commencement of John Dos Passos' third novel, Streets
of Night, *is in itself a short story, but the style shows few of the characteristics of the writer's later work. There is a rather pleasing immaturity
about this little freshman adventure which would be lost in the larger
canvas of the trilogy,* U. S. A. *Dos Passos is a superb reporter and his
writing method has been much imitated by young, ambitious literary men,
many of them from Harvard. For Harvard consumption (his 25th Anniversary Class Report) he listed only four books as published by him;*
Streets of Night *was not among them, but this excerpt deserves recall
from oblivion. "Harvard," wrote Dos Passos in* Nineteen Nineteen, *"stood*

for the broad a *and those contacts so useful in later life and good English prose . . . if the hedgehog cant be cultured at Harvard the hedgehog cant . . ."*

BUT I don't think I want to, Cham." "Come along, Fanshaw, you've got to." "But I wouldn't know what to say to them." "They'll do the talking . . . Look, you've got to come, date's all made an' everything."

Cham Mason stood in his drawers in the middle of the floor, eagerly waving a shirt into which he was fitting cuff-links. He was a pudgy-faced boy with pink cheeks and wiry light hair like an Irish terrier's. He leaned forward with pouting lips towards Fanshaw, who sat, tall and skinny, by the window, with one finger scratching his neck under the high stiff collar from which dangled a narrow necktie, blue, the faded color of his eyes.

"But jeeze, man," Cham whined.

"Well, what did you go and make it for?"

"Hell, Fanshaw, I couldn't know that Al Winslow was going to get scarlet fever . . . Most fellers 'ld be glad of the chance. It isn't everybody Phoebe Sweeting'll go out with."

"But why don't you go alone?"

"What could I do with two girls in a canoe? And she's got to have her friend along. You don't realize how respectable chorus girls are."

"I never thought they were respectable at all."

"That shows how little you know about it."

Cham put on his shirt with peevish jerks and went into the next room. Fanshaw looked down at Bryce's *American Commonwealth* that lay spread out on his knees and tried to go on reading: This decision of the Supreme Court, however . . . But why shouldn't he? Fanshaw stretched himself yawning. The sunlight seeped through the brownish stencilled curtains and laid a heavy warm hand on his left shoulder. This decision of the Supreme . . . He looked down into Mount Auburn Street. It was June and dusty. From the room below came the singsong of somebody playing "Sweet and Low" on the mandolin. And mother needn't know, and I'm in college . . . see life. A man with white pants on ran across the street waving a tennis racket. Stoddard, on the *Lampoon*, knows all the chorines.

Cham, fully dressed in a tweed suit, stood before him with set lips, blinking his eyes to keep from crying.

"Fanshaw, I don't think you're any kind of a . . ."

"All right, I'll go, Cham, but I won't know what to say to them."

"Gee, that's great." Cham's face became cherubic with smiles. "Just act natural."

"Like when you have your photograph taken," said Fanshaw, laughing shrilly.

"Gee, you're a prince to do it . . . I think Phoebe likes me . . . It's just that I've never had a chance to get her alone."

Their eyes met suddenly. They both blushed and were silent. Fanshaw got to his feet and walked stiffly to the bookcase to put away his book.

"But Cham." He was hoarse; he cleared his throat. "I don't want to carry on with those girls. I don't . . . I don't do that sort of thing."

"Don't worry, they won't eat you. I tell you they are very respectable girls. They don't want to carry on with anybody. They like to have a good time, that's all."

"But all day seems so long."

"We won't start till eleven or so. Phoebe won't be up. Just time to get acquainted."

From far away dustily came the bored strokes of the college bell.

"Ah, there's my three-thirty," said Fanshaw.

It was hot in the room. There was a faint smell of stale sweat from some soiled clothes that made a heap in the center of the floor. The strokes of the bell beat on Fanshaw's ears with a dreary, accustomed weight.

"How about walking into town instead?"

Fanshaw picked up a notebook out of a patch of sun on the desk. The book was warm. The beam of sunlight was full of bright, lazy motes. Fanshaw put the book up to his mouth and yawned. Still yawning, he said:

"Gee, I'd like to but I can't."

"I don't see why you took a course that came at such a damn-fool time."

"Can't argue now," said Fanshaw going out the door and tramping down the scarred wooden stairs.

.   .   .   .

"You ask the clerk to call up and see if they're ready," said Cham. They stood outside the revolving door of the hotel, the way people linger shivering at the edge of a pool before diving in. Cham wore a straw hat and white flannel pants and carried a corded luncheon basket in one hand.

"But Cham, that's your business. You ought to do that." Fanshaw felt a stiff tremor in his voice. His hands were cold.

"Go ahead, Fanshaw, for crissake, we can't wait here all day," Cham whispered hoarsely.

Fanshaw found himself engaged in the revolving door with Cham pushing him from behind. From rocking chairs in the lobby he could see the moonfaces of two drummers, out of which eyes like oysters stared at him. He was blushing; he felt his forehead tingle under his new tweed cap. The clock over the desk said fifteen of eleven. He walked firmly over to the desk and stood leaning over the registry book full of blotted signatures and dates. He cleared his throat. He could feel the eyes of the drummers, of the green bellboy, of people passing along the street boring into his back. At last the clerk came to him, a greyfaced man with a triangular mouth and eyeglasses, and said in a squeaky voice:

"Yessir."

"Are Miss . . . Is Miss . . .? Say, Cham, what are their names, Cham?" Guilty perspiration was trickling on Fanshaw's temples and behind his ears. He felt furiously angry at Cham for having got him into this, at Cham's back and straw hat tipped in the contemplation of the Selkirk Glacier over the fireplace. "Cham!"

"Miss Montmorency and Miss Sweeting," said Cham coolly in a businesslike voice.

The clerk had tipped up one corner of his mouth. Leaving Cham to talk to him, Fanshaw walked over to a rocker by the fireplace and hunched up in it sulkily. With relief he heard the clerk say:

"The young ladies will be down in a few minutes; would you please wait?"

Fanshaw stared straight ahead of him. He'd never speak to Cham again after this. When the bellboy leaned over the desk to say something to the clerk, the eight brass buttons on his coattails flashed in the light. The clerk laughed creakily. Fanshaw clenched his fists. Damn them, what had he let himself be inveigled into this for? He looked at the floor; balanced on the edge of a spittoon a cigar stub still gave off a little wisp of smoke. The temptations of college life; as he sat with his neatly polished oxfords side by side, making the chair rock by a slight movement of the muscles of his thin calves, he thought of the heart-to-heart talk Mr. Crownsterne had given the sixth form this time last year about the temptations of college life. The soapy flow of Mr. Crownsterne's voice booming in his ears: You are now engaged, fellows, in that perilous defile through which all of us have to pass to reach the serene uplands of adult life. You have put behind you the pleasant valleys and problems of boyhood, and before you can assume the duties and responsibilities of men you have to undergo — we all of us have had to undergo — the supreme test. You all know, fellows, the beautiful story of the Holy Grail . . . Galahad . . . purity and continence . . . safest often the best course . . . shun not the society of the lovely girls of our own class . . . honest and healthy entertainment . . . dances and the beautiful flow of freshness and youth . . . but remember to beware in whatever circle of life the duties and responsibilities of your careers may call you to move, of those unfortunate women who have rendered themselves unworthy of the society of our mothers and sisters . . . of those miserable and disin-

herited creatures who, although they do not rebuff and disgust us immediately with their loathsomeness as would common prostitutes, yet
. . . Remember that even Jesus Christ, our Saviour, prayed not to be led
into temptation. O, fellows, when you go out from these walls I want
you to keep the ideals you have learned and that you have taught by your
example as sixth formers . . . the spotless armor of Sir Galahad . . .

The rocking chair creaked. The clock above the desk had ticked its
way to eleven fifteen. Old Crowny's phrases certainly stayed in your
mind. Suppose we met mother on the trolley? No, she'd be at church.
Nonsense, and these were respectable girls anyway; they wouldn't lead
into temptation. A heap lot more respectable than lots of the girls you
met at dances. Why don't they come?

"Gee, I bet they weren't up yet," said Cham giggling.

"What, at eleven o'clock?"

"They don't usually get up till one or two."

"I suppose being up so late every night." Fanshaw could not get his
voice above a mysterious whisper. He sat in the rocking chair without
moving and stared at the clock. Eleven thirty-six. The bellboy stood in
front of the desk, his eyes fixed on vacancy. The bellboy grinned and
drew a red hand across his slick black hair.

"Did ye think we'd passed out up there?" came a gruff girl's voice
behind him, interrupted by a giggle. He smelt perfume. Then he was on
his feet, blushing.

They were shaking hands with Cham. One had curly brown hair and
a doll's pink organdy dress and showed her teeth, even as the grains on
an ear of sweet corn, in a continual smile. The other had a thin face and
tow hair and wore the same dress in blue.

"I was coming up to help," shouted Cham.

"Ou, what's that?"

"It's a present." The blue dress hovered over the lunch basket.

"A case of Scotch!" They all shrieked with laughter.

"That's our eats," said Cham solemnly.

"And this is Mr. ——— ?"

"Beg pardon, this is my friend, Mr. Macdougan . . . answers to the
name of Fanshaw."

Fanshaw shook their hands that they held up very high.

"This is Miss Phoebe Sweeting and this is Miss Elise Montmorency."

"We'll never be able to eat all that," said the blue girl tittering.

"We'll drink some of it," said Cham. "There's some Champagny water."

"My Gawd!"

"You carry it now, Fanshaw," said Cham in a hurried undertone, and
pushed the pink girl out in front of him through the revolving door.

Fanshaw picked up the basket. It was heavy and rattled.

"O, I just do love canoeing," said the blue girl as they followed. "Don't you?"

.   .   .

They stood on the landing at Norumbega. A man in a seedy red sweater torn at the elbows was bringing a canoe out of the boathouse. A cool weedy smell teasing to the nostrils came up out of the river.

"Ou, isn't it deep?" said Elise, pressing her fluffy dress against Fanshaw's leg.

"Stop it, I tell you . . . You'll push me in the water . . . Ow!" Cham was brandishing a bullrush at the pink girl, tickling her with it. She was protesting in a gruff baby lisp full of titters. "If you spoil my dress . . ."

"I'm sure you paddle beautifully . . . D'you mind if I call you Fanshaw . . . It's a funny name like a stage name. Look at them!"

Phoebe had snatched the bullrush and was beating Cham over the head. The brown fluff fell about them bright in the streaming sunlight. Fanshaw found himself picking up Cham's straw hat, palping a dent in the rim with his finger. Cham's hair shone yellow; he grabbed the pink girl's hand. The bullrush broke off and the head fell into the river, floated in the middle of brown bright rings.

"Ow, damn it, you hurt," she cried shrilly. "There now, you made me say damn."

"Momma kiss it an' make it well."

Fanshaw found the blue girl's grey glance wriggling into his eyes.

"Silly, ain't they? Kids, are they not?"

The ain't stung in Fanshaw's ears. The girl was common. The thought made him blush.

"Come along, let's get started. Man the boats," cried Cham.

"I'm scared o' canoes. You can paddle all right, can't you, Fanshaw?" The blue girl pressed his hand tight as they stood irresolute a moment looking down into the canoe. The other canoe was off, upstream into the noon dazzle.

"Come along," shouted Cham. The sun flashed on his paddle. He began singing off key:

> I know a place where the sun is like gold
> And the cherryblooms burst with snow
> And down underneath . . .

"All right, Missy, step in," said the man in the red sweater who was holding the canoe to the landing with a paddle. "Easy now."

"Let m-m-me get in first," said Fanshaw stuttering a little "I hope this isn't a tippy one."

"I'll help you in Missy," said the man in the red sweater. Fanshaw, from the stern seat he had plunked down in, saw the man's big red hand, like a bunch of sausages against the blue dress, clasp her arm, press against the slight curve of her breast as he let her down among the cushions. "Thanks," she said, as she tucked her dress in around her legs, giving the man a long look from under the brim of her hat.

"Ou, I'm scared to death," she said, leaning back gingerly. "If you tip me over . . ."

Fanshaw had pushed the canoe out from the landing. Over his shoulder he caught a glimpse of a grin on the face of the man with the red sweater. He paddled desperately. The other canoe was far ahead, black in the broad shimmering reach of the river. He was sweating. He splashed some water into the canoe.

"Ou you naughty . . . Don't. You've gotten me all wet."

"I think I'll take my coat off if you don't mind."

"Don't mind me, go as far as you like," giggled Elise.

Fanshaw took off his coat and rolled up his sleeves. He was trying not to look at the pink legs in stockings of thin black silk with clocks on them that stretched towards him in the canoe, ending in crossed ankles and bronze high heel slippers.

"Warm, isn't it?"

"Hot, I call it. I hope they don't go awfully far. I don't want to get all sunburned . . . A boy swiped my parasol." Her grey eyes flashed in his. She was giggling with her lips apart.

"How was that?" How solemn I sound, thought Fanshaw.

"I dunno, one o' them souvenir hunters out at the Roadside Inn." She pulled down her babyish-looking hat that had blue and pink roses on it so that it shaded her eyes.

"Whew, smell that!" she cried.

"Must be a sewer, or marshgas."

"Clothespins! Clothespins!" Elise was holding her nose and wriggling in the bottom of the canoe. Then she burst into giggles again and cried: "Gee, this little girl loves the country, nit!"

"Now it's better, isn't it?"

"I want to eat. Cham's crazy to go so far."

"They've got the picnic basket, so I don't see what we can do but follow."

"Follow on, follow on," sang Elise derisively.

Upstream Cham's canoe had drawn up to the bank under a fringe of trees grey in the noon glare. Behind it a figure in white and a figure in pink, close together, were disappearing into the shadow.

"They'll have every single thing eaten up," wailed Elise.

"I'm afraid I'm not a very good paddler," said Fanshaw through clenched teeth.

"There you go again."

"Well, I didn't mean to. I'm sorry."

"You'll have to get me a new dress, that's all."

The canoe ran into the bank with a sliding thump.

Phoebe was looking at them from behind a clump of maples. She cooed at them in her most dollish voice.

"What have you kids been doing all by yourselves out in the river?"

"We saw you, don't you worry dearest," said Elise balancing to step out of the canoe. "O murder, I got my foot in it!"

"Bring the cushions, Fanshaw," shouted Cham, who was kneeling beside the open picnic basket with a bottle in his hand.

Fanshaw's hands were sticky. The warm champagne had made him feel a little sick. He sat with his back against a tree, his knees drawn up to his chin, looking across the gutted lunch basket at Cham and Phoebe, who lay on their backs and shrieked with laughter. Beside him he was conscious of the blue girl sitting stiff on a cushion, bored, afraid of spoiling her dress. Overhead the afternoon sun beat heavily on the broad maple leaves; patches of sunlight littered the ground like bright torn paper. Through the trees came the mud smell and the restless sheen of the river. Fanshaw was trying to think of something to say to the girl beside him; he daren't turn towards her until he had thought of something to say.

"Doggone it I've got an ant down my back," cried Cham, sitting up suddenly, his face pink.

"Momma catch it," spluttered Phoebe in the middle of a gust of laughter.

Cham was scratching himself all over, under his arm, round his neck, making an anxious monkey face till at last he ran his hand down the back of his neck.

"Yea, I got him."

"He's a case, he is," tittered Elise.

Cham was on his hands and knees whispering something in Phoebe's ear, his nose pressed into her frizzy chestnut hair.

"Stop blowin' in my ear," said the pink girl, pushing him away, "Wouldn't that jar you?"

"What we need is juss a lil more champagny water." Cham picked the two bottles out of the basket and tipped them up to the light. "There's juss a lil drop for everybody."

"Not for me . . . I think you're trying to get us silly," said the blue girl.

"God did that."

"Well, I never."

"Ou something's ticklin' me . . . Did you put that ant on me?" The pink girl scrambled to her feet and made for Cham.

"Honest, I didn't . . ." cried Cham, jumping out of her way and doubling up with glee: "Honest, I didn't. Cross my heart, hope I may die, I didn't."

"Cham, you're lyin' like a fish. I got an ant down my dress. Ou, it tickles!"

"I'll catch it, Phoebe."

"Boys, don't look now. I'm goin' fishin' . . . Ou . . . I got him. O it's just a leaf . . . O he looked. He's a cool one. I'm goin' to smack your face."

"Catch me first, Phoebe deary," cried Cham, running off up a path. She lit out after him. "Look out for your dress on them bushes," cried Elise.

"I should worry."

Fanshaw watched the pink dress disappear down the path, going bright and dull in the patches of sun and shadow among the maple trees. Their laughing rose to a shriek and stopped suddenly. Fanshaw and Elise looked at each other.

"Children must play," said Fanshaw stiffly.

"What time are we goin' home, d'you know?" said Elise yawning.

"You don't like — er — picnicking."

There was a silence. From down river came the splash of paddles and the sound of a phonograph playing "O Waltz Me Around Again Willie." Fanshaw sat still in the same position with his knees drawn up to his chin, as if paralyzed. With tightening throat he managed to say:

"What can they be doing . . . They don't seem to be coming back."

"Ask me something hard," said the blue girl jeeringly.

Fanshaw felt himself blushing. He clasped his hands tighter round his knees. He felt the sweat making little beads on his forehead. Ought he to kiss her? He didn't want to kiss her with her rouged lips and her blonde hair all fuzzy like that, peroxide probably. A fool to come along, anyway. What on earth shall I say to her?

She got to her feet.

"I'm goin' to walk around a bit . . . Ou, my foot's gone to sleep."

Fanshaw jumped up as if a spring had been released inside him.

"Which way shall we go?"

"I guess we'd better go the other way," said Elise tittering and smoothing out the back of her fluffy dress.

They walked beside the water; along the path were mashed cracker boxes, orange peel, banana skins. The river was full of canoes now. Above the sound of paddles occasionally splashing and the grinding undertone of phonographs came now and then a giggle or a man's voice shouting. Elise was humming "School Days," walking ahead of him with mincing steps. He saw a woodpecker run down the trunk of an oak.

"Look, there's a woodpecker." Elise walked ahead, still humming, now and then taking a little dance step. "It's a red-headed woodpecker." As she still paid no attention, he walked behind her without saying anything, listening to the tapping of the woodpecker in the distance, watching her narrow hips sway under the pleats of her dress as she walked. A rank, heavy smell came from the muddy banks. He looked at his watch. Only four o'clock. She caught sight of the watch and turned round.

"What time is it, please?"

"It's only four o'clock. . . . We have lots of time yet."

"Don't I realize it? Say, what's the name of this old damn-fool park?"

"Norumbega."

"It's never again for me," she cried giggling. Then all at once she dropped down on the ground at the foot of a tree and began to sob with her dress all puffed up about her.

"But what's the matter?"

"Nothing . . . My God, shut up and go away!" she whined through her sobs.

"All right, I'll go and see nobody swipes the canoe."

Biting his lips, Fanshaw started slowly back along the path.

.　　.　　.　　.

The air of the examination room was heavy and smelt of chalk. Through the open windows from the yard drifted the whir of lawnmowers and the fragrance of cut grass. Fanshaw had just finished three hundred words on "The Classical Subject in Racine." He found himself listening to the lawnmowers and breathing in the rifts of warm sweetness that came from the mashed grass. It almost made him cry. The spring of Freshman year, the end of Freshman year. The fragrance of years mown down by the whirring, singsong blades. He stared at the printed paper: Comparative Literature 1. Devote one hour to one of the following subjects . . . And the girl in the blue dress had plunked herself down under a tree and cried. What a fool I was to walk away like that. "What's that perfume?" "Mary Garden," she had said, and her grey glance had wriggled into his eyes and his hands had moved softly across the fluffy dress, feeling the whalebone corsets under the blue fluff. No, that's when I helped her back into the canoe. Elise Montmorency, the girl in the blue dress, had plunked herself down under a tree and cried because he hadn't kissed her. But he had kissed her; he had come back and lain on the grass beside her and kissed her till she wriggled in his arms under the blue fluff and the sunshine had lain a hot tingling coverlet over his back.

He sat stiff in his chair staring in front of him, his hands clasped tight under the desk. All his flesh was hot and tingling. He breathed deep of the smell of cut grass that drifted in through the window, under the smell of mashed grass and cloverblossoms, sweetness, heaviness, Mary Garden perfume. Gee, am I going to faint?

> And there on beds of violets blue
> And freshblown roses washed in dew,
> Filled her with thee a daughter fair
> So buxom blithe and debonair.

Fanshaw felt the blood suddenly rush to his face. If the proctor sees me blushing he'll think I've been cribbing. He hung his head over his paper again.

Devote one hour . . . She was common and said ain't. That was not the sort of girl. He was glad he hadn't kissed her . . . The spotless armor of Sir Galahad. Maybe that was temptation. Maybe he'd resisted temptation. And lastly, Mr. Crownsterne's voice was booming in his ears: And lastly, fellows, let me wish each one of you the best and loveliest and most flower-like girl in the world for your wife. A lot old Crowny knew about it. Marriage was for ordinary people, but for him, love, two souls pressed each to each, consumed with a single fire.

> Not the angels in heaven above
> Nor the demons down under the sea
> Can ever dissever my soul from the soul
> Of the beautiful Annabel Lee.

The moth's kiss, dearest. He was in a boat with red sails, in the stern of a boat with red lateen sails and she was in his arms and her hair was fluffy against his cheek, and the boat leapt on the waves and they were drenched in droning fragrance off the island to windward, wet rose gardens, clover fields, fresh-cut hay, tarry streets, Mary Garden perfume. That perfume was common like saying ain't.

Sudden panic seized him. The clock was at twenty-five past. Gosh, only thirty-five minutes for those two questions! The nib of his fountain pen was dry. He shook a drop out on the floor before he began to write.

John Dos Passos, *Streets of Night* (New York, 1923).

Lucius Beebe

NOTES ON A DRY GENERATION

(1927)

Lucius Beebe went to Harvard for a while (1924–25) and to Yale for a while (1926). He got his A.B. degree at Harvard (1927) and still later in life was elected an honorary member of Princeton's Triangle Club. These academic facts are cited to show Beebe's varied intellectual taste which has run to such things as poetry, criticism, food and drink, local history and legend, and railroading (with a camera). The comments following were written at the time of the Harvard Tercentenary when Beebe found Harvard little changed from his day. The gilded youth of Cambridge was still in possession of the Ritz, of Locke's, and of The Country Club.

AN EARLIER and wittier commentator once made the remark that "Harvard University was pleasantly and conveniently situated in the bar-room of Parker's in School Street," and what was to all intents and purposes the focal point of valor and the humanities as the class of 1927 went about absorbing the higher learning (through the agency of what always seemed a sort of process of osmosis) was only a short distance down the line in Winter Place. In other words, the University, ever aware of change and prompt to keep abreast of the latest movement, contrived, in the interval between Josh Billings * and Bob Benchley, to move precisely four city blocks, where, of course, it again found itself in a saloon.

I refer, as you have surmised, to the most gracious and comforting tavern that ever survived an era of outrage, pillage and Federal barbarism, Frank Locke's Winter Place Wine Rooms. It has been variously known as the Dutchman's, as Winter Place Restaurant, as Locke's and as Locke-Ober's, and even, to irreverent undergraduates, as the Nekked Lady, but by any other name it smells the same; fragrant and holy in the souvenirs of many discerning men of several generations.

Jack Wheelwright (the elder) once remarked that he had designed the West Boston Bridge "so that he could get from State Street to the bar in the Lampoon Building, get stiff and back to State Street again in half an hour." The undergraduates of the middle twenties improved on this short sighted formula. Being youths of vision, their design for living called for using the West Boston Bridge to get to Winter Place, get crocked and get back to Cambridge in four years. Once established in the shadow of the mahogany bar beneath the cheerful aspect of the nude on the wall, they found themselves strangely persuaded by the philosophy of Dr. Holmes's Beacon Street young lady who, when urged to go abroad, remarked "Why should I travel when I'm already there?"

During the years of the Great Foolishness Locke's never sold a drop, although now and then a waiter maintained a private concession without the knowledge of the management. Massachusetts, apparently subscribing to the appalling bigotry of the times, was willing to place the citizens of the Commonwealth in double jeopardy by maintaining a "Baby Volstead Act" while in more patriotic New York posses of outraged burghers were gouging the eyes out of Federal officers and throwing their carcasses into refuse barrels in Fifty-second Street. Bostonians wrote letters to the editor of the *Transcript* and drank in the butler's pantry at home.

*See page 329.

But if Locke's never violated the law, that is a far cry from saying nobody ever felt better after leaving the premises, and diners always seemed to arrive burdened with parcels, brief cases, and even swag-bellied portmanteaux, which were placed under the table, and for the rest of the evening caused any shifting of feet to be accompanied with the ginger precision of a cigar smoker in a powder mill.

Locke's was (and for the matter of that, still is) a temple of robust and masculine good cheer, a resort of dining *au serviette au cou* where the menu is overwhelmed with Kansas City steaks, lobster thermidor, sweetbreads Eugénie, shad, mutton chops, Cape oysters, jack rabbit stews and pigeon pies. If you didn't order a full portion from every classification on the bill of fare, from shellfish, through turtle soup, flounder, rack of lamb and a fancy dessert, Nick Stuhl, the manager, knew there was something the matter with you. It took a lot of Jamaica rum to float what you were supposed to eat in Winter Place, and all the management, from Emil Camus, the urbane proprietor, to Charlie, Maurice and Eddie, the waiters, took an interest in what you ate. When you had placed your order Charlie would lay a knowing finger along his nose and say: "The chef, he works but very hard tonight," and you sent out a highball glass of straight rum for the chef and whoever else Charlie favored in the offices out back. And if it was a special occasion and you were drinking wine, you asked Mr. Camus to have a glass, but you hardly dared accost so august a personage as the proprietor with anything less than hock.

The undergraduate group which most favored Locke's was a gathering of chivalry known as the Michael Mullins Chowder and Marching Society which met at unstated but frequent intervals in a private room upstairs. Whatever secret ends the order may have served, they included neither marching nor the consumption of chowder. The members invariably arrived in top hats and evening tail coats, and a sort of self-limiting rule of the organization was that each new member provide a lavish champagne dinner for the already elected members. As the capacity of the adherents of Mullins was apparently unbounded, this served to keep membership within decently exclusive limits.

Next to the delights of Locke's on winter nights when the wind hastened down the Avenue in a tangible, gelid wall and the Arlington Street roundsman found it expedient to seek the shelter of the Sears's carriage house, was an ageless gaffer named Freddy. Freddy was the proprietor of the last of the town's horse drawn hacks, a valiant Jehu and a Bostonian of note whose origins antedated by a generation or so the brave days when Sam Shaw, miraculous in a white top hat and fawn paddock coat, was accustomed to tool a gleaming red and yellow coach to the Country Club races in Brookline, or when Tommy Taylor's "Whitechapel" hansom cab was a marvelous thing to behold. Freddy rolled up and down the Boulevards of Boston, ancient, blasphemous and trailing clouds of glory from Honest Parker Shannon's bar, an undismayed coda to the saga of horse-cabs which had its origins two hundred years before in Jonathan Wardell, who held the town's first hackney license and kept his rig on the rank outside the Orange Tree Inn in Hanover Street. Freddy was a figure out of the past whose silver side lamps were an oriflamme of the night. He was, too, a caution.

Nobody ever saw Freddy in a condition even remotely approximating sobriety, but, within the definition of the Scotch magistrate, nobody ever saw him gone in wine. He could always wiggle a finger, and usually he contrived to mount the box of his herdic without the aid of more than a mere handful of assistants. He maintained three equipages: a victoria, a closed coach of the genus growler, and a magnificent arrangement, but rarely brought into service, a coupé on runners known as the "booby," and reserved for the most social snowstorms. To have been wafted home from a ball at the Somerset in the booby, amidst an early morning blizzard, your *chapeau claque* tilted over your nose to avoid smashing against the low roof, the fine snow drifting in over the buffalo robe through the chinks in the door, and your last measure of S. S. Pierce's overproof rum reserved as defense (for you and Freddy) against the elements while crossing the Harvard Bridge is a lyric memory not to be ranked with any of the other exquisite souvenirs of this world.

Nobody knew where Freddy made his headquarters or how he sensed party doings, but he never missed a debutante party along the reaches of the Avenue or a club dinner in Mount Auburn Street. When in the middle twenties the Iroquois Club burned up one night (and a very social fire it was, too, what with the pompiers waited on by a liveried club steward with glasses of chilled champagne), Freddy drove a fiacre load of top hatted youths through the firelines and to a point of vantage just as the roof fell in. "My patrons don't like the set pieces," he told bystanders as the cheering subsided, "so I allus get 'em there for the sky bombs and such!" There was a school of thought which maintained that Charlie Alexander, pontifical society editor of the *Transcript*, kept Freddy posted on major events of the Back Bay calendar.

Nobody ever learned, either, where or how Freddy lived. It was reported that he maintained housekeeping arrangements all the year round in the inner economy of the growler, tethering his horse to the trunk rack and sleeping with his feet out the window. He asserted that he had taught Theodore Roosevelt, while at Harvard, the essentials of boxing, and nobody would have batted an eye if he had claimed to have taught Grant the use of strong waters. For you could pay Freddy in cash or in trade, and six in the morning was entirely apt to find him seated, whip in hand, in your sitting room, his wicked white eyebrows working up and down with delight, as he put away the most amazing quantities of spirits. The fare from Boston to the vicinage of Harvard Square came to approximately a bottle of rye. Heart of oak and watchman of the night, undergraduates will not look upon his like again.

Utopia came to Harvard in 1924 through the agency of John Clement, Bradley Fisk and a dozen gallons of what was generally known as "Medford" rum. John was part proprietor, with Maurice Firuski, of the Dunster House Bookshop when it was located in Mount Auburn Street directly opposite the Phoenix-S. K. Club, and he lived in what then seemed Babylonish elegance in a three-room suite upstairs. Bradley was an undergraduate of some means, many clubs and a vast imagination, who lived round the corner in Apthorp House with Bydie Kilgour and John Rosecranz. The antecedents of the rum were never closely enquired into, but it was reputed to have been the fruit of a raid on a bonded warehouse in South Boston. Whether or not it was authentic Medford spirits nobody we knew was qualified to judge; certainly it was magnificent stuff, uncut, overproof, clear and with the bouquet of a great Cognac. It served its purpose.

The reordering nearer to our hearts' desire of an even then vaguely unsatisfactory world was planned nightly in John's rooms. John and Bradley smoked pipes, and the flue in the stove was a source of perpetual grief, with the result that Utopia was born in an atmosphere suggestive of nothing so much as the Burning of Rome. John was a Vermont Yankee with red hair and yellow Norseman's mustaches, and once it was agreed that he was to be supreme head of the wonderstate, a decision usually unanimously arrived at about midnight, there was nothing left but a few details before we went in town to the Lamb's Club for the night. Our principal thesis, if memory serves, held that central authority existed for maintaining an army, issuing currency against a reserve of proof spirits, and the collection and disposal of garbage. Beyond that we had little use for government, although occasionally Pierre LaRose, mystery man and Merlin of Harvard Yard and a herald of the Catholic Church, was consulted on problems of purely ritual significance. He knew, for instance, about the construction of Savannah Artillery Punch, and there was talk of making him chamberlain of the realm, but nothing much came of it. There were to have been three poet laureates, Barry Bingham, Robert Hillyer and Jack Wheelwright (the younger), but Wheelwright came back from Paris wearing a broad brimmed black hat and reading "transition" and was blackballed after an all night session in the course of which a window was broken and the stovepipe detached from the chimney. The Utopians nearly perished of asphyxiation.

From the Harvard Tercentenary Supplement of the *Boston Herald*, September 13, 1936.

George Weller

ELEVEN O'CLOCK IN NOVEMBER

(1933)

The search for the great American college novel will always come back to George Weller's Not to Eat, Not for Love. *Its prestige has grown rather than dwindled with the years. In 1946 Richard C. Boys called it the "best of all our college novels" and fifteen years after publication Frederick L. Gwynn termed it "the very best of college fiction, and one of the most engaging and thoughtful novels of the interwar period." The author, now a distinguished foreign correspondent and former Nieman Fellow, worked himself through Harvard College with the Class of 1929. He played a little football, waited on table at the Pi Eta Club and in Gore Hall, sold his blood, addressed envelopes for the Harvard University Press, worked afternoons as a tutor and playground supervisor, and even read proof for pay while serving as editorial chairman of the* Crimson. *The result is a remarkably broad picture of Harvard life in the early thirties, and yet character has not been neglected for the sake of the panoramic and historical purposes of the novel. Weller has described his book as an account of "one man's change against the period of Harvard's change." Thus Epes Todd is the leading character, but what happens to Epes is blended with all the happenings of a Harvard year. The brief section "eleven o'clock in November" describes the atmosphere in Cambridge on the morning of a football game. Weller established the pattern of his novel before he began work, and spent a year as a teacher in Arizona thinking about it. The book was started in Vienna in 1931 while Weller was a student at Max Reinhardt's theater school, and the manuscript was completed on the island of Capri in 1932.*

AT THE SIDEDOOR of the Lampoon the stink of the tenement beyond Central Square assaults the nose of circulation manager Waugh. In a smelly cloud above the unwashed boys hangs the rotten clothing smell of being poor, renewed each moment from those who wait, in sweatshirts and gray flannel skullcaps fantastically perforated, for Waugh to give out Lampoons. The Game Number lies piled high beside the door, red, blue, orange, green spluttered on slick white. He reads names. "Corcoran." A tall thin boy with rotten teeth, a baseball shirt with PELICANS showing under the unbuttoned sweater that just hangs on his shoulders, razors himself through the crowd. "What happened to your other four copies at the West Point game? You didn't come back." "I lost two." "Well?" "I say I lost them." "I know, but godammit, the other two?" "They got dirty when it rained." His excuse is amended anonymously by other salesmen. Alexander McCoomb, business manager of the Lampoon, comes suddenly out of the building. "How about a line here?" he says to the boys, grinning at them. They make him a line, and he brushes past circulation manager Waugh with a quick nod.

"What did you put for psycho-physical parallelism?" asks Abraham Eckstein, who lives in a Dorchester threedecker and whose father did piecework in Brooklyn but now owns his own little shop, of Harold Radman, whose father did piecework in the Bronx and now owns platoons of duplicate dwellings near Hell Gate Bridge and is building a skyscraper whose shadow lattices Brooklyn City Hall. Radman, anxious to be away, mumbles in the slurring accent of the Manhattan arriviste, "See you later. Forgot to get my tickets from the H. A. A." They leave the Saturday section in philosophy and part, the janitor locking Emerson Hall behind them.

A man in black about sixty or seventy years old enters Doctor Prentiss' Sever Hall section of first year Italian just as it begins, crosses the room and seats himself quietly at the end of the benches by the windows. Philip Hofstetter watches him, trying to remember what title has been underneath when he has seen the picture of that brown face, so wonderfully seamed with wrinkles. Briggs. Dean Briggs. There were two biographies on sale in the Coop. The new Briggs baseball cage. And before that the biggest dormitory at Radcliffe, Briggs Hall. But who was he, who was Dean Briggs? He was a man who was Dean under Eliot, wasn't he? And who was Eliot? A man who said: "The summer camp is America's greatest single contribution to education." But who was he? who were they?

At 11.17 traffic officer Joe Lang greets traffic officer Joe Doherty, tells him to watch the equipment on the broad driving a big blue boat when she comes out of the corner shoeshine parlor, picks from the traffic box floor the rolled morning paper that the guy in the new Ford about quarter-past nine always passes him, and from a telephone booth in the bank calls his wife. "I'm handling the machine this aft for the captain. On the game squad. Harvard and somebody else. Some big one. It sounds like a real break to me, the captain being in the side car, because all the sergeants are pretty old and next year they'll be needing one that knows all the rules, nothing over the Anderson Bridge after 12.15 and all like that." Emerging through the greasy folding door he looks past the subway entrance islanded in the middle of the Square over toward Straus Hall, but the big blue boat has gone.

Bill Galt, down for the game, stomach feeling dried out from seven hours' dancing, remembers that in Cambridge they call the campus the Yard. Last night he dressed at the chapter house over at Boston Tech, but all the beds there are gone and to change from the wrinklearmed dinner coat in which he was found by a breakfast maid of the Boston Wellesley Club, caved in a wicker chair near the front door innocent and asleep, he now must discover Mower Hall, a fellow named Wells Fargo. He rests his suitcase to buy a feather for his derby. "Red?" "No," he says, and picks one to match his tie. "A quarter," says the vender, "and I hope you beat hell out of them. That's the way we feel about the Hahvad boys."

In an alley behind one of the big garages Teddy has propped up his big board covered with green felt against a hydrant. From a black rubberoid weekend case with the lock broken he takes two big kewpie dolls with lampshade skirts, the crimson and the green, and behind the frilly pink lining of the case he folds away the gray and yellow skirt that the West Point doll wore last week. In rows he pins to the board tin footballs hung on crimson silk, armbands thick-lettered in white felt, hatbands, handkerchiefs, and celluloid dogs with red ribbon plumply sashed. In the top left hand corner he affixes the fishtail banners with their slender reedy varnished standards and under it the wire holder for the bootleg programs. In his pockets he puts two pairs of opera glasses, the gold and the pearl. Through the broken half window of a cellar next the garage he reaches a bending explorative arm, feels around, scans the alley for enemies, then shoves the weekend case inside. Twelve cushions of straw covered with speckly butcher's paper go under one arm and holding the loaded board away from his shapeless blue serge knees he moves slowly out of the alley.

Wells Fargo, sent down from the lyke wake bridge game in the room of Farnsworth the tutor in economics to buy more lemons and a piece of ice in two paper bags, is addressed in the Square by a tall thin boy in a baseball shirt who tries to sell him a Lampoon and a football program. He is reminded that there is a football game, that he has not breakfasted except at four that morning, that he has not lunched, that none of the lyke wake bridge players is aware that flesh is soon to be torn asunder in the crimson name. He considers them: unbelieving, cynical, fractious, embittered, dubitative, rejective not reflective, subjunctive (the mood of doubt), deniers and repudiators all. Only in proof's august presence would their tongues, loose all night in the room of Timothy Farnsworth, cleave to their mouths. Seeing, they believe; unseeing, they heckle. His lips move: "I, Wells the winged, rainbowcolored messenger, manytongued, I saw the lemons pyramided beside the morning paper, I saw the lemons and I turned aside, and I bought of the football Lampoons two, and of the unofficial football programs two." Hymning through the Yard the merit of his deed he returns and first giving them gifts he breaks asunder that game of bridge, for he will sleep in his tent ere wardrums roll.

From a window of Claverly open on Linden Street pips a clarinet:

> Look where the crimson banners fly,
> Hark to the sound of tramping feet,
> There is a host approaching nigh,
> Harvard is marching up the street;

breathes a moment, and then begins:

> Hit the line for Harvard
> For Harvard wins today,
> And we'll show the sons of Eli
> That the crimson still holds sway.

A man in a white sailor hat, crimson sweater and white flannels comes to the window and cranes around the reddish cornice to ask the man in the next room the right time.

Two men stand on the edge of the Westmorly pool rubbing themselves dry. "Pretty lucky to be able to swim in your dormitory," says the visitor, watching the green waves grow calm. "I know," answered the host. "There's a story about Ann Pennington and this pool, but no one seems to tell it the same way."

Tex decides to wait until tomorrow to close his trunk. It's liable to be right cold in their big gray stadium, and he'd better tote his furcoat anyway, might have to wear it as far as Nashville. They and their hour examinations! Ought to give a boy a chance on a long pull, not bust him because he gets three Ds and a couple of Es the first time, before he's hardly got his parcels undone. Hope he doesn't meet Mr. Ogden from the Harvard Club of Dallas first off. Along about January-February he'll end up at State, just as he always thought. Anyway he met a lot of nice boys and that's something.

Of the two student waiters, Al and Wheatman, eating cream soup in the basement kitchen of the clubhouse while John the head student waiter hustles rice pudding with raisins to the last few members hastening gameward, Al the big redhead thinks about the members and Wheatman the sharpnosed blonde little Yankee thinks about the cream soup. They never talk while they eat. The redhead is always wondering whether the members think it is fresh for him to call some of them by their first names. The little Yankee watches for John's trips into the diningroom, because he does not like to blow healingly upon his soup spoon when John is around. And John, for the sixth time trying to drive the chef's cat out of the dark corners of the diningroom, is saying to himself: "The hardest thing I know is not to be a snob, either a snob downward, or a snob upward."

Six freshmen, two sophomores, three Business School and two Law School men are eating round mosqueshaped buns and drinking coffee inside the gates of Soldiers Field. Several wear the green pasteboard badges of head ushers. The sophomores are discussing whether it is better to see the game in full as a head usher or to earn a couple of dollars as ticket taker and miss the first half. Fallon, a law student who says he has been ticket taking for five years, tells them that all rainy day games and some others, all the big games anyway, begin with a kicking duel for the first quarter. Better take two dollars whenever they can get it for two hours' soft work.

In Mower Hall Mrs. Magillicuddy goes to the iron rail of the landing and sees that it is Mr. Fargo ascending, who lives in number 17.

Hat over his eyes, hands deep in the sagged pockets of his winter overcoat, the fifty yearold man is on the corner saying in a voice low, intimate and whining, "Tickets, boys? Tickets?" Past him go all the twenty yearold men, luncheonbound before the game. They exchange stories of the blacklisted who, having sold their tickets to a speculator, will never again be able to see a Harvard game. But the fifty yearold man, safety razor salesman, shell and pea player, sideshow barker, dip, counterman, bum, concession artist, skating rink ticketman, hijacker, filling station handyman, shillaber, marathon dance timekeeper, gobetween, bookmaker, though it is almost too late for him to hope more from this day or more from this lifetime, goes on whining while he watches the traffic cop, "Tickets, boys? Tickets?"

And then as east in Boston harbor, in Kendall and Central Squares, in the Brighton stockyards the screaming wild white gnomes of steam dance around the sweatdrops on the whistles the sullen boom of Harvard's deep bell in the cupola of Harvard Hall, over all the hurriers in the restless Square, over all the walkers in the peaceful Yard, tolls down the cinder of the halfday, down into memory, down into forgetfulness.

George Weller, *Not to Eat, Not for Love* (New York, 1933).

Alistair Cooke

A LESSON FOR YALE

(1951)

Despite Harvard's historical indebtedness to British tradition, cricket as played on Smith Field at the Harvard Business School and cricket as played at Lord's bear very little resemblance. Just to check this point the Manchester Guardian sent its American correspondent to Cambridge one May afternoon, and he duly made his report under the heading "A Lesson for Yale . . . Magnificent Losers — by An Innings." Alistair Cooke, who briefly attended both Harvard and Yale, has been commentator on American affairs for the British Broadcasting Corporation since 1938 and, since 1948, Chief Correspondent in the United States for the Guardian. Before joining the Guardian's American staff in 1945, he was special correspondent on American Affairs for The Times. He is the author of A Generation on Trial: U.S.A. v. Alger Hiss (1950) and of Letters from America (1951).

THE RIVALRY of Yale and Harvard is going into its third century and has been bloodied down the years by many a student riot and pitched battle on each other's campus, to say nothing of the more routine muscle-matching of football games.

By the end of the last century the typical Yale man had evolved into a human type as recognisable as a Cossack or the Pitcairn skull, and there was a tense period in the late twenties and early thirties when Harvard could no longer bear close proximity with these well-developed anthropoids and primly refused to play them at anything. The football and chess fixtures were summarily cancelled. But by now even a Harvard man has heard of "one world," though of course he recognises no obligation to belong to it. So today, in a wild lunge of global goodwill, Harvard recalled the sons of Elihu Yale to their common heritage by suggesting a revival of the ancient joust known as cricket.

Not for 44 years have Yale and Harvard together attempted anything so whimsical. But a far-sighted alumnus lately gave $100 to revive the match and encouraged Harvard men to learn how the other half lives. Accordingly, with this bequest, pads and bats were fetched from Bermuda and Canada, and a roll of coconut matting was bought wholesale in Philadelphia. These props were assembled to-day on Smith Field, which is a dandelion enclosure lying west of the Harvard football stadium.

Here at 1.30 in the afternoon came ten of the visiting Yale men, various sets of white and grey gentlemen's pantings, a score-book and a couple of blazers for the sake of morale. Fifteen minutes later, and two hundred yards away, the Harvard team arrived in two old Chevrolets and a Cadillac. They carried the matting out to a weedy airstrip devoid of dandelions; stretched it out and pegged it down; made Indian signs at the glowering Yale men and, discovering that they understood English, formally challenged them to a match; spun a dime, won, and chose to go in first.

The eleventh Yale man was still missing and the Harvard captain, a mellifluous-spoken gentleman from Jamaica, offered to lend them a Harvard man. The Yale captain suspected a trap and said they would wait. Ten minutes later the eleventh man came puffing in, swinging from elm to elm. Everything was set. It was a cloudless day. It had been 92 the day before, but Providence obliged with a 35-degree drop overnight and we nestled down into a perfect English May day — sunny and green, with a brisk wind. The eleven spectators stomped and blew on their hands at the field's edge. And the game began.

Mr. Conboy and Mr. Cheek put on the purchased pads. Conboy took centre and faced the high lobbing off breaks of Mr. Foster, who delivered six of these nifties and was about to deliver a seventh but saw that Mr. Cheek had turned his back and was off on a stroll around the wicket. This mystery turned into a midfield conference at which it was found out that Yale expected to play an eight-ball over and Harvard a six. An Englishman on the Harvard side kindly acquainted the Yale men with the later history of cricket, and they settled for a six-ball over.

This shrewd act of gamesmanship effectively rattled the Harvard team for a while, and Conboy was soon out for three and Cheek for a duck. But Frank Davies, from Trinidad, knew a sophisticated play that shortly demoralized the Yale men. He came in slowly, hefted his pads, squinted at the coconut matting, patted it, rubbed his right shoulder, exercised his arm and, while the Yale men were still waiting for him to get set, started to cut and drive the Yale bowling all over the field.

Yale retorted by occasionally bowling an over of seven balls and once an over of five. It had no effect. They were now thoroughly cowed by Davies's professional air — once he cleverly feigned a muscle spasm and had the Yale side clustered round him terrified at the prospect of a doctor's bill. They were so trembly by now that they thought it only decent to drop any fly ball that came their way. Davies hooked a ball high to leg, but the Yale man obligingly stumbled, pawed the air, and gave a masterly — and entirely successful — performance of a man missing an easy catch.

Davies tried another hook with the same result, but the agreement was now so firmly understood that no Yale man would hold anything. Davies accordingly cut with flashing elbows, secure in the new-found knowledge that considered as a slip fielder a Yale man is a superlative bridge player. Davies went on to cut fine and cut square and drive the ball several times crack against the cement wall on which two mystified little boys were sitting. This, it was decided, was a boundary, and the scorer was told to put down four runs.

Davies did some more shrugs and lunges with his shoulder-blades, and, though there was a fairly constant trickle of bating partners at the other end, Davies had scored never less than two-thirds of the total. Suddenly he let go with a clean drive to mid-on for two and the astonished scorer discovered that the total was now 68 and Davies had reached his half-century.

There had been so far a regrettable absence of English spirit but Bruce Cheek, a civil servant, formerly of Peterhouse, Cambridge, was signed up to repair this omission by shouting "Well played, sir!" — an utterly alien sound to the two Boston small fry on the cement wall. This cued the growing crowd to rise and applaud the incomparable Davies. All fourteen of them joined in the ovation.

Ten minutes later the Rev. Bill Baker, a Baptist from Manchester, went in to receive his baptism of fire from Foster, who had suddenly found his off-break again. The result was that Mr. Baker was walking back right after walking out. Then Davies hit a short ball into a Yale man's hands. He failed to drop it in time. And the whole side was out. Harvard, 102 — Davies, 70.

The two small fry dropped off the cement wall and came into the field to investigate the ritual. One of them stayed in the outfield and the tougher one came on and asked a question of the retreating umpire. It was a simple question. It was: "What game you playin', mister?" He was told, and turned round and bawled: "Cricket!" at his pal. The pal shrugged his little shoulders and went off and picked up two Boston terriers from somewhere, for no reason that anyone discovered then or since. They did manage to invade the field during the Yale innings and had to be shooed off.

Meanwhile we had taken tea, from a steel thermos about the size of a city gas tank. From nowhere a parson arrived, wearing an old straw caddie. It was a heart-warming sight, and I found myself mumbling through a tear the never-to-be forgotten lines ". . . some corner of a foreign field that is forever Lipton's."

With a knightliness that cannot be too highly praised, Yale maintained the dogged pretense that they were playing cricket. It entitled their going out to the matting and back again in a slow though spasmodic procession. The continuity of this parade was assured by one Jehingar Mugaseth, a dark supple young man from Bombay, who had one of those long, beautiful, unwinding runs that would have petrified even the nonchalant Mr. Davies. At the other end was a thin, blond man with another long run, an American who distrusted breaks but managed a corkscrew baseball swerve in mid-air.

Between them the Yale team fell apart, and your reporter had no

sooner looked down to mark "McIntosh caught" than he looked up to
see Allen's middle stump sailing like a floating coffin past the wicket-
keeper's right ear. Yale were suddenly all out — for 34. They followed on,
more briskly this time — they were catching on to the essential tempo
of the game — and were out the second time in record time for 24 runs.
It was all over at 6.40.

No excuses were offered from the Yale team. They had fine English
names — such as Grant, West, Allen, Foster, Parker, and Norton — and
true to the Old Country traditions they lost magnificently. Nobody mentioned the mean Colonial skill recruited by the Harvard side. Nobody,
that is, except a Yale man who dictated to me the exact tribal composition
of the Harvard team: one Indian, one Jamaican, one Australian, one
Egyptian, one Argentinian, one from Trinidad, one from Barbados, a
Swiss New Yorker, two Englishmen, and a stranger from Connecticut.

But after all it's not the winning that matters, is it? Or is it? It's — to
coin a word — the amenities that count: the smell of the dandelions, the
puff of the pipe, the click of the bat (when Harvard are batting), the rain
on the neck, the chill down the spine, the slow, exquisite coming on of
sunset and dinner and rheumatism.

Manchester Guardian, May 21, 1951.

VI

HER SOLITARY SONS

At the age of sixteen I turned my steps towards these venerable halls, bearing in mind, as I have ever since done, that I had two ears and but one tongue. . . Suffice it to say, that though bodily I have been a member of Harvard University, heart and soul I have been far away among the scenes of my boyhood. Those hours that should have been devoted to study have been spent in roaming the woods, and exploring the lakes and streams of my native village.

HENRY D. THOREAU (1837)

Henry Adams

THE EDUCATION OF A HARVARD MAN

(1856 and 1907)

*Until the publication of Ernest Samuels' The Young Henry Adams in
1948, those who had read the autobiographical Education of Henry
Adams only knew that the bitter and disappointed author looked back on
his life at Harvard with no dislike but little enthusiasm. It was not ever
thus, for the undergraduate Henry Adams showed himself to be as properly sentimental and youthful in his enthusiasm as the older Henry Adams
pictured himself failing and intellectually misplaced. Adams — the grandson and great grandson of an American president — was the son of Charles
Francis Adams. He was for seven years Assistant Professor of History at
Harvard (1870–1877), and his historical contribution was the History of
the United States of America [1801 to 1817]. His reflections on his college room come from The Harvard Magazine (1856); his mature conclusions about Harvard from the Education (1918).*

MY OLD ROOM

IT IS DUSTY and dirty and dingy. Spiders have spun their webs on
the ceiling. The paper is faded with age, and discolored with
stains of many hues. Long experience in Cambridge has taken
away from my furniture all that was breakable, and my chairs
are marked deeply with the initials of half my classmates and a host of
friends. Queer odors linger about the closets and the bedrooms, as though
their former contents had been embalmed and laid on the shelves, like
the urns in the old Roman tombs.

In winter the winds howl around me, and rush over my head, without the slightest regard to the walls which should keep them away. No
amount of heat yet attained will prevent the water which stands in my
pitcher from freezing inches deep in the cold weather of the winter term.
In short, my room is the coldest, the dirtiest, and the gloomiest in Cambridge.

But what do I care for the cold, so long as a good fire burns in the
grate? Or what do I care for the dust that whitens my pictures and hats

and books, or the stains that mark my walls, or the cracks that run through the ceiling, so long as they stay on the walls and ceiling, and give no discomfort to me? Or what do I care for the darkness and gloom, when, in the long December evenings, the cannel snaps and blazes in the fire-place, and shines merrily on the gilded books that line my shelves? . . .

My room is in an old house which seems to have witnessed guest after guest come within its doors when Freshmen, full of ambition and hope, and leave them at last when Seniors, downcast and disappointed. . .

In this old room, have I lived while years have passed by. In the winter I have set up my household gods upon this hearth, and many a time when in the bright, frosty forenoons the sun has cheerfully shone into my room, and the fire blazed warmly in the grate, I have asked myself whether life here is not as full of enjoyment as life can be, and whether negative happiness, the absence of all real discomfort, is not, after all, the best that is granted to man. . .

The philosophy of College rooms! How many misunderstand it! How many take their degrees, and depart, without having such an idea enter their heads! Yet few satires would be more bitter than a history of the thoughts of the inhabitants of these rooms, of their actions, and of their failures or successes, as the case may be. How great a proportion of those who have left their names on the catalogues should we find acknowledging that here they have wasted their time, have thrown away their opportunities and have disappointed their friends? Not that they have done wrong. No. They have simply done nothing.

But College has been very much abused; much more so than it deserves. Stories of the past — told by fathers and grandfathers over their walnuts and wine, or handed down in venerable manuscripts, or laughed at in the works of brilliant and famous writers for centuries back — have cast a shade of doubt upon the respectability of College life. Visions of midnight suppers and Deipnosophoi Clubs, spectres of irreligion and blasphemy, of utter and irretrievable corruption, of sensuality and brutalizing debauchery, in the imaginations of very many who live near and among us, would rightly be the only recollections that a College room could call up. They insist upon condemning the whole upon the testimony against a few, and must have it that I am thoughtless and extravagant, because such may have been the vices of my predecessors.

All students know that these ideas are mistaken ones. We all know that dissipation is the exception, and not the rule. Here and there a person may be led away, or lead himself away. The bright air-castle that his friends built for him may be undermined. That great column of fire and cloud that led him forward always, when he first trod these College paths, the vast outline of his hopes filled in by his boyish ambition, may be overthrown and vanish for ever. But was a rational system ever invented that admitted of no failure? Did ever the most earnest enthusiast, even in his wildest conceptions of universal happiness, imagine a world where temptation should exist, and yet no sin? With such a system Paradise would indeed be regained.

One of the common systems of education is little better than another. If the College is dangerous and hurtful, the store or the counting-room is as bad, or worse. Fortune does not favor alone their occupants, but her cornucopia showers its gifts equally upon all men. The standard of morality, which some say is so low among us, is not raised by confinement to the counter and the ledger. Temptation and vice are citizens of the world, and wander at will, — no more confined within College walls than shut away from monks and nuns by their deep vows, or by the bolts and bars of their cloisters.

I am about leaving my old room to seek another resting-place, and I hope a better one. It has been very pleasant to me, however, and I am very sorry to go. To me it will always be haunted by my companions who have been there, by the books that I have read there, by the pleasure and the pain that I have felt there, and by a laughing group of bright, fresh faces, that have rendered it sunny in my eyes for ever. I have learned there what College really is. I have learned there one part of the great secret of life. I have learned, too, however late, that College rank is *not* a humbug, as some pretend; also, that nothing can be done without study, though some suppose that "smartness" is sufficient. If a boy appreciated all this before he entered College, his life there might be a success, and not, what it usually is, a failure.

And so I have bidden my room good-by. I have spent my last evening there. I have studied my last lesson there. I have seen the pictures taken down from the walls, and the carpet torn up from the floor. Since I entered it, the world has not stood still. Many of the greatest events of the century will be associated in my mind with my old room. . .

The Harvard Magazine, September 1856.

THE GRADUATE HAD FEW STRONG PREJUDICES

The next regular step was Harvard College. He was more than glad to go. For generation after generation, Adamses and Brookses and Boylstons and Gorhams had gone to Harvard College, and although none of them, as far as known, had ever done any good there, or thought himself the better for it, custom, social ties, convenience, and, above all, economy, kept each generation in the track. Any other education would have required a serious effort, but no one took Harvard College seriously. All went there because their friends went there, and the College was their ideal of social self-respect.

Harvard College, as far as it educated at all, was a mild and liberal school, which sent young men into the world with all they needed to make respectable citizens, and something of what they wanted to make useful ones. Leaders of men it never tried to make. Its ideals were altogether different. The Unitarian clergy had given to the College a character of moderation, balance, judgment, restraint, what the French called *mesure*; excellent traits, which the College attained with singular success, so that its graduates could commonly be recognized by the stamp, but such a type of character rarely lent itself to autobiography. In effect, the school created a type but not a will. Four years of Harvard College, if successful, resulted in an autobiographical blank, a mind on which only a water-mark had been stamped.

The stamp, as such things went, was a good one. The chief wonder of education is that it does not ruin everybody concerned in it, teachers and taught. Sometimes in after life, Adams debated whether in fact it had not ruined him and most of his companions, but, disappointment apart, Harvard College was probably less hurtful than any other university then in existence. It taught little, and that little ill, but it left the mind open, free from bias, ignorant of facts, but docile. The graduate had few strong prejudices. He knew little, but his mind remained supple, ready to receive knowledge.

The Education of Henry Adams (Boston and New York: Houghton Mifflin Company, 1918).

W. E. Burghardt Du Bois

THAT OUTER WHITER WORLD OF HARVARD
(c. 1890)

One of Harvard's most famous Negro alumni is W. E. B. Du Bois, who graduated from the College in 1890 and received the doctorate of philosophy in political science in 1895. Now in his mid-eighties, a noted teacher of economics and history, Dr. Du Bois is a convinced disciple of Marxian socialism and insists on unity of racial action in carrying out the social reforms which he feels are necessary before the Negro will ever attain full freedom. From 1910 to 1933 Dr. Du Bois edited The Crisis, *a magazine devoted to the social betterment of the Negro. He also served as director of publicity and research for the American Association for the Advancement of Colored People but resigned in disagreement in 1933 over the direction which he felt the Association's policies should take. Since that time he has been head of the sociology department at Atlanta University. He is the author of many books, largely scholarly interpretations of various Negro problems, but they include his "essay toward an autobiography of a race concept,"* Dusk of Dawn (1940), *which outlines his radical*

*philosophy. "I was not and am not a communist," Dr. Du Bois has asserted.
"I do not believe in the dogma of inevitable revolution in order to right
economic wrong. I think war is worse than hell, and that it seldom or
never forwards the advance of the world."*

I WAS HAPPY at Harvard, but for unusual reasons. One of these unusual
circumstances was my acceptance of racial segregation. Had I gone from
Great Barrington high school directly to Harvard I would have sought
companionship with my white fellows and been disappointed and embittered by a discovery of social limitations to which I had not been
used. But I came by way of Fisk and the South and there I had accepted
and embraced eagerly the companionship of those of my own color. It
was, of course, no final end. Eventually with them and in mass assault,
led by culture, we were going to break down the boundaries of race;
but at present we were banded together in a great crusade and happily
so. Indeed, I suspect that the joy of full human intercourse without res-
ervations and annoying distinctions, made me all too willing to consort
with mine own and to disdain and forget as far as was possible that
outer, whiter world.

Naturally it could not be entirely forgotten, so that now and then I
plunged into it, joined its currents and rose or fell with it. The joining
was sometimes a matter of social contact. I escorted colored girls, and as
pretty ones as I could find, to the vesper exercises and the class day and
commencement social functions. Naturally we attracted attention and
sometimes the shadow of insult as when in one case a lady seemed determined to mistake me for a waiter. A few times I attempted to enter student organizations, but was not greatly disappointed when the expected
refusals came. My voice, for instance, was better than the average. The
glee club listened to it but I was not chosen a member. It posed the re-
curring problem of a "nigger" on the team.

In general, I asked nothing of Harvard but the tutelage of teachers
and the freedom of the library. I was quite voluntarily and willingly outside its social life. I knew nothing and cared nothing for fraternities and
clubs. Most of those which dominated the Harvard life of my day were
unknown to me even by name. I asked no fellowship of my fellow students. I found friends and most interesting and inspiring friends among
the colored folk of Boston and surrounding places. With them I carried
on lively social intercourse, but one which involved little expenditure of
money. I called at their homes and ate at their tables. We danced at
private parties. We went on excursions down the Bay. Once, with a group
of colored students gathered from surrounding institutions, we gave Aris-
tophanes' "The Birds" in a colored church.

So that of the general social intercourse on the campus I consciously missed nothing. Some white students made themselves known to me and a few, a very few, became life-long friends. Most of them, even of my own more than three hundred classmates, I knew neither by sight nor name. Among my Harvard classmates many made their mark in life: Norman Hapgood, Robert Herrick, Herbert Croly, George A. Dorsey, Homer Folks, Augustus Hand, James Brown Scott, and others. I knew practically none of these. For the most part I do not doubt that I was voted a somewhat selfish and self-centered "grind" with a chip on my shoulder and a sharp tongue.

Something of a certain inferiority complex was possibly present: I was desperately afraid of not being wanted; of intruding without invitation; of appearing to desire the company of those who had no desire for me. I should have been pleased if most of my fellow students had desired to associate with me; if I had been popular and envied. But the absence of this made me neither unhappy nor morose. I had my "island within" and it was a fair country.

Only once or twice did I come to the surface of college life. First, by careful calculation, I found that I needed the cash of one of the Boylston prizes to piece out my year's expenses. I got it through winning a second oratorical prize. The occasion was noteworthy by the fact that the first prize went to a black classmate of mine, Clement Morgan. He and I became fast friends and spent a summer giving readings along the North Shore to help our college costs. Later Morgan became the center of a revolt within the college. By unwritten rule, all of the honorary offices of the class went to Bostonians of Back Bay. No Westerner, Southerner, Jew, nor Irishman, much less a Negro, had thought of aspiring to the honor of being class day official. But in 1890, after the oratorial contest, the students of the class staged an unexpected revolt and elected Morgan as class orator. There was national surprise and discussion and later several smaller Northern colleges elected colored class orators.

This cutting of myself off from my fellows did not mean unhappiness nor resentment. I was in my early young manhood, unusually full of high spirits and humor. I thoroughly enjoyed life. I was conscious of understanding and power, and conceited enough still to think, as in high school, that they who did not know me were the losers, not I. On the other hand, I do not think that my classmates found in me anything personally objectionable. I was clean, not well-dressed but decently clothed. Manners I regarded as more or less superfluous and deliberately cultivated a certain brusquerie. Personal adornment I regarded as pleasing but not important. I was in Harvard but not of it and realized all the irony of "Fair Harvard." I sang it because I liked the music.

The Harvard of 1888 was an extraordinary aggregation of great men. Not often since that day have so many distinguished teachers been together in one place and at one time in America. There were William James, the psychologist; Palmer in ethics; Royce and Santayana in philosophy; Shaler in geology; and Hart in history. There were Francis Child, Charles Eliot Norton, Justin Winsor, and John Trowbridge; Goodwin, Taussig, and Kittredge. The president was the cold, precise but exceedingly just and efficient Charles William Eliot, while Oliver Wendell Holmes and James Russell Lowell were still alive and emeriti.

By good fortune, I was thrown into direct contact with many of these men. I was repeatedly a guest in the house of William James; he was my friend and guide to clear thinking; I was a member of the Philosophical Club and talked with Royce and Palmer; I sat in an upper room and read Kant's *Critique* with Santayana; Shaler invited a Southerner, who objected to sitting by me, out of his class; I became one of Hart's favorite pupils and was afterwards guided by him through my graduate course and started on my work in Germany.

It was a great opportunity for a young man and a young American Negro, and I realized it. I formed habits of work rather different from those of most of the other students. I burned no midnight oil. I did my studying in the daytime and had my day parceled out almost to the minute. I spent a great deal of time in the library and did my assignments with thoroughness and with prevision of the kind of work I wanted to do later. I have before me a theme which I wrote October 3, 1890, for Barrett Wendell, then the great pundit of Harvard English. I said:

> Spurred by my circumstances, I have always been given to systematically planning my future, not indeed without many mistakes and frequent alterations, but always with what I now conceive to have been a strangely early and deep appreciation of the fact that to live is a serious thing. I determined while in the high school to go to college — partly because other men went, partly because I foresaw that such discipline would best fit me for life. . . I believe foolishly perhaps, but sincerely, that I have something to say to the world, and I have taken English 12 in order to say it well.

Barrett Wendell rather liked that last sentence. He read it out to the class.

It was at Harvard that my education, turning from philosophy, centered in history and then gradually in economics and social problems. Today my course of study would have been called sociology; but in that day Harvard did not recognize any such science. I had taken in high school and at Fisk the old classical course with Latin and Greek, philosophy and some history. At Harvard I started in with philosophy and then turned toward United States history and social problems. The turning was due to William James. He said to me, "If you must study philosophy, you will; but if you can turn aside into something else, do so. It is hard to earn a living with philosophy."

So I turned toward history and social science. But there the way was difficult. Harvard had in the social sciences no such leadership of thought and breadth of learning as in philosophy, literature, and physical science. She was then groping and is still groping toward a scientific treatment of human action. She was facing at the end of the century a tremendous economic era. In the United States, finance was succeeding in monopolizing transportation, and raw materials like sugar, coal, and oil. The power of the trust and combine was so great that the Sherman Act was passed in 1890. On the other hand, the tariff at the demand of manufacturers continued to rise in height from the McKinley to the indefensible Wilson tariff of 1894. A financial crisis shook the land in 1893 and popular discontent showed itself in the Populist movement and Coxey's Army. The whole question of the burden of taxation began to be discussed and England barred an income tax in 1894.

These things were discussed with some clearness and factual understanding at Harvard. The tendency was toward English free trade and against the American tariff policy. We reverenced Ricardo and wasted long hours on the "Wages-fund." The trusts and monopolies were viewed frankly as dangerous enemies of democracies, but at the same time as inevitable methods of industry. We were strong for the gold standard and fearful of silver. On the other hand, the attitude of Harvard toward labor was on the whole contemptuous and condemnatory. Strikes like that of the anarchists in Chicago, the railway strikes of 1886; the terrible Homestead strike of 1892 and Coxey's Army of 1894 were pictured as ignorant lawlessness, lurching against conditions largely inevitable. Karl Marx was hardly mentioned and Henry George given but tolerant notice. The anarchists of Spain, the Nihilists of Russia, the British miners — all these were viewed not as part of the political development and the tremendous economic organization but as sporadic evil. This was natural. Harvard was the child of its era. The intellectual freedom and flowering of the late eighteenth and early nineteenth centuries were yielding to the deadening economic pressure which made Harvard rich but reactionary. This defender of wealth and capital, already half ashamed of Sumner and Phillips, was willing finally to replace an Eliot with a Lowell. The social community that mobbed Garrison, easily hanged Sacco and Vanzetti.

Edwin Arlington Robinson

BEGINNING TO FEEL AT HOME
(1891)

A small-town boy from Gardiner, Maine, Edwin Arlington Robinson came to Harvard in the autumn of 1891 for two years as a special student. He was lonely and blue; his finances worried him; and he was handicapped by poor eyesight and painful ear trouble. Yet at Harvard the shy and discriminating Robinson found friends, those who would sit and smoke a pipeful or two in stimulating conversation, those who liked to share a bottle over some good talk about recent books. To him this was satisfaction. "I have two more examinations yet to take, French and English, and then my Harvard career will be at an end," he wrote his friend, Harry de Forest Smith, in 1893. "I have no particular desire to come another year, but I would hate to part with the experience of the past two. I have lived, upon the whole, a very quiet life, but for all that I have seen things that I could not possibly see at any other place, and have a different conception of what is good and bad in life. From the standpoint of marks, my course here has been a failure, as I knew well enough it would be; but that is the last thing in the world I came here for." And later, he reflected, "I wonder more and more just where I might have come out if I had never seen Harvard Square as I did. . . There was something in the place that changed my way of looking at things." The record of this change is contained in his long and faithful correspondence with Harry Smith — then a student at Bowdoin but later Professor of Greek at Amherst — from which these excerpts are taken.

November 15, 1891

I AM beginning to feel at home and am in a better frame of mind than when I wrote you that half lugubrious epistle telling you of my woes and uncertainties. Of course there is some uncertainty now, and will be until after the mid-years, but I am not going to trouble myself any more about it. "Sufficient unto the day, etc."

. . . . .

Last evening I went into town to see the Russell Comedy Co. in the *City Directory*. I think it is a little the flattest thing I ever witnessed on any stage. I cannot understand how the Athenians can support such stuff. Cheap farce-comedy is undermining the whole dramatic scheme and God only knows what we shall have in a few years to come. Richard Mansfield plays *Dr. Jeckyll and Mr. Hyde* next Sat. evening and if nothing happens I shall be on hand to see it.

Last Wednesday, Dr. Schuman came to see me and I went in to see him in the evening. Beer, oysters, pipes, cigars, and literary conversation were in order. It was the most thoroughly Bohemian evening I ever passed and one of the most satisfactory. The Doctor "uttered nothing base" during the whole time. I wished you were with us more than once; you would have enjoyed it.

For some reason or other I cannot take any particular interest in Harvard athletics, though I am as much a member of the University as any Senior. And I will say here that there is remarkably little feeling between the students of different grades. I am on comparatively good terms with a Senior, a Soph and two or three Specials. They are all alike, and all seem to be fellows of good common-sense. The "fast set" we hear so much about is not a fictitious body, but they keep themselves severely away from the common herd. I can generally tell one when I see him, and he is not much to see either.

The Professors are gentlemen; but when some upper-class man is temporarily promoted to some petty office like superintendent of exams, or assistant registrar, then authority is agonizing. They are harmless, however, and I rather enjoy watching them after I get used to their ways. I might do the same thing myself, unconsciously, should the opportunity present itself. But it will not.

There are eight bowling courts in the gym, and I am quite a fiend for that rather antiquated sport. As to the other appliances, I have not touched them. I fear I am not an enthusiast on the subject of physical culture, though I am an excellent subject to [be] experimented with. My stooping shoulders are disfiguring, but I cannot bring myself to a regular course of training. In fact, I cannot find the time. . .

November 22, 1891

The banners of Harvard are still crimson, but the air is blue — in a double sense. You could not well picture a more melancholy gang than came home from Springfield Saturday night. There was no enthusiasm, no yelling, and practically no drinking. Sorrow was drowned in thought rather than in booze. I am drowning mine in self-hatred, for this reason:

I was fool enough to sacrifice the Springfield game for *Dr. Jeckyll and Mr. Hyde.* It was Mansfield's only performance of the play in Boston this season and I was determined to take it in. *Hinc illae*, etc. The play was totally disappointing. Beyond the transformation scenes it does not amount to much anyway; and much to my surprise and disgust, the stage was in total darkness whenever they took place, and all the time that Hyde was personated. It might as well have been performed by an usher, as far as scenic effect was concerned. Of course we had the voice, but that was hardly satisfactory.

Just now, as I am writing, the Sabbath stillness is broken by a gang of four fellows riding by in a carriole yelling "Ya-a-ale! Ya-a-a-le!" It seems surprising that a Yale man should be in Cambridge today and perhaps they are only friends of the New Haven boys. They are making noise enough, whoever they are. If I could have the money that has changed hands through the game I should invite you down for a year or two. It would have done your soul good to see the scramble for tickets. As high as twenty and twenty-five dollars was paid for seats on the Harvard Side. I might have bought a seat in the centre section for three dollars Saturday morning, but I was set on *Dr. Jeckyll*. In consequence, I am now in a fierce humor for having made such an unconscionable fool of myself. Read the Sunday *Herald* and judge for yourself what I missed, while I might have taken it in as well as not. Experience is no doubt a good thing but I hate to think of spending a whole life in acquiring it.

I am beginning to feel blue already, thinking that I have but one year in Cambridge. And yet it is a little strange that I should feel so. I have made no intimate friends, in fact I have not yet met a single soul to whom I have been in any manner drawn. Literature is at a discount here, but I may find some damned fool yet who will read and smoke with me. The satisfaction I derive is doubtless due to the absolute change and the college atmosphere, which is enormous. I think of the old gray-headed buffers who have climbed the stairs of Massachusetts and Harvard Halls, and dream of a room in classic Holworthy. This is foolishness, but there is no great harm in it. . .

December 8, 1891

I suppose about this time you are wondering where in the devil my letter is; and in view of this state of things I will explain. Last Sunday I was (to use a worldly expression) sick enough to kill. I did nothing but lie around my room and feel blue and nasty. If I had written a letter I should probably [have] put the pessimism of our friend Omar Khayyam completely in the shade; so I concluded to let it go till I was in a better humor. I trust I am now and will try to make up for my failure to keep up the agreement.

This is the first opportunity this evening I have had a chance [*sic*] to write, though I have been intending to do so since I came out of Memorial from dinner at six o'clock. As soon as I got settled for a ruminative smoke in walked Mr. H. A. Cutler, business manager for the *Advocate*, and a rattling good fellow. He had the proof of my latest poetical (?) effusion, — a rondeau entitled "In Harvard 5." The subject is Shakespeare and you will see it in due time. I have not sent the last number containing the "Villanelle of Change," as I was hoping to send you a copy of the *Monthly* with one of my productions; but in this my hopes were blasted.

After Cutler left, my cousins from Cambridgeport came and staid till nine
o'clock. Then came a knock at the door; and at my yell of "Come!" in
stepped Robert Morss Eliott [Lovett], perhaps the leading spirit of Harvard outside of athletics. Of course Capt. Trafford and his crew are with
the immortals. Eliott [Lovett] is a Senior and in many respects a remarkable man. Without any "gushing," I actually felt honored to receive a
call from him, being a Special and a first year man at that. He is editor
in chief of the *Monthly* and brought back the manuscript of my sonnet
on Thomas Hood. At a meeting of the board of editors it was weighed in
the balance and found wanting. (Perhaps I have some foolish opinions of
my own, but they are of no value in this case). We talked of college papers
and kindred matters for about half an hour, when he left with a request
for another contribution — which I have decided to make — and an urgent
request to call on him. If I succeed in getting in with such fellows as that,
college life will prove most agreeable. I think the best way to do it will be
to keep silence on the matter of contributions. I may change my mind
but these are my feelings at present. I was sailing along in such elegant
shape, putting whatever I chose into the *Advocate*, that I must confess
this declination put a slight "damper" on me; but Mr. Lovett (I wrote
Eliott before by mistake — must have been thinking of the President) —
showed himself to be such a gentleman and "white man" that I could not
feel offended. If I am a little foxy I may get in with the whole gang,
which will be rather more pleasant than my present situation. Of course
I have found some good fellows — but you will understand precisely what
I mean. I will send you the *Advocate* with Villanelle tomorrow with this
letter. Perhaps I have tired you with talk of my own affairs, but you know
that I am prone to enter into confidence with now and then a fellow spirit
[*sic*]. Of course I need not ask you not to mention anything that I have
written.

Our blue books in French came due today, and as I was badly prepared I shall get a low mark. But will work up in the review and ought
not to get into trouble. The courses here in elementary French are conducted in a rather peculiar manner, and in my own poor opinion call for
much unnecessary work on the part of the student; but I foresee good
results in the future if I half do myself justice. My rank on the last blue-
book was 9—, scale same as G.H.S. That was not bad, but quite a number got 10. The exams go by letters — A-B-C, etc. I have not yet heard
from my English 9 exams. At last I am through with that most estimable
lady, Jane Austen. Next week we go to work on the essayists — Hazlitt
first, then Lamb and Leigh Hunt. When DeQuincey and Carlyle come,
there will be trouble. They are two writers of whom I am absolutely ignorant. I have read *Sartor Resartus*, but should hate to be called upon
to write a review of it.

I am afraid that this letter will prove rather dry picking. I am sure it would to anyone *but* you, and feel a little guilty as it is. Rec'd a letter from Gledhill today. He is going on swimmingly and is apparently one of the "big guns" of St. L. University. That is one advantage, as I have said before, of a small college. For the leaders it is clover, but for the others it cannot be so pleasant if they are at all sensitive. Here at Harvard there is less of the real college spirit, but there is more equality. I have been treated first rate by everyone I have seen and have tried to do the same myself. Lovett said that my sonnet was about the first contribution on record by a first year man to the *Monthly*. I have an idea that that fact was instrumental in its restoration to its "inventor."

I have been writing for three quarters of an hour, and begin to feel sleepy. Will have a little smoke and turn in. Wish you were here with me.

December 13, 1891

This time I will endeavor to be prompt in my weekly letter and give you a page or two of my usual drool so that it may reach you the first of the week. I also hope to hear from you, as usual. Your letters form no inconsiderable item in my college existence. A letter from a human being who realizes the fact that there is some breadth to human sympathy, and that all men are in a way themselves, is a matter not to be disregarded. I think you give me much credit when you tell me that I know a different Smith from that popularly regarded as "Smithy" — at least that was the former title you bore. At present you are Mr. Smith, of Rockland, and as such I send you greeting. By your permission, or I suppose more properly "with your permission," I shall make you a Christmas present in the form of Wm. Hazlitt's essays. Some of them will please you — if they don't you need not read them. You may be amused at my freedom in this announcement, but you must remember that Robinson is writing and Robinson sometimes says strange things. . .

Last night I went to the "Globe" with Barnard to see Agnes Huntington in *Captain Thérèse*. Agnes was well enough but the opera was painful in its vacuity, if I may use the word. We left at the end of the second act, and repaired to Herr Engelhart's beer shop where [we] spent the remainder of the evening quite pleasantly and I think profitably. If you could come up here for a week or so this spring I should be more than happy; and I think you would manage to enjoy yourself too. Harvard University is a great place to set a man's thoughts going. Yesterday I watched two able-bodied men spreading fragrant New England dung on the campus. I began to wonder if they were not deriving quite as much benefit from Harvard as some of its more scholarly inmates. I think they were, and I have an idea that I felt a kind of envy for their lot. There is a kind of poetry in scattering dung — if the dung is good — that must needs awaken a fine sentiment in the mind of a man of any imagination. The excrement gives the increment to the emerald grass, etc., and when the spring zephyrs begin to blow the transformation becomes apparent. It is great stuff, and the faculty are obviously poets. They use no prepared fertilizer whatever, but cling to the mushy manure of our, and their, ancestors. And shades of Cincinnatus, doesn't it stink! The odor made me homesick, I think; never before have I realized what a real countryman I am. No man of feeling can smell the odors of his native land two hundred miles from home without experiencing a tender surge of emotion within his breast. . .

Denham Sutcliffe, ed., *Untriangulated Stars: Letters of Edwin Arlington Robinson to Harry de Forest Smith, 1890–1905* (Cambridge: Harvard University Press, 1947).

Charles Macomb Flandrau

A DEAD ISSUE
(1897)

Few books so much annoyed the 100 per cent Harvard men of the nineties as Charles M. Flandrau's Harvard Episodes *(1897). The trouble was that it hit home, and loyal Harvard men did not like to think that readers outside Cambridge might get the wrong picture of Harvard life. No good Harvard man, commented the* Graduates' Magazine, *"would wish . . . to hear it quoted from unfriendly lips." And even Dean Briggs, as late as 1912, was saying that he thought it would have been much better if Flandrau had never written his broad condemnation of college snobs and butterflies. To modern eyes and ears Flandrau's book has the universal ring that approaches truth. Despite the fact that he retrieved some of his lost repute among his contemporaries with his later books, his lasting literary monument will probably be* Harvard Episodes, *from which comes this sharp story of a lonely and inexperienced teacher and his relations with his undergraduate club.*

MARCUS THORN, instructor in Harvard University, was thirty-two years old on the twentieth of June. He looked thirty-five, and felt about a hundred. When he got out of bed on his birthday morning, and pattered into the vestibule for his mail, the date at the top of the *Crimson* recalled the first of these unpleasant truths to him. His mirror — it was one of those detestable folding mirrors in three sections — enabled him to examine his bald spot with pitiless ease, reproduced his profile some forty-five times in quick succession, and made it possible for him to see all the way round himself several times at once. It was this devilish invention that revealed fact number two to Mr. Thorn, while he was brushing his hair and tying his necktie. One plus two equalled three, as usual, and Thorn felt old and unhappy. But he didn't linger over his dressing to philosophise on the evanescence of youth; he didn't even murmur, —

> Alas for hourly change! Alas for all
> The loves that from his hand proud youth lets fall,
> Even as the beads of a told rosary.

He could do that sort of thing very well; he had been doing it steadily for five months. But this morning, the reality of the situation — impressed upon him by the date of his birth — led him to adopt more practical measures. What he actually did, was to disarrange his hair a little on top, — fluff it up to make it look more, — and press it down toward his temples to remove the appearance of having too much complexion for the size of his head. Then he went out to breakfast.

Thorn's birthday had fallen, ironically, on one of those rainwashed, blue-and-gold days when "all nature rejoices." The whitest of clouds were drifting across the bluest of skies when the instructor walked out into the Yard; the elms rustled gently in the delicate June haze, and the robins hopped across the yellow paths, freshly sanded, and screamed in the sparkling grass. All nature rejoiced, and in so doing got very much on Thorn's nerves. When he reached his club, he was a most excellent person not to breakfast with.

It was early — half-past eight — and no one except Prescott, a sophomore, and Wynne, a junior, had dropped in as yet. Wynne, with his spectacles on, was sitting in the chair he always sat in at that hour, reading the morning paper. Thorn knew that he would read it through from beginning to end, carefully put his spectacles back in their case, and then go to the piano and play the "Blue Danube." By that time his eggs and coffee would be served. Wynne did this every morning, and the instructor, who at the beginning of the year had regarded the boy's methodical habits at the club as "quaint," —suggestive, somehow, of the first chapter of "Pendennis," — felt this morning that the "Blue Danube" before breakfast would be in the nature of a last straw. Prescott, looking as fresh and clean as the morning, was laughing over an illustrated funny paper. He merely nodded to Thorn, although the instructor hadn't breakfasted there for many months, and called him across to enjoy something. Thorn glanced at the paper and smiled feebly.

"I don't see how you can do it at this hour," he said; "I would as soon drink flat champagne." Prescott understood but vaguely what the man was talking about, yet he didn't appear disturbed or anxious for enlightenment.

"I'll have my breakfast on the piazza," Thorn said to the steward who answered his ring. Then he walked nervously out of the room.

From the piazza he could look over a tangled barrier of lilac bushes and trellised grapevines into an old-fashioned garden. A slim lady in a white dress and a broad brimmed hat that hid her face was cutting nasturtiums and humming placidly to herself. Thorn thought she was a young girl, until she turned and revealed the fact that she was not a young girl — that she was about his own age. This seemed to annoy him in much the same way that the robins and Wynne and the funny paper had, for he threw himself into a low steamer-chair where he wouldn't have to look at the woman, and gave himself up to a sort of luxurious melancholy.

In October, nine months before, Thorn had appeared one evening in the doorway of the club dining-room after a more or less continuous absence of eight years from Cambridge. It was the night before college opened, and the dining-room was crowded. For an instant there was an uproar of confused greetings; then Haydock and Ellis and Sears Wolcott and Wynne — the only ones Thorn knew — pushed back from the table and went forward to shake hands with him. Of the nine or ten boys still left at the table by this proceeding, those whose backs were turned to the new arrival stopped eating and waited without looking around, to be introduced to the owner of the unfamiliar voice. Their companions opposite paused too; some of them laid their napkins on the table. They, however, could glance up and see that the newcomer was a dark man of thirty years or more. They supposed, correctly, that he was an "old graduate" and a member of the club.

"You don't know any of these people, do you?" said Haydock, taking him by the arm; "what a devil of a time you've been away from this place."

"I know that that's a Prescott," laughed the graduate. In his quick survey of the table, while the others had been welcoming him back, his eyes had rested a moment on a big fellow with light hair. Everybody laughed, because it really was a Prescott and all Prescotts were simply more or less happy replicas of all other Prescotts. "I know your brothers," said the graduate, shaking hands with the boy, who had risen.

"It's Mr. Thorn." Haydock made this announcement loud enough to be heard by the crowd. He introduced every one, prefixing "Mr." to the names of the first few, but changing to given and even nicknames before completing the circuit of the table. The humour of some of these last, — "Dink," "Pink," and "Mary," for instance, — lost sight of in long established usage, suggested itself anew; and the fellows laughed again as they made a place for Thorn at the crowded table.

"It's six years, isn't it?" Haydock asked politely. The others had begun to babble cheerfully again of their own affairs.

"Six! I wish it were; it's eight," answered Thorn. "Eight since I left college. But of course I've been here two or three times since, — just long enough to make me unhappy at having to go back to Europe again."

"And now you're a great, haughty Ph.D. person, an 'Officer of Instruction and Government,' announced in the prospectus to teach in two courses," mused Ellis, admiringly. "How do you like the idea?"

"It's very good to be back," said Thorn. He looked about the familiar room with a contented smile, while the steward bustled in and out to supply him with the apparatus of dining.

It was, indeed, good to be back. The satisfaction deepened and broadened with every moment. It was good to be again in the town, the house, the room that, during his life abroad, he had grown to look upon more as "home" than any place in the world; good to come back and find that the place had changed so little; good, for instance, when he ordered a bottle of beer, to have it brought to him in his own mug, with his name and class cut in the pewter, — just as if he had never been away at all. This was but one of innumerable little things that made Thorn feel that at last he was where he belonged; that he had stepped into his old background; that it still fitted. The fellows, of course, were recent acquisitions — all of them. Even his four acquaintances had entered college long since his own time. But the crowd, except that it seemed to him a gathering decidedly younger than his contemporaries had been at the same age, was in no way strange to him. There were the same general types of young men up and down the table, and at both ends, that he had known in his day. They were discussing the same topics, in the same tones and inflections, that had made the dinner-table lively in the eighties, — which was not surprising when he considered that certain families belong to certain clubs at Harvard almost as a matter of course, and that some of the boys at the table were the brothers and cousins of his own classmates. He realized, with a glow of sentiment, that he had returned to his own people after years of absence in foreign lands; a performance whose emotional value was not decreased for Thorn by the conviction, just then, that his own people were better bred, and better looking, and better dressed than any he had met elsewhere. As he looked about at his civilised surroundings, and took in, from the general chatter, fragments of talk, — breezy and cosmopolitan with incidents of the vacation just ended, — he considered his gratification worth the time he had been spending among the fuzzy young gentlemen of a German university.

Thorn, like many another college antiquity, might have been the occasion of a mutual feeling of constraint had he descended upon this under-

graduate meal in the indefinite capacity of "an old graduate." The ease
with which he filled his place at the table, and the effortless civility that
acknowledged his presence there, were largely due to his never having
allowed his interest in the life of the club to wane during his years away
from it. He knew the sort of men the place had gone in for, and, in many
instances, their names as well. Some of his own classmates — glad, no
doubt, of so congenial an item for their occasional European letters — had
never failed to write him, in diverting detail, of the great Christmas and
spring dinners. And they, in turn, had often read extracts from Thorn's
letters to them, when called on to speak at these festivities. More than
once the graduate had sent, from the other side of the world, some
doggerel verses, a sketch to be used as a dinner-card, or a trifling addition
to the club's library or dining-room. Haydock and Ellis and Wolcott and
Wynne he had met at various times abroad. He had made a point of
hunting them up and getting to know them, with the result that his
interest had succeeded in preserving his identity; he was not unknown
to the youngest member of the club. If they didn't actually know him,
they at least knew of him. Even this crust is sweet to the returned graduate
whose age is just far enough removed from either end of life's measure
to make it intrinsically unimportant.

"What courses do you give?" It was the big Prescott, sitting opposite,
who asked this. The effort involved a change of colour.

"You'd better look out, or you'll have Pink in your class the first thing
you know," some one called, in a voice of warning, from the other end
of the table.

"Yes; he's on the lookout for snaps," said some one else.

"Then he'd better stay away from my lectures," answered Thorn,
smiling across at Prescott, who blushed some more at this sudden con-
vergence of attention on himself. "They say that new instructors always
mark hard — just to show off."

"I had you on my list before I knew who you were," announced
another. "I thought the course looked interesting; you'll have to let me
through."

"Swipe! swipe!" came in a chorus from around the table. This banter-
ing attitude toward his official position pleased Thorn, perhaps, more than
anything else. It flattered and reassured him as to the impression his
personality made on younger — much younger — men. He almost saw in
himself the solution of the perennial problem of "How to bring about a
closer sympathy between instructor and student."

After dinner Haydock and Ellis took him from room to room, and
showed him the new table, the new rugs, the new books, *ex dono* this,
that, and the other member. In the library he came across one of his own
sketches, prettily framed. Some of his verses had been carefully pasted

into the club scrap-book. Ellis and Haydock turned to his class photo-graph in the album, and laughed. It was not until long afterwards that he wondered if they had done so because the picture had not yet begun to lose its hair. When they had seen everything from the kitchen to the attic, they went back to the big room where the fellows were drinking their coffee and smoking. Others had come in in the interval; they were condoling gaily with those already arrived, on the hard luck of having to be in Cambridge once more. Thorn stood with his back to the fireplace, and observed them.

It was anything but a representative collection of college men. There were athletes, it was true, — Prescott was one, — and men who helped edit the college papers, and men who stood high in their studies, and others who didn't stand anywhere, talking and chaffing in that room. But it was characteristic of the life of the college that these varied dis-tinctions had in no way served to bring the fellows together there. That Ellis would, without doubt, graduate with a *magna*, perhaps a *summa cum laude*, was a matter of interest to no one but Ellis. That Prescott had played admirable foot-ball on Soldiers' Field the year before, and would shortly do it again, made Prescott indispensable to the Eleven, perhaps, but it didn't in the least enhance his value to the club. In fact, it kept him away so much, and sent him to bed so early, that his skill at the game was, at times, almost deplored. That Haydock once in a while contributed verses of more than ordinary merit to the "Monthly" and "Advocate" had nearly kept him out of the club altogether. It was the one thing against him, — he had to live it down. On the whole, the club, like all of the five small clubs at Harvard whose influence is the most powerful, the farthest reaching influence in the undergraduate life of the place, rather prided itself in not being a reward for either the meritorious or the energetic. It was composed of young men drawn from the same station in life, the similarity of whose past associations and experience, in addition to whatever natural attractions they possessed, rendered them mutually agreeable. The system was scarcely broadening, but it was very delightful. And as the graduate stood there watching the fellows — brown and exuberant after the long vacation — come and go, discussing, com-paring, or simply fooling, but always frankly absorbed in themselves and one another, he could not help thinking that however much such institu-tions had helped to enfeeble the class spirit of days gone by, they had a rather exquisite, if less diffusive spirit of their own. He liked the liveliness of the place, the broad, simple terms of intimacy on which every one seemed to be with every one else, the freedom of spech and action. Not that he had any desire to bombard people with sofa-cushions, as Sears Wolcott happened to be doing at that instant, or even to lie on his back in the middle of the centre-table with his head under the lamp, and read the "Transcript," as some one else had done most of the evening; but he enjoyed the environment that made such things possible and un-objectionable.

"I must make a point of coming here a great deal," reflected Thorn.

The next day college opened. More men enrolled in Thorn's class that afternoon than he thought would be attracted by the subject he was announced to lecture in on that day of the week. Among all the students who straggled, during the hour, into the bare recitation-room at the top of Sever, the only ones whose individualities were distinct enough to impress themselves on Thorn's unpractised memory, were a Negro, a stained ivory statuette of a creature from Japan, a middle-aged gentleman with a misplaced trust in the efficacy of a flowing sandy beard for con-cealing an absence of collar and necktie, Prescott, and Haydock. Prescott surprised him. There was a crowd around the desk when he appeared, and Thorn didn't get a chance to speak to him; but he was pleased to have the boy enroll in his course, — more pleased somehow than if there had been any known intellectual reason for his having done such a thing; more pleased, for instance, than he was when Haydock strolled in a moment or two later, although he knew that the senior would get from his teachings whatever there was in them. Haydock was the last to arrive before the hour ended. Thorn gathered up his pack of enrollment cards, and the two left the noisy building together.

"Prescott enrolled just a minute or two before you did," said Thorn, as they walked across the Yard. He was a vain man in a quiet way.

"Yes," answered Haydock drily, "he said your course came at a con-venient hour"; he didn't add that, from what he knew of Prescott, com-plications might, under the circumstances, be looked for.

"Shall I see you at dinner?" Thorn asked before they separated.

"Oh, are you going to eat at the club?" Haydock had wondered the night before how much the man would frequent the place.

"Why, yes, I thought I would — for a time at least." No other arrange-ment had ever occurred to Thorn.

"That's good — I'm glad," said the senior; he asked himself, as he walked away, why truthful people managed to lie so easily and so often in the course of a day. As a matter of fact, he was vaguely sorry for what Thorn had just told him. Haydock didn't object to the instructor. Had his opinion been asked, he would have said, with truth, that he liked the man. For Thorn was intelligent, and what Haydock called "house broken," and the two had once spent a pleasant week together in Germany. It was not inhospitality, but a disturbed sense of the fitness of things that made Haydock regret Thorn's apparent intention of becoming so inti-mate with his juniors. The instructor's place, Haydock told himself, was with his academic colleagues, at the Colonial Club — or wherever it was that they ate.

Thorn did dine with the undergraduates that night, and on many nights following. It was a privilege he enjoyed for a time exceedingly. It amused him, and, after the first few weeks of his new life in Cambridge, he craved amusement. For in spite of the work he did for the college — the preparing and delivering of lectures, the reading and marking of various written tasks, and the enlightening, during consultation hours, of long haired, long winded seekers after truth, whose cold, insistent passion for the literal almost crazed him — he was often profoundly bored. He had not been away from Cambridge long enough to outlive the conviction, acquired in his Freshman year, that the residents of that suburb would prove unexhilarating if in a moment of inadvertence he should ever chance to meet any of them. But he had been too long an exile to retain a very satisfactory grasp on contemporary Boston. Of course he hunted up some of his classmates he had known well. Most of them were men of affairs in a way that was as yet small enough to make them seem to Thorn aggressively full of purpose. They were all glad to see him. Some of them asked him to luncheon in town at hours that proved inconvenient to one living in Cambridge; some of them had wives, and asked him to call on them. He did so, and found them to be nice women. But this he had suspected before. Two of his classmates were rich beyond the dreams of industry. They toiled not, and might have been diverting if they hadn't — both of them — happened to be unspeakably dull men. For one reason or another, he found it impossible to see his friends often enough to get into any but a very lame sort of step with their lives. Thorn's occasional meetings with them left him melancholy, sceptical as to the depth of their natures and his own, cynical as to the worth of college friendships — friendships that had depended, for their warmth, so entirely on propinquity — on the occasion. His most absorbing topics of conversation with the men he had once known — his closest ties — were after all issues very trivial and very dead. Dinner with a classmate he grew to look on as either suicide, or a post mortem.

It was the club with its fifteen or twenty undergraduate members that went far at first toward satisfying his idle moments. Dead issues, other than the personal traditions that added colour and atmosphere to the every day life of the place, were given no welcome there. The thrill of the fleeting present was enough. The life Thorn saw there was, as far as he could tell, more than complete with the healthy joy of eating and drinking, of going to the play, of getting hot and dirty and tired over athletics, and cold and clean and hungry again afterwards. The instructor was entranced by its innocence — its unconscious contentment. It was so unlike his own life of recent years, he told himself; it was so "physical." He liked to stop at the club late in the winter afternoons, after a brisk walk on Brattle Street. There was always a crowd around the fire at that hour, and no room that he could remember had ever seemed so full of warmth and sympathy as the big room where the fellows sat, at five o'clock on a winter's day, with the curtains drawn and the light of the fire flickering up the dark walls and across the ceiling. He often dropped in at midnight, or even later. The place was rarely quite deserted. Returned "theatre bees" came there to scramble eggs and drink beer, instead of tarrying with the mob at the Victoria or the Adams House. In the chill of the small hours, a herdic load of boys from some dance in town would often stream in to gossip and get warm, or to give the driver a drink after the long cold drive across the bridge. And Thorn, who had not been disposed to gather up and cling to the dropped threads of his old interests, who was not wedded to his work, who was not sufficient unto himself, enjoyed it all thoroughly, unreservedly — for a time.

For a time only. For as the winter wore on, the inevitable happened — or rather the expected didn't happen, which is pretty much the same thing after all. Thorn, observant, analytical, and — where he himself was not concerned — clever, grew to know the fellows better than they knew themselves. Before he had lived among them three months, he had appreciated their respective temperaments, he had taken the measure of their ambitions and limitations, he had catalogued their likes and dislikes, he had pigeon-holed their weaknesses and illuminated their virtues. Day after day, night after night, consciously and unconsciously, he had observed them in what was probably the frankest, simplest intercourse of their lives. And he knew them.

But they didn't know him. Nor did it ever occur to them that they wanted to or could. They were not seeking the maturer companionship Thorn had to give; they were not seeking much of anything. They took life as they found it near at hand, and Thorn was far, very far away. For them, the niche he occupied could have been filled by any gentleman of thirty-two with a kind interest in them and an affection for the club. To him, they were everything that made the world, as he knew it just then, interesting and beautiful. Youth, energy, cleanliness were the trinity Thorn worshipped. And they were young, strong, and undefiled. Yet, after the first pleasure at being back had left him, Thorn was not a happy man, although he had not then begun to tell himself so.

The seemingly unimportant question presented by his own name began to worry him a little as the weeks passed into months. First names and the absurd sounds men had answered to from babyhood were naturally in common use at the club. Thorn dropped into the way of them easily, as a matter of course. Not to have done so would, in time, have become impossible. The fellows would have thought it strange — formal.

Yet the name of "Marcus" was rarely heard there. Haydock, once in a while, called him that, after due premeditation. Sears Wolcott occasionally used it by way of a joke — as if he were taking an impertinent liberty, and rather enjoyed doing it. But none of the other men ever did. On no occasion had any one said "Marcus" absentmindedly, and then looked embarrassed, as Thorn had hoped might happen. It hurt him a little always to be called "Thorn"; to be appealed to in the capacity of "Mr. Thorn," as he sometimes was by the younger members, positively annoyed him. Prescott was the most incorrigible in this respect. He had come from one of those fitting schools where all speech between master and pupil is carried on to a monotonous chant of "Yes, sir," "No, sir," and "I think so, sir." He had ideas, or rather habits, — for Prescott's ideas were few, — of deference to those whose mission it was to assist in his education that Thorn found almost impossible to displace. For a long time — until the graduate laughed and asked him not to — he prefixed the distasteful "Mr." to Thorn's name. Then, for as long again, he refrained markedly from calling him anything. One afternoon he came into the club where the instructor was alone, writing a letter, and after fussing for a time among the magazines on the table, he managed to say, —

"Thorn, do you know whether Sears has been here since luncheon?"

Thorn didn't know and he didn't care, but had Prescott handed him an appointment to an assistant professor's chair, instead of having robbed him a little of what dignity he possessed, he would not have been so elated by half. Prescott continued to call him "Thorn" after that, but always with apparent effort, — as if aware that in doing it he was not living quite up to his principles. This trouble with his name might have served Thorn as an indication of what his position actually was in the tiny world he longed so much to be part of once more. But he was not a clever man where he himself was concerned.

Little things hurt him constantly without opening his eyes. For instance, it rarely occurred to the fellows that the instructor might care to join them in any of their hastily planned expeditions to town after dinner. Not that he was ostracised; he was simply overlooked. When he did go to the theatre, he bought the tickets himself, and asked Prescott or Sears, or some of them, to go with him. The occasion invariably lacked the charm of spontaneity. When he invited any of them to dine with him in town, as he often did, they went, if they hadn't anything else to do, and seemed to enjoy their dinner. But to Thorn these feasts were a series of disappointments. He always got up from the table with a sense of having failed in something. What? He didn't know — he couldn't have told. He was like a man who shoots carefully at nothing, and then feels badly because he hits it. He persisted in loitering along sunny lanes, and growing melancholy because they led nowhere. It was Sears Wolcott who took even the zest of anticipation out of Thorn's little dinners in town, by saying to the graduate one evening, —

"What's the point of going to the Victoria for dinner? It's less trouble, and a damned sight livelier, to eat out here." Sears had what Haydock called, "that disagreeable habit of hitting promiscuously from the shoulder." The reaction on Thorn of all this was at last a dawning suspicion of his own unimportance. By the time the midyear examinations came, he felt somehow as if he were "losing ground"; he hadn't reached the point yet of realising that he never had had any. He used to throw down his work in a fit of depression and consult his three-sided mirror apprehensively.

The big Prescott, however, became the real problem, around which the others were as mere corollaries. It was he who managed, in his "artless Japanese way," as the fellows used to call it, to crystallise the situation, to bring it to a pass where Thorn's rather unmanly sentimentality found itself confronted by something more definite and disturbing than merely the vanishing point of youth. Prescott accomplished this very simply, by doing the poorest kind of work — no work at all, in fact — in the course he was taking from Thorn. Barely, and by the grace of the instructor, had he scraped through the first examination in November. Since then he had rested calmly, like a great monolith, on his laurels. He went to Thorn's lectures only after intervals of absence that made his going at all a farce. He ignored the written work of the course, and the reports on outside reading, with magnificent completeness. Altogether, he behaved as he wouldn't have behaved had he ever for a moment considered Thorn in any light other than that of an instructor, an officer of the college, a creature to whom deference — servility, almost — was due when he was compelled to talk to him, but to whom all obligation ended there. His attitude was not an unusual one among college "men" who have not outgrown the school idea, but the attendant circumstances were. For Thorn's concern over Prescott's indifference to the course was aroused by a strong personal attachment, one in which an ordinary professorial interest had nothing to do. He smarted at this failure to attract the boy sufficiently to draw him to his lectures; yet he looked with a sort of panic toward the approaching day when he should be obliged, in all conscience, to flunk him in the midyear examination. He admired Prescott, as little, intelligent men sometimes do admire big, stupid ones. He idealised him, and even went the length, one afternoon when taking a walk with Haydock, of telling the senior that under Prescott's restful, olympic exterior he thought there lurked a soul. To which Haydock had answered with asperity, "Well, I hope so, I'm sure," and let the subject drop. Later in the walk, Haydock announced, irrelevantly, and with a good deal of vigour, that if he ever made or inherited millions, he would establish a chair in the university, call it the "Haydock Professorship of Common Sense," and respectfully suggest to the President and Faculty that the course be made compulsory.

Thorn would have spoken to the soulful Prescott, — told him gently that he didn't seem to be quite in sympathy with the work of the course, — if Prescott had condescended to go to his lectures in the six or seven weeks between the end of the Christmas recess and the examination period. But Prescott cut Tuesday, Thursday, and Saturday, at half-past two o'clock, with a regularity that, considered as regularity, was admirable. Toward the last, he did drop in every now and then, sit near the door, and slip out again before the hour was ended. This was just after he had been summoned by the Recorder to the Office for "cutting." Thorn never got a chance to speak to him. He might have approached the boy at the club; but the instructor shrank from taking advantage of his connection with that place to make a delicate official duty possible. He had all along avoided "shop" there so elaborately, — had made so light of it when the subject had come up, — that he couldn't bring himself at that late day to arise, viper like, from the hearthstone and smite. A note of warning would have had to be light, facetious, and consequently without value, in order not to prove a very false and uncalled for note indeed. The ready coöperation of the Dean, Thorn refrained from calling on; he was far from wishing to get Prescott into difficulties.

By the time the examination day arrived, the instructor was in a state of turmoil that in ordinary circumstances would have been excessive and absurd. In the case of Thorn, it was half pathetic, half contemptible. He knew that in spite of Prescott's soul (a superabundance of soul is, as a matter of fact, a positive hindrance in passing examinations), the boy would do wretchedly. To give him an E — the lowest possible mark, always excepting, of course, the jocose and sarcastic F — would be to bring upon himself Prescott's everlasting anger and "despision." Of this Thorn was sure. Furthermore, the mark would not tend to make the instructor wildly popular at the club; for although everybody was willing to concede that Prescott was not a person of brilliant mental attainments, he was very much beloved. One hears a good deal about the "rough justice of boys." Thorn knew that such a thing existed, and did not doubt but that, in theory, he would be upheld by the members of the club if he gave Prescott an E, and brought the heavy hand of the Office down on him. But the justice of boys, he reflected, was, after all, rough; it would acknowledge his right to flunk Prescott, perhaps, and, without doubt, hate him cordially for doing it. Thorn's aversion to being hated was almost morbid.

If, on the other hand, he let the boy through, — gave him, say, the undeserved and highly respectable mark of C, — well, that would be

tampering dishonestly with the standards of the college, gross injustice to
the rest of the students, injurious to the self-respect of the instructor, and
a great many other objectionable things, too numerous to mention. Altogether, Thorn was in a "state of mind." He began to understand something of the fine line that separates instructor from instructed, on whose
other side neither may trespass.

When at length the morning of the examination had come and gone,
and Thorn was in his own room at his desk with the neat bundle of blue-
covered books before him, in which the examinations are written, it was
easy enough to make up his mind. He knew that the question of flunking
or passing Prescott admitted of no arguments whatever. The boy's work
in the course failed to present the tiniest loophole in the way of "extenuat-
ing circumstances," and Prescott had capped the climax of his past record
that morning by staying in the examination-room just an hour and a
quarter of the three hours he was supposed to be there. That alone was
equivalent to failure in a man of Prescott's denseness. Not to give Prescott
a simple and unadorned E would be holding the pettiest of personal
interests higher than one's duty to the college. There was no other way
of looking at it. And Thorn, whose mind was perfectly clear on this point,
deliberately extricated Prescott's book from the blue pile on his desk,
dropped it carelessly — without opening it — into the glowing coals of
his fireplace, and entered the boy's midyear mark in the records as C.

No lectures are given in the college during the midyears. Men who
are fortunate enough to finish their examinations early in the period can
run away to New York, to the country, to Old Point Comfort, to almost
anywhere that isn't Cambridge, and recuperate. Haydock went South.
Ellis and Wynne tried a walking trip in the Berkshire Hills, and, after
two days' floundering in the mud, waded to the nearest train for a city.
Boston men went to Boston — except Sears Wolcott and Prescott, who
disappeared to some wild and inaccessible New England hamlet to snow-
shoe or spear fish or shoot rabbits; no one could with authority say which,
as the two had veiled their preparations in mystery. So it happened that
Thorn didn't see Prescott for more than a week after he had marked his
book. In the mean time he had become used to the idea of having done it
according to a somewhat unconventional system — to put it charitably.
He passed much of the time in which the fellows were away, alone; for
the few who went to the club, went there with note-books under their
arms and preoccupied expressions in their eyes. They kept a sharp look-
out for unexpected maneuvres on the part of the clock, and had a general
air of having to be in some place else very soon. Thorn, thrown on his
own resources, had a mild experience of what Cambridge can be without
a crowd to play with, and came to the conclusion that, for his own interest
and pleasure in life, he had done wisely in not incurring Prescott's ill-will

and startling the club in the new role of hard-hearted, uncompromising pedagogue. The insignificant part he played in the lives of the under-graduates was far from satisfying; but it was the sort of half a loaf one doesn't willingly throw away. By the time Prescott came back, Thorn had so wholly accepted his own view of the case that he was totally un-prepared for the way in which the boy took the news of his mark. He met Prescott in the Yard the morning college opened again, and stopped to speak to him. He wouldn't have referred to the examination — it was enough to know that the little crisis had passed — had not Prescott, blush-ing uneasily, and looking over Thorn's shoulder at something across the Yard, said, —

"I don't suppose you were very much surprised at the way I did in the exam, were you?"

"It might have been better," answered Thorn, seriously. "I hope you will do better the second half year. But then, it might have been worse; your mark was C."

Prescott looked at him, a quizzical, startled look; and then realising that Thorn was serious, that there had been nothing of the sarcastic in his tone or manner, he laughed rudely in the instructor's face.

"I beg your pardon," he said, as politely as he could, with his eyes still full of wonder and laughter; "I had no idea I did so well." He turned abruptly and walked away. Thorn would have felt offended, if he hadn't all at once been exceedingly scared. Prescott's manner was extraordinary for one who, as a rule, took everything as it came, calmly, unquestioningly. His face and his laugh had expressed anything but ordinary satisfaction at not having failed. There was something behind that unwonted aston-ishment, something more than mere surprise at having received what was, after all, a mediocre mark. Thorn had mixed enough with human kind to be aware that no man living is ever very much surprised in his heart of hearts to have his humble efforts in any direction given grade C. Men like Prescott, who know but little of the subjects they are examined in, usually try to compose vague answers that may, like the oracles, be interpreted according to the mood of him who reads them. No matter how general or how few Prescott's answers had been — Thorn stopped suddenly in the middle of the path. The explanation that had come to him took hold of him, and like a tightened rein drew him up short. Prescott had written nothing. The pages of his blue book had left the examination-room as virgin white as when they had been brought in and placed on the desk by the proctor. There was no other explanation possible, and the instructor tingled all over with the horrid sensation of being an unspeakable fool. He turned quickly to go to University Hall; he meant to have Prescott's mark changed at once. But Prescott, at that moment, was bounding up the steps of University, two at a time. He was undoubtedly on his way to the Office to verify what Thorn had just told him. Thorn walked rapidly to his entry in Holworthy, although he had just come from there. Then, with short, nervous steps, he turned back again, left the Yard, and hurried in aimless haste up North Avenue. He had been an ass, — a bungling, awful ass, — he told himself over and over again. And that was about as coherent a meditation as Mr. Thorn was able to indulge in for some time. Once the idea of pretending that he had made a mistake did suggest itself for a moment; but that struck him as wild, impossible. It would have merely resulted in forcing the Office to regard him as stupid and careless, and, should embarrassing questions arise, he no longer had Prescott's book with which to clear himself. More than that, it would give Prescott reason to believe him an underhand trickster. The boy now knew him to be an example of brazen partiality; there was no point in incurring even harsher criticism. Thorn tried to convince himself, as he hurried along the straight, hideous highway, that perhaps he was wrong, — that Prescott hadn't handed in a perfectly blank book. If only he could have been sure of that, he would have risked the bland assertion that the boy had stumbled on more or less intelligent answers to the examination questions, without perhaps knowing it himself. This, practically, was the tone he had meant to adopt all along. But he couldn't be sure, and, unfortunately, the only person who could give information as to what was or wasn't in the book, was Prescott. But Prescott had given information of the most direct and convincing kind. That astounded look and impertinent laugh had as much as said: —

"Well, old swipe, what's your little game? What do you expect to get by giving a good mark to a man who wasn't able to answer a single question?" And Thorn knew it. At first he was alarmed at what he had done. He could easily see how such a performance, if known, might stand in the light of his reappointment to teach in the college, even if it didn't eject him at once. But before he returned to his room, after walking miles, he scarcely knew where, fear had entirely given way to shame, — an over-powering shame that actually made the man sick at his stomach. It wasn't as if he had committed a man's fault in a world of men where he would be comfortably judged and damned by a tribunal he respected about as much as he respected himself. He had turned himself inside out before the clear eyes of a lot of boys, whose dealings with themselves and one another were like so many shafts of white light in an unrefracting medium. He had let them know what a weak, characterless, poor thing he was, by holding himself open to a bribe, showing himself willing to exchange, for the leavings of their friendships, something he was bound in honour to give only when earned, prostituting his profession that they might continue to like him a little, tolerate his presence among them.

And he was one whom the college had honoured by judging worthy to stand up before young men and teach them. It was really very sickening.

Thorn couldn't bring himself to go near the club for some days. He knew, however, as well as if he had been present, what had probably happened there in the meanwhile. Prescott had told Haydock and Wolcott, and very likely some of the others, the story of his examination. They had laughed at first, as if it had been a good joke in which Prescott had come out decidedly ahead; then Haydock had said something — Thorn could hear him saying it — that put the matter in a pitilessly true light, and the others had agreed with him. They usually did in the end. It took all the "nerve" Thorn had to show himself again.

But when he had summoned up enough courage to drop in at the club late one evening, he found every one's manner toward him pretty much as it always had been; yet he could tell instinctively as he sat there, who had and who hadn't heard Prescott's little anecdote. Wolcott knew; he called Thorn, "Marcus," with unnecessary gusto, and once or twice laughed his peculiarly irritating laugh when there was nothing, as far as Thorn could see, to laugh at. Haydock knew; Thorn winced under the cool speculative stare of the senior's grey eyes. Wynne knew; although Thorn had no more specific reason for believing so, than that the boy seemed rather more formidably bespectacled than usual. Several of the younger fellows also knew; Thorn knew that they knew; he couldn't stand it. When the front door slammed after him on his way back to his room, he told himself that, as far as he was concerned, it had slammed for the last time.

He was very nearly right. He would have had to be a pachyderm compared to which the "blood sweating behemoth of Holy Writ" is a mere satin-skinned invalid, in order to have brazened out the rest of the year on the old basis. He couldn't go to the club and converse on base-ball and the "musical glasses," knowing that the fellows with whom he was talking were probably weighing the pros and cons of taking his courses next year, and getting creditable marks in them, without doing a stroke of work. He couldn't face that "rough justice of boys" that would sanction the fellows making use of him, and considering him a pretty poor thing, at the same time. So he stayed away; he didn't go near the place through March and April and May. When his work didn't call him elsewhere, he stayed in his room and attempted to live the life of a scholar, —an existence for which he was in every conceivable way unfitted. For a time he studied hard out of books; but the most profitable knowledge he acquired in his solitude was the great deal he learned about himself. He tried to write. He had always thought it in him to "write something," if he ever should find the necessary leisure. But the play he began amounted to no

more than a harmless pretext for discoursing in a disillusioned strain on
Life and Art in the many letters he wrote to people he had known abroad,
— people, for whom, all at once, he conceived a feeling of intimacy that
no doubt surprised them when they received his letters. His volume of
essays was never actually written, but the fact that he was hard at work
on it served well as an answer to: —

"Why the devil don't we ever see you at the club nowadays?"

For the fellows asked him that, of course, when he met them in the
Yard or in the electric cars; and Haydock tarried once or twice after his
lecture and hoped politely that he was coming to the next club dinner.
He wasn't at the next club dinner, however, nor the next, nor the next.
Haydock stopped reminding him of them. The club had gradually ceased
to have any but a spectacular interest for Thorn. His part at a dinner
there would be — and, since his return, always had been — that of decorous audience in the stalls, watching a sprightly farce. The club didn't
insist on an audience, so Thorn's meetings with its members were few.
He saw Haydock and Prescott, in a purely official way, more than any
of them. Strangely enough, Prescott seemed to be trying to do better in
Thorn's course. He came to the lectures as regularly as he had avoided
them before the midyears. He handed in written work of such ingenious
unintelligence that there was no question in Thorn's mind as to the boy's
having conscientiously evolved it unaided. The instructor liked the spirit
of Prescott's efforts, although it was a perpetual "rubbing in," of the memory of his own indiscretion; it displayed a pretty understanding of
noblesse oblige.

The second half year was long and dreary and good for Thorn. It
set him down hard, — so hard that when he collected himself and began
to look about him once more, he knew precisely where he was — which
was something he hadn't known until then. He was thirty-two years old;
he looked thirty-five, and he felt a hundred, to begin with. He wasn't
an undergraduate, and he hadn't been one for a good many years. He
still felt that he loved youth and sympathised with its every phase, —
from its mindless gambolings to its preposterous maturity. But he knew
now that it was with the love and sympathy of one who had lost it.
He had learned, too, that when it goes, it bids one a cavalier adieu, and
takes with it what one has come to regard as one's rights, — like a saucy
house-maid departing with the spoons. He knew that he had no rights;
he had forfeited them by losing some of his hair. He wouldn't get any
of them back again until he had lost all of it. He was the merest speck
on the horizon of the fellows whom he had, earlier in the year, tried to
know on a basis of equality, — a speck too far away, too microscopic
even to annoy them. If he had only known it all along, he told himself,
how different his year might have been. He wouldn't have squandered

the first four months of it, for one thing, in a stupid insistence on a relation that must of necessity be artificial — unsatisfying. He wouldn't have spent the last five of it in coming to his senses. He wouldn't have misused all of it in burning — or at least in allowing to fall into a precarious state of unrepair — the bridges that led back to the friends of his own age and time.

"I have learned more than I have taught, this year," thought Thorn.

To-day was Thorn's birthday. Impelled by a tender, tepid feeling of self-pity the instructor had come once more to the club to look at it and say good-bye before leaving Cambridge. He would have liked to break-fast on the piazza and suffer luxuriously alone. But just at the moment he was beginning to feel most deeply, Sears Wolcott appeared at the open French window, and said he was "Going to eat out there in the landscape too." So Thorn, in spite of himself, had to revive.

"What did you think of the Pudding show last night?" began Sears. Talk with him usually meant leading questions and their simplest answers.

"It was very amusing — very well done," said Thorn. What was the use, he asked himself, of drawing a cow-eyed stare from Wolcott by saying what he really thought — that Strawberry Night at the Pudding had been "exuberant," "noisy," "intensely young."

"I saw you after it was over," Sears went on; "why didn't you buck up with the old grads around the piano? You looked lonely."

"I was lonely," answered Thorn, truthfully this time.

"Where were your classmates? There was a big crowd out."

"My classmates? Oh, they were there, I suppose. I haven't seen much of them this year."

Wolcott's next question was: —

"Why the devil can't we have better strawberries at this club, I wonder? Where's the granulated sugar? They know I never eat this damned face powder on anything." He called loudly for the steward, and Thorn went on with his breakfast in silence. After Sears had been appeased with granulated sugar, he asked: —

"Going to be here next year?"

"I've been reappointed; but I think I shall live in town. Why do you ask?"

"Oh, nothing — I was thinking I might take your courses. What mark is Prescott going to get for the year?"

Thorn looked up to meet Wolcott's eyes unflinchingly; but the boy was deeply absorbed in studying the little air bubbles on the surface of his coffee.

"I don't know what mark he'll get. I haven't looked at his book yet," said Thorn. Sears remarked "Oh!" and laughed as he submerged the bubbles with a spoon. It was unlike him not to have said, "You do go through the formality of reading his books then?"

Prescott and Wynne joined them. They chattered gaily with Wolcott about nothing out there on the piazza, and watched the slim lady on the other side of the nodding lilac bushes cut nasturtiums. Thorn listened to them, and looked at them, and liked them; but he couldn't be one of them, even for the moment. He couldn't babble unpremeditatedly about nothing, because he had forgotten how it was done. So, in a little while, he got up to leave them. He had to mark some examination books and pack his trunks and go abroad, he told them. He said good-bye to Prescott and Wolcott and Wynne and some others who had come in while they were at breakfast, and hoped they would have "a good summer." They hoped the same to him.

As he strolled back to his room with the sounds of their voices in his ears, but with no memory of what they had been saying, he wondered if, after all, they hadn't from the very first bored him just a little; if his unhappiness — his sense of failure when he talked to young people — didn't come from the fact that they commended themselves to his affections rather than to his intellect. Thorn was a vain man in a quiet way.

Prescott's final examination book certainly didn't commend itself to his intellect. It was long, and conscientious, and quite incorrect from cover to cover. The instructor left it until the last. He almost missed his train in deciding upon its mark.

Charles M. Flandrau, *Harvard Episodes* (Boston, 1897).

Lee Simonson

MY COLLEGE LIFE WAS AN INNER ONE

(c. 1908)

Lee Simonson, a founder and for more than twenty years a director of the Theater Guild, is one of America's foremost designers for the stage. His autobiography, Part of a Lifetime, *is a sensitive chronicle of the development of an artistic personality, for Simonson can write as well as paint and build. Of him it has been said "no other artist of our time can surpass him in making the technical details of a production fit the play so accurately and harmonize with the ideas of the author and director." At Harvard he was one of the founders of the Dramatic Club, won the Bowdoin Prize, and graduated* magna cum laude *in philosophy. Through his own testimony he is revealed as one of those highly individual personalities which the Harvard atmosphere occasionally nurtures. He is the author of* The Stage is Set (1932).

WILLIAM JAMES, George Santayana, Josiah Royce, George Herbert Palmer, Hugo Münsterberg, Ralph Barton Perry, William Allan Neilson, Charles Townsend Copeland, George Pierce Baker — this Olympian roster evokes a Harvard that in retrospect seems to be a Harvard of a golden age, or rather a golden afternoon, for the college seemed like some well-kept orchard, cooled by the first lengthening shadows and warmed by the sun of a benign enlightenment, where the fruits of knowledge and culture hung ripe, waiting to be plucked for the asking. A kind of peace of infinite intellectual plenty seemed to lie even over the dingiest of our academic halls, though Emerson Hall, the center of philosophy, was, as Münsterberg reminded us, "new and insofar esthetically satisfying." Of William James I had only a glimpse when he gave the opening lecture of an introductory course, Philosophy 1. But the largest lecture hall was packed when Münsterberg asked those of us "who had fountain pens not to ejaculate any ink upon the floor." The excitement of new knowledge was in the air and pervaded us even as we imbibed his more mechanical version of the mind's processes and followed as best we could his buzzing accent and rolling r's — "ze zenz zenzationz zemzelvez . . . ze nerf imbulses fr-r-rom ze ber-r-ipher-r-ry to ze occzzipital zenter of ze brr-rain, gendlemen . . ." It seemed important that, according to a rumor, there was an elevator large enough to hoist cows to the laboratory. Royce appeared to be a formidable legal mind retained as *amicus curiae* in the interests of the Deity. Since the New England heart no longer panted along the water brooks of theological injunction, Royce's "system" could be relied upon to demonstrate that God and the Absolute were metaphysical necessities. If neither had existed it would have had to be invented. The intellectual apparatus employed was formidable. I still get slightly dizzy recalling that as part of a final examination I regurgitated the proof that two infinities could be equal — or unequal. I can no longer remember which. But the realization of what it meant to live in the mind came from George Santayana.

When I am asked where I went to college, I am always inclined to reply, "I went to Santayana." He was a foreign presence, with the punctiliousness and the elegance of a courtier in his speech, his manner, his gait, elegant even in a sack suit, small and neat-footed, his cane and gloves hung in one hand as he made his exit from the lecture room. His face with its pointed beard, full, sensuous lips, and the dark humid eyes, so dark that the pupil and the iris were indistinguishable, was a portrait of a Spanish grandee by Velasquez incarnated. His speech was exactly like his printed prose, exquisitely articulated, balanced and modulated, without an instant's blur of casual conversation. (It was Walter Lippmann,

I think, who later complained that Santayana wrote English as though it were a learned language.) He seemed a prince marooned among savages, whiling away his exile in attempting to civilize them, his eyes never clearly focused on us, gazing slightly above our heads as if looking for the sail that was to bear him home. But the warmth and the clarity of gift as an expositor held every one of us under a spell. Here Reason was no stern daughter-in-law of the Absolute, no frigid instrument, but an organic part of our faculties of apprehension, the dominating factor in the functioning of human personality. Truth might not be beauty, but as one apprehended it, it had the appropriateness of a beautiful object, and there was an almost sensuous satisfaction to the process of learning. One garnered the wisdom and culture of the past as one might live with a being one loved. There was a warmth, a glow and a living pulse, to Santayana's expositions, whether of Plato, Lucretius, Dante, or Goethe, that sets them apart in my memory from the form of exegesis known as philosophic discourse. I reminded him of this twenty years later in Paris over a table d'hôte. He was deprecatory of his career as a teacher at Cambridge. "There, my dear Simonson, I was a mere young lady, practicing the pianoforte." His metaphysical system, the Realm of Essence, had already claimed him and alone seemed to him of any importance.

These days, whenever I stay on a university campus for even an afternoon I have a sense that each faculty member, particularly every younger one, is a timid and intimidated intelligence, hunched in his mental coat collar, looking over his shoulder furtively for fear that a Board of Regents or a Board of Overseers will put the evil eye on him, unless the teacher is already a full professor; then, as the dean of one Middle Western faculty once remarked to me, "They can't get us out at any price except on statutory charges of rape." In the Harvard of my time academic freedom seemed part of the very air of the place. "Opinion in good men," as Milton said, "is but knowledge in the making." Knowledge and wisdom seemed coextensive. No doubt the patina of retrospect lends a possibly false glow and mellowness to the scene, as successive coats of varnish do to a painting which they are intended to preserve. It seemed a stable world. No philosophic heresy could flutter the pulses of State Street, let alone its strongboxes. In the department of economics, the Economic Man, the Charley McCarthy of the day, performed dutifully on every professor's knee. And Lawrence Lowell in his course on government failed to discern anywhere any possible pattern of a revolution.

The sense of security was such that Harvard of that day, as it no longer seems able to do, could tolerate a heretic: George Pierce Baker. The critical analysis of contemporary plays is now so much the order of the day, an opinion of O'Neill, Shaw, Sherwood, or Odets seems so much more important than a revaluation of *A New Way to Pay Old Debts* or *The Way of the World*, that it is difficult to convey what it meant to an undergraduate to be told that it was important to study Henry Arthur Jones and Arthur Wing Pinero even though none of their work might eventually qualify as literature or possibly ever be a seasoned strut in the ceiling of permanent literary values that crowned an academic Pantheon. What Baker reminded us of, not once, but insistently, was that Jones, Pinero, Shaw, Barrie, and Clyde Fitch were important to study, whatever their ultimate shortcomings might prove to be from the point of view of dramatic history, because they were the best we had. This was our theater in the making, ours to make by a critical understanding of it. We could go on only from where we were. We were not the assenters to historic achievements or partisans of lost causes but, as potential audiences, critics, playwrights, the arbiters of living issues. The immense influence that Baker had on so many generations of students was not due primarily to his taste or to his particular opinions as to what was good play-writing and what was not, for much of which some of us had scant respect, but to the sense of our effective importance that he instilled in us. We were living intelligences who could affect actual issues before they were irrevocably decided one way or the other. We mattered. He cultivated consistently and successfully the sense of alternatives that William James had evoked.

No doubt the amount of time we spent analyzing the progress in structure and characterization displayed in *The Second Mrs. Tanqueray* compared with *The Profligate*, or *Michael and His Lost Angel* in contrast to *Mrs. Dane's Defense*, now seems ludicrous. I remember trying unsuccessfully to convince him that Shaw was worth more than two lectures. But the particular instances mattered less than the method of approach. Baker had the air less of a professor than of a celebrated actor, or rather an actor-manager who had been knighted. He was something of a snob as well, and his gift for discovering talent and imagination was often less than he was credited with. Robert Edmond Jones, who was later exhibited at testimonial banquets as one of Baker's prize products, was almost completely ignored and never admitted to the immediate circle of his disciples known as Baker's Dozen. But in Baker's presence the theater became a living art and remained so, I think, for everyone who ever sat under him.

Within sight of Sever Hall where I studied the dramatizations of sex and society, across Harvard Square another realm began. At the "Co-op" I found first editions of the Abbey Theatre and the Celtic revival, the dirge and wonder of Synge's *Riders to the Sea*, the miracle of *The Well of the Saints*, and drifted with Yeats upon *The Shadowy Waters*. . . . At the same time I came upon a volume of Paul Verlaine, whose lyrics I literally took to my bosom, learning them by heart — *Clair de Lune, Streets, Chanson d'Automne, Sagesse*. I apostrophized myself more than once in my shaving mirror with:

> Qu-as-tu fait, ô toi que voilà
> Pleurant sans cesse,
> Dis, qu'as-tu fait, toi que voilà
> De ta jeunesse?

Having a romantic notion of what round-table camaraderie of college intellectuals should be like and being, by Harvard standards, socially a complete failure, I solaced myself with the wind that blew out of the gates of the day, fountains in polished marble basins that sobbed with ecstasy, and the violins of autumn wounding my heart with a languorous monotone, as I took my solitary walks under russet elms or through winter slush along Brattle Street to the reservoir and back again. My college life was largely an inner and introspective one. . . .

Lee Simonson, *Part of a Lifetime* (New York: Duell, Sloan & Pearce. Copyright 1943 by Lee Simonson).

John Reed

"COLLEGE IS LIKE THE WORLD"

(c. 1910)

John Reed caught typhus and died in Moscow in October 1920. It is a temptation to borrow here from Dos Passos' "Playboy" in Nineteen Nineteen. *It is worth recalling the personal sketch which Reed's classmate, Edward E. Hunt, wrote about him in 1935: "None of his Classmates can ever forget John Reed. He came bursting on the scene at Harvard with a noise and a grin that could not be ignored. Large, athletic, exuberant and humorous, he seemed to be on earth for the motion he got out of it. . . Nothing he did could be taken quite seriously for there was always a strain of the grotesque in his undertakings. He laughed at himself and the rest of us laughed with him." But after the war came the* Ten Days That Shook the World. *A new John Reed was born, died in Moscow, and was buried under the Kremlin wall. The amazing story of John Reed the Soviet saint, and the symbol of attacks on the social order, seems all the more amazing after reading Reed's account of his College days at Harvard written in 1917 shortly before sailing for Russia.*

IN 1906 I went up to Harvard almost alone, knowing hardly a soul in the University. My college class entered over seven hundred strong, and for

the first three months it seemed to me, going around to lectures and meetings, as if every one of the seven hundred had friends but me. I was
thrilled with the immensity of Harvard, its infinite opportunities, its august history and traditions — but desperately lonely. I didn't know which
way to turn, how to meet people. Fellows passed me in the Yard, shouting gayly to one another; I saw parties off to Boston Saturday night,
whooping and yelling on the back platform of the street car, and they
passed hilariously singing under my window in the early dawn. Athletes
and musicians and writers and statesmen were emerging from the ranks
of the class. The freshman clubs were forming.

And I was out of it all. I "went out" for the college papers, and tried
to make the freshman crew, even staying in Cambridge vacations to go
down to the empty boat-house and plug away at the machines — and was
the last man kicked off the squad before they went to New London. I
got to know many fellows to nod to, and a very few intimately; but most
of my friends were whirled off and up into prominence, and came to see
me no more. One of them said he'd room with me sophomore year —
but he was tipped off that I wasn't "the right sort" and openly drew away
from me. And I, too, hurt a boy who was my friend. He was a Jew,
a shy, rather melancholy person. We were always together, we two outsiders. I became irritated and morbid about it — it seemed I would never
be part of the rich splendor of college life with him around — so I drew
away from him. . . It hurt him very much, and it taught me better. Since
then he has forgiven it, and done wonderful things for me, and we are
friends.

My second year was better. I was elected an editor of two of the
papers, and knew more fellows. The fortunate and splendid youths, the
aristocrats who filled the clubs and dominated college society, didn't seem
so attractive. In two open contests, the trial for editor of the college daily
paper and that for assistant manager of the varsity crew, I qualified easily
for election; but the aristocrats blackballed me. However, that mattered
less. During my freshman year I used to *pray* to be liked, to have friends,
to be popular with the crowd. Now I had friends, plenty of them; and I
have found that when I am working hard at something I love, friends
come without my trying, and stay; and fear goes, and that sense of being
lost which is so horrible.

From that time on I never felt out of it. I was never popular with the
aristocrats; I was never elected to any clubs but one, and that one largely
because of a dearth of members who could write lyrics for the annual
show. But I was on the papers, was elected president of the Cosmopolitan
Club, where forty-three nationalities met, became manager of the Musical
Clubs, captain of the water-polo team, and an officer in many undergraduate activities. As song-leader of the cheering section, I had the supreme

blissful sensation of swaying two thousand voices in great crashing chor-
uses during the big football games. The more I met the college aristocrats,
the more their cold, cruel stupidity repelled me. I began to pity them for
their lack of imagination, and the narrowness of their glittering lives —
clubs, athletics, society. College is like the world; outside there is the
same class of people, dull and sated and blind.

Harvard University under President Eliot was unique. Individualism
was carried to the point where a man who came for a good time could
get through and graduate without having learned anything; but on the
other hand, anyone could find there anything he wanted from all the
world's store of learning. The undergraduates were practically free from
control; they could live pretty much where they pleased, and do as they
pleased — so long as they attended lectures. There was no attempt made
by the authorities to weld the student body together, or to enforce any
kind of uniformity. Some men came with allowances of fifteen thousand
dollars a year pocket money, with automobiles and servants, living in
gorgeous suites in palatial apartment houses; others in the same class
starved in attic bedrooms.

All sorts of strange characters, of every race and mind, poets, philosophers, cranks of every twist, were in our class. The very hugeness of it
prevented any one man from knowing more than a few of his classmates,
though I managed to make the acquaintance of about five hundred of
them. The aristocrats controlled the places of pride and power, except
when a democratic revolution, such as occurred in my senior year, swept
them off their feet; but they were so exclusive that most of the real life
went on outside their ranks — and all the intellectual life of the student
body. So many fine men were outside the charmed circle that, unlike
most colleges, there was no disgrace in not being a "club man." What is
known as "college spirit" was not very powerful; no odium attached to
those who didn't go to football games and cheer. There was talk of the
world, and daring thought, and intellectual insurgency; heresy has always
been a Harvard and a New England tradition. Students themselves criticized the faculty for not educating them, attacked the sacred institution
of intercollegiate athletics, sneered at undergraduate clubs so holy that
no one dared mention their names. No matter what you were or what you
did — at Harvard you could find your kind. It wasn't a breeder for masses
of mediocrely educated young men equipped with "business" psychology;
out of each class came a few creative minds, a few scholars, a few "gentlemen" with insolent manners, and a ruck of nobodies . . . Things have
changed now. I liked Harvard better then.

Toward the end of my college course two influences came into my
life, which had a good deal to do with shaping me. One was contact with
Professor Copeland, who, under the pretense of teaching English composition, has stimulated generations of men to find color and strength and

beauty in books and in the world, and to express it again. The other was what I call, for lack of a better name, the manifestations of the modern spirit. Some men, notably Walter Lippmann, had been reading and thinking and talking about politics and economics, not as dry theoretical studies, but as live forces acting on the world, on the University even. They formed the Socialist Club, to study and discuss all modern social and economic theories, and began to experiment with the community in which they lived.

Under their stimulus the college political clubs, which had formerly been quadrennial mushroom growths for the purpose of drinking beer, parading and burning red fire, took on a new significance. The Club drew up a platform for the Socialist Party in the city elections. It had social legislation introduced into the Massachusetts Legislature. Its members wrote articles in the college papers challenging undergraduate ideals, and muckraked the University for not paying its servants living wages, and so forth. Out of the agitation sprang the Harvard Men's League for Women's Suffrage, the Single Tax Club, an Anarchist group. The faculty was petitioned for a course in socialism. Prominent radicals were invited to Cambridge to lecture. An open forum was started, to debate college matters and the issues of the day. The result of this movement upon the undergraduate world was potent. All over the place radicals sprang up, in music, painting, poetry, the theatre. The more serious college papers took a socialistic, or at least progressive tinge. Of course all this made no ostensible difference in the look of Harvard society, and probably the clubmen and the athletes, who represented us to the world, never even heard of it. But it made me, and many others, realize that there was something going on in the dull outside world more thrilling than college activities, and turned our attention to the writings of men like H. G. Wells and Graham Wallas, wrenching us away from the Oscar Wildean dilettantism that had possessed undergraduate littérateurs for generations.

John Reed, "Almost Thirty," *The New Republic*, April 29, 1936.

Thomas Wolfe

EUGENE GANT'S HARVARD
(c. 1923)

In the Houghton Library at Harvard there is a cheap ruled notebook containing jottings made by Thomas Wolfe in planning Of Time and the River. They are simply rough phrases separated by dashes: "My bewilderment and my despair — I close up suddenly — the lust for knowledge and for recognition — the feeling of impotence — the books in the Widener

*Library — the hordes of people on the pavements — to know all things
and to try all places — the recourse to poetry — the vulgar definition of
the Workshop people into creator and critic . . . My enormous feats of
reading — the ceaseless questing everywhere — the impact of loneliness —
the ineradicable stain of solitude upon my spirit — the wild eyes — the
flowing hair — utter rebellion from the group — sullen resentment for the
group. . ." In a few words these thoughts sum up Wolfe's feelings about
Harvard when he studied here as a graduate student between 1920 and
1923, and the impressions and discouragements which pressed down upon
an artistic conscience ever striving to burst out of control. Eugene Gant is,
of course, Wolfe himself, and much of the novel Of Time and the River
(1935) concerns Gant's experiences in Cambridge and Boston, particularly with the 47 Workshop of George Pierce Baker. Wolfe was a member
of that group, and three plays remain as examples of Wolfe's writing in
this period. Wolfe has also left a manuscript fragment, "The River
People," a portion of a projected work which has as its initial setting
the steps of Widener.*

THE TRAIN rushed on across the brown autumnal land, by wink of water
and the rocky coasts, the small white towns and flaming colors and the
lonely, tragic and eternal beauty of New England. It was the country of
his heart's desire, the dark Helen in his blood forever burning — and now
the fast approach across October land, the engine smoke that streaked
back on the sharp gray air that day!

The coming on of the great earth, the new lands, the enchanted city,
the approach, so smoky, blind and stifled, to the ancient web, the old
grimed thrilling barricades of Boston. The streets and buildings that slid
past that day with such a haunting strange familiarity, the mighty engine
steaming to its halt, and the great train-shed dense with smoke and acrid
with its smell and full of the slow pantings of a dozen engines, now passive
as great cats, the mighty station with the ceaseless throngings of its
illimitable life, and all of the murmurous, remote and mighty sounds of
time forever held there in the station, together with a tart and nasal voice,
a hand's breadth off that said: "There's hahdly time, but try it if you
want."

He saw the narrow, twisted, age-browned streets of Boston, then, with
their sultry fragrance of fresh-roasted coffee, the sight of the man-swarm
passing in its million-footed weft, the distant drone and murmur of the
great mysterious city all about him, the shining water of the Basin, and
the murmur of the harbor and its ships, the promise of glory and of a
thousand secret, lovely and mysterious women that were waiting somewhere in the city's web.

He saw the furious streets of life with their unending flood-tide of a million faces, the enormous library with its million books; or was it just one moment in the flood-tide of the city, at five o'clock, a voice, a face, a brawny lusty girl with smiling mouth who passed him in an instant at the Park Street station, stood printed in the strong October wind a moment — breast, belly, arm, and thigh, and all her brawny lustihood — and then had gone into the man-swarm, lost forever, never found?

Was it at such a moment — engine-smoke, a station, a street, the sound of time, a face that came and passed and vanished, could not be forgotten *here* or *here* or *here*, at such a moment of man's unrecorded memory, that he breathed fury from the air, that fury came?

He never knew; but now mad fury gripped his life, and he was haunted by the dream of time. Ten years must come and go without a moment's rest from fury, ten years of fury, hunger, all of the wandering in a young man's life. And for what? For what?

What is the fury which this youth will feel, which will lash him on against the great earth forever? It is the brain that maddens with its own excess, the heart that breaks from the anguish of its own frustration. It is the hunger that grows from everything it feeds upon, the thirst that gulps down rivers and remains insatiate. It is to see a million men, a million faces and to be a stranger and an alien to them always. It is to prowl the stacks of an enormous library at night, to tear the books out of a thousand shelves, to read in them with the mad hunger of the youth of man.

It is to have the old unquiet mind, the famished heart, the restless soul; it is to lose hope, heart, and all joy utterly, and then to have them wake again, to have the old feeling return with overwhelming force that he is about to find the thing for which his life obscurely and desperately is groping — for which all men on this earth have sought — one face out of the million faces, a wall, a door, a place of certitude and peace and wandering no more. For what is it that we Americans are seeking always on this earth? Why is it we have crossed the stormy seas so many times alone, lain in a thousand alien rooms at night hearing the sounds of time, dark time, and thought until heart, brain, flesh and spirit were sick and weary with the thought of it; "Where shall I go now? What shall I do?"

He did not know the moment that it came, but it came instantly, at once. And from that moment on mad fury seized him, from that moment on, his life, more than the life of any one that he would ever know, was to be spent in solitude and wandering. Why this was true, or how it happened, he would never know; yet it was so. From this time on — save for two intervals in his life — he was to live about as solitary a life as a modern man can have. And it is meant by this that the number of hours, days, months, and years — the actual time he spent alone — would be immense and extraordinary.

And this fact was all the more astonishing because he never seemed

to seek out solitude, nor did he shrink from life, or seek to build himself
into a wall away from all the fury and the turmoil of the earth. Rather,
he loved life so dearly that he was driven mad by the thirst and hunger
which he felt for it. Of this fury, which was to lash and drive him on for
fifteen years, the thousandth part could not be told, and what is told may
seem unbelievable, but it is true. He was driven by a hunger so literal,
cruel and physical that it wanted to devour the earth and all the things
and people in it, and when it failed in this attempt, his spirit would drown
in an ocean of horror and desolation, smothered below the overwhelming
tides of this great earth, sickened and made sterile, hopeless, dead by the
stupefying weight of men and objects in the world, the everlasting flock
and floodings of the crowd.

Now he would prowl the stacks of the library at night, pulling books
out of a thousand shelves and reading in them like a madman. The thought
of these vast stacks of books would drive him mad: the more he read, the
less he seemed to know — the greater the number of the books he read,
the greater the immense uncountable number of those which he could
never read would seem to be. Within a period of ten years he read at least
20,000 volumes — deliberately the number is set low — and opened the
pages and looked through many times that number. This may seem unbelievable, but it happened. Dryden said this about Ben Jonson: "Other
men read books but he read libraries" — and so now was it with this boy.
Yet this terrific orgy of the books brought him no comfort, peace, or wisdom of the mind and heart. Instead, his fury and despair increased from
what they fed upon, his hunger mounted with the food it ate.

He read insanely, by the hundreds, the thousands, the ten thousands,
yet he had no desire to be bookish; no one could describe this mad assault upon print as scholarly: a ravening appetite in him demanded that
he read everything that had ever been written about human experience.
He read no more from pleasure — the thought that other books were waiting for him tore at his heart forever. He pictured himself as tearing the
entrails from a book as from a fowl. At first, hovering over book stalls,
or walking at night among the vast piled shelves of the library, he would
read, watch in hand, muttering to himself in triumph or anger at the
timing of each page: "Fifty seconds to do that one. Damn you, we'll see!
You will, will you?" — and he would tear through the next page in twenty
seconds.

This fury which drove him on to read so many books had nothing to
do with scholarship, nothing to do with academic honors, nothing to do
with formal learning. He was not in any way a scholar and did not want
to be one. He simply wanted to know about everything on earth; he
wanted to devour the earth, and it drove him mad when he saw he could
not do this. And it was the same with everything he did. In the midst of

a furious burst of reading in the enormous library, the thought of the streets outside and the great city all around him would drive through his body like a sword. It would now seem to him that every second that he passed among the books was being wasted — that at this moment something priceless, irrecoverable was happening in the streets, and that if he could only get to it in time and see it, he would somehow get the knowledge of the whole thing in him — the source, the well, the spring from which all men and words and actions, and every design upon this earth proceeds.

And he would rush out in the streets to find it, be hurled through the tunnel into Boston and then spend hours in driving himself savagely through a hundred streets, looking into the faces of a million people, trying to get an instant and conclusive picture of all they did and said and were, of all their million destinies, and of the great city and the everlasting earth, and the immense and lonely skies that bent above them. And he would search the furious streets until bone and brain and blood could stand no more — until every sinew of his life and spirit was wrung, trembling, and exhausted, and his heart sank down beneath its weight of desolation and despair.

Yet a furious hope, a wild extravagant belief, was burning in him all the time. He would write down enormous charts and plans and projects of all that he proposed to do in life — a program of work and living which would have exhausted the energies of 10,000 men. He would get up in the middle of the night to scrawl down insane catalogs of all that he had seen and done: — the number of books he had read, the number of miles he had travelled, the number of people he had known, the number of women he had slept with, the number of meals he had eaten, the number of towns he had visited, the number of states he had been in.

And at one moment he would gloat and chuckle over these stupendous lists like a miser gloating over his hoard, only to groan bitterly with despair the next moment, and to beat his head against the wall, as he remembered the overwhelming amount of all he had not seen or done, or known. Then he would begin another list filled with enormous catalogs of all the books he had not read, all the food he had not eaten, all the women that he had not slept with, all the states he had not been in, all the towns he had not visited. Then he would write down plans and programs whereby all these things must be accomplished, how many years it would take to do it all, and how old he would be when he had finished. An enormous wave of hope and joy would surge up in him, because it now looked easy, and he had no doubt at all that he could do it.

He never asked himself in any practical way how he was going to live while this was going on, where he was going to get the money for this gigantic adventure, and what he was going to do to make it possible.

If he thought about it, it seemed to have no importance or reality whatever — he just dismissed it impatiently, or with a conviction that some old
man would die and leave him a fortune, that he was going to pick up a
purse containing hundreds of thousands of dollars while walking in the
Fenway, and that the reward would be enough to keep him going, or
that a beautiful and rich young widow, true-hearted, tender, loving, and
voluptuous, who had carrot-colored hair, little freckles on her face, a snub
nose and luminous gray-green eyes with something wicked, yet loving
and faithful in them, and one gold filling in her solid little teeth, was going
to fall in love with him, marry him, and be forever true and faithful to
him while he went reading, eating, drinking, whoring, and devouring his
way around the world; or finally that he would write a book or play every
year or so, which would be a great success, and yield him fifteen or twenty
thousand dollars at a crack. Thus, he went storming away at the whole
earth about him, sometimes mad with despair, weariness, and bewilderment; and sometimes wild with a jubilant and exultant joy and certitude
as the conviction came to him that everything would happen as he wished.
Then at night he would hear the vast sounds and silence of the earth
and of the city, he would begin to think of the dark sleeping earth and
of the continent of night, until it seemed to him it all was spread before
him like a map — rivers, plains, and mountains and 10,000 sleeping towns;
it seemed to him that he saw everything at once.

VII

THESE FESTIVAL RITES

In the hot sultry month that's called July,
(Forever famous to posterity)
A day is yearly kept, no doubt with zeal
By some, who to New England's common weal
Wish well, in these apostatizing days,
Wherein religion sensibly decays.
No doubt for noble ends this day's observed
By some, who have to learning just regard;
Whose souls (bright as the light) would grieve to see
These regions buried in obscurity.

A SATYRICAL DESCRIPTION OF COMMENCEMENT (1718)

Maria Sophia Quincy

"*I NEVER SAW SUCH A SPLENDID SCENE*"
(*1829*)

The Quincy girls were the five daughters of Josiah Quincy, Member of Congress, State Senator, Mayor of Boston, and President of Harvard. They were the "articulate sisters" — as their editor, M. A. DeWolfe Howe, has called them — and between 1814 and 1834 they kept "profuse" journals which described for their own delectation (especially if one of them was absent from home) the doings of the Quincy family. Because of their close connection with Harvard College during the term of their father's presidency, it has been thought fitting to include in this anthology documentary evidence that the woman's influence in Harvard writing was present long before the advent of Radcliffe. The author of this excerpt, Sophia, was the third of the sisters; she was twenty-four years old when she described the events of her father's first Commencement as President and the lively doings in Wadsworth House.

Friday, 28th August, 1829.

WE HAVE ENJOYED a great deal of pleasure during the three last days and so constantly has the time been occupied that I have not been able to continue my regular journal. I shall now give a sketch of what we have been seeing and doing. . .

On Wednesday the weather was delightful for the occasion [Commencement], as cool as in October. We were all arrayed at an early hour. I wore blue [word illegible] blonde gauze handkerchief, and cameo comb. Abby wore white and her hat, Susan a beautiful yellow dress made for this day — Mama in black with her blonde lace cap new trimmed with broad white ribbon. I never saw her look so handsome before. Ladies Margy and Anna preferred to stay at home. We were scarcely drest when a cry was heard through the mansion from the President and daughters, to us to assemble and tie up the degrees with blue ribbon, and write the names on them. It was now half past eight, and at nine the doors were to open. We surrounded Susan's bed on which were strewn a heap of degrees, Abby wrote the names, I held the scrolls, while Susan, Anna, and Margy tied them with ribbon. The hurrying exceeded all former experiences. The Corporation waited in the library. Papa flew in every other minute to snatch the rolls from our hands as soon as finished. The two pair of scissors perversely hid themselves among the papers, and the pieces of blue ribbon that came flying from Mrs. Farwell's were speedily exhausted. A fit of laughter assailed some of the ti-ers, while the impatience of others (who shall be nameless) retarded instead of forwarding the work. However, just in time all was finished and deposited in the library, and at that moment we were summoned to the parlour.

Margy and I descended and were soon followed by Mama, Susan, and Abby. Col. and Mrs. Morse, "Edward," and Mrs. Ford were therein seated. The ladies and the Colonel were introduced in due form to us. Mrs. Morse is a very plain but genteel, ladylike woman. Mrs. Ford in deep black, rather interesting. The Colonel a fine-looking man. The ladies said they would take off their bonnets if we thought best, and had bro't headdresses. We advised them certainly to do it, and upstairs we all ran, as there was no time to be lost. Mrs. Morse placed on her head a yellow toque, and Mrs. Ford a pretty, fashionable cap trimmed with black.

As soon as they were ready, attended by the gentlemen, and preceded by Horace, we all went through our back stable yard and stationed ourselves at a side door, at which was already planted Mrs. Farrar, and Mrs. Ripley. The other doors were thronged with ladies. Here we waited for a few minutes and as soon as the doors opened "caught up our frocks and ran." The rush of ladies was very great, and as they uplifted their voices and screamed as they ran, it was really frightful. I got into the gallery among the first and flew into the "King's Box," as Uncle Morton denominated our pew. Our party followed me like lightning, and if I had only shut the door as soon as they were all in, we should have been delightfully accommodated; but I was so confused and frightened with the noise and running that before I was aware two other ladies had packed in. We were very much crowded, but beckoning one of the Constables, we sent him to our house for a music-stool, which we placed at the foot of the pew, and on which I was perched in the most conspicuous place possible. It was an excellent seat, however, and I found my two neighbors (who had inserted themselves much against our wish) very agreeable people. One was Miss Ward from Salem, whose only brother had a part on this occasion, the other a Mrs. Fay from Alabama, a relation of the Hedge family. I had a great deal of pleasant conversation with them and with Nancy Perkins, Anna Higginson, and Mrs. Clarke. The three last-mentioned ladies were standing at the outside of our pew, and a happy thought came into my head, and when Mr. Chamberlain bro't the music-stool, I conveyed to him a request that he would furnish these ladies with chairs. Four chairs soon appeared and they were comfortably seated, and many were their acknowledgements to me for my kindness.

The galleries were filled from the lowest to the highest seat with ladies. I never saw such a splendid scene. It surpassed even the Inauguration. There were a greater number of beautiful women collected together than I ever saw before, and dressed with great elegance, and in the most shewy style. The house below equally filled with the lords of the Creation. We waited some time before the welcome sounds of the full band announced the approach of the procession, and soon the President in full costume sailed up the aisle, followed by the Governor [Levi Lincoln] and his aids in full uniform (Josiah looked elegantly), and all the dignitaries, civil and ecclesiastical, of the land, and strangers filled the house in a fine style. Mrs. Morse was delighted with the scene, and said she had never imagined such a crowd before, nor such a splendid spectacle.

Dr. [Eliphalet] Porter opened the services with a very fine prayer, which affected Mrs. Morse to tears. Papa then took his seat in the pulpit and the young men commenced speaking. Charles Fay was the first, and went through a Latin address with a very good air and graceful manner. Sixteen or seventeen young men spoke in succession with various degrees of merit — Wm. Channing and young Robbins the best. Mr. Storrow had the first part and of course spoke the last, and in truth everybody was excessively fatigued. I did not hear much of the first part of the oration, and the latter part I lost entirely, for poor Mrs. Fay, our new acquaintance, began to feel very faint, grew paler and paler. Miss Ward supported her, the Miss Hills wafted smelling bottles from behind us, while Abby and I fanned on each side, and soon the attention of the multitude was fixed on our pew. The poor lady grew worse and worse however. Luckily her husband beheld her from below and hastened upstairs, and reached the door just as she was going off entirely. The crowd was so great that we could scarcely get the door open. However, the people were very accommodating, and Mr. Colman and her husband with some other gentlemen bore her from our sight after we had played our parts before the audience for some ten or fifteen minutes.

When the oration was finished Papa took his seat in the antiquated arm chair before the pulpit with the degrees of hurried memories by his side, and the class came up on the stage in sixes and sevens. He addressed them in Latin, presented them to the Governor, and gave them their degrees in a very graceful style. A year from this day I was seated in the Library at Quincy penning a letter to Sophia Morton while all the rest of the family had come over here to Copley Greene's Commencement. What would we have thought if the curtain of Fate had been raised, and we had beheld the splendid scene exhibited on this day, and Papa seated on the stage in the costume of President of the University!

The degrees having been given, we had some delightful music from the band which had played at intervals during the morning, and then

Mr. Walker from Northampton delivered the English Oration. It was a very fine one, but his style of speaking so exactly resembled Josiah's burlesquing different orators, that Abby and I were entirely overset, and laughed rather indecorously. A Latin Address closed the performances, spoken very well by Mr. Page, and at four o'clock the Assembly broke up. The procession formed and departed to the Dinner Hall, and as soon as possible our party left the church and entered our delightful residence. The crowd around the doors, the groups of carriages and rows of chaises really surpassed what I had seen before. . .

We found Margy, Anna and Mary Jane in the parlour, Margy arrayed in Anna's pink Battiste, and blonde gauze handkerchief, Anna in Margy's beautiful sheer muslin, and Mary Jane in black with carved comb and ornaments, and blonde gauze mantle — all three ladies looking very handsome. Mr. Greene and Edmund had met us at the door.

They were, as well may be imagined, half famished, and declared they thought we never were coming out; it was then half past four. Dinner was soon on the table, and added to our family were Mrs. Morse and her son, and Mrs. Ford. We went into the Freshmen's room, where York and another black attendant had spread the table with great elegance. The dinner was beautiful, dessert ornamented with flowers and all in the best style. Conversation during the repast turned on the pleasures of the morning. Anna and Margy had had a variety of people flitting in and out. Mr. Robbins, the father of the young man who spoke, was brought fainting from the church and comfortably put to bed up in our room. He had just recovered sufficiently to be carried off in his chaise as we came home.

We were at table till half past five, and had just got into the drawing room, which together with the dining room was beautifully decorated with flowers, when gentlemen and ladies began to pour in. One room was crowded, and a number of walkers in the entry and opposite room. The band were stationed in the back parlour, and animated the company with their delightful strains. The Governor and his train of course paid their respects. Eight or nine foreigners, among whom were Mr. Santag and Mr. Wallenstein, Sir Isaac Coffin, &c. &c. &c. Mrs. Derby and her two pretty nieces, all very much drest, the Miss Whites and Miss Silsbee, very handsome, and Miss Sumner and Miss Griffith, very genteel, sailed in and out. Marie Upham, who really looked beautiful, and of course drest with the best taste in the world in an elegant black dress, blonde gauze scarf and pearl ornaments, her hair put up with an ornamental comb, and a beautiful blonde gauze toque trimmed with blonde lace on her head. A great many gentlemen, young and old. I conversed with Messrs. Santag and Wellenstein, Stackpole, Mr. Bethune, Wm. Payne, Mr. Adams, the

Editor of the *Centinel*, Col. Merrick (who declared I was the only lady in the whole church whom he recognized) &c. &c. Mr. Stackpole introduced me to Miss Silsbee, who in her turn introduced to me a youth whose name I have forgotten and then I presented her to Mary Jane. Mrs. Gorham Parsons and Mary Ann Lee also came from Brighton, and a number of others whom I cannot enumerate. Mrs. Morse and her friend seemed to enjoy the scene very much.

The company were arriving and departing till half past seven, ice-creams and coffee circulating all the time. The Governor took leave early, and was escorted off by the troop of horse in a tempest of drums and dust, and by half after seven almost all had departed. A pretty Spanish Lady drest in black with a black toque on her head staid till the last, and by Mama's request played a beautiful piece on the piano. Old Mr. Hedge and I were conversing, and so interesting was our converse that we prosed on long after the Lady had began and thereby excited various shakes of the head, and warning looks from many of the auditors. The piece was very long, but well executed, and soon after the conclusion the lady and her husband, and another light-haired unknown departed. Mr. Coit, Mr. Pickering, Mr. Robinson (the tenant of No. 1. Hamilton Place) and Eliot Dwight came after all the rest had departed, and we had a very pleasant evening, as usual.

On Thursday morning at the breakfast table the party was formed for the church. Margy had not intended going, but on the whole thought she would, and prepared accordingly — Anna the only one who remained, and she said she would wait till twelve and then try to get in with Josiah. I wore green silk, pointed skirt, handkerchief, and white scarf, nothing on my head, — Abby and Margy their hats. We all repaired to the same door. No one was there but the Miss Hills and others soon joined us. The other doors very much crowded. We stood some time, Mama on the upper step holding an umbrella over our heads, and all conversing pleasantly. The moment the bolt was pushed, the umbrella was thrown afar off, and we all rushed in. There was more strife than yesterday, but pale and trembling, we all found ourselves in our accustomed pew. It was really surprising to see the ladies leap over the tops of the pews. A number of female forms were seen rushing through our pew, and leaping over the highest side of it to those adjoining. They were headed by Mrs. Abbott Lawrence, who certainly deserved to have a degree given her for her powers of jumping. Mrs. Bigelow (the sister or aunt of Mrs. L.) was the last of the train, and she was just half over the pew when Mama entered, and catching her round the waist, pulled her back and insisted on her keeping her place with us. The poor lady was so agitated and frightened that she could scarcely speak, but appeared very much obliged for the permission to remain with us. They seemed to have no idea of remaining in our seat, imagining it was reserved particularly for us. The two Miss Hills again sat with us, and we again sent for the music stool on which Abby sat at the foot of the pew. There was not nearly as many ladies as were collected on Commencement day, but still the galleries were well filled, and all the intervening spaces filled with gentlemen. Margy and I sat together and had a great deal of amusement in looking at the various figures in the opposite gallery and chatting with each other.

The prize speaking commenced at ten, Papa and seven or eight other gentlemen as Judges occupied the seat in front of the organ. Ten youths spoke in succession, all very respectable, but young Simmons the best. He spoke admirably an extract from "Ringan Gilhaize" and carried off the first prize, a medal of twenty dollars. I think his speaking gave us as much pleasure as anything of the kind I ever heard. He spoke very finely at the last Exhibition. Papa announced the distribution of Prizes from the stage when the speaking was over. The second prizes were awarded to others of the orators. They concluded speaking at half past eleven, and the Phi Beta Society were not to enter till twelve, so we conversed with a variety, Mr. Merriam among the rest, and listened to music during the intermission. Josiah brought Anna in with some difficulty and got her down to our pew, and then went for another music stool, on which I was enthroned at the head of the pew.

At twelve the Society entered. An unusual number turned out on this occasion, and the stage and pews on the broad aisle were filled with them, while the rest of the church was completely filled with the people in general. It was a fine scene, and the stage presented a striking assemblage of gentlemen of every age, from Dr. Prince of Salem (who has attended on these occasions for nearly sixty years) to the Marshals of the day, Mr. Tower and Mr. Andrews, two handsome young men who were very elegantly dressed and ornamented with their pink and blue ribbons and medals, and sat at the foot of the antiquated old chair, which has seen so many equally interesting groups around it, now passed from the stage of Life forever.

Mr. [Convers] Francis commenced speaking at twelve and never concluded till a quarter past *two*. His oration was a fine one, but so unconscionably and unwarrantably long that of course the whole audience were wearied out. Their impatience was so great that I believe they would have left the house, had not their desire to hear Mr. Sprague overbalanced their wish to leave Mr. Francis. At length he did conclude, and we had some music while we rose and got rid of some of our fatigue before Mr. [Charles] Sprague commenced. He pronounced an excellent Poem on "Curiosity," combining the severity of well merited censure and the drollery of ludicrous description in a very happy manner. It was curious to observe the faces of this crowded audience, now laughing and expressing great delight and clapping with might and main, and then silent, grave and thoughtful as the orator changed the picture from a gay to a grave subject. He spoke an hour, and closed with an elegant compliment to Papa, and when he concluded received a thunder of applause. It was indeed a gratifying moment for the Quincy family. Papa sat concealing his face with his hand, as he fronted the whole audience and must have felt somewhat embarrassed. The whole was concluded by half past three o'clock, and all the audience left the Church with expedition, the Society and orators of the day to dine at the University Hall, and the Judges of the prize speaking and other dignitaries adjourning to the President's House.

We waited till the crowd was gone, and received the compliments and congratulations of the surrounding ladies and from Mr. Bigelow and Mr. Cranch from the stage below. The latter was at our house the preceding evening, and seemed to have highly enjoyed these days, said he had now seen the glory of New England, and seemed to understand "what was what" (to use an elegant expression) perfectly well. He has been travelling about since he took leave of us six weeks since, and returned here to be present on these occasions. He goes to-morrow. I like him very much.

We received the thanks of Mrs. Bigelow and the Misses Hill for all our politeness, and returned to our mansion just after all the dinner party had assembled in the drawing room.

York and his co-partner had spread an elegant table in the dining room for two and twenty, and so only Susan could join the party. It was quite an amalgamation dinner and, as Susan said, composed of curious contrasts. There was Mr. Coit and Dr. Holmes, Isaac P. Davis and Mr. Bowditch, Daniel Davis and Dr. Porter, contrasted in the inward man certainly, and Mr. Harding and Mr. Coit presented a singular diversity in outward appearance. Besides these there were Judge Story, who talks all the time, and Dr. Popkin who never says a word; Mr. John Pickering and Mr. Callender, Mr. Francis and Mr. Willis, Frank Gray and Mr. Farrar, and Mr. Ritchie.

We ladies retired to our room during the dinner, and listened to Sarah's account of Miss Goldsboro' and Miss Coolidge being brought in here after fainting in the church — accompanied by six gentlemen and four ladies. We saw them carried out of the gallery, but little thought of their being deposited in our beds. However, they were recovered and departed before our return. Josiah came up to our room, saying he could get no seat at the Society's dinner, nor at the President's either, so came to us. We had a table spread in the little back parlour, and a great deal of amusement with our flying repast. The gentlemen in the dining room made a great noise laughing and talking, and all seemed to be going very well. We then retired to our room and Margy laid down while Abby prepared a dress for Mrs. Derby's this evening. I was dreadfully fatigued, body and mind.

The dinner party broke up at half past six, and we all ran down to hear accounts and regale on the ice-creams and fruits left on the table. Mr. Callender came in while we were in the height of conversation, upon which Margy [Mrs. Greene] cried out, "Mr. Callender, I am invisible," and he returned with his accustomed readiness, "My dear *Miss Quincy*, I am very happy to see you." He is very droll and added greatly to the brilliancy of the party. They had a delightful dinner, the entertainment elegantly got up, and the company extremely animated and agreeable.

As soon as all had departed the carriage was ordered, and Margy, Susan and Abby with their evening costumes whirled off to the city and Mrs. Derby's. The chaise bore away Josiah and Edmund to the metropolis and York and John in our *gig* followed in the rear. Mamma, Anna and I spent the evening in talking over the various events of the day, and the pleasure we had enjoyed during this week. The gentlemen declared to-day that these were "three of the proudest days old Harvard had ever seen," and they have certainly been "highly gratifying" to the Quincy family.

The girls remained in town all night — Anna recounted the visitors she had received while we were in church this morning. Mr. Pollard, Mr. Haydn, Mr. McCleary, and Mr. Sprague, the poet, among the rest. The first entertainment given by the President went off in the best style possible in every respect.

M. A. DeWolfe Howe, ed., *The Articulate Sisters* (Cambridge: Harvard University Press, 1946).

Josiah Quincy, Jr.

PRESIDENT JACKSON GIVES 'EM
A LITTLE LATIN
(1833)

When President Andrew Jackson made his triumphal tour of New England in 1833, his aide-de-camp in Massachusetts was Josiah Quincy, Jr., son of the President of Harvard and later Mayor of Boston. Young Quincy well remembered General Lafayette's enthusiastic reception at Harvard in 1824, for Quincy had had to deliver a Latin greeting in honor of the great Frenchman; he had also served as Lafayette's aide-de-camp dur-

*ing the official welcome of the Commonwealth. The visit of General
Jackson and Vice-President Van Buren was different; it was deplored by
conservative, Federalist Boston, and it was something of a shock for the
Old Guard, like John Quincy Adams, to have Harvard give an honorary
degree to Old Hickory, who was never noted for his erudition. The details
of the visit were humorously revealed by "Major Jack Downing" (Seba
Smith of the Portland* Courier) *and many of Smith's imitators, among
them Charles Augustus Davis of the New York* Advertiser *who made
Major Jack tell in a fictitious report the now famous story of the Harvard
ceremony. When Jackson acknowledged Harvard's honor, Jack Downing recorded, "the General was going to stop, but I says in his ear, 'You
must give 'em a little Latin, Doctor!' . . . 'E pluribus unum,' says he,
'my friends, sine qua non.'"*

THE MORNING of Wednesday, the 25th, was chilly and overcast, not at all
the sort of day for an invalid to encounter the fatigues of travel and
reception. At ten o'clock, nevertheless, the President appeared, and took
his seat in the barouche, and was greeted with the acclamations which
will always be forthcoming when democratic sovereignty is seen embodied
in flesh and blood. Very little flesh in this case, however, and only such
trifle of blood as the doctors had thought not worth appropriating. But the
spirit in Jackson was resolute to conquer physical infirmity. His eye
seemed brighter than ever, and all aglow with the mighty will which can
compel the body to execute its behests. He was full of conversation, as
we drove to Cambridge, to get that doctorate whose bestowal occasioned
many qualms to the high-toned friends of Harvard. College degrees were
then supposed to have a meaning which has long ago gone out of them;
and to many excellent persons it seemed a degrading mummery to dub a
man Doctor of Laws who was credited with caring for no laws whatever
which conflicted with his personal will. John Quincy Adams, I remember,
was especially disturbed at this academic recognition of Jackson and
actually asked my father, who was then president of the College, whether
there was no way of avoiding it. "Why, no," was the reply. "As the people
have twice decided that this man knows law enough to be their ruler, it
is not for Harvard College to maintain that they are mistaken." But Mr.
Adams was not satisfied, and the bitter generalization of his diary that
"time-serving and sycophancy are the qualities of all learned and scientific
institutions" was certainly not to be modified by his successor's visit to
Cambridge. It did not require Jack Downing's fun to show the delicious
absurdity of giving Jackson a literary degree; but the principle that
wandering magistrates, whether of state or nation, might claim this distinction had been firmly established, and there were difficulties in limiting
its application.

There is a familiar expression by which newspaper reporters denote the strong current of feeling which sometimes runs through an assembly, and yet reaches no audible sound of applause of censure. It has been decided that the word [*sensation*], put in brackets as it is here printed, shall convey those tremors of apprehension or criticism which cannot be exhibited with definiteness. Nobody who knows anything about Harvard College can doubt that there will be *sensation* whenever the people decide that Governor B. F. Butler shall appear upon the stage of Sanders Theatre to receive the compliment of the highest degree which can there be offered; but I will venture to say that an emotion much stronger than this was felt by the throng which filled the College Chapel when Andrew Jackson, leaning upon the arm of my father, entered the building from which he was to depart a Doctor of Laws. Fifty years have taught sensible men to estimate college training at its true worth. It is now clear that it does not furnish the exclusive entrance to paths of the highest honor. The career of Abraham Lincoln has made impossible a certain academic priggishness which belonged to an earlier period of our national existence. Jackson's ignorance of books was perhaps exaggerated, and his more useful knowledge of things and human relations was not apparent to his political opponents to whom the man was but a dangerous bundle of chimeras and prejudices; but I do not need the testimony of a diary now before me to confirm the statement that his appearance before that Cambridge audience instantly produced a toleration which quickly merged into something like admiration and respect. The name of Andrew Jackson was, indeed, one to frighten naughty children with; but the person who went by it wrought a mysterious charm upon old and young. Beacon Street had been undemonstrative as we passed down that Brahmin thoroughfare on our way to Cambridge; but a few days later I heard an incident characteristic enough to be worth telling. Mr. Daniel P. Parker, a well-known Boston merchant, had come to his window to catch a glimpse of the guest of the State, regarding him very much as he might have done some dangerous monster which was being led captive past his house. But the sight of the dignified figure of Jackson challenged a respect which the good merchant felt he must pay by proxy, if not in person. "Do some one come here and salute the old man!" he suddenly exclaimed. And a little daughter of Mr. Parker was thrust forward to wave her handkerchief to the terrible personage whose doings had been so offensive to her elders.

The exercises in the Chapel were for the most part in Latin. My father addressed the President in that language, repeating a composition upon which he somewhat prided himself, for Dr. Beck, after making two verbal corrections in his manuscript, had declared it to be as good Latin as a man need write. Then we had some more Latin from young Mr. Francis

Bowen, of the senior class, a gentleman whose name has since been associated with so much fine and weighty English. There were also a few modest words presumably in the vernacular, though scarcely audible, from the recipient of the doctorate.

But it has already been intimated that there were two Jacksons who were at that time making the tour of New England. One was the person who I have endeavored to describe; the other may be called the Jackson of comic myth, whose adventures were minutely set forth by Mr. Jack Downing and his brother humorists. The Harvard degree, as bestowed upon this latter personage, offered a situation which the chroniclers of the grotesque could in no wise resist. A hint of Downing was seized upon and expanded as it flew from mouth to mouth until, at last, it has actually been met skulking near the back door of history in a form something like this. General Jackson, upon being harangued in Latin, found himself in a position of immense perplexity. It was simply decent for him to reply in the learned language in which he was addressed; but, alas! the Shakespearian modicum of "small Latin" was all that Old Hickory possessed, and what he must do was clearly to rise to the situation and make the most of it. There were those college fellows, chuckling over his supposed humiliation; but they were to meet a man who was not to be caught in the classical trap they had set for him. Rising to his feet just at the proper moment, the new Doctor of Laws astonished the assembly with a Latin address, in which Dr. Beck himself was unable to discover a single error. A brief quotation from this eloquent production will be sufficient to exhibit its character: "Caveat emptor: corpus delicti: ex post facto: dies irae: e pluribus unum: usque ad nauseam: Ursa Major: sic semper tyrannis: quid pro quo: requiescat in pace."

Now this foolery was immensely taking in the day of it; and mimics were accustomed to throw social assemblies into paroxysms of delight by imitating Jackson in the delivery of his Latin speech. The story was, on the whole, so good, as showing how the man of the people could triumph over the crafts and subtleties of classical pundits, that all Philistia wanted to believe it. And so it came to pass that, as time went on, part of Philistia did believe it, for I have heard it mentioned as an actual occurrence by persons who may not shrink from a competitive examination in history whenever government offices are to be entered through that portal. . .

To return to the real Jackson, who held what Dickens says Americans call a le-vee, after the exercises in the chapel. He stood at one end of the low parlor of the President's house, and bowed to the students as they passed him. "I am most happy to see you, gentlemen," he said; "I wish you all much happiness"; "Gentlemen, I heartily wish you success in life"; and so on, constantly varying the phrase, which was always full of feeling. The President had begun his reception by offering his hand to all who approached; but he found that this would soon drain the small strength which must carry him through the day. He afterward made an exception in favor of two pretty children, daughters of Dr. Palfrey. He took the hands of these little maidens, and then lifted them up and kissed them. It was a pleasant sight, — one not to be omitted when the events of the day were put upon paper. This rough soldier, exposed all his life to those temptations which have conquered public men whom we still call good, could kiss little children with lips as pure as their own.

Josiah Quincy, Jr., *Figures of the Past* (Boston, 1884).

Josiah Quincy

THE CENTENNIAL CELEBRATION

(1836)

Lawyer by profession, former Congressman and later Mayor of Boston, Josiah Quincy became President of Harvard in 1829 at the age of fifty-seven. An able administrator who materially strengthened the growing University, he was less successful in his relations with students than in making current teaching methods more attractive. Morison has called him "the most unpopular President in Harvard history since Hoar." Yet "brave 'old Quin'" was a stanch advocate of academic freedom and under his administration progress was made toward allowing students a choice of subjects. One of the big events of the Quincy period was the bicentennial celebration of September 8, 1836. On this occasion President Quincy delivered a two-hour address which was later expanded into his two-volume history of the University, from which the following official account is taken.

AS THE DAY of the Celebration approached, extensive and tasteful arrangements were . . . made by the Undergraduates for the decoration of the College edifices. The entrance to Harvard Hall, and the porticos of Dane and University Halls, were wreathed with evergreens and flowers; and arches decorated in the same manner were erected over the three principal entrances to the College grounds. The name of HARVARD was placed over the centre arch, between Massachusetts and Harvard Halls, while those of DUNSTER and CHAUNCY, the first two Presidents of the University, surmounted respectively the two side arches. Arrangements were also made for a general illumination of the College buildings.

On the morning of the 8th of September, 1836, a white banner, on which the device of the first seal of the University was emblazoned, was raised on the summit of the pavilion. At an early hour all the avenues leading from the city of Boston and its environs to Cambridge were thronged; and by nine o'clock the Alumni and invited guests, to the number of more than fifteen hundred, assembled in University Hall.

There were venerable and reverend divines, — grave and dignified judges, — statesmen and lawyers, — learned, intellectual, and eminent men of other professions and pursuits in life, — exchanging cordial salutations after years of separation. There were the young and ardent, looking forward in imagination to a brilliant future, and men of maturer age pleased with the retrospection of the past. The greetings of companions of early days, the efforts at recognition, the fond and fervent recollections not untinged with melancholy, which the meeting occasioned, the inquiries more implied than uttered after the absent, the inquisitive glances, rather than words, by which each seemed to ask of the other's welfare, constituted a scene not to be forgotten by any individual who witnessed it. . .

When the Chief Marshal named the classes of the Alumni, it was deeply interesting to mark the result. The class of 1759 was called, but their only representative, and the eldest surviving Alumnus, Judge Wingate, of New Hampshire, being ninety-six years of age, was unable to attend. The classes from 1763 to 1773 were successively named, but solemn pauses succeeded; they had all joined the great company of the departed, or, sunk in the vale of years, were unable to attend the high festival of their Alma Mater. At length, when the class of 1774 was named, Mr. Samuel Emery came forward; a venerable old man, a native of Chatham, Barnstable County, Massachusetts, who, at the age of eighty-six, after an absence of sixty years from the Halls of Harvard, had come from his residence in Philadelphia to attend this celebration. The Rev. Dr. Ripley, of Concord, of the class of 1776, and the Rev. Dr. Homer, of Newton, of the class of 1777, were followed by the Rev. Dr. Bancroft, of Worcester, and the Rev. Mr. Willis, of Kingston, of the class of 1778; and, as modern times were approached, instead of solitary individuals, twenty or thirty members of a class appeared at the summons.

On leaving University Hall, the procession moved along the principal avenues within the College grounds, through the gateway between Massachusetts and Harvard Halls, and, passing through the lines of the escort formed by the Undergraduates, entered the Congregational Church. The galleries of the edifice had been reserved for the ladies, and, after the entrance of the procession, every part of the building was filled by a crowded audience. After a voluntary on the organ, the Rev. Dr. Ripley offered a solemn and fervent prayer. Although more than eighty years of age, he spoke in a clear and powerful voice. Like the Jewish leader, "his eye was not dim, nor his natural force abated."

An Occasional Ode, written by the Rev. Samuel Gilman, of Charleston, S. C., was then sung.

> FAIR HARVARD! thy sons to thy Jubilee throng,
>   And with blessings surrender thee o'er
> By these festival-rites, from the Age that is past,
>   To the Age that is waiting before.
> O Relic and Type of our ancestors' worth,
>   That hast long kept their memory warm!
> First flower of their wilderness! Star of their night,
>   Calm rising through change and through storm!
>
> To thy bowers we were led in the bloom of our youth,
>   From the home of our free-roving years,
> When our fathers had warned, and our mothers had prayed,
>   And our sisters had blest, through their tears.
> *Thou* then wert our parent, — the nurse of our souls, —
>   We were moulded to manhood by thee,
> Till, freighted with treasure-thoughts, friendships, and hopes,
>   Thou didst launch us on Destiny's sea.
>
> When, as pilgrims, we come to revisit thy halls,
>   To what kindlings the season gives birth!
> Thy shades are more soothing, thy sunlight more dear,
>   Than descend on less privileged earth:
> For the Good and the Great, in their beautiful prime,
>   Through thy precincts have musingly trod,
> As they girded their spirits, or deepened the streams
>   That make glad the fair City of God.
>
> Farewell! be thy destinies onward and bright!
>   To thy children the lesson still give,
> With freedom to think, and with patience to bear,
>   And for Right ever bravely to live.
> Let not moss-covered Error moor *thee* at its side,
>   As the world on Truth's current glides by;
> Be the herald of Light, and the bearer of Love,
>   Till the stock of the Puritans die.

The touching allusions of this beautiful Ode excited a deep and solemn enthusiasm, and the Address of President Quincy commanded, during two hours, the attention of the audience. A prayer was afterwards offered by the Rev. Dr. Homer, and then the whole congregation united their voices in the solemn strains of "Old Hundred."

> From all that dwell below the skies,
> Let the Creator's praise arise;
> Let the Redeemer's name be sung
> Through every land, by every tongue.
>
> Eternal are thy mercies, Lord;
> Eternal truth attends thy word;
> Thy praise shall sound from shore to shore,
> Till suns shall rise and set no more.

No one could look around at this moment, without thrilling emotions, on this crowded assembly of educated and intelligent men, convened on the high festival of this ancient literary institution, and soon to be separated never to meet again.

The benediction was given by the Rev. Dr. Ripley; and, on leaving the church, the procession was formed in the same order as when it entered. The classes of the Alumni were again summoned, and solemn pauses again succeeded, until Mr. Emery walked down the aisle alone, and was greeted by testimonies of applause from his younger brethren. On leaving the church, the procession, including more than fifteen hundred individuals, proceeded to the left across the Common, and then, turning to the right, passed in front of the College edifices. By this arrangement, the graduates of the various classes passed in review before each other. After passing Dane Hall, the procession turned to the left, proceeded through Harvard Street, in front of the President's House, and entered the College grounds opposite the pavilion. . .

The tables were prepared to accommodate about fifteen hundred persons, and they were completely filled by the Alumni and their invited guests, except a division on the left of the President's chair, reserved for, and occupied by, the Undergraduates.

It was extraordinary to see how soon and how quietly fifteen hundred persons found places, each one seated and duly provided for the feast. On the left of the chair, the Undergraduates of the University were seated, and thence to the extreme right extended row above row, and class after class, of Alumni, embracing every period of life, from the youth fresh from the studious hall, to the octogenarian, who seemed to live again in the memories of the distant past. When all were seated, a prayer was offered by the Rev. President Humphrey, of Amherst College. For a time the dining quietly proceeded; but soon the busy hum of many voices, the laugh, the joke, animated the scene. All were again hushed, as if by magic, when Mr. Everett, the President of the Day, rose to address them. To say that he was most happy, is feeble praise. He was eloquent, brilliant, touching; — and as he read, in the sea of intelligent faces around him, the effect of his own unrivalled declamation, his fancy seemed to burst away on freshened pinion, and to pour forth lavishly the riches of his well-fraught mind. . . .

Josiah Quincy, *The History of Harvard University* (1840).

Horace Howard Furness

PRESIDENT WALKER TAKES THE HELM
(1853)

*One of the world's great Shakespearean scholars, Horace Howard Fur-
ness is known to our time for the compilation of the New Variorum Edition of the plays of William Shakespeare. In addition, however, he was a
man of wide knowledge and interests, a correspondent par excellence.
Of him, H. H. F. Jayne, the collector of his letters, has written: "The
letters . . . beginning as they do with Furness's years at Harvard preserve sufficient continuity to mark the events of his crowded life . . .
they reveal the expansion of his mind, the subtleties of his nature . . .
his rare good humor and his kindly sympathy. He devoted much time to
his correspondence, especially in his later years, and he always looked
upon letter-writing as an art. He infused the merest note of acknowledg-
ment with a twinkle of wit or a beguiling touch of his personality. His
longer letters . . . are veritable mines for sparkling gems of observation
and reflection." Furness entered Harvard at sixteen and came self-pre-
pared in every subject except mathematics. He earned part of his way
by tutoring and teaching school. The following letter was written to his
sister at home, after the inauguration of President Walker following the
resignation of President Sparks because of ill health.*

Cambridge, May 29, 1853

THIS WEEK has passed most delightfully. I felt perfectly free, & mingled
study & recreation in the most delicious confusion. As time by no means
hung heavy on my hands I was under no sort of obligations to teach
the orphan girl to read or the orphan boy to sew. I read, wrote, slept, and
smoked to my heart's content. Yesterday afternoon I read a "History of
the Inquisition" & gradually dreamed off & awoke maintaining that some
one or other, I couldn't remember the name, would make a most capital
General Inquisitor. The event of the week, however, was the Inauguration of Pres't Walker. There was none of the pomp and magnificence of
preceding years, yet it was still quite imposing. The first ceremony was
the planting of a young tree, which ever after bears Dr. Walker's name.
This is a time-honored custom and is performed as follows. In the morning about ten o'clock the Senior class marched in a body to Pres't Sparks'
& presented a handsome bouquet to Lady S.; thence to Dr. Walker's &
gave a similar bouquet to Lady W. Retiring from Dr. Walker's, the
President-elect accompanied them and was escorted into the College yard
to where a hole had been dug, into which was placed a fine young pine
tree; the Chief Marshal then steps forward and addresses a flowery,

spooney speech to Dr. Walker, who replies somewhat similarly, about children's children (i.e., grandchildren) sitting under the shade of it & reflecting with pleasure upon its planting. (Now if there are the same laws in force then, as now, they will be very quickly dispersed as a "parietal group.") Dr. Walker then advances & throws in the first shovelful of earth, & is followed by each member of the class, doing the same in turn; "and now," said the Doctor as he threw down the shovel, "where are your 'digs'?" What hand-clapping and what laughter! (But between you and me, I think it was a joke that he heard among the bystanders at President Sparks' or Everett's Inauguration.) The worthy Doctor was then accompanied home and the crowd dispersed to celebrate the day in uproarious carousals. And upon my word, I never saw such almost universal, what shall I call it —intoxication is too gross a term to apply to such good fellows & yet it was nothing more nor less. One of my classmates was not far from the truth, when he said that "there was not more than fifteen fellows out of our class, who were not 'tight' that day"; and what was true of our class was true of the other three also. You know my penchant for such scenes, & I assure you that that day I saw some rich ones. I hate to have any one get "tight," but if he must & will do so, why, pray let me see him, & when he is getting over it I will administer soda water & good advice to his heart's content. On the day in question, at about eleven o'clock I was lying reading on my sofa, now and then interrupted by bursts of merriment, when a real good friend of mine, who is, however rather fond of getting elevated semioccasionally & then comes & confesses to me, so to speak, rushed into my room, bawling out: "Furness, you old fool you! get up! come round to D.'s; you must come; all the fellows are round there & we're having a glorious time!" This speech was interspersed with adjectives "immentionable to ears perlite." I complied, & truly it was the most ludicrous sight I ever witnessed. There were about fifteen or twenty fellows scarcely conscious of what they were about, & in shaking hands with them I was obliged to dodge the wine & punch which they would otherwise have spilt over me. I could fill sheets with description of the ridiculous scenes; one, however, will suffice. One of the company happening to find himself in front of a looking-glass inquired "who was that spooney fellow looking at him"; receiving no reply he aimed a blow & shivered the glass to atoms, & turning around with a satisfied look said, he "thought *that* rather knocked him!"

So much for the forenoon; in the afternoon we were marshalled class by class & joined in the grand procession which escorted Dr. Walker to the church. Here the Governor (Clifford) made a very neat speech & delivered to Dr. W. the old Charter & seal & large silver keys of the College. Dr. W. replied, & there was an oration in Latin by Carroll, the first

scholar of the Senior class. After that followed Dr. Walker's address, &
a splendid one it was; it answered all the charges which of late have been
brought against colleges. Its length was its only fault; it will be printed
& will I think make quite a sensation. After the address followed the
Doxology. And you'd better believe I put in vigorously. Every one joined
& it did sound grandly. After that we again marched round Cambridge
& finally dispersed, & night & carousals began to thicken. In the eve'g
W. & myself went up to the H. P. C. room and he read the last number
of "Bleak House" to me, & we came to the conclusion that it was a fine
one — *splenndid* . . .

My desire to see you all is inexpressible . . . Oceans of love to Father
& Mother, & continents for yourself, & believe me, darling sister,

Yours

HORACE

H. H. F. J. (H. H. F. Jayne), ed., *The Letters of Horace Howard Furness*
(Boston: Houghton Mifflin, 1922). Copyright 1922 by H. H. F. Jayne.

William Lawrence

BRET HARTE AND THE GREEN GLOVES
(1871)

*William Lawrence, "the great alumnus of his Harvard generation" (as the
Harvard Alumni Bulletin referred to him), found time in his life of a busy
and distinguished churchman to serve his University with devotion and
with skill. He was successively Preacher to the University, Overseer, and
Fellow of Harvard College. At various times he was a one-man fund-
raising committee and he twice played a leading part in large fund-raising
campaigns in behalf of the University. This retrospective and amusing
account of another Phi Beta Kappa Day was written in 1940 when he was
ninety years of age.*

CAMBRIDGE can be hot and, if ever there was a hottest day in Cambridge,
that day was Thursday, June 29, 1871, Phi Beta Kappa Day. It was as
hot perhaps as that July day in 1775 when General Washington un-
sheathed his sword in command of the American Army. You may recall
that the prudent George — just from sunny Virginia — retired to the shade
of his great elm while his future army, the "embattled farmers" of Lexington, Concord, and other parts of Middlesex County, sweltered in the
sun upon the treeless plain called "Cambridge Common."

The Phi Beta Kappa exercises were to be held in the Unitarian Church,
as was usual before the erection of Memorial Hall. The program as an-

nounced was of exceptional interest; everybody in Cambridge was on the tiptoe of expectation.

The President of Alpha Chapter was the author and hero of perhaps the most widely read book of the seas, *Two Years Before the Mast*, Richard Henry Dana, Jr., 1837, whose ancestors, by the way, rested in the graveyard hard by. The orator, Dr. Noah Porter, was Professor, later President, of Yale University and was thought to be the leading philosopher in the country. Then and finally, to top off this feast of reason and flow of soul, the poet was to be Bret Harte, who was in the heyday of his popularity. After some fifteen years in the West, he had just returned from San Francisco. His journey across the country was a veritable triumphal progress. The press hailed him as he passed from city to city. Everyone was familiar with *The Luck of Roaring Camp*. Men, women, and even children chuckled at *The Heathen Chinee*. And now, as the guest in Cambridge of William Dean Howells, editor of the *Atlantic*, he was welcomed by Longfellow, Emerson, Norton, and Agassiz. He dined with the Saturday Club and was the center of interest to all the literary groups of Cambridge and Boston. It was a queer mixture. Scholars, scientists, editors, and judges were intrigued and amused. So was Bret Harte — and also somewhat bored. What would be the topic of the poem, what its style, was the question of the members of Chapter A of the P.B.K. Would he attempt a classic or would his atmosphere savor of Hell's Kitchen? Cambridge was agog.

At eleven o'clock the exercises began. At noon I was to be at Christ Church in attendance upon the marriage of my classmate, Henry Cabot Lodge, to Nannie, daughter of Admiral Davis. They had been engaged since our sophomore winter vacation, two years and a half. Undergraduates were forbidden to marry in those days, and Cabot, determined to lose no time, was to be married within 24 hours of the time that he received his diploma at the hands of Harvard's young President, Charles Eliot.

I went with the crowd and at eleven o'clock was packed in the rear of the Unitarian Church. Richard Henry Dana, Jr., who was always most precise in his manner, opened the ceremonies and introduced Dr. Noah Porter, who announced his subject, "The Sciences of Nature or the Science of Man." His personality was so solemn and his voice so deep that, as he repeated the weighty subject, the air became unbearably oppressive. However, he went on. I believe that the scholars thought it a great oration. My impressions were those of dullness, confusion, and length. But that was my fault.

Twelve o'clock was approaching, and I slipped out for the wedding in Christ Church. The sun blazed as I passed by the graveyard; the marriage service with the wedding march was as usual. Cabot and his bride walked down the aisle and out through the porch and drove off. How little we realized that in forty and then fifty years I should be reading the burial service in the same church, first over Nannie and then over Cabot, and their bodies be carried out through the same porch.

Time, however, was precious. I must hear Bret Harte and then hurry on to the reception at the bride's house. So back to the Unitarian Church I went and, to my dismay, found Noah Porter still discussing the Sciences of Nature and Man. Soon he finished; and now the audience bristled with anticipation.

The Poet stood up and placed his manuscript upon the desk; Bret Harte at last! Of medium height, 35 years of age, to quote Mr. Howells, "He was then, as always, a child of extreme fashion as to his clothes and the cut of his beard, which he wore in a moustache with the dropping side whiskers of the day, and his joyful physiognomy was as winning as his voice. . ." He was frightened, doubtless, for his voice was so weak that few heard it; being in the rear of the church, I heard almost nothing. But as Bret Harte went on, I could feel the dismay, the shock, the amusement, and the wrath of the several groups in the audience.

Newspaper accounts of the day only complicate the question of just what the Poet read. From the report in the Boston *Daily Advertiser* of June 30, it appears that Harte's poem was similar to one included in the same year in *East and West Poems* (James R. Osgood, Boston, 1871). Now called "The Aspiring Miss De Laine: A Chemical Narrative," the poem is part of the accepted works of Harte. . . Whatever the variance in the first lines, the tale is the same, and the finished work concludes:

> . . . for Miss Addie was gone! . . .
> Gone without parting farewell; and alas!
> Gone with a flavor of Hydrogen Gas.
>
> When the weather is pleasant you frequently meet
> A white-headed man slowly pacing the street;
> His trembling hand shading his lack-lustre eye,
> Half blind with continually scanning the sky.
> Rumor points him as some astronomical sage,
> Reperusing by day the celestial page;
> But the reader, sagacious, will recognize Brown,
> Trying vainly to conjure his lost sweetheart down,
> And learn the stern moral this story must teach,
> That Genius may lift its love out of its reach.

One of the best comments about the occasion is that contained in *Bret Harte, Argonaut and Exile*, by George R. Stewart, Jr. (Houghton Mifflin, 1931):

> Harte had been asked to compose and read the Phi Beta Kappa poem at the Harvard Commencement — a real honor undoubtedly and to Bostonians probably the highest honor which an American poet could receive. But Harte was fatally careless about the whole matter, and proceeded throughout with bad taste. In the first place, with foolish temerity he de-

cided to be humorous. Now a second *Heathen Chinee* would undoubtedly have been successful even at a Harvard Commencement, but rather than anything less uproarious he should have taken refuge in the usual pompous windiness of Phi Beta Kappa poems. And Harte, apparently confident that people would eulogize anything which he happened to give them, did not even go to the trouble to write a new poem. Instead, he took some old verses in the style of Tom Hood which he had written and published nine years before * during his salad days with the *Era* [*The Golden Era*, December 28, 1862, a San Francisco literary magazine]. These he refurbished without improving greatly, and renamed *Aspiring Miss De Laine*. Then on Commencement Day he dressed himself somewhat more glaringly even than usual and took his seat on the platform. When he rose and began to read, all Boston's and Cambridge's assembled social and intellectual leaders grew, according to individual temperament, cold with vicarious embarrassment and hot with choler. His *green* gloves! His poem — flippant and silly without being really funny! His manner, too, was unfortunate. He placed both green-gloved hands on the table and spoke in so low a voice as to be heard only with difficulty.

Whatever the true story, Harte was so imperfectly heard that there was no applause at the end. My interpretation of the incident was then and still is that Bret Harte was so bored by the scholastic atmosphere that he reacted and sprang what he thought was a joke upon his solemn audience, with the result that, shocked, amazed and angry, the members of Harvard Chapter Alpha of the P. B. Kappa departed to their homes in silence, uttering in an undertone language that was not fit to print.

Meanwhile I slipped off to the wedding reception on Quincy Street; joined with the guests in covering the bridal couple with rice as they drove off. Cabot was at the opening of his career of over half a century as historian, statesman, and United States Senator.

Harvard Alumni Bulletin, December 14, 1940.

James Russell Lowell

WHAT A GLORIOUS OBJECT IS A SENIOR!
(1875)

Poet, essayist, editor, diplomat, James Russell Lowell had a distinguished career that brought him international repute. Yet Lowell, with his Cambridge connections, was never very far, spiritually or physically, from Cambridge and his home "Elmwood." For more than thirty years he was a member of the Faculty, and he held the Smith Professorship of French and Spanish Languages and Literatures, a chair occupied before him by

---

* This poem was entitled "The Lost Beauty," as was the Phi Beta Kappa version, and signed "Bret."

Ticknor and Longfellow. His "Commemoration Ode" was delivered at the memorial services honoring the Harvard students and graduates who gave their lives in the Civil War; and his oration at the 250th anniversary of the College in 1886 became a notable part of his collected works. Among his minor writings is this description of the Class Day revels around the tree in Holden Quadrangle.

THE COLLEGE YARD is cheery with music and gay with a quietly moving throng. The windows from groundsill to eaves bloom thick with young and happy faces. At half past four the sound of marching music in quick time is heard, passing at longer or shorter intervals for the *rah-rah-rah* with which the class bid good-bye to the buildings, and the waiting crowd are consoled by knowing that the last great show of the day is drawing nigh. At five o'clock comes the dance round the Liberty Tree, but long before that every inch of vantage-ground whence even a glimpse at this frenzy of muscular sentiment may be hoped for has been taken up. The trees are garlanded with wriggling boys, who here apply the skill won by long practice in neighboring orchards and gardens, while every post becomes the pedestal of an unsteady group. In the street a huddled drove of carriages bristle with more luxurious gazers. The Senior class are distinguished by the various shapes of eccentric ruin displayed in their hats, as if the wildest nightmares of the maddest of hatters had suddenly taken form and substance. First, the Seniors whirl hand in hand about the tree with the energy of excitement gathered through the day; class after class is taken in, till all College is swaying in the unwieldy ring, which at last breaks to pieces of its own weight. Then come the frantic leaping and struggling for a bit of the wreath of flowers that circles the tree at a fairly difficult height. Here trained muscle tells; but sometimes mere agility and lightness, which know how to climb on others' shoulders, win the richest trophy. . .

Perhaps the prettiest part of the day is its close. The College yard, hung with varicolored Chinese lanterns, looks (to borrow old Gayton's word) *festivously* picturesque, while the alternating swells and falls of vocal and instrumental music impregnate the cooler evening air with sentiment and revery. Youths and maidens, secluded by the very throng, wander together in a golden atmosphere of assured anticipation. Life is so easy in the prospect when a pair of loving eyes hold all of it that is worth seeing, and are at once both prophecy and fulfilment! Fame and fortune are so lightly won (in that momentary transfiguration of commonest things into the very elements of poetry and passion) by the simple jugglery of taking everything for granted! And what a glorious object is a Senior on Class Day to the maiden of sixteen!

F. O. Vaille and H. A. Clark, eds., *The Harvard Book* (Cambridge, 1875).

David McCord

ENTER A FORMER NAVAL PERSON
(1943)

In the decade of the forties the most famous visitor to the Harvard Yard was Prime Minister Winston Churchill. Tremendous secrecy surrounded his coming, but of course the inevitable rumors about the famous guest did leak through the official censorship. This is how the Harvard Alumni Bulletin *described the event, in the words of its editor, David McCord.*

WITH the suddenness of the coming of autumn leaves, there returned to the Yard on September 6 much of the color and excitement of three historic Harvard events: the Tercentenary celebration of 1936, the memorable Oxford Convocation of June, 1941, and the great military Commencement of last May. A blend of these three festivals marked the dignified and delightful ceremony at which . . . the Harvard degree of Doctor of Laws was conferred on the Right Honorable Winston Leonard Spencer Churchill, Great Britain's Prime Minister, and man of the hour. Indeed, the surprise of the occasion brought it sharply into focus; and the time of the year — when the Yard is poised for first flight into fall days — enhanced the sense and feel of adventure. To learn overnight that within a few hours one might see and hear the man whose character and eloquence have been the inspiration of the free world in its darkest hour, brought professors home from vacations, and cheerfully cancelled hundreds of family plans for spending Labor Day away from Cambridge.

Early Monday morning those fortunate enough to hold one of the limited number of Yard tickets began to filter through the main gates. They were still not too sure as to just what was about to happen, for Mr. Churchill's name had so far appeared in print only in a brief announcement in the national press to the effect that he was to broadcast at noon from an unnamed American city. No official word of him had escaped in Cambridge. But the heavy ropes which marked off the large area of the Yard now known as the Tercentenary Theatre, and the battery of microphones on the steps of the Memorial Church, more than confirmed the suspected probability of the impending event. By 11 A.M., Harvard military units were gathering in formations in the old part of the Yard; Overseers and other dignitaries in morning dress were hurrying across diagonal paths, silk hats shining in the sun. Crowds of civilians — mostly women — were finding places on the steps of the Widener Library, members of the Navy Band began to assemble near the west porch of the Church; police were in view. At a quarter to twelve the specially and hurriedly invited to the academic exercises had entered Sanders Theatre; a few moments later began the exercises themselves, in which — now no surprise — the Prime Minister, in the brilliant red of his Oxford gown, played to great applause the leading part. Then the principals emerged from the south door of Memorial Hall, hurried across to the Church, and a minute later from the south steps President Conant was introducing to Harvard's six or seven thousand military, and five or six thousand students, Faculty, alumni, guests, and employees, the man who recently told the world that we have reached "the end of the beginning."

Up to the very last the secret had been well kept. Even those in the next-but-one of the University's inner circles knew nothing whatever of the event until a week before it occurred; and in many cases then there was indication only that an honorary degree was to be conferred. So, in fact, the invitations read to Overseers, alumni officials, the military, and distinguished guests. They were doubly marked *confidential.* The tickets which followed indicated Sanders Theatre, a time, a seat — no more. Yard passes were not generally thought to exist until the Saturday previous. There was suspicion; there were ultimate hints in the public press, such as that of Mr. Churchill's broadcast and something about his keeping "a long-standing engagement." Secrecy extended even to running off the programs late at night. The University Printing Office recalls that when copy was submitted, it appeared that only a Mr. X was to be honored; his name would come later. But at the end of the copy stood the text for *God Save the King!* By and large, one can now half believe that the potential audience *willed* that it prove to be the Prime Minister who was coming to the Yard.

He came. It was a long-standing invitation, to be accepted when opportunity offered. The opportunity had arrived, but there was no time for the University to invite an audience remote from Cambridge. It is remarkable, rather, that the staff in Massachusetts Hall was able to notify the immediate Harvard family to carry through so many complicated details — from secret service to broadcasting arrangements — in so short a time. But it was done, and here now at a little before noon in familiar Sanders Theatre sat and stood more than 1,200 people in what one man described as "the most exciting fever of a lifetime."

On the platform ranged the empty seats for 118 members of the academic procession. On the floor were set aside seats for the remainder of the procession — the Faculty and the Board of Overseers. At the right and left of the stage, underneath the balcony, sat the higher ranking members of the Army and Navy units at the University. At the back of the Theatre in semicircle stood a group of undergraduates. (Students were permitted to apply for a limited block of tickets, filled in the order of request.) Three or four WAVE officers took seats with the Navy. A number of ladies — wives of members of the Governing Boards and administrative officers — occupied the center balcony. In this group were Mrs. Conant, Mrs. Churchill, and Subaltern Mary Churchill.

A bugle sounded. Three minutes later, to the *Second Connecticut March*, the academic procession entered the Theatre — the Faculty by the south entry, the Overseers and dignitaries by the north. Ascending the platform, the Deans took places in the front row left, facing the House Masters. Robe after robe scattered a rainbow over the stage. Some of the most brilliant were those of the *Emeriti*, among them Professors Merriman and Rand.

At noon sounded the fanfare * from the balcony overlooking the transept. This was indeed the moment. The now standing audience broke into prolonged applause and cheers as the Prime Minister, with President Conant, preceded by the Secretary to the University and members of the Corporation, and followed by Jerome D. Greene, '96, LL.D. '37, Honorary Keeper of the Corporation Records, the Governor of the Commonwealth, Commander C. R. Thompson of the Royal Navy, and Brigadier General William J. Keville, the Governor's Aide, entered the Theatre and ascended the center steps. From the press bank at the right flashed the camera bulbs. The applause continued. The President and Fellows took seats at the back center underneath the three crimson shields; the Prime Minister found his place at the left between the Governor (on his right) and George H. Chase, Dean of the University. Principals, Faculty, and audience then were seated. Throughout the exercises, six Secret Service men stood inflexible at strategic positions at the back of, and in front of, the stage.

The University Marshal, Dr. Reginald Fitz, said: "Mr. Sheriff, pray give us order"; and the Sheriff of Middlesex County, top-hatted and gold-braided, arose, thrice pounded the stage with his sword-in-scabbard, and said in the tradition: "The meeting will be in order." The Rev. Henry Bradford Washburn, '91, S.T.D. '30, offered prayer:

> . . . And we most heartily beseech Thee, with Thy favour to behold and bless Thy servants the President of the United States, the gracious sovereign King George, his First Minister, and all to whom Thou hast entrusted the destinies of the United States of America and the British Commonwealth of Nations. . .

The University Choir, in black gowns with broad red facing, seated at the extreme left under the balcony, sang the anthem — the final chorus from Handel's *Samson*, with the magnificent words by Milton:

---

* Written by Walter H. Piston, '24, Walter W. Naumburg Professor of Music, first played at the Oxford Convocation in 1941.

> Let their celestial concerts all unite,
> Ever to sound his praise in endless morn of light.

Twenty members of the Boston Symphony Orchestra accompanied them, under the direction of Associate Professor G. Wallace Woodworth, Organist and Choirmaster. The Orchestra also played the fanfare and played for the subsequent Seventy-Eighth Psalm and Paine's Commencement Hymn. This was the Orchestra's first participation in a Harvard ceremony since the Tercentenary, and many of those present returned from their vacations just for the one day. Mr. Churchill, it was noted, turned far around in his chair to observe and hear the music.

Leverett Saltonstall, '14, LL.D. '42, Governor of the Commonwealth, gave the brief address of welcome. When he had finished and resumed his seat, the Prime Minister turned and laid his hand on the Governor's arm. One could see his lips move. "Very good," he said. The Governor had concluded:

> Mr. Churchill: You are an inspiring example of the motto of our great President, Thomas Jefferson:
>
> Ye shall know the truth, and the truth shall make you free.*

The audience rose and joined in the singing of the Psalm. When all were again seated, the President stood up in his place and called Mr. Churchill by name. The Prime Minister also arose, and the President conferred on him the degree of Doctor of Laws, reading the citation.

WINSTON LEONARD SPENCER CHURCHILL

> An historian who has written a glorious page of British history; a stateman and warrior whose tenacity and courage turned back the tide of tyranny in freedom's darkest hour.

When the University Marshal had handed Dr. Churchill his diploma, applause broke out in new strength. It is doubtful if anything in Sanders Theatre ever surpassed it. Again bulbs flashed. Mr. Churchill bowed and smiled, and bowed again. He was visibly touched by the reception.

Taking his manuscript from his pocket, he moved forward to the lectern and the battery of five microphones. On either side of him towered the white marble statues of President Quincy and the Colonial patriot, James Otis. He searched for his glasses with hands that reach more happily for a cigar. He looked constantly right and left. His mobile face and restless arms gave fluid emphasis to what he said. Chancellor of Bristol University, honorary Alumnus of Oxford and Harvard, his dramatic address nonetheless led out unerringly from academic groves to Anglo-American relations. There is no need to summarize. The radio and

* John. 8.32.

the press of the Nation have already done that and more. But beyond the objective, fraternal point of his speech, we may quote this paragraph:

> And here let me say how proud we ought to be, young and old, to be living in a tremendous, thrilling, formative epoch in the human story, and how fortunate it was for the world that when these great trials came upon us there was a generation that terror could not conquer and brutal violence could not enslave.

He was cheered to the echo of the old Theatre. The power of his words had found a mark. He looked pleased.

There followed the Commencement Hymn and the Benediction. To more applause, the Prime Minister, the dignitaries, and Faculty left the platform and the audience immediately followed.

Most of the audience hastened at once across to the Yard and arrived there to find President Conant on the south steps of the Memorial Church introducing the man for whom the massed crowds had patiently waited. The sun was fainting hot. Our visitor saw the whole Tercentenary Theatre filled, the Army and Navy in the center, a large group of WAVES among them. On the steps of Widener stood hundreds. Nearly ten thousand voices cheered him. The Prime Minister, now, robe discarded — in short black jacket, gray trousers, gray unmatching waistcoat, black bow tie with dots, a black Homburg, and a light cane in his hand. This was the familiar figure; no gown to hide his British squareness, no black velvet cap to shield his eyes. The crowd was delighted. Soldier, to soldiers and sailors. The veteran of older wars and this war spoke briefly to young men who had yet to go out. Cameras clicked and whirred. He rapped with his cane to drive home a point. He looked fiercely into the sun. He looked down and smiled. In his talk he was optimistic, but he emphasized that the end of the war is not yet round any visible corner. Closing, he made the sign of the V twice with the first two fingers of his right hand. The crowd voiced mighty concurrence, and V's appeared everywhere in answer.

From there the President escorted Mr. Churchill to the Fogg Museum to attend a small luncheon given by the University. Here he met members of the governing boards, administrative officers, and their wives, and members of the official party. In honor of the occasion, Harvard's 17th-century state silverware was used for service. President Conant made some brief remarks:

> Today Harvard welcomes the Prime Minister of Great Britain. We also welcome the Chancellor of Bristol University, a fellow academician. But most significant of all, we welcome a man whose inspiring leadership of a gallant people has preserved for us and our children that liberty without which no university can survive.
>
> Those of us of the Harvard family who are gathered here this afternoon have the special pleasure and high honor of greeting Mr. and Mrs.

Churchill and the members of their official party. I trust our guests realize how deeply we appreciate this visit. It is no simple matter for a man who carries Mr. Churchill's burdens to find the time to attend an academic festival. This day will be long remembered in Harvard history. I am sure that I am speaking on behalf of all of you . . . when I express our deep gratitude to the Prime Minister for the honor he has done us.

Mr. Churchill has already spoken twice today. I shall not therefore trouble him by a request to make another speech. I am venturing, however, to take the liberty of asking him to propose the toast to the President of the United States.

Ladies and gentlemen — Mr. Churchill.

A toast and some unrecorded words and a witticism followed.

Crowds trailed to the west entrance of the Museum and waited patiently back of circulating police until the Prime Minister and President Conant — each now with a long Churchill cigar — emerged. In final response to final cheers, Harvard's newest Alumnus made the familiar sign and hoisted on his stick the familiar black hat.

In the little while that he was long with us — to turn about a poet's phrase — the dominant impression of Mr. Churchill is the kindliness and brightness in his great vitality. It is true that he probably carried in his head that day the knowledge that the first of the Axis partners had given up. But that need not be counted. In a wearied world there was no weariness in that face. He smiled often. He caused his guardians great uneasiness by insisting twice on saluting the crowd through an open window of Memorial Hall before the academic procession had gathered. His informality was continually evident. On the platform he would hitch up the folds of his red gown, and his hands appeared frequently to stray through invisible slits to his pockets. He sat comfortably. When his wife and daughter lingered on the steps of the Museum before entering, he turned around and came out unaffectedly after them. There was no pose to anything that he said or did. He stood equally and four-square among us, and we shall not forget him.

Harvard Alumni Bulletin, September 15, 1943.

VIII

THE ALUMNI

I have not much cause, I sometimes think, to wish my Alma Mater well, personally; I was not often highly flattered by success, and was every day mortified by my own ill fate or ill conduct. Still, when I went today to the ground where I had had the brightest thoughts of my little life and filled up the little measure of my knowledge, and had felt sentimental for a time, and poetical for a time, and had seen many fine faces, and traversed many fine walks, and enjoyed much pleasant, learned, or friendly society, — I felt a crowd of pleasant thoughts, as I went posting about from place to place, and room to chapel.

RALPH WALDO EMERSON (1822)

Why has this throng come up, out of the bustle and strife of the forum and the market-place, to our academic seat? What spirit stirs this multitude today? You have come to pay homage to the University of your love, and through it to all universities.

CHARLES W. ELIOT (1886)

"This," said Mr. George, "you will learn to know as your Alma Mater — which are two Greek words, meaning 'Go as you please.'"

ROLLO'S JOURNEY TO CAMBRIDGE (1880)

It is very pleasant to do you a kindness, and every one is glad of a chance to serve the dear old College. She needs help, and thought, and devotion, and gratitude from us all, for she has given us and our land more than any one of us will give back. She will keep on giving.

HENRY LEE HIGGINSON (1890)

Charles Francis Adams

THE ALUMNI MEET
(1857)

The son and grandson of a president of the United States, Charles Francis Adams (1807–1886) was one of the most distinguished public servants of his time. After an unusual childhood spent partly in Russia and England, he went through the Boston Latin School and graduated from Harvard in 1825 at the age of eighteen. He was trained in the law by Daniel Webster and admitted to practice in Boston four years later. Thereafter he was never out of the public eye. He served as a Whig in the Massachusetts House and Senate, prepared a biography and edited the works of his grandfather, wrote articles on American history, ran for vice-president on the Free Soil ticket, managed a Boston daily paper, helped organize the Republican party, and served as American minister to Britain during the Civil War. Throughout his life he showed himself to be a citizen of conviction whose public career was above party and politics. In his detailed journals he recorded his many trips from Quincy to Cambridge on matters connected with the University and its Alumni. He spoke frequently of making the journey not because so much he wanted to as because he felt he ought to. For years active in the Alumni Association, he also served as Overseer and President of the Board from 1869 to 1881.

 THURSDAY 16th — July [1857] Not quite so hot. I went to the city at the usual time, passed through it, and reached the Colleges at Cambridge just at the moment when the association of the alumni was expected to assemble at Gore Hall. But at that time very few had arrived, and I began to doubt what might be the matter, but the members soon filed in until the library was filled. Among the members however I saw but very few familiar faces. Only five or six of my Class, and a sprinkling of acquaintance, independently of official people. There was a formal meeting at which the process was gone through of an election of officers, but it was only a form. The old set was continued for another year. And it will be continued just so long as Mr. Winthrop fancies the place; when he does not another sweep will be made, just like the last, so that I may be got rid of in the same way that Sumner was. For such distinctions I have no ambitions, so that it makes no difference to me — and I should never attend such exhibitions, but for the feeling that sometimes I ought to do so, if for no other reason, as representative of opinion. It was this that brought me here today.

At eleven o'clock the procession was formed and we marched to the church which was very soon filled up, though it struck me with a very small proportion of men. Of the alumni I think there could not have been more than eight-hundred. Of others it seemed as if there could not be more than a quarter as many. The galleries and remaining pews below swarmed with women. After a brief prayer by Mr. Mason, Mr. Everett made his speech. The main topic was college culture, which he undertook to defend on its three most disputed divisions, the dead languages, mathematics and metaphysics. But it was not so much a logical argument, as a brilliant series of illustrations rhetorically presented with all the gorgeousness of an oriental imagination. As an Orator for this species of labor Mr. Everett stands at the head of his class in this age. He has all the requisites for producing effects *ad libitum*. But after all it is not the highest species of eloquence. It wants depth of convictions, and earnestness of heart, and force of will. I witnessed this exhibition with just as much satisfaction as I should a very fine display of pyrotechnics, warm and brilliant and dazzling to the *eye*, but productive of not a single internal emotion. And as Mr. Everett grows older his imagination gains upon his reasoning powers, so that what he produces is more effective for a temporary purpose, and less valuable for permanent use. As a defence of the higher walks of education I do not think this will add a feather weight to the present opinion.

The ceremonies finished at half past one. Fifteen minutes later the alumni were once more called together at Gore Hall and marched to the philosophy rooms, (as they used to be called), where we dined. Here was Mr. Winthrop's turn, and he did very well. His own introduction was happy, and his mode of drawing out others would have been equally so, but for the drawback of extravagant compliment showered upon all around. This drew out in succession, the Governor, President Walker, Lord Napier, the British Minister, President Quincy, who was most vociferously cheered, President King of Columbia College, and Mr. Everett. He ended by introducing a gentleman from St. Louis. Mr. Winthrop had warned me that I was next in order. But I saw that the serious and grave thoughts which I had in my mind to present were not at all in harmony with all this, and that perhaps they might imply an invidious and very unwelcome lecture, which I did not mean. My wish was to say a single word in behalf of enthusiasm as a colaborer with knowledge in the support of high education against the inroads of materialism. This is the element the College wants. It has never had it since the decline of the Puritan fervor which founded it. In the last half century it has been in the cold embrace of commercial conservatism, which has piled up wealth on it but has taught it incredulity in all the earnest movements of the country. The representatives of it are such men as Mr. Everett and Mr. Winthrop, fine "chevaux de bataille" for a parade field day, but utterly incompetent to cope with the great moral struggles of the world. Had I touched such a thing as this, it would only have been discordant noise, jangling and out of tune, at best not understood; and if I did not touch that, I was a little disposed to join in the race of compliments, so I made up my mind to depart in season, to escape the alternative. I sent a line to Mr. Winthrop telling him not to call me, and went off. This may be a little cowardice on my part too, for I am not ashamed to confess my utter aversion to this species of display, as foreign as possible from all my habits and feelings. I can speak when my mind and heart are full of a subject, and I have had too many proofs of the effect produced at such times to be distrustful of my power — but in cases like these I feel no confidence and therefore never accomplish any success. I took the car to the city and from thence after whiling away an hour at the Athenaeum, to Quincy at seven o'clock.

Adams Manuscript Trust.

Edward A. Weeks, Jr.

REUNION

(1933)

While editing the "Graduates' Window," a column in the Harvard Graduates' Magazine, *Edward Weeks turned one June to the thoughts rising in the mind of an alumnus who returns to Harvard for the festivities of Class Day and Commencement. The result, said only as Weeks could say it, appears below. One of the most versatile of those in the field of American letters today, Weeks has been editor of the* Atlantic Monthly *since 1938 and is himself known also as a lecturer, radio broadcaster, and member of the "trade" of writers.*

FROM a seat high in the bleachers — those bleachers which were seemingly designed for a legless generation — gazing down at the assembly of the homecoming classes, the Graduate (whose class this year had not come home to roost) let his thoughts ruminate on Commencement. The turf of Soldiers Field stretched away to the furthest extremity of a home run. The sharp regular thud of the pitch was now and again broken by a hit, when the murmur of the crowd would break into a shout.

Bands blared and the skirling of bagpipes opposite first base indicated the youngest graduates preparing to give every assistance to the Yale pitcher when the inevitable blow-up should occur. Nearer the plate sat the ten- and fifteen-year veterans, a little thinner on top, a little fuller at the bottom, a little less excited by the ball game, a little more interested in each other. Beyond the Yale bench rose the family phalanx of the twenty-fifth reunion and beyond them clustered the Old Guard. In the intervals of play the eye traversed the Charles to the green boundary of the trees, and above, Memorial and the towers of new Harvard.

The prospect of beating Yale is always inviting but, thought the Graduate, it certainly needs a deeper persuasion than this to fetch these people together. The meeting of friends long separated can be, and too often is, an embarrassing affair: the reunion of war veterans demonstrates how painfully self-conscious such things may be. College friendships are more homogeneous and less compulsory than those of 1917, yet up to the occasion of the twenty-fifth reunion it is an exceptional class that can call back more than one man in every seven. Of the delinquent six some — an unhappily high proportion these days — stay at home for the sake of economy; others because of a constitutional aversion to the "glad hand"; others, a few perhaps, being disappointed in their expectation of a career, prefer to avoid their contemporaries; and still others are too careless or too remote to make the effort.

Reunion begins as a network of small independent intimacies but as glasses are filled and emptied a feeling of cordiality extends from group to group. The glass that cheers is surely the most valuable means of banishing shyness and of obliterating those superficial partitions which college erects between its undergraduates. John Barleycorn is an Honorary Member of every good class.

The Graduate still relishes the remembrance of how the "spark" of 19— resolutely unwound the fire hose and with it washed a mercenary hotel manager out of his own lobby. He remembers a once-famous stroke rowing a dinghy around and around and around Marblehead harbor *with one oar* while the class on the lawn of the Rockmere performed as a coxswain should. Why this was so unspeakably funny is hard to say, but it was. Yet on soberer reflection the Graduate takes some satisfaction in the thought that the breaking and entering which seemed to characterize so many reunions directly after the war (and for which the hard stuff of Prohibition was no little responsible) has calmed down. It is no longer necessary to break three hundred glasses and fifteen windowpanes in order to prove that you've been college graduates for six years. Amen! Amen! sigh the hotel proprietors on the Cape.

It requires, of course, something more than equal parts of gin and sentiment to make a reunion attractive. It requires in the first place a good Class Secretary, a man with a friendly memory and an indefatigable grasp of detail. It requires a Class Bible, a *Who's Who* which whether its entries be reticent or fulsome has the singular virtue of being honest. It requires an old *Lampoon* editor to point up the publicity. It requires a brass band and a soiled Roman toga and the chance of beating Yale. But most of all it requires a man (some classes have more than one) with a genius for loyalty — "one of those individuals" as Carroll Perry says

> who fall in love with an *institution* and never get over it: one of those to whom Alma Mater means also wife and children. . . He knew every man who had graduated and all the sometime members of the class as well. These last he managed to fetch back to the reunions in equal proportions to the graduates. He knew just who had died in the quarter-century and how it all happened, and in what condition they had left their families.

Mr. Perry was writing of Williams College but his words fit an occasional Harvard man in our memory.

Judging from what he hears of the Old Guard and from what he has experienced in his own time the Graduate concludes that reunions improve with age. The forced conviviality, the almost ostentatious exclusiveness of certain individuals, the shy reticence of others fade from the scene as time goes on. This is not because we learn the secret of Rotarians as we grow older. It is simply the mellow effect of an evolutionary process. In the process of maturity talents latent in college are discovered. Integrity and unswerving purpose that were once suspected by the few are now recognized by the many. Men have emerged, as it were, from the hidden recesses of their ambition, the doors of social indifference no longer shut them apart, they are, as the saying goes, ready "to take off their hats and tell their right names."

This evolution of a Class, this slow appraisal of the other fellow, is hardly complete before middle life. Some Classes attain a quicker perception than others but not till men have been twenty — twenty-five — years "out" do they come back to Cambridge eagerly and with that mingling of affection, respect — and tolerance! — which is best to be seen in the midst of the Old Guard. From that time forward professional entertainers are no longer necessary to top off the banquet; the class would rather hear from its own members especially those who "have done things." And even though this may result in such plain speaking as Mr. Sinclair Lewis indulged in at New Haven, the effect, once the shock has subsided, is for the good. In college we saw as through a glass darkly, but now face to face.

It is habitual for young men to gauge their efforts by the past and to put complete confidence in the future. Thus a young writer may say to himself "when Keats was my age he had written *Hyperion*" or "a year from now I shall be as old as Dickens when he wrote *Pickwick*" and spur himself on accordingly. But by mid-life the future has ceased to beckon with such sure promise; it is the present which holds us fast. "Getting and spending we lay waste our powers." And what a relief it is to shake off the traces, to rest in the green shade and chew the cud of experience. A wife of '07, Mrs. Helen Garnsey Haring, attending her first Harvard reunion, the twenty-fifth, saw this instantaneously, and wrote it down for others to remember. "The men of our generation" she wrote,

> twenty-five years out of College have borne the major weight of the late War and of the economic débâcle. We have become accustomed to weary and tense faces. But those June days of holiday-making, of relaxing in intimate companionship with others whose hopes, experiences, and fears had exactly paralleled theirs through the years, gradually eased the intolerable strain. There must have been more than one wife who knew that "it was months since she'd heard her husband laugh like that."

To recognize as we do at reunions that we have kept step with our contemporaries is a fine and heartening thing, yet there is more to the Cambridge return than mere personal gratification. To the Old Guard, to those who have gone thirty — forty — fifty years onwards, there is a special significance in Commencement Day. The class dinners, of course, are more than dinners, for as the members decrease and the ranks close up there is more occasion than ever to revive the days of the past and the names that are memories. But on Commencement Day itself, as one passes down between the ranks of the Seniors, as one listens to President Lowell (more impressive than ever on this, his last appearance) confer the degrees, as one "spreads" on the perennial salad and then goes marching past the dignitaries on the steps of Widener, the feeling arises that we are part of something bigger than ourselves, of something more durable than the trees in the yard or the bricks of the buildings. In these days of shaken confidence and little faith it is good to come back to a firm foundation . . .

Harvard Graduates' Magazine, September 1933.

John P. Marquand

MR. HILLIARD TELLS ALL

(1941)

It seems superfluous to introduce John Phillips Marquand, A.B. 1915, to a Harvard audience or any audience. His preoccupation with the foibles of a certain stratum of our American society is so widely known that no remarks are necessary, save to say that he seems to have the matter well in hand. "Harvard is a subject that I still face with mixed emotions," he wrote to his Class secretary in 1940. "I brought away from it a number of frustrations and illusions which have handicapped me through most of my life. Yet, on the other hand, Harvard taught me the value of intellectual enthusiasm. In spite of the efforts of Drs. Lowell and Conant, I still observe that one of its best known products is a type with which I find myself identified that has difficulty in surviving or making itself understood west of the Appalachians or south of New Jersey. This, I think, is as it should be. All institutions of learning, even the greatest, should have a local flavor." Here then is a little of the local flavor as a group of Marquand's characters, Mr. Harry Pulham included, go about planning their 25th anniversary celebration.

THE PRIVATE dining room contained an oval table. There was a picture of the Grand Canyon on one wall and a yellowed photograph of Boston after the fire of 1872 on the other.

"All right, boys," Bo-jo said. "Sit down anywhere. And get the soup on. We're all hungry."

First there was oxtail soup, and then came breaded veal cutlets, and then came a choice of blueberry pie or ice cream — a heavy lunch, more than I was used to eating, more than any of us wanted to eat — except Chris Evans, who looked hungry. The conversation was scattered as though we had come to realize that we were not there to talk. Curtis was telling me about his boat. Bo-jo was talking to Charley Roberts at the end of the table.

"Charley," he said, "what do you do for exercise these days?"

"I think about it mostly," Charley said.

"That's the way it is," said Bo-jo. "Doctors never take care of themselves."

"There isn't any time," Charley answered.

"Now, don't pull that on me," Bo-jo said. "Every doctor I know is always on a cruise or amusing himself whenever someone is having a baby. You doctors always consider yourselves as a class apart."

"We don't," Charley said.

"You doctors," Bo-jo told him, "always pretend you know everything. Now, actually, there are just as many boneheads in the medical profession as there are in business.. Why, I damned near went to the medical school myself."

"That ought to bear your statement out," said Charley.

"I'm just saying," Bo-jo said, "that doctors don't know everything."

"Well, they don't," Charley said.

"They either assume they know everything," said Bo-jo, "or else they take the other tack. They say they just don't know."

John Phillips Marquand, *H. M. Pulham, Esquire* (Boston: Little, Brown & Company, 1941). Copyright 1940, 1941 by John P. Marquand and Adelaide H. Marquand.

"Well, what do you want us to do?" Charley asked.

"Now, that's begging the question," Bo-jo said. "And you've got plenty of time to exercise if you want to. Look at me. Sometimes I don't get home till ten o'clock, but I always have time for exercise. If I can't do anything else I get on the rowing machine."

"Whose rowing machine?" Charley asked.

"My rowing machine," Bo-jo said. "I have one in my dressing room in town and one out in the country. If all you boys had rowing machines you'd be better off. Every morning of my life I get on it for half an hour before breakfast, and when I get home I get on it and get up a good sweat before I change, and frankly I'm just as fit as I ever was. Do you know what I did last night?"

Faces turned toward him. No one knew what he had done.

"I was up at Joe Royce's for dinner, and I don't know how it came up, but somehow he bet me that I couldn't walk downstairs on my hands. I walked down two flights of stairs on my hands."

"Did you get corns on them?" Charley asked. Bo-jo began to laugh, and he beckoned to the waiter.

"You can pass around the Scotch-and-soda now," he said. "We'll have brandy with the coffee."

Curtis Cole had stopped talking about the boats, and Bob Ridge leaned across the table.

"Curtis, before we forget it we might make an appointment."

"What for?" Curtis asked.

"What we were talking about, Curtis. It's just a formality. What time do you get up in the morning?"

Curtis Cole's eyes opened wider.

"Now, look here, Bob," he said. "I know you've got to make a living —"

"You just tell me what time you get up in the morning," Bob said, "and I'll be right there."

"What the deuce are you boys talking about?" Bo-jo asked.

"Nothing," said Bob. "It's just a business matter, Bo-jo."

"Well, what are you going to do to Curtis in the morning?"

Curtis Cole pushed back his chair.

"He isn't going to do one damned thing to me in the morning."

"It's just a matter of business, Bo-jo," Bob said.

"Now, we're not here to talk business," Bo-jo said.

"I'm glad to hear you say it," Curtis said.

"What are you so sore about?" Bo-jo asked. "What's the matter with you, Curtis?"

"We'd better skip it," Curtis said. "But I'm just tired of having my classmates try to sell me things."

"Now, listen, boys," said Bo-jo, "let's not talk about business."

After the dessert was taken away we had coffee and brandy and cigars. I looked at my watch. It was two o'clock.

"Bo-jo," I said, "this has been perfectly swell, but I ought to be getting back."

"Now, listen," said Bo-jo, "no one has to go back for a while, anywhere. If you boys just relax and lean back and listen, I've got something to say that's important. We've got to put aside personal matters. We've all got to do something for the Class."

Bo-jo leaned his elbow on the table. He passed one of his hands over his close-cropped head and his eyebrows drew together.

"I don't know how it is," Bo-jo said, and he gave a quick short laugh, "that I always get things put over on me. I'm always the one who has to do all the work. Now when we have to get ready for the Twenty-fifth here I am and everybody comes around to me and says, Well, go ahead, get it started, you're elected. Well, all right. I'm going to get it started. There'll be a lot of committees before we get through — entertainment committees and God knows what; but in the end it's going to come down to the graduates who live around here. It's up to us whether or not our Twenty-fifth is going to be something to remember, and when I thought it over I wondered how it would be if we started with just a small, informal committee, made up of people who didn't want to blow their own horns, but who are loyal to the Class, and who aren't afraid to work. That's why I picked you men. We're just our own little committee and by God we're going to take our coats off and pitch in." No one said anything.

"Now, don't look so blank," Bo-jo said. "It isn't going to be tough when we get started. We're all going to get right behind this and push it through, and we're all going to have a damned good time. Of course the whole system is pretty well worked out. The classmates and their wives and kids arrive and we put them into dormitories. But then the wives have to be entertained, and the kids have to be entertained, and we have to be entertained. Someone's got to see that the kids don't all get mixed up. Well, the wives can do that. But the thing that's bothering me is the big final entertainment, the one the whole class takes part in, the wives and kids and everybody. Now, last year they had a band playing popular tunes and the kids sang the old songs. Everybody had a good time except some of the kids got lost. Now, has anybody got suggestions about an entertainment?"

There was another silence.

"Come on — come on," Bo-jo said. "Naturally there'll be a ball game and a men's dinner and an outing at some country club or else at someone's place at Brookline, if anyone at Brookline has a place big enough.

But what worries me is what about the entertainment. How about it, boys?"

"Someone might write a show," Curtis said. "I hear they did that once."

"All right," said Bo-jo. "Who can write a show? Can anyone here write one?"

No one seemed able to write one. Bo-jo's glance, level and confident, turned diagonally across the table toward Chris Evans.

"How about it, Chris?" he asked. "Can't you write a show?"

Chris put both his elbows on the table.

"I don't know how, and besides I haven't got the time."

"Well, go ahead and try," Bo-jo said. "That's the least anyone can do."

"I haven't got the inclination," Chris said, and his voice grew edgy. "And I haven't got the time because I work for my living."

"Well, we've all got to take a little time out and work for this," said Bo-jo, "and it's going to be like a vacation. We're all going to recapture something of the old days. Frankly, now, doesn't everyone agree that the happiest time he ever spent was those four years back at Harvard?"

No one replied, and it was hard to tell whether the silence meant agreement or not.

"And there's one thing more," Bo-jo said, "that I know you'll agree with. Our Class is the best damned class that ever came out of Harvard, and the reason is that we've always pulled together. Now, it's been suggested that someone in the class write a show. Well, that's a good suggestion, and that's what we're here for. Well, who can write it — someone who was in the Lampoon or the Pudding or something? We had one of the best damned Pudding shows I ever saw. Do you remember Spotty Graves doing the tight-rope act? We've got to have Spotty in the show."

"Spotty Graves has passed on," Bob Ridge said.

"Passed on where?" said Bo-jo.

"He passed on the year before last," Bob Ridge said. "He left a wife and four children, and only five thousand dollars in insurance. Not enough to clean up with."

"Oh, yes," said Bo-jo. "That's right. I remember now, but that's beside the point. Now, we certainly have a lot of literary birds in the Class if we try to think of them, a lot of quiet birds who didn't distinguish themselves much. That's one of the things that gripes me about Yale. The Elis are always wheeling out the Yale poets and the Yale literary group. Why, hell, we have a lot of the same thing in the Class, except we don't shout about them. Now, who is there who can write a show?"

"There's Bill King," I said. "Bill always has a lot of ideas."

"It's my personal opinion," Bo-jo said, "That Bill King's a bastard. I wouldn't be surprised if he were a Communist, and we don't want any smart, unconstructive cracks. What we want is something full of pep and good nature. Who else is there?"

Bo-jo looked around the table.

"Well," he said, "can't anybody think of anybody else? All right. I'll tell you what we'll do. We'll let Chris think about it for us. Chris, you think up the names of five people who can write a show and let me know the first of the week."

"All right," said Chris.

"And now we've got to keep our minds open," said Bo-jo. "Are there any other suggestions?"

"How about getting one of those professionals," Curtis Cole asked, "who organize song and dance shows?"

"All right," said Bo-jo. "Now we're talking. You make it a business to look it up, Curt. Send me in a memorandum of five of those professionals the first of the week. And now I've got an idea."

"Go ahead," said Charley. "It must be good."

Bo-jo glanced at the ceiling and flicked his cigar ash into his coffee cup.

"The main problem as I see it," he said, "is to get everyone in the proper spirit. Now, I don't know anything that makes people more happy than a good fight."

"A fight?" Bob Ridge asked. "What sort of a fight?"

"Boxing," said Bo-jo. "Two good game, fast lightweights, to fight ten exhibition rounds. We ought to get them cheap just for the publicity."

Charley Roberts looked at Bo-jo with interest. "Are you serious about that?" he asked.

"It surprises you, doesn't it?" Bo-jo inquired. "Well, it did me too when I thought of it first, but the more you think of it the better you'll like it. Two good game boys, right on a platform in the Harvard Yard, pasting each other. Why, it'll drive everybody crazy! It'll take them out of themselves. They won't remember where they are."

"But I thought the whole object of this thing was for everyone to remember where he was," Chris Evans said.

"That's beside the point," said Bo-jo.

"If you're going to get them," Charley Roberts said, "why not pick heavyweights?"

"Now you've got the spirit," said Bo-jo. "I've thought of that. They're too expensive, Charley."

"Well, why not get ten niggers in a battle royal?" Charley asked. "That ought to take the boys and girls out of themselves."

Bo-jo Brown wrinkled up his forehead.

"Now, look here, boys," he said, "we didn't come here to throw water on good ideas. There's nothing easier than knocking. Bob, I want you to go down to Mike's Gymnasium on Scollay Square. Just go and see Mike personally and ask Mike for the names of some good boys who want publicity, and let me know what you find first thing next week. Got it, Bob?"

"All right," Bob said, "if you really want me to, Bo-jo."

"Now we're getting somewhere," Bo-jo said. "Now, suppose we don't have boxing. That gets us back to song and dance stuff, doesn't it? Charley, you haven't got a job yet. Suppose you get busy and ask around about talent in the class — boys, girls, everybody — tap dancers, saxophones, stunts — We've got to have a lot of stunts — people who can do card tricks or impersonations."

"I haven't got much time," said Charley.

"You told us that before," Bo-jo said. "Just get off your fanny and get busy."

Bo-jo pushed back his chair and rose.

"Well," he said, "I've got to be getting back to the office now. We're all started — set to go. There's nothing like a talk around a table to get ideas. I've had a swell time and I hope you all have, and we'll get together sometime soon. Oh, Harry — "

"Yes," I said.

Bo-jo slapped me on the back and took a firm hold on my arm.

"Harry, here, thought he was going to get off easy. Well, I haven't forgotten Harry. You're coming right down to the office with me now."

"Now, listen, Bo-jo," I said. "It's three o'clock."

"Don't I know it's three o'clock?" Bo-jo asked me. "I'm not crabbing about the time, am I? Besides, it won't take long — your job hasn't really started yet. All right, boys, is everything all straight? All right. Let's go."

The club was nearly deserted when Bo-jo and I got our hats from the checkroom. The only members left in the newspaper room were four old gentlemen who would have been my father's age if my father had been living. They sat in black leather armchairs rustling the papers, and I heard one of them speaking querulously.

"You can blame it all on Wilson," he said, "and the League of Nations."

Outside on the sidewalk Bo-jo took me by the arm again.

"Well," Bo-jo said, "it's a great life, isn't it?"

"How do you mean it's a great life?" I asked.

"Exactly what I say," Bo-jo answered, "a great life. What's the matter? Are you sore about something?"

"I was just thinking," I said. "I never realized that I'd been alive so long."

"What the hell's the matter with you?" Bo-jo asked. "What got that idea into your head?"

"Up there at lunch," I said. "I'd never realized that we were all so old."

"Now, that's a hell of a way to talk," Bo-jo said. "We're not old."

"We're in our middle forties," I said.

"That isn't old," Bo-jo said. "You're just as old as you feel. I'm just as good as I ever was, and so are you, but I see what you mean. Those other people up there looked terrible. It's because they don't take care of themselves. Not enough exercise. Too much worry."

"Maybe they have to worry," I said.

"No one has to worry. Look at me. I never worry."

His grip on my arm tightened. He began walking faster with the swift, elastic step of youth, drawing deep breaths of the humid spring air. There was still a crowd in front of the subway station, sailors talking to girls in tight silk dresses, two or three newsboys, a blindman and the old lady feeding the pigeons bread crumbs out of a brown paper bag.

"There's one thing I can always do," Bo-jo said. "I can always get people to work."

"I know you can," I said. "It's a gift, Bo-jo."

"It's just knowing how to handle them," Bo-jo went on. "Now, those boys are going to wear their fingers off. There's nothing like class spirit. It gets you out of yourself. If you want to be happy, get out of yourself."

On Washington Street in front of the news bulletins the paper boys were shouting. Their voices rose above the scuffling of shoe leather on the pavements.

"London Cabinet in session," they were shouting. "All about it. Braintree woman burned to death. All about it."

"It would be funny," I said, "wouldn't it, if it started all over again? It's about the same time of year."

"Forget it," Bo-jo said. "Get it out of your mind."

Bo-jo's offices were large and newly decorated. There was a rail with a boy sitting behind a table. Bo-jo pushed me in front of him.

"Come on," he said. "Come on."

"All right," I said, "but I can't stay long, really."

"Come on," said Bo-jo. "It won't take a minute. It's about the lives."

"You mean about the lives of the Class," I asked, "the biographies?"

"What's the matter with you?" Bo-jo asked. "Do you think I'm talking French? Come inside here and look."

Bo-jo opened the door of a long room. There were two large tables against the walls heaped with papers and form letters and two girls were seated at desks typing.

"Look here," I said. "This anniversary of ours is more than a year off, isn't it?"

Bo-jo slapped me on the shoulder.

"Now you're talking," he answered. "But we're not going to get caught out. It's time we began organizing."

I still could not understand him.

"All these papers," I said, "all these pictures — they haven't got anything to do with our Class, have they?"

"Now you're getting it," Bo-jo answered. "Of course it isn't *our* Class. This is the year ahead of us, this year's Twenty-fifth. Their Class Secretary works right in this office — you know him, Jake Meek — this is his staff and we're using the same girls for our book. This is Miss Ferncroft, Mr. Pulham. This is Miss Josephs, Mr. Pulham."

The girls turned around in their swivel chairs and smiled.

"Where do I come in?" I asked.

Bo-jo slapped me on the shoulder again and nearly threw me off balance.

"Why," he answered, "you're the one who's going to chase everybody and get their lives. You're going to have general oversight of the book — all the paper work, all the editing — someone's got to do it."

"Why doesn't our Class Secretary do it?" I asked. "That's what he's meant for."

Bo-jo frowned.

"Now, that isn't the right way to look at it, Harry," he said. "You know Sam Green. Sam's the best damned secretary any class has ever had, but he's got to have help, hasn't he? Now, let's get this straight. Are you going to let the Class down, or aren't you?"

"But look here, Bo-jo," I said. "I'm not accustomed to doing anything like this, and besides I haven't got the time."

Bo-jo gave my chest a playful push, causing me to take two steps backward.

"Now you're talking," he said. "I knew you'd get into the spirit of it. Time — why, the job doesn't really begin until next autumn. All you have to do now is to go over the general organization with Miss Ferncroft."

"But look here," I said. "This will take hours and hours."

"And when you take off your coat and start pitching in," Bo-jo went on as though he had not heard me, "you're going to be fascinated by it, and we're all going to have a swell time working together. I'm busy now and I've got to duck out. It's great to have seen you, Harry. I haven't had such a good time in years."

"Wait a minute, Bo-jo," I said.

Bo-jo pulled the door open and waved his other hand.

"It's a big meeting down the street," he said. "I'll see you later, boy" — and then the door closed, and I was on one side of it and Bo-jo was on the other.

I looked at the papers for a moment and then I looked at Miss Ferncroft. It was only right that someone should do this for the Class, but I did not see why it was up to me particularly; and yet I did not want to be disagreeable.

I picked up some of the typewritten sheets which were clipped together. They began with a printed form, dealing with the life of someone in college just about my time.

"And then there are the photographs," Miss Ferncroft said. "We're having a great deal of trouble collecting the photographs of before and after."

They would be the pictures of young men in high collars taken from the first Class Report, and then there would be the pictures of the way we were today, bald-headed, gray-headed, weary — and what had it all been about?

"So you can see," Miss Ferncroft said, "why Mr. Brown needs help."

"Yes, I can see," I said.

Then I began to read the manuscript which I was holding. It was written by someone whom I had never known. The name was Charles Mason Hilliard.

BORN: Ridgely, Illinois, March 23rd, 1893; son of Joseph, Gertrude (Jessup) Hilliard.
PREPARED AT: Ridgely High School and Brock Academy.
COLLEGE DEGREES: A.B., LL.B.
MARRIED: Martha Gooding, New York City.
CHILDREN: Mary Gooding, Roger, Thomas.
OCCUPATION: Lawyer.
ADDRESS: *(Business)* Mortgage Building, New York.
          (Home) Mamaroneck, New York.

"He doesn't give any dates," I said.

"That's the trouble," said Miss Ferncroft. "No one ever follows instructions."

I continued reading John Mason Hilliard's personal history.

After leaving Law School I joined the firm of Jessup and Goodrich in New York. Five years later I was employed by the firm of Jones and Jones. I am now a partner in the firm of Watkins, Lord, Watkins, Bondage, Green, Smith and Hilliard. I have been very busy all this time practising corporation law and trying to raise a family. My work at Law School was interrupted by the war in which I served as a First Lieutenant, Engineer Corps. This seems to me a strange interlude, unrelated to my other activities. I still like to go to the football games and cheer for Harvard. My chief avocation is watching my children grow up. I am an Episcopalian, and I bowl occasionally and sometimes play golf. In politics I am a Republican, hoping that the day will come when Mr. Roosevelt leaves the White House. Ten years ago it was my good fortune to be sent on business to the Pacific Coast. I made the most of this opportunity for travel and still hope sometime, if I ever have a long enough vacation, to take the family to see the Grand Canyon. Harvard has always seemed to me the best educational institution in the world, and I can hope for nothing better than that my sons will follow my footsteps (which I trust they will do, if we can get Mr. Roosevelt out of the White House) and gain from our old Alma Mater what I have gained, both in experience and peace of mind. I have not had the time which I have wished for reading good books. On leaving college I started Gibbon's *Decline and Fall of the Roman Empire* and Nicolay and Hay's *Lincoln*. I am still working on them in my spare time and hope to report to those who are interested at the reunion that I have finished this self-imposed stint.

"Is this characteristic?" I asked Miss Ferncroft.

"Well, they all seem to be pretty much like that," Miss Ferncroft answered. "It's funny. Most of them have been so busy working that they haven't had time to do anything."

"Would you give me a sheet of note paper, please, Miss Ferncroft," I asked her, "and have you a fountain pen?" She handed me a sheet of note paper, and I sat down in front of it. I did not like what I was going to do, because in a sense it was disloyal to the Class. Nevertheless, I had been making up my mind. It was an imposition.

Dear Bo-jo [I wrote],

It was perfectly swell seeing you at lunch, and as you say, the idea of working on our Class Book is fascinating. I can't tell you how much I wish I could go ahead the way you ask me, but, as a matter of fact, I am going to be very busy, especially toward autumn, and I do not feel I am quite the person to undertake the responsibility. I can't tell you how flattered I am that you feel I am up to it.

What I had written sounded weak. I tore the paper up and put it in the wastebasket and started out again.

Dear Bo-jo,

You shoved this job off on me, because you thought I'd be flattered and because you think I am easily imposed upon. Though I accept you and eat your lunch, I can see that you are a fathead. What do I care what happens to the Class Report?

This was more what I wanted to say, but somehow you can't say things like that. I tore the paper up and tried another sheet.

Dear Bo-jo,

I forgot to tell you that it looks as though I shall have to take a long business trip to New York and Kay and I have been talking about going out to the Pacific Coast next autumn and next winter. Fascinating as all this work will be, I am sure you can see how I can't readily undertake it, but thanks ever so much for asking me.

I was aware that none of this was true. It might be possible that I could suggest to Kay that we go away somewhere, but if I did so it was doubtful whether she would do it, with bills coming in the way they were. I tore the letter up and threw it in the wastebasket.

Dear Bo-jo [I wrote again],
Before I really start out on this perhaps we'd better talk about it a little more.

Yours,
Harry

I folded the letter and placed it in an envelope and handed it to Miss Ferncroft.

"Will you please give this to Mr. Brown?" I said. "Sometime when he isn't too busy. And I'm afraid I'll have to be going now."

"But you'll be back, won't you?" Miss Ferncroft asked.

Willard L. Sperry

THE ALUMNUS
(1947)

Familiarity with English university life (he was a Rhodes scholar at Oxford) gives Willard L. Sperry the proper perspective to comment on the Alumnus as a phenomenon of the American educational scene. Dean Sperry has a universality of alumni experience with which few are blessed, since in addition to Oxford he has academic ties with Olivet College, Yale, Amherst, Brown, Williams, and Boston University, as well as Harvard. For thirty years Dean of the Harvard Divinity School, he has been Plummer Professor of Christian Morals at Harvard since 1929. Dean Sperry has written fifteen books, among them a delightful volume of reminiscent sketches, Summer Yesterdays in Maine, *which established him as a master in the art of the familiar essay.*

I SUPPOSE the real trouble was that I was coming down with a bad cold. I knew that I was already running a temperature. What is more I was some hundreds of miles from home. I had written the local Pullman office weeks earlier asking for a lower berth on that night. I had gone to the station that afternoon to pick up my reservation. After inching along in line for half an hour, I had been told that there was nothing for me. My protest that I had applied some time ago elicited only the threadbare liturgical response, "My God! Haven't you heard there's a war on?"

I then made the round of the hotels near the station. Nothing doing. The lobbies were filled with men in uniform, and the desk clerk used the same liturgy as the man at the Pullman window. *In extremis* I called up a friend of other years and asked could he possibly get me in at his University Club? After ten minutes the answer came back: Yes, there would be a room for me.

This welcome news mitigated the mood of self-pity, though it did not entirely dispel it. These colds; one never knows. It might be some sort of galloping pneumonia of which one dies within 36 hours. But at any rate I should not be found dead on a bench in the park. If I were to die, it would be decently in bed at the Club. A stubborn residual childishness did not prevent me from picturing my wife arriving too late to receive my whispered benediction and having to deal only with the cheerless business of hunting up the nearest mortician and getting "the remains" shipped home.

However, the first glimpse of the Club lobby was reassuring. I realized that I was a privileged person in being admitted at all, and I tried to rise to the occasion. The lounges lying beyond the lobby, lined with intimate nooks like the apsidal chapels of a cathedral, had an air of high seriousness. Architecturally they were in the best Tudor tradition, matching the fabric of the institution they served. Plainly, it is increasingly improbable that any American can hope to get an education hereafter in any building other than Perpendicular Gothic.

Elderly club servants in somewhat moth-eaten vestments — these too in the best English baronial tradition — were shuffling about with trays of ritual cocktails being served to what President Eliot once called — and his successors still call — "the society of educated men." Even the olives and cherries, the orange peel, and toothpicks in the glasses seemed to have taken on moral dignities and a sense of mission which they can never hope to attain in the outer illiterate world where they are at the best the unashamed symbols of candid self-indulgence.

The desk clerk handed me my guest card, and I found that I was assigned to "The 1894 Room"; he mentioned the assignment to the porter with a kind of reverent awe. This aged lackey delivered me there in due time and seemed not unwilling to honor the usual club rule about no tips in its breach rather than its observance. So there I was for the night, if not longer — indeed until the end.

I had forgotten the '90s. At that time I was not much concerned with aesthetics, being in the Philistine years of adolescence. But somehow the initial view of the room rang a far-off bell. The bed was larger than these straitened years now allow; it was a shameless out-size double bed. It was made of rosewood and had lush curlicues on the headboard and footboard. A poke at the mattress suggested honest horsehair, but the apparatus beneath the mattress plainly antedated the years of beauty rest. There were two Morris chairs, pseudo-mahogany, to match the rosewood; the bars at the back of both were in the nearest slots, suggesting decorum rather than abandon. A rather fragile writing table bespoke a feminine hand, presumably the gift of some devoted wife, intended to add a light home touch to the otherwise heavy masculine air of the room.

Then there was a period bookcase, made of built-up units with tilting glass doors. I forget the name of the firm that used to make those things. It was something like "Globe Wobberke." They were "period" pieces. The shelves had not been dusted for some time, but then, had I forgotten that there is a man-power shortage; "My God, haven't you heard. . . . !" A glimpse through the dusty glass discovered a few imperfectly correlated objects, by no means all bookish. Item, a class flag of '94 tacked against a back wall; item, two steins with the college arms surmounted by the mystical figures " '94"; item, framed menus of the dinners at the tenth, twenty-fifth, and fortieth reunions; item, several books cowering apologetically in the left-hand corner of the lowest shelf.

There was a history of the University up to 1908 as written by the then President; a history of the Civil War, written by himself and donated by a professor who had been made an honorary member of the Class; then three sober-looking volumes by members of the Class who had gone on to take their doctorates, dealing variously with "The Mating Habits of the Lower Lepidoptera," "The Active Properties of the Trihydrobenzocarbonates and their Derivatives," and "The Influence of the Pre-Dionysiac Orgies upon the Art of the Later Sumerians." There was something very reassuring about those volumes. They ballasted that bookcase. The flag and the mugs and the menus had suggested a society riding high, not down to a proper Plimsoll line.

But the striking thing about the room was the pictures. There were 39 of them. I counted them twice to be sure. They covered the entire wall space. They were all photographs, a kind of fifty-year family album of the Class in its totality, or in groups. My first view of them was a tremendous personal relief, like water on parched ground. I had come out of college with a precious freight of just such photographs: the college, the class, the crew, the debating society, the dinner club. They seemed to me to humanize my sheepskin, which assured me that the college had honored itself in honoring me, a generous bit of overstatement about which, by the way, I have never been quite certain. My wife, who is a disciple of Clive Bell and who believes in "significant form," will have none of them. They have been wrested from me, one by one, and relegated to the attic. So the '94 room was, at first glance, a kind of lost Eden given back again. I could imagine members of the Class escaping from home, where at the most a discreet copy of Picasso or Van Gogh hangs on the walls, to have their uninhibited hour of reminiscent self-indulgence here.

However, truth is a hard mistress, and if the truth be told, this gallery was not of itself, objectively viewed, a thing of unutterable beauty. Some of the photographs were very large and had been assembled plate by plate to cover an entire scene. They were coming unglued at the abutting edges. Some had been taken by a revolving camera, and prompted a feeling of dizziness as the right and left wings seemed to be closing in upon one — these wings were like tanks by-passing one. The earliest were "glossy prints" which had been light-struck here and there in developing, or else the fixing bath had been weak. Most of them had originally been brown — and what could be more appropriate, since Spengler says that brown is the "historical" color — but many had faded to a kind of jaundiced yellow. No, they were not loveliness incarnate.

However, the scenes and the persons could still be distinguished. There was the Class in its entirety as first gathered in front of Founders' Hall on a September day in 1890, patently callow and self-conscious. There were the Class teams over four years: football, baseball, tennis, track; there were the crews — and in a world which prides itself upon improvement of its models year by year, how little an eight-oared shell has changed. There was the Class on graduation; in sailor straw hats, blue coats, and white flannels. And then the sequence of reunion pictures, with the successful few beginning to emerge from the ruck, seated always somewhere near the center of the group, or snap-shotted by select two's and three's: a Senator, a judge, the founder of the Whalebone Corporation, the president of a bank, and the cheery fellow who was always "the life and soul of the party." At the tenth reunion this group had been caught by the camera on a golf green, armed with prehistoric implements, putting across a terrain not unlike the Himalayas. The twentieth reunion seemed to have taken place by some lakeside; members of one-time crews were stripping again for action in rival barges; but their bags no longer buttoned at the top. The twenty-fifth must have been a great occasion. It convened at a country club, and the bank president had stood the crowd a clambake. The clams and lobsters and seaweed had been shipped from very far. Somehow those clams suggested intimations of mortality;

> Hence in a season of calm weather
> Though inland far we be. . .

One wondered whether they had really been fresh. In any case, there was the druidical stone circle required by a clambake, a chef in a high white cap, and the hungry crowd gathering around with plates.

As the sequence began to wear thin with the years, the numbers fell away, until finally a handful were convened for the fiftieth; bald, urbane, inscrutable, indomitable. But one could feel the spell of man's brief span over the scene; '94 was under sentence of death. Looking at this final picture, as the late Mr. Browning has it, "I felt chilly and grown old." I suspected the chills of being bodily as well as spiritual and I was right; my temperature was now 102° (there is always a clinical thermometer in my travelling case), I found myself wishing that there had been a room in the local Statler, where the art gallery is less likely to prompt morbid reflections; where the unfailing pair of pictures by Greuze hang over the bed, "La jeune fille à l'agneau" and "La jeune fille qui pleurt son oiseau mort" — with the omnipresent prints of Amiens and Beauvais cathedrals matching them on the opposite wall. At least Greuze's young ladies have life ahead of them, not behind them; and the French cathedrals have at any rate lasted longer than the members of '94. I put out the light and went to bed, to meditate through a white night upon the mystery of the alumnus. What sort of a person is he after all, what is his place in the cosmos? At least I lived to tell the tale.

II

Well, at any rate he is indubitably American. There is nothing like him in any other land. In the older English universities you are dated as of the year of your entrance, not of your graduation. Over there '94 would have been '90. But that means little or nothing; it is simply a bookkeeping entry on the ledgers, to show when you opened your account with higher learning. Indeed neither the university as a whole, nor a college in particular, seem to mean as much to an Englishman as does his school. His heart beats faster at the memory of Eton or Winchester, than at that of Christ Church or King's. In the continental universities nothing of the sort, either first or last, obtains. The class of 1194 at Bologna, or that of 1394 at Paris, is perished as though it had never been. Insofar as it ever existed by the calendar it did not become corporately self-conscious; it never "jelled."

No, '94 is as American as a Hopi dance or a ten-gallon hat. As was said of Lincoln, so one can say of '94, "Nothing is here of Europe." One wonders why the Class, even more than the college itself, should have become here the core around which the affections and memories of academic life have crystallized. Is it because members of a class usually lived together, moving en bloc from less favored to more favored quarters over the four years? In any case we accept the member of 1894, indeed for all his affectation we like him, because he is a creature of our culture, not a would-be copy of some outworn Old World model.

As for himself, over the on-going years, there is no doubt what his reunions mean to him. They are his instinctive protest against the way in which the world inevitably depersonalizes him, as it either invests him with dignities and public functions or takes the heart out of him on some treadmill. In a little Scottish cemetery there is a headstone which says, "Here lies the body of Tammas Jones who was born a man and died a grocer." One is prepared to rewrite that epitaph in countless other terms. There was once some warm humanity to him; but he died a banker or a surgeon, a parson or a lawyer. Against this stain and slow contagion of the trades and professions — particularly under the hard driving pressure of modern life — his reunion is his one best chance to reassert his authentic human self, if it is not gone beyond recall.

The reunion is just a bit pathetic and always rather liable to be ludicrous. George Meredith tells us that we make a mistake when "our hearts hold longings for the buried day"; the wisdom of the ages tells you that you cannot recover '94 as it originally was. "The moving finger writes, and having writ moves on." After fifty years, or even twenty-five, the bodily machine won't take it. The sober aftermath of the reunion proves it to you when you are back home; indigestion, a twinge of rheumatism in some new spot, an inordinate sunburn, perhaps even an ominous oppression across the chest. It was too high a price to pay for one day's fun. And yet there was something right in the intention, an instinctive hunger to be, even at this late date, one's unofficial authentic self.

Indeed, there may have been a strain of masochism in the decision to attend the reunion in the first place, a perverse determination to know how far one had allowed the machinery of the world to get one hopelessly enmeshed in its gears. Has one anything left to talk about save one's professional shop? Can one escape from the lock-step of one's vocational chain gang? The fear that this may not be so is a devastating emotion. The willingness to put oneself to the test in the presence of one's classmates of years gone by is in itself an ascetic exercise. We all dimly realize that the motives behind our homecoming to the college town are mixed and its transactions subtle. Beneath the surface festivities lie some of our darkest fears and dearest hopes.

Thus, there is the need of reassuring oneself from time to time as to one's identity, as well as one's independence. Has there been over the years a consecutive and reasonably consistent self? Why we should bother our heads over such a question is a riddle, but we do. We do so, probably, because we know that divided selves, disrupted selves, are the prelude to madness. There is no known subjective device by which we can gain any such assurance. Introspection, so far from reassuring us, only tends to alarm us. You have to take the self you now are back into the presence of some objective fact which is itself enduring, which you have known well and loved over a lifetime. You have to go back, for example, to some bit of external nature that has long been your mental second nature. That was what Wordsworth did when he went back to Grasmere in 1799. He had had an orphaned and homeless childhood, a desultory youth, alarms and excursions and an inconclusive amour in France during the days of the Revolution. He had returned to England a man of divided loyalties and for the moment a man without a country. Before he could settle down to work he had to satisfy himself as to his integrity and identity. This he did by putting himself in the presence of the bit of earth he knew best, the Lake District. The ten lines to the Rainbow (1802) are proof of his need and of the answer to his urgent self-imposed question. For this is not a poem about a rainbow at all — it rather is a poem like Emily Dickinson's "Single Hound" — concerned with the soul's "own identity." The danger, as Emily knew, is that the hound may slip its leash. When Wordsworth saw the rainbow over Helvellyn he knew that he was all right; he could honestly say that his days were "bound each to each by natural piety";

> So was it when my life began;
> So is it now I am a man;
> So be it when I shall grow old.

The other way of getting this reassurance is to go back to the enduring societies of which one has been a part. For this purpose such a society must be concrete, intimate, manageable by the human heart. The state is always there, but save in times of national emergency it is too complex or too abstract. The church and the college serve us better. You go to your reunion, prompted by the same imperious necessity which sent Wordsworth to Cumberland and Westmoreland. If all is well, you come away able to say, "So was it . . . so is it . . . so shall it be."

III

Then there is the problem of repaying a debt. No man, even the un-scholarshipped and economically self-sufficient man, ever pays for the cost of his education. He goes out owing about half the bill to those shadowy figures known as "the founders and benefactors of this institution." One of my friends says that we begin life wondering whether the world is worthy of us and we go on humbly to wonder whether we are worthy of the world. We go to college wondering whether it is good enough for us; we look back on it wondering if we were good enough for it. Therefore very few of us, who have any conscience in these matters, can go through later years without trying to repay at least something of the balance of the account still standing against us.

If the truth be told, all the skills of American business, its ingenuity in advertising, and its shameless appeal to sentiment as well, are employed by the institution in building up its endowments from living alumni. The thing has become a vocation by itself, a recognized and necessary part of the life of the privately endowed American college and university. At its worst the procedure borders dangerously on something like blackmail or a professional racket. We resent the day when in the order of nature it becomes our duty to hand over a bigger check than we think we can at the moment afford, in response to the high-powered salesmanship of some classmate, who is insistent that "good old '94" shall not fall behind the gift of '93 and shall set the bar a bit higher for '95. It is, however, the method that irks us, not the cause. For unless we are wayward and thankless sons of the alma mater, we know that the homestead has this claim on us. This temper, too, is indigenous and wholly American. There is nothing like it in the Old World. The colleges and universities in England hark back to the days when the properties of despoiled abbeys were handed over to them. Their endowments still live on in the terms of ancient feudal lands, rather than as railroad bonds in the bank. The supposition is that the income from these lands still suffices. The suggestion that any living person should give anything to his university or his college has been, within the last few years, little short of a revolution in the mores of that people. We Americans have had to teach them how to do it. Yet in the twanging of this iron string of economic self-reliance we have achieved, even with our slick and streamlined methods of solicitation, a certain vigor and virtue which we identify as our very own.

IV

Then there is finally the more difficult problem of the attitude which the alumnus will take toward the ongoing and maturing apparatus for education in the institution. It is here, of course, that the alumnus, unless he is more than common generous, is apt to be a liability rather than an asset. The very reasons that endear the place to him and bring him back to his reunions make him cherish the college as it was in his time, not as he finds it now. There were great teachers in those days; he delights to remember them and to tell the well-worn tales about them. Today there are only pedants and specialists. The place has deteriorated. He does not understand the price which has now to be paid in the terms of strict specialization for the steady increment of sound knowledge, which must be the constant backlog for the pleasant hearth fire of a living culture. In want of that backlog the fire dies.

The president of one of our greatest universities once said,

I could run this university if I had only the trustees and the faculty and the students and the general public to deal with. It is the alumni that make the job hard. There is at the entrance of the campus a pair of iron gates. Those gates swing a little in the wind. For years they have given off a rusty squeak, and no one has done anything about it. So the other day I took an oil can and went down and oiled the hinges myself. But I know what is going to happen at the next Commencement. The alumni are going to come back and say, "The dear old college isn't what it used to be; the gates to the campus don't squeak the way they did in our time."

When it comes to oiling the academic machinery, or what is worse, replacing it altogether by new devices when the old methods have served their day, the protest becomes more vocal and more serious. The people who are running the place now are trying to spoil it. They don't understand what a college is for. They are making dry-as-dust prigs out of the students; they have gone off after false gods of their own devising. The more the drink flows at the reunion, the more lachrymose this plaint. We were the people, and, alas, wisdom is perishing with us. This muddled mood of self-congratulation and self-pity is very pleasant for the romantic and anachronistic alumnus. What he fails to understand is that, in colleges, as in industries and as in war, skills have been immeasurably tempered and sharpened since he left college, that we live in an age of precision instruments and that mental sloppiness is not enough. It's all very like the pious deacon who makes unthinking use of every latest physical device for his comfort and then goes to church on Sunday to sing that "the good old time religion," which was good enough for all the generations gone, is good enough for him. He has no sense of incongruity between the plane reservation he holds for tomorrow's thousand-mile hop and his horse-and-buggy piety. Upon these matters the alumnus will do well to ponder, when he is corporately gathered for his next reunion. He can afford to deny himself too much conviviality for the sake of a sobriety of mind, to be intelligently addressed to the question of what the dear old place is trying to do for the needy present and the vastly perplexing future. It is no longer '94.

In the year 1790 Edmund Burke indulged in certain "Reflections on the Revolution in France." In the course of these reflections he says,

> To be attached to the subdivision, to live in the little platoon we belong to in society, is the first principle (the germs as it were) of publick affections. It is the first link in the series by which we proceed towards a love to our country and to mankind. The interest of that portion of social arrangement is a trust in the hands of all those who compose it; and as none but bad men would justify it in abuse, none but traitors would barter it away for their own personal advantage.

The alumnus in his more sober moments knows that this is so. The little academic platoon, in which he first learned what the "public affections" are, is dear and necessary to him for what it taught him about life and the world. Burke did not let the case rest there. He went on to describe the nature and structure of society in its entirety. What he said of "society" may be said with equal truth of all our serious institutions of learning, our colleges and universities:

> Society is indeed a contract. Subordinate contracts for objects of mere occasional interest may be dissolved at pleasure — but the state (and likewise the college) ought not to be considered as nothing better than a partnership agreement in a trade of pepper and coffee, callico or tobacco, or some other such low concern, to be taken up for a little temporary interest and to be dissolved by the fancy of the parties. It is to be looked upon with reverence; because it is not a partnership in things subservient only to the gross animal existence of a temporary and perishable nature. It is a partnership in all science; a partnership in all art; a partnership in every virtue, and in all perfection. As the ends of such a partnership cannot be obtained in many generations, it becomes a partnership not only between those who are living, but between those who are living, those who are dead, and those who are to be born. Each contract of each particular state is but a clause in the great primeval contract of eternal society, linking the lower with the higher natures, connecting the visible and invisible worlds.

"The Alumnus," *Harvard Alumni Bulletin*, April 26, 1947.

Alan Gregg

FORTY YEARS AFTER
(1951)

Alan Gregg is a scientist who has never lost sight of the humanities, a physician whose first concern is the person he is treating rather than the disease. After twenty years' concentrating on "the methods and problems of medical education and research," Dr. Gregg retired as Director for the Medical Sciences of the Rockefeller Foundation. He has also served as Chairman of the Advisory Committee for Biology and Medicine of the Atomic Energy Commission. At the time of his fortieth anniversary of graduation from Harvard College, Dr. Gregg told his Classmates: "All streets crossed without injuries or death to self or others. No parking tickets or arrests for my style of driving. Blood pressure still normal. Stopped cigarette smoking several times. Amazed and amused to reach my sixtieth birthday . . . intact, having survived both the agony of my family's illnesses and the exhaustion of their well being. Insurance paid up and prepared to meet inflation by decreasing my needs."

REMEMBER? There you were a little boy of eight, standing at the side of a broad sandy avenue in a Colorado town watching a parade. Not a circus parade, nor a military parade, but the parade of the Society Circus, a sort of summer horse show. In August 1898, or thereabouts.

Your beautiful eldest sister was going to be riding in the Harvard carriage. So many people you knew seemed to be actually in the parade. Lots of floats. A detachment of police, some G.A.R.'s led by Captain John Potter, then the Elks, the Modern Woodmen, the Daughters of Rebekah, and the Colorado Midland Band. And right after the Band came suddenly the Yale carriage, wheels and spokes wrapped with blue bachelors' buttons, with one side draped in a big blue Yale banner. The Yale boys of the town with bright blue hat bands and blue neckties and the girls carrying huge bouquets of violets. Cheers and laughter and smiles from the people on the sidewalk as the carriage came along.

Then you spied a much warmer color coming along, a carriage hardly visible as a carriage, so covered it was with red hollyhocks, crimson streamers, and ribbons, and — why there she was! Your own sister in it, carrying red American Beauty roses, laughing and happy with her friends. Such a warm color, red. And then something quite astonishing happened. Your whole family burst into cheers! You had never seen them so noisily happy and carefree — Mother smiling and clapping. Even Father took off his hat and cheered — which is a very unusual thing for a Congregational minister to do. This was the Harvard carriage.

It was your first experience of allegiance, acknowledged and expressed, open and unashamed — unadulterated and unqualified. Even you could feel you belonged! Then and there, for the rest of your life, the letter H became the naturally balanced symbol of dependability, of beauty and steadfast romance. The letter Y was like an arrow's tip, swift, neat, intense — but untrustworthy, all but dangerous. You even resented the Y in Y.M.C.A. Y — a symbol to put you on guard! And you could think, with deepest satisfaction, after the Harvard carriage had passed, that home and happy and heart and Heaven all began with H, too.

You were the youngest in a family of seven, and your brothers one by one "went East" — to Harvard. You were going, too. That was why you were going to school — to get to Harvard. Very sober business. You were going to leave everything else behind — Colorado and Pike's Peak and all your friends . . . everything. Twenty-six points required for entrance, but your school's schedule didn't allow for French as well as Latin, Greek, and German. So for three years your father read French with you every afternoon at 5.30 for an hour.

On Sunday afternoons, out of fascination with what your three older brothers seemed to know about Harvard, you pored over the *Harvard University Catalogue*, forwards and backwards. There were lots of strange and impressive things in it. There were "courses primarily for graduates." There was a Professor of French named de Sumichrast. It was clear that President Charles William Eliot had graduated in 1853, even earlier than your father's Class of 1866. It was stated that you could get entrance credit for a course in Chipping, Filing, and Fitting. Also there was a professor named Louis Grandgent — what an elegant name! And there were courses even in Sanskrit, given by Charles R. Lanman, who had translated from Sanskrit books you'd never seen mentioned anywhere. It was hard to believe, but the gymnasium was in charge of a man whose first name was Dudley. No cowboy in Colorado would have admitted to such a name — ever. But there it was! Dudley Allen Sargent . . . Sargent, of course, suggested something military and manly and that helped a little bit. It still was hard to believe the Dudley part. But, after all, Harvard was a place for Great Minds. Father kept talking about James and Royce and George Herbert Palmer — though a man named Santayana sounded more mysterious and alluring. From the excitement of all these names you could return to reality via George Washington Cram, the Recorder, a title that carried more than the overtones of factual finality.

One day you learned that your oldest brother had been elected to Phi Beta Kappa — a piece of intelligence obviously justifying your father's kissing your mother in sheer gratitude almost before the postman had left the front porch. A few years later your next oldest brother's letter referred to "going to the Pudding" — incomprehensible but evidently a very sweet privilege indeed. You soon learned that it was a Club, and an ineffable wonder crept into your mind despite the disquiet it brought you — could there be gradations of Perfection? Could there be a quintessence of Harvard itself — the Hasty Pudding Club?

Sneers at "Easterner" and tenderfoot were the rule in those days in the West. All through the Academy you were teased by your classmates in the name of "Hahvud." "Thweee wowsing cheahs for deah old Hahvud"! A martyrdom borne in the silent loyalty of determined and Spartan conviction. "Veritas" could still count on defenders even when they were sadly outnumbered. Even your friends would have to go their ways, while you went yours, to Harvard — pronounced as it is written — Harvard.

Then one bitterly cold winter's night at 10.45 — when you thought your father was going to tell you to go to bed, he gave you a letter that had come from the East addressed to "Dean LeBaron Russell Briggs," and told you to go down to the Santa Fé station, where Dean Briggs was to arrive at the wild hour of 11.55, and deliver that letter to him. It was important, and you knew you were just a kid. You got on Father's Hartford Columbia chainless bicycle and rode at top speed, almost bursting with a sense of consecration and your own first service to Harvard University. You delivered that letter to an almost disconcertingly genial man in a huge yellow-brown overcoat. You said "My Father wants you to have this now." It was done. To your speechless embarrassment you

were thanked by Dean LeBaron Russell Briggs of Harvard. My! He had
a lot of wrinkles in his face, and they all worked when he smiled.

There was a good deal of worry at home about finances. Father wore
his winter suit all one hot summer because that would save $35. The
Christmas of 1903, when you went into Mother's and Father's room to say
Merry Christmas, they opened their presents from the children, and it
was soberly happy and tender. Then Mother gave Father an envelope
from the East. He began reading the letter and suddenly, to your utter
consternation and anguish, he gasped loudly, threw himself on the bed
and lay there — your own Father — sobbing and sobbing — with relief.
It was a check from an admirer. You never knew how much it was for, but
it would clear the mortgage, Mother said, as she patted him on the
shoulder and said, "There! there! Bartlett don't cry." You never knew
there had been a mortgage to send the boys to Harvard and one of the
girls to Radcliffe — and what exactly was a mortgage — did it mean a
deadly promise? Of all wonders your own father sobbing without control
and your mother in perfect control of herself! All that Christmas day you
wondered if you had not come pretty near missing Harvard. Of course
you wouldn't have not gone to Harvard . . . but, you knew you might
not have been actually able to *get* there. What then? Gosh!

September 1907 finally came. At seventeen and two months you were
being called a Harvard man. Do you remember the first meeting of the
freshman class in Upper Massachusetts Hall? What an extraordinarily
shabby building! How much longer could it last? All those fellows milling
around, some of them so extremely well dressed in clothes that had been
bought for them — not hand-me-downs from older brothers. Such self-
assured dignity. It made you feel gawky. Then one asked you, holding out
a registration form, "Say, what does this mean, 'Mother's maiden name'?"
With a reassuring upsurge of maturity you told him. Oh infinite aplomb!
You became a Harvard man.

Do you remember the excitement of having the chance to choose your
courses? And of having men teachers in every single course! It was
exhilarating. Names you had read a hundred times in the dog-eared
catalogue at home in Colorado. These were they! This was it! Think of
making your own choice of Abbott Lawrence Lowell, Charles Homer
Haskins, Bliss Perry, William Morton Wheeler, George Santayana, T. W.
Richards, Josiah Royce, Charles Townsend Copeland, William Morris
Davis, George Lyman Kittredge — and many many more. It was like
choosing from a tray of jewels. But these were men — all men — and
expecting you to be grown up, too.

But in your Class — well, there you hardly knew anybody. Some of
them behaved as though their friends were already made. So formal.
Not at all like Colorado where everybody would be more likely to admit

they were greenhorns and start from scratch. No — not here — not warm or casual but distant and cool. But of course you couldn't expect Olympians to chatter or be unbuttoned. In the Yard, on the street, in Gore Hall, at Boston dances, in classes, everybody seemed to know just what to do, just how to behave. When they were introduced they said "How do you do?" but never "Pleased to meet you" or just "Hello." They all seemed to have their friends — or maybe they didn't want to be bothered. Remember the sophomore you rowed behind on a scrub crew who just stared blankly at you when you said "Hello" to him on Massachusetts Ave.? It never occurred to you that he, too, might be toughing it out, a long way from, say, the Springfield High School and people he could be at ease with.

And the garret room at Miss Dudley's at 53 Dunster St., on the fourth floor. Forty-five dollars for the year. Perfectly comfortable, and if not more . . . well, after all, it helped in letting you go to Harvard. In the center of the room you could stand up. A cot, a chair, and a table — with which to receive the visit of Robert DeCourcy Ward, your Freshman Adviser, whose subject, meteorology, you were so interested in you didn't dare mention it for fear he might think you were pretending.

You went out for freshman football but all the others were so big that, with the overpowering sense of shame that only an adolescent can experience, you suddenly thought you had gotten into the varsity dressing room by a horrible mistake. You asked an enormous man named Maguire. No, you were in the freshman locker room and thence you betook your 119 pounds out to the field, glad to be tackled, for the earth at least had a somewhat familiar feel, though it was moist and soft as no Colorado football field had ever been.

Then there was the first day you saw President Eliot. He was crossing the Yard, and you had to pass him — close. Father had said once that President Eliot had a birthmark on his face. But this was stupendous. It flashed into your mind that this was another proof that Harvard was as great in what it ignored as in what it stood for. Meanwhile, on he came toward you. Off came your hat in bewildered reverence that increased as you passed such a demigod of dignity and fortitude.

Do you remember the Freshman night at Brooks House when you asked Professor Royce what his idea of Heaven was? He replied: "It would be my idea of Heaven to understand the full meaning of anything I was doing." Thereupon, you had that strange conviction that here was something you didn't in the least understand, but nonetheless it was probably overwhelmingly important. You thought about it, and thought about it, and, at long last you understand it — on your fortieth anniversary.

Harvard Alumni Bulletin, April 7, 1951.

IX

SOME VISITORS FROM AFAR

Cambridge is situated about 2 miles west of Boston. It is a large and handsome town, but derives its principal importance from Harvard University, which is located here, and is one of the oldest and most celebrated literary institutions in the United States.

The Fashionable Tour in 1825

Harvard College: This celebrated institootion of learnin' is pleasantly situated in the Bar-room of Parker's, in School street, and has poopils from all over the country.

Artemus Ward; His Travels (1865)

Cambridge, one of the two most renowned of academic cities lies about 3 miles W. of Boston (horse-cars from Bowdoin Square and Park Square). . . . Its greatest attraction is Harvard University, the oldest and most richly endowed institution of learning in America.

Appleton's General Guide to the United States and Canada (1886)

Cambridge (no good hotels), an academic city with 70,028 inhab., lies on the N. bank of the Charles River, opposite Boston, with which it is connected by several bridges traversed by electric and other tramways. Its interest centres in the fact that it is the seat of Harvard University, the oldest, richest, and most famous of American seats of learning.

Baedeker's United States (1893)

Edward Johnson

OF THE FIRST PROMOTION OF LEARNING
IN NEW ENGLAND

(c. 1654)

Edward Johnson (1598–1672) captain of militia, colonial historian, and stalwart Puritan founder of Woburn, Massachusetts, chronicled some of the early history of New England in an anonymous work The Wonder-Working Providence of Sions Saviour in New England *(1654). This homely but vigorous narrative describes in straightforward fashion the major happenings of the author's time interpreted as the struggle of the faithful against the satanic forces of the new world exemplified in the wilderness of the country. The work abounds with the author's own particular brand of "rustical rime" and is full of printer's errors, the result of publication without the author's revisions. Some of the nice phrases in his comments about Harvard have been attributed to the unknown author of* Good News from New England *(1648). Yet despite these apparent defects the work has a strength and directness of approach which is especially appealing to the reader in view of the fact that Captain Johnson was much more a man of action than a man of letters.*

THE SITUATION of this College is very pleasant, at the end of a spacious plain, more like a bowling green, than a wilderness, near a fair navigable river, environed with many neighbouring towns of note, being so near, that their houses join with her suburbs. The building [is] thought by some to be too gorgeous for a wilderness, and yet too mean in others' apprehensions for a College. It is at present enlarging by purchase of the neighbour houses; it hath the conveniences of a fair hall, comfortable studies, and a good library, given by the liberal hand of some magistrates and ministers, with others. The chief gift towards the founding of this College was by Mr. John Harnes [Harvard], a reverend minister; the country being very weak in their public treasury, expended about £500 towards it, and for the maintenance thereof gave the yearly revenue of a ferry passage between Boston and Charles Town, which amounts to about £40 or £50 per annum. The commissioners of the four united colonies also taking into consideration (of what common concernment this work would be, not only to the whole plantations in general, but also to all our English Nation), they endeavoured to stir up all the people in the several colonies to make a yearly contribution toward it, which by some is observed, but by the most very much neglected; the Government hath endeavoured to grant them all the privileges fit for a College, and accordingly the Governour and magistrates, together with the President of the College, for the time being, have a continual care of ordering all matters for the good of the whole: This College hath brought forth, and nursed up very hopeful plants, to the supplying some churches here, as the gracious and godly Mr. Wilson, son to the grave and zealous servant of Christ, Mr. John Wilson, this young man is Pastor to the Church of Christ at Dorchester; as also Mr. Buckly, son to the reverend M. Buckly of Concord; as also a second son of his, whom our native country hath now at present help in the ministry, and the other is over a people of Christ in one of these colonies, and if I mistake not, England hath I hope not only this young man of N. E. nurturing up in learning, but many more, as M. Sam. and Nathanael Mathers, Mr. Wells, Mr. Downing, Mr. Barnard, Mr. Allin, Mr. Bruster, Mr. William Ames, Mr. Jones. Another of the first fruits of this College is employed in these western parts in Mevis, one of the summer islands; beside these named, some help hath been had from hence in the study of physick, as also the godly Mr. Sam. Danforth, who hath not only studied divinity, but also astronomy; he put forth many almanacks, and is now called to the office of a teaching elder in the Church of Christ at Roxbury, who was one of the fellows of this College; the number of students is much increased of late, so that the present year 1651 on the twelfth of the sixth month, ten of them took the degree of Bachelors of Art, among whom the sea-born son of Mr. John Cotton was one. Some gentlemen have sent their sons hither from England, who are to be commended for their care of them, as the judicious and godly Doctor Ames, and divers others. This hath been a place certainly more free from temptations to lewdness than ordinarily England hath been, yet if men shall presume upon this to send their most exorbitant children intending them more especially for God's service, the justice of God doth sometimes meet with them, and the means doth more harden them in their way, for of late the godly Governors of this College have been forced to expel some, for fear of corrupting the fountain . . .

Mr. Henry Dunster is now President of this College, fitted from the Lord for the work, and by those that have skill that way, reported to be an able proficient, in both Hebrew, Greek, and Latin languages, an orthodox preacher of the truths of Christ, very powerful through his blessing to move the affection; and besides he having a good inspection into the well-ordering of things for the students' maintenance (whose commons hath been very short hitherto) by his frugal providence hath continued them longer at their studies than otherwise they could have done; and verily it's great pity such ripe heads as many of them be, should want means to further them in learning. But seeing the Lord hath been pleased to raise up so worthy an instrument for their good, he shall not want for encouragement to go on with the work . . .

The "College" referred to is the second Harvard Hall, burned in 1764. Rev. Urian Oakes was then Acting President and the student body numbered about seventeen.

Jasper Danckaerts

THEY KNEW HARDLY A WORD OF LATIN (1680)

During the year 1679–80 two Dutch Labadists, the followers of the French Protestant theologian and preacher, Jean de Labadie, came to North America in search of a suitable location for a colony of their sect. They found the place they desired in Delaware and on their way home visited Boston. Their names were Jasper Danckaerts (1639–c. 1704) and Peter Sluyter (1645–1722). Bartlett B. James, who edited Danckaerts' Journal of the trip, commented that the Dutchman "viewed his surroundings through the eyes of a fanatical self-satisfaction. For this reason his criticisms or strictures upon persons and conditions are to be received with much discount. But he was an intelligent man, and a keen-eyed and assiduous note-taker.

WE STARTED OUT to go to Cambridge, lying to the northeast of Boston, in order to see their college and printing office. We left about six o'clock in the morning, and were set across the river at Charlestown. We followed a road which we supposed was the right one, but went full half an hour out of the way, and would have gone still further, had not a Negro who met us, and of whom we inquired, disabused us of our mistake. We went back to the right road, which is a very pleasant one. We reached Cambridge about eight o'clock. It is not a large village, and the houses stand very much apart. The college building is the most conspicuous among them. We went to it, expecting to see something unusual, as it is the only college, or would-be academy of the Protestants in all America, but we found ourselves mistaken. In approaching the house we neither heard nor saw anything mentionable; but, going to the other side of the building, we heard noise enough in an upper room to lead my comrade to say, "I believe they are engaged in disputation." We entered and went up stairs, when a person met us, and requested us to walk in, which we did. We found there eight or ten young fellows, sitting around, smoking tobacco, with the smoke of which the room was so full, that you could hardly see; and the whole house smelt so strong of it that when I was going up stairs I said, "It certainly must be also a tavern." We excused ourselves, that we could speak English only a little, but understood Dutch or French well, which they did not. However, we spoke as well as we could. We inquired how many professors there were, and they replied not one, that there was not enough money to support one. We asked how many students there were. They said at first thirty, and then came down to twenty; I afterwards understood there are probably not ten. They knew hardly a word of Latin, not one of them, so that my comrade could not converse with them. They took us to the library where there was nothing particular. We looked over it a little. They presented us with a glass of wine. This is all we ascertained there. The minister of the place goes there morning and evening to make prayer, and has charge over them; besides him, the students are under tutors or masters. Our visit was soon over, and we left them to go and look at the land about there. We found the place beautifully situated on a large plain, more than eight miles square, with a fine stream in the middle of it, capable of bearing heavily laden vessels. As regards the fertility of the soil, we consider the poorest in New York superior to the best here. As we were tired, we took a mouthful to eat, and left. We passed by the printing office, but there was nobody in it; the paper sash however being broken, we looked in, and saw two presses with six or eight cases of type. There is not much work done there. Our printing office is well worth two of it, and even more. We went back to Charlestown, where, after waiting a little, we crossed over about three o'clock.

Journal of Jasper Danckaerts, 1679–168 (New York: Barnes & Noble, Inc., 1952).

Francisco de Miranda

AN INSTITUTION BETTER DESIGNED TO TURN OUT CLERGYMEN THAN WELL-INFORMED CITIZENS

(1784)

The "precursor of the independence of Spanish-America," Francisco de Miranda (1750–1816), visited Harvard College in 1784 and was not generally impressed. His memories of his visit were recorded in one of the many volumes of his voluminous diary, part of his legacy to his beloved Venezuela and the world. Miranda, who has been called "martyr to the cause of which Bolívar was the hero," was a tireless worker and propagandist for the independence of the Spanish colonies throughout the whole period of revolutionary ferment in the late eighteenth century. From 1811 to 1812 he was the ruler of Venezuela, but he was ultimately betrayed to the royalists and spent the remainder of his life in Spanish prisons.

DR. WATERHOUSE and I set aside one day to visit the University of Cambridge. We left at 8:00 in the morning, crossed on the Charlestown Ferry in ten minutes, and taking a post chaise we set out on our literary journey to Cambridge, about four miles distant . . . where in the company of some Tutors (the President was not at home) we set about to see the College. The rooms of the Tutors, and those of the students, are reasonably comfortable, and have no taste or adornment. The Library is rather well organized and is neat. Some 12,000 volumes now compose its collection, English books for the most part, although not badly selected. The room, or museum, of natural history, hardly merits the name. There are a few badly arranged exhibits, and among them is a *diente monstruoso* [or a monstrous tooth, or tusk], one of those which belonged to those extraordinary carnivorous animals, bigger than the elephant and unknown to us, according to what the Society of London has declared, after studying the skeletons found in various parts of this continent and sent to London for such examination.

Afterwards, we went on to the Hall of Philosophy, as they call it, which is a well-equipped spacious room, decorated with several portraits of the principal benefactors of the College, some engravings by Copley (a native of this city), and a marble bust of Lord Chatham, a work of passing merit. The key to the philosophical apparatus was not to be found, and it being the students' dinner hour we went down to the refectory where we all ate rather frugally. The meal consisted of a piece of salt pork, potatoes, cabbages, a bit of bread and cheese, with a little cider as the beverage. Our meal was finished rapidly, as is the custom among scholars, and I returned with my companion, the Doctor, to Boston.

It was necessary to return to see what we had missed on the first visit, and, in fact, that is what we did the following week, visiting in the company of Professor Williams (a man of science and intelligence) the philosophical apparatus, which is certainly very good, and sufficiently complete for its purpose; there is lacking, however, an observatory, and therefore the astronomical instruments are scattered about in one place and another. Afterwards, we went to the top of the building where a lovely view is unfolded.

Since there was nothing more for us to see we went down to the house of the President, who had invited us to dine; and so we had dinner in the company of His Reverence. I made them a present of a silver medallion wrought in Mexico by Gil on the occasion of the establishing of the Academy of National and Public Law, and they esteemed it highly. And so I returned home with my companion.

It seems to me that the institution is more designed to turn out clergymen than able and informed citizens. It is certainly an extraordinary thing that there is not a single course in the modern languages and that theology is the principal course of study in the College. The manner of dress and the manner of conducting oneself and of being polite in society, etc., are sciences to which not the least attention is paid; and the outward appearance of the students is the most slovenly that has ever been seen in students of this kind. The President is lean, austere, and of an insufferable circumspection.

The Diary of Francisco de Miranda. Tour of the United States, 1783–1784 (New York, 1928).

J. P. Brissot de Warville

THE AIR OF CAMBRIDGE IS PURE

(1788)

J. P. Brissot de Warville (1754–1793), journalist, pamphleteer, and French revolutionist, disciple of Rousseau and Voltaire, visited the United States through his interest in the abolitionist movement and wrote one of the most penetrating of the early commentaries on the new nation. The author of two books on the philosophy of law, Brissot edited the Patriote française *during the French Revolution and took a leading part in the public affairs of the time. He served successively as a member of the municipality of Paris, of the legislative assembly, and then of the convention. As a member of the diplomatic committee, he is held to have been largely responsible for France's foreign policy of the time, including the declaration of war against the emperor and against England. When his party fell, he was executed on the guillotine. "However unfortunate the intelligent and philanthropic writer of these Travels may have been at the conclusion of his earthly career," remarks the translator and editor of the* New Travels, *"It is a tribute due to his memory from every liberal mind, to acknowledge, that no traveller of our own times has made a more valuable present to the enlightened part of Europe than M. Brissot, by his account of the present state of the people, of their manners and trade, of the United States of America. . . Brissot has taught his countrymen to think very differently of that people. I believe every reader of these travels, who understands enough of America to enable him to judge, will admit that his remarks are infinitely more judicious, and more candid, than those of any other gentleman who has lately visited that country."*

BOSTON has the glory of having given the first college or university to the new world. It is placed on an extensive plain, four miles from Boston, at a place called Cambridge; the origin of this useful institution was in 1636. The imagination could not fix on a place that could better unite all the conditions essential to a seat of education; sufficiently near to Boston to enjoy all the advantages of a communication with Europe and the rest of the world, and sufficiently distant not to expose the students to the contagion of licentious manners common in commercial towns.

The air of Cambridge is pure, and the environs charming, offering a vast space for the exercise of the youth.

The buildings are large, numerous, and well distributed. But, as the number of the students augments every day, it will be necessary soon to augment the buildings. The library, and the cabinet of philosophy, do honour to the institution. The first contains 13,000 volumes. The heart of a Frenchman palpitates on finding the works of Racine, of Montesquieu, and the Encyclopaedia, where, 150 years ago, rose the smoke of the savage calumet.

The regulation of the course of studies here is nearly the same as that at the university of Oxford. I think it impossible but that the last revolution must introduce a great reform. Free men ought to strip themselves of their prejudices, and to perceive, that, above all, it is necessary to be a man and a citizen; and that the study of the dead languages, of a fastidious philosophy and theology, ought to occupy few of the moments of a life which might be usefully employed in studies more advantageous to the great family of the human race . . .

But to return to the university of Cambridge, superintended by the respectable president Willard. Among the associates in the direction of the studies are distinguished Dr. Wigglesworth and Dr. Dexter. The latter is professor of natural philosophy, chemistry, and medicine; a man of extensive knowledge, and great modesty. He told me, to my great satisfaction, that he gave lectures on the experiments of our schools of chemistry. The excellent work of my respectable master, Dr. Fourcroy, was in his hands, which taught him the rapid strides that this science has lately made in Europe.

In a free country everything ought to bear the stamp of patriotism. This patriotism, so happily displayed in the foundation, endowment, and encouragement of his university, appears every year in a solemn feast celebrated at Cambridge in honour of the Sciences. This feast, which takes place once a year in all the colleges of America, is called the *commencement*: it resembles the exercises and distribution of prizes in our colleges. It is a day of joy for Boston; almost all its inhabitants assemble in Cambridge. The most distinguished of the students display their talents in the presence of the public; and these exercises, which are generally on patriotic subjects, are terminated by a feast, where reign the freest gaiety, and the most cordial fraternity.

It is remarked, that in countries chiefly devoted to commerce the sciences are not carried to any high degree. This remark applies to Boston. The university certainly contains men of worth and learning; but science is not diffused among the inhabitants of the town. Commerce occupies all their ideas, turns all their heads, and absorbs all their speculations. Thus you find few estimable works, and few authors . . . The arts, except those that respect navigation, do not receive much encouragement here.

J. P. Brissot de Warville, *New Travels in the United States of America* (1794).

Harriet Martineau

THE STATE OF THE UNIVERSITY WAS A SUBJECT OF GREAT MOURNING

(1838)

The English writer, Harriet Martineau (1802–1876), produced two books as a result of her visit to the United States in 1834–1836. The first was Society in America (1837), an economic, political, and social critique of the United States, and the second Retrospect of Western Travel (1838), a series of descriptive sketches recording personal impressions of her experiences. While she was widely attacked, especially by southern critics, for her views on slavery and the south, Retrospect of Western Travel, from which the following selection is taken, was a popular success. In her comments on Harvard, wisely and sometimes amusingly stated, may be seen the underlying development of the political and ethical ideas which made her an important influence on the intellectual life of the Victorian era.

IF HARVARD is ever to recover her supremacy, to resume her station in usefulness and in the affections of the people, it must be by a renovation of her management, and a change in some of the principles recognized by her. Every one is eager to acknowledge her past services. All American citizens are proud of the array of great men whom she has sent forth to serve and grace the country; but, like some other universities, she is falling behind the age. Her glory is declining, even in its external manifestations; and it must decline as long as the choicest youth of the community are no longer sent to study within her walls.

The politics of the managers of Harvard University are opposed to those of the great body of the American people. She is the aristocratic college of the United States. Her pride of antiquity, her vanity of pre-eminence and wealth, are likely to prevent her renovating her principles and management, so as to suit the wants of the period; and she will probably receive a sufficient patronage from the aristocracy, for a considerable time to come, to encourage her in all her faults. She has a great name; and the education she affords is very expensive, in comparison with all other colleges. The sons of the wealthy will therefore flock to her. The attainments usually made within her walls are inferior to those achieved elsewhere; her professors (poorly salaried, when the expenses of living are considered), being accustomed to lecture and examine the students, and do nothing more. The indolent and the careless will therefore flock to her. But, meantime, more and more new colleges are rising up, and are filled as fast as they rise, whose principles and practices are better suited to the wants of the time. In them living is cheaper; and the professors are therefore richer with the same or smaller salaries; the sons of the yeomanry and mechanic classes resort to them; and, where it is the practice of the tutors to work with their pupils, as well as lecture to them, a proficiency is made which shames the attainments of the Harvard students. The middle and lower classes are usually neither Unitarian nor Episcopalian, but "orthodox," as their distinctive term is: and these, the strength and hope of the nation, avoid Harvard, and fill to overflowing the oldest orthodox colleges; and when these will hold no more, establish new ones.

When I was at Boston, the state of the University was a subject of great mourning among its friends. Attempts had been made to obtain the services of three gentlemen of some eminence as professors; but in vain. The salaries offered were insufficient to maintain the families of these gentlemen in comfort, in such a place as Cambridge; though, at that very time, the managers of the affairs of the institution were purchasing lands in Maine. The Moral Philosophy chair had been vacant for eight years. Two of the professors were at the time laid by in tedious illnesses; a third was absent on a long journey; and the young men of the senior class were left almost unemployed. The unpopularity of the president among the young men was extreme; and the disfavour was not confined to them. The students had, at different times within a few years, risen against the authorities; and the last disturbances in 1834, had been of a very serious character. Everyone was questioning what was to be done next, and anticipating a further vacating of chairs which it would be difficult to fill. I heard one merry lady advise that the professors should strike for higher wages, and thus force the council and supporters of the university into a thorough and serious consideration of its condition and prospects in relation to present and future times.

The salary of the president is above 2000 dollars. The salaries of the professors vary from 1500 dollars to 500; that is, from £375 to £125. Upon this sum they are expected to live like gentlemen, and to keep up the aristocratic character of the institution. I knew of one case where a jealousy was shown when a diligent professor, with a large family, made an attempt by a literary venture to increase his means. Yet Harvard college is in buildings, library, and apparatus, in its lands and money, richer than any other in the Union.

The number of undergraduates, in the year 1833–4 was two hundred and sixteen. They cannot live at Harvard for less than 200 dollars a-year, independently of personal expenses. Seventy-five dollars must be contributed by each to the current expenses; fuel is dear; fifteen dollars are charged for lodging within the college walls, and eighty are paid for board by those who use their option of living in the college commons. The fact is, I believe, generally acknowledged, that the comparative expensiveness of living is a cause of the depression of Harvard in comparison with its former standing among other colleges; but this leads to a supposition which does not to all appear a just one, that if the expenses of poor students could be defrayed by a public fund, to be raised for the purpose, the sons of the yeomanry would repair once more to Harvard.

It may be doubted whether, if a gratis education to poor students were to be dispensed from Harvard tomorrow, it would rival in real respectability and proficiency the orthodox colleges which have already surpassed her. Her management and population are too aristocratic, her movement too indolent, to attract young men of that class; and young men of that class prefer paying for the benefits they receive; they prefer a good education, economically provided, so as to be within reach of their means, to an equally good education furnished to them at the cost of their pride of independence. The best friends of Harvard believe that it is not by additional contrivances that her prosperity can be restored; but by such a renovation of the whole scheme of her management as shall bring her once more into accordance with the wants of the majority, the spirit of the country and of the time.

Harriet Martineau, *Retrospect of Western Travel* (1838).

Charles Dickens

THE QUIET INFLUENCE OF CAMBRIDGE
(1842)

Charles Dickens' triumphant tour of the United States took place when he was but twenty-nine years old, and he celebrated his thirtieth birthday while in the States. He was the author of a half-dozen successful books, including Pickwick Papers, Oliver Twist, *and* Nicholas Nickleby. *The enthusiasm which greeted him knew no bounds. He met the President and all the most important people; tickets for the public receptions in his honor sold for fabulous prices. It was partly the warmth of his welcome and the resulting public idolization which caused the swift adverse reaction to his perfectly justified criticisms of America contained in the* American Notes, *published on his return to England. There was little, however, about Boston and New England that did not appeal to him, including his glimpse of Harvard.*

THERE is no doubt that much of the intellectual refinement and superiority of Boston, is referable to the quiet influence of the University of Cambridge, which is within three or four miles of the city. The resident professors at that university are gentlemen of learning and varied attainments; and are, without one exception that I can call to mind, men who would shed a grace upon, and do honor to, any society in the civilised world. Many of the resident gentry in Boston and its neighborhood, and I think I am not mistaken in adding, a large majority of those who are attached to the liberal professions there, have been educated at this same school. Whatever the defects of American universities may be, they disseminate no prejudices; rear no bigots; dig up the buried ashes of no old superstitions; never interpose between the people and their improvement; exclude no man because of his religious opinions; above all, in their whole course of study and instruction, recognise a world, and a broad one too, lying beyond the college walls.

It was a source of inexpressible pleasure to me to observe the almost imperceptible, but not less certain effect, wrought by this institution among the small community of Boston; and to note at every turn the humanising tastes and desires it has engendered; the affectionate friendships to which it has given rise; the amount of vanity and prejudice it has dispelled. The golden calf they worship at Boston is a pigmy compared with the giant effigies set up in other parts of that vast counting-house which lies beyond the Atlantic; and the almighty dollar sinks into something comparatively insignificant, amidst a whole Pantheon of better gods.

Charles Dickens, *American Notes* (London, 1842).

Lady Emmeline Stuart-Wortley

MONSIEUR AGASSIZ WAS VERY MUCH OCCUPIED

(1849)

Lady Emmeline (1806–1855), second daughter of the fifth Duke of Rutland and friend of Queen Victoria, composed her first important piece of prose at the age of ten when she chronicled "the dreadful fire at Belvoir Castle" and reported realistically the nursemaid's cry to the children of the family, "Oh, for God's sake get up, the Castle is all in a blaze, you will be burnt in your beds." In later life she was as prolific and detailed a reporter as she was an avid traveler. With her husband, Lady Emmeline visited Russia, Italy, Holland, the Balkan countries, Hungary, and Turkey. After his death she traveled with her daughter to Europe, and America. She was in Mexico during the revolution of 1848 and she crossed the Isthmus of Panama by dugout canoe. It might be said that Lady Emmeline even met death in character, for despite a broken leg she insisted on a particularly dangerous and difficult journey through the Holy Land in 1855 and died in Damascus. Lady Emmeline was exceptionally prolific in both verse and prose and was the author of many long poems celebrating her travels, as well as several verse dramas, including Angiolina del Albano, or Truth and Treachery *(1841) and* Eva, or The Error *(1840). A pleasant account of her life is given in* Wanderers: Episodes from the Travels of Lady Emmeline Stuart-Wortley and Her Daughter Victoria, 1849–1855, *edited by her granddaughter, Mrs. Henry Cust.*

THE FIRST time we went to Cambridge we went to see our amiable friends Mrs. and Miss Everett. They are in the President's house, and are to continue there for the present. After sitting a little while with Mrs. Everett, we went with Mr. and Miss Everett in their carriage to Mount Auburn, the spacious and beautiful cemetery. The finely diversified grounds occupy about one hundred acres, in general profusely adorned with a rich variety of trees, and in some places planted with ornamental shrubbery: there are some tombs graced with charming flower-beds. There are also some pretty sheets of water there: it is divided into different avenues and paths, which have various names. Generally they are called after the trees or flowers that abound there, such as lily, poplar, cypress, violet, woodbine, and others. It is indeed a beauteous city for the dead. The birds were singing most mellifluously and merrily — it was quite a din of music that they kept up in these solemn but lovely shades. The views from Mount Auburn are fine and extensive. There are some graceful and well-executed monuments within its precincts.

Afterward we went with Mr. Everett to see a little of the colleges, and then visited the mineralogical cabinet. Harvard University is the most ancient, and is reckoned the best endowed institution in the Union. It was founded in 1638, and from a donation made to it by the Rev. John Harvard it was called after him. We paid a brief visit to the great telescope, merely to look at it, however, and not through it, for it was then dull, and very cloudy, with no prospect of its being otherwise during the evening — it is a refracting telescope. Mr. Bond himself was not there, but his son was, who is already a distinguished and enthusiastic astronomer. Mr. Bond, senior, was one of the discoverers of the eighth satellite of Saturn.

Another time we went to the *soirée*, which Mr. and Mrs. Everett gave on the occasion of the meeting of the American Association of Science at Cambridge.

There I saw, of course, many learned celebrities. Among them — Professor Peirce, Professor Silliman, Professor Guyon, Professor Sparks (the new President of Harvard University), and Professor Agassiz, the celebrated naturalist (I found he was a cousin of my old governess, Mademoiselle Anne Agassiz).

This very distinguished man — one of the great contributors to the world's stores of science and knowledge — is an extremely agreeable member of society, and a very popular one. His manners are particularly frank, pleasing, cordial, and simple; and though deeply absorbed, and intensely interested in his laborious scientific researches, and a most thorough enthusiast in his study of natural philosophy, yet he rattled merrily away on many of the light topics of the day with the utmost gayety, good-humor, and spirit.

He has succeeded, after great trouble and persevering indefatigable care, in preserving alive some coral insects, the first that have ever been so preserved, and he kindly promised me an introduction to those distinguished architects. We accordingly went, accompanied by Mr. Everett, the following day. M. Agassiz was up-stairs very much occupied by some scientific investigation of importance, and he could not come down, but he allowed us to enter the all but hallowed precincts devoted to the much-cherished coral insects.

M. Agassiz had been away a little while previously, and left these treasures of his heart under the charge and superintendence of his assistant. This poor care-worn attendant, we were told, almost lost his own life in preserving the valuable existence of these little moving threads, so much did he feel the weighty responsibility that devolved upon him, and with such intense anxiety did he watch the complexion, the contortions, all the twistings and twirlings, and twitchings, and flingings and writhings of the wondrous little creatures, most assiduously marking any indications of *petite santé* among them. They were kept in water carefully and frequently changed, and various precautions were indispensably necessary to be taken in order to guard their exquisitely delicate demisemi existences.

Glad enough was the temporary gentleman-in-waiting, and squire-of-the-body to these interesting zoophytes to see M. Agassiz return, and to resign his charge into his hands. With him this exceeding care and watchfulness was indeed nothing but a labor of love, and probably no nurse or mother ever fondled a weakly infant with more devoted tenderness and anxious attention than M. Agassiz displayed toward his dearly-beloved coral insects.

As to me, I hardly dared breathe while looking at them for fear I should blow their precious lives away, or some catastrophe should happen while we were there, and we should be suspected of *coralicide!* However, the sight was most interesting. We watched them as they flung about what seemed their fire-like white arms, like microscopic opera dancers or windmills; but these apparent arms are, I believe, all they possess of bodies. How wonderful to think of the mighty works that have been performed by the fellow-insects of these restless little laborers. What are the builders of the Pyramids to them? What did the writers of the "Arabian Nights" imagine equal to their more magical achievements? Will men ever keep coral insects by them to lay the foundations of a few islands and continents when the population grows too large for the earthy portion of the earth? People keep silkworms to spin that beautiful fabric for them: and M. Agassiz has shown there is no impracticability. I looked at the large bowl containing the weird workers with unflagging interest, till I could almost fancy minute reefs of rock were rising up in the basin.

What a world of marvels we live in, and alas that the splendid wonders of science should be shut out from so many myriads of mankind . . . Penny Magazines and such works have done much, but much there remains to be done to bring the subjects not only within reach, but to make them more universally popular and attractive, and less technical.

At last we took leave of those marine curiosities, and wended our way back, sorry not to have seen M. Agassiz (who was still absorbed in dissecting or pickling for immortality some extraordinary fish that he had discovered), but delighted to have had the opportunity of seeing his *protégés.*

"M. Agassiz ought indeed to have an extensive museum," said ———— "for I believe every body in the States makes a point of sending off to him, post haste, every imaginable reptile, and monster, and nondescript that they happen to find." I should, assuredly not like to have the opening of his letters and parcels if that is the case.

Lady Emmeline Stuart-Wortley, *Travels in the United States, etc., During 1849 and 1850* (New York, 1851).

Anthony Trollope

I DID NOT VISIT THE MUSEUM
(1861)

In the midst of the chaotic Civil War period Anthony Trollope came to these shores. His North America, *published in England and the United States, contains the result of his impressions — neutral toward the "irrepressible conflict" but reservedly realistic on matters of the traveler's experiences in America. Trollope's own self-criticism of his report was confirmed in the judgment of later critics. The novelist wrote of* North America: *"It was tedious and confused, and will hardly, I think, be of future value to those who wish to make themselves acquainted with the United States." Trollope was genuinely fond of America, however, and his book enabled him to repair many of the wounds left by his mother's sharp criticism as a result of her stay in the United States from 1827 until 1831. Trollope's comments about Harvard are among the most interesting passages in the book.*

CAMBRIDGE is not above three or four miles from Boston. Indeed, the town of Cambridge properly so called begins where Boston ceases. The Harvard College — that is its name, taken from one of its original founders — is reached by horsecars in twenty minutes from the city. An Englishman feels inclined to regard the place as a suburb of Boston; but if he so expresses himself, he will not find favor in the eyes of the men of Cambridge.

The University is not so large as I had expected to find it. It consists of Harvard College, as the undergraduates' department, and of professional schools of law, medicine, divinity, and science. In the few words that I will say about it I will confine myself to Harvard College proper, conceiving that the professional schools connected with it have not in themselves any special interest. The average number of undergraduates does not exceed 450, and these are divided into four classes. The average number of degrees taken annually by bachelors of art is something under 100. Four years' residence is required for a degree, and at the end of that period a degree is given as a matter of course if the candidate's conduct has been satisfactory. When a young man has pursued his studies for that period, going through the required examinations and lectures, he is not subjected to any final examination as is the case with a candidate for a degree at Oxford and Cambridge. It is, perhaps, in this respect that the greatest difference exists between the English Universities and Harvard College. With us a young man may, I take it, still go through his three or four years with a small amount of study. But his doing so does not insure him his degree. If he have utterly wasted his time he is plucked, and late but heavy punishment comes upon him. At Cambridge in Massachusetts the daily work of the men is made more obligatory; but if this be gone through with such diligence as to enable the student to hold his own during the four years, he has his degree as a matter of course. There are no degrees conferring special honour. A man cannot go out "in honours" as he does with us. There are no "firsts" or "double firsts"; no "wranglers"; no "senior opts" or "junior opts." Nor are there prizes of fellowships and livings to be obtained. It is, I think, evident from this that the greatest incentives to high excellence are wanting at Harvard College. There is neither the reward of honour nor of money. There is none of that great competition which exists at our Cambridge for the high place of Senior Wrangler; and, consequently, the degree of excellence attained is no doubt lower than with us. But I conceive that the general level of the University education is higher there than with us; that a young man is more sure of getting his education, and that a smaller percentage of men leaves Harvard College utterly uneducated than goes in that condition out of Oxford or Cambridge. The education at Harvard College is more diversified in its nature, and study is more absolutely the business of the place than it is at our Universities.

The expense of education at Harvard College is not much lower than at our colleges; with us there are, no doubt, more men who are absolutely extravagant than at Cambridge, Massachusetts. The actual authorized expenditure in accordance with the rules is only £50 per annum, *i.e.*, 249 dollars; but this does not, by any means, include everything. Some of the richer young men may spend as much as £300 per annum, but the largest number vary their expenditure from £100 to £180 per annum; and I take it the same thing may be said of our Universities. There are many young men at Harvard College of very small means. They will live on £70 per annum, and will earn a great portion of that by teaching in the vacations. There are thirty-six scholarships attached to the University varying in value from £20 to £60 per annum; and there is also a beneficiary fund for supplying poor scholars with assistance during their collegiate education. Many are thus brought up at Cambridge who have no means of their own, and I think I may say that the consideration in which they are held among their brother students is in no degree affected by their position. I doubt whether we can say so much of the sizars and bible clerks at our Universities.

At Harvard College there is, of course, none of that old-fashioned, time-honoured, delicious, mediaeval life which lends so much grace and beauty to our colleges. There are no gates, no porter's lodges, no butteries, no halls, no battels, and no common rooms. There are no proctors, no bulldogs, no bursers, no deans, no morning and evening chapel, no quads, no surplices, no caps and gowns. I have already said that there are no examinations for degrees and no honours; and I can easily conceive that in the absence of all these essentials many an Englishman will ask what right Harvard College has to call itself a University.

I have said that there are no honours, — and in our sense there are none. But I should give offence to my American friends if I did not explain that there are prizes given — I think, all in money, and that they vary from 50 to 10 dollars. These are called *deturs*. The degrees are given on Commencement Day, at which occasion certain of the expectant graduates are selected to take parts in a public literary exhibition. To be so selected seems to be tantamount to taking a degree in honours. There is also a dinner on Commencement Day, — at which, however, "no wine or other intoxicating drink shall be served."

It is required that every student shall attend some place of Christian worship on Sundays; but he, or his parents for him, may elect what denomination of church he shall attend. There is a University chapel on the University grounds which belongs, if I remember right, to the Episcopalian Church. The young men for the most part live in College, having rooms in the College buildings; but they do not board in those rooms. There are establishments in the town under the patronage of the University, at which dinner, breakfast, and supper are provided; and the young men frequent one of these houses or another as they, or their friends for them, may arrange. Every young man not belonging to a family resident within a hundred miles of Cambridge, and whose parents are desirous to obtain the protection thus provided, is placed, as regards his pecuniary management, under the care of a patron, and this patron acts by him as a father does in England by a boy at school. He pays out his money for him and keeps him out of debt. The arrangement will not recommend itself to young men at Oxford quite so powerfully as it may do to the fathers of some young men who have been there. The rules with regard to the lodging and boarding houses are very stringent. Any festive entertainment is to be reported to the President. No wine or spirituous liquors may be used, &c. It is not a picturesque system, this; but it has its advantages.

There is a handsome library attached to the College, which the young men can use; but it is not as extensive as I had expected. The University is not well off for funds by which to increase it. The new museum in the College is also a handsome building. The edifices used for the undergraduates' Chambers and for the lecture-rooms are by no means handsome. They are very ugly red-brick houses standing here and there without order. There are seven such, and they are called Brattle House, College House, Divinity Hall, Hollis Hall, Holsworthy Hall, Massachusetts Hall, and Stoughton Hall. It is almost astonishing that buildings so ugly should have been erected for such a purpose. These, together with the library, the museum, and the chapel, stand on a large green, which might be made pretty enough if it were kept well mown like the gardens of our Cambridge colleges; but it is much neglected. Here, again, the want of funds — the *res angusta domi* — must be pleaded as an excuse. On the same green, but at some little distance from any other building, stands the President's pleasant house.

The immediate direction of the College is of course mainly in the hands of the President, who is supreme. But for the general management of the Institution there is a Corporation, of which he is one. It is stated in the laws of the University that the Corporation of the University and its Overseers constitute the Government of the University. The Corporation consists of the President, five Fellows, so called, and a Treasurer. These Fellows are chosen, as vacancies occur, by themselves, subject to the concurrence of the Overseers. But these Fellows are in nowise like to the Fellows of our colleges, having no salaries attached to their offices. The Board of Overseers consists of the State Governor, other State officers, the President and Treasurer of Harvard College, and thirty other persons, — men of note, chosen by vote. The Faculty of the College, in which is vested the immediate care and government of the undergraduates, is composed of the President and the Professors. The Professors answer to the tutors of our colleges, and upon them the education of the place depends. I cannot complete this short notice of Harvard College without saying that it is happy in the possession of that distinguished natural philosopher, Professor Agassiz. M. Agassiz has collected at Cambridge a museum of such things as natural philosophers delight to show, which I am told is all but invaluable. As my ignorance on such matters is of a depth which the Professor can hardly imagine, and which it would have shocked him to behold, I did not visit the museum. Taking the University of Harvard College as a whole, I should say that it is most remarkable in this, —

that it does really give to its pupils that education which it professes to give. Of our own Universities other good things may be said, but that one special good thing cannot always be said.

Anthony Trollope, *North America* (London and New York, 1862).

David Macrae

HARVARD AND HER TWO HUMORISTS

(c. 1868)

David Macrae (1837–1907) traveled in America during 1867–68, observing the progress of reconstruction after the Civil War. A Scottish minister and writer, Macrae had a sharp eye for detail and a shrewd wit which makes his travel report, The Americans at Home, *a most entertaining and well-written document, even though the reader may feel a certain glibness about the author's commentary. One of the best chapters in the book is that describing his visit to Longfellow and his "auditing" of lectures by Lowell and Holmes.*

A FEW days after my first interview with Longfellow, he was kind enough to take me to hear one of Lowell's lectures at Harvard, where the author of the *Biglow Papers* occupies the Chair of Modern Languages and Literature.

We went first and had a glance through the University Library. Harvard's ambition was to make this an American Bodleian; but the destruction of the library by fire in 1764 was a heavy blow; and the number of books since collected does not exceed 150,000. I noticed several old donations from Scotland, and the librarian said he was anxious to see more of the Scottish element, and wished that Scottish authors and publishers knew the desire of Harvard that everything published in this country should put in an appearance there — a desire which I am glad of this opportunity of making to some extent known. As for the kind of books wanted, Harvard is omniverous. "I should be glad," the librarian said, "if every Scotchman who puts an idea or half an idea in print would send it to this library." To illustrate the importance that might attach to even the pettiest publication, he told me a story (which I hope was not apocryphal) about some man who would have lost a large fortune, had it not been that a funeral sermon preserved at Harvard enabled him to supply a missing link in the chain of evidence.

On leaving the library, and crossing the grassy square towards Lowell's class-room, we saw, rambling towards the same point from the other side, an undersized gentleman in a Highland cloak, carrying a portfolio under his arm. It turned out to be the author of the *Biglow Papers* himself.

We accompanied him to his class-room, where 100 to 150 students were assembled, most of them keen, dark-eyed youths, and many of them wearing double eye-glasses — a phenomenon about New England (and especially about Boston) ladies and gentlemen which I never got to the bottom of.

Lowell stepped up to the platform, opened his portfolio on the desk, and without ceremony began his lecture. American professors, like American ministers, abjure gowns. Lowell, in plain shooting-coat and light speckled necktie; long curling brown hair, parted in the middle; corner of white handkerchief sticking out of his breast-pocket, stood leaning with his elbows on his desk, and one leg bent back and swaying itself easily on the point of his boot as he went on.

He read in a pleasant, quiet, gentlemanly way, and enlivened his lecture with continual sallies of wit, that threatened at times to disturb the decorum of the class. The main topic related to the poetry of the Troubadours: but the introduction had some remarks on the Saxons — "of whom, however," said he, "as was said of the gods, 'the less we have to do with them the better.'" He described them as a sturdy people, "sound of stomach," "with no danger of liver complaint" — a shrewd people, "endowed with an acute sense of settling on the land and sticking like alluvial deposits in the levels" — practical men "with no notion that two and two ever make five." "The solidity of these people," he said, "makes them terrible when fairly moved." "But there could be no poet in a million such. Poetry is not made of such materials — of minds in which the everlasting question is, 'What is this good for?' — a question which would puzzle the rose and be answered triumphantly by the cabbage."

When he came to speak of the old Metrical Romances, he said, describing the career of one of their knight-errants, — "It was delightful. No bills to pay. Hero never brought to a stand-still for want of cash." "Then there are the giants who are admitted to all the rights of citizenship, and serve as anvils for knights, who sometimes belabour them for three days in succession, and stop, not for want of breath on the part of the combatants, but of the minstrel, who, when he found himself or his audience becoming exhausted, managed to make the giant's head loose on his shoulders."

In these glorious days of the Metrical Romance, said the professor, "you have a fine time of it, living in your castle on the top of a rock, enjoying a sort of independence, such as man enjoys in jail." Your horse, too, is a wonderful animal, "whose skeleton Professor Owen would have given his ears for." You have a summary way of dealing with your subjects. "If they are infidels you take all their heads off and bring them to more serious views." Finally, at the end of a glorious career, "you die deeply regretted by your subjects, if there are any of them left with their heads on."

Enlivening his lecture with little sparkling bits of fun of this sort, he went on for nearly an hour, in quiet, easy style, rarely looking up from his manuscript; his hands looped behind his back, or fingering the edges of his desk, raising the lid half an inch and letting it softly down again. At the comical bits there was a "pawky" look in his face and a comical twinkle of the eye, as if he were enjoying the fun just as much as we. . .

Since Longfellow's resignation of his Chair at Harvard, some eighteen years ago, Lowell has occupied his place. The two poets live near each other, and are intimate friends. In manner, voice, and appearance, Lowell, like Longfellow, would not be distinguished from a cultured English gentleman. Both of them are indispensable members of what the envious New Yorkers call the Mutual Admiration Society of Boston — the circle that has done so much to give America a classic literature of her own, and that represents a class of the scholarly men whom America will produce in greater numbers when the work of breaking up the boundless prairies and hunting incessantly after the almighty dollar is sufficiently over to afford time for quiet intellectual growth.

I was glad to hear that the opening of the medical classes would give me an opportunity of hearing Oliver Wendell Holmes deliver the inaugural lecture. Mr. Fields, the publisher, who went with me, took me round to the museum behind the lecture-hall, where we found a number of the literary and scientific men of Boston assembled to accompany Dr. Holmes to the platform. The doctor himself was there, but was altogether a different-looking man from what I supposed him to be. I had conceived of him, for what reason I know not, possibly from his poetry, as a tall, thin, dark-eyed, brilliant-looking man. This is not, perhaps, the conception one gets from his *Autocrat of the Breakfast Table;* but I read his poems first, and first impressions are apt to remain. Holmes is a plain little dapper man, his short hair brushed down like a boy's, but turning gray now; a trifle of furzy hair under his ears; a powerful jaw, and a thick, strong under lip that gives decision to his look, with a dash of pertness. In conversation he is animated and cordial — sharp too, taking the word out of one's mouth. When Mr. Fields said, "I sent the boy this — " "Yes; I got them," said Holmes. He told me I should hear some references to Dr. John Brown of Edinburgh in his lecture; also some thoughts he had taken from Dr. Brown's fine essay on Locke and Sydenham. "But, you see," he added, with a smile, "I always tell when I steal anything!"

Near us, under one of the lofty windows, two men were standing whom I would have travelled many a league to meet. One of them was

Professor Louis Agassiz — big, massive, genial-looking; the rich healthy colour on his broad face still telling of the Old World from which he came — altogether a man who, but for his dark, keen eyes, would look more like a jovial English squire than a devotee of science. Beside him stood a man of strangely different build — a gaunt, long-limbed man, dressed in a high-collared surtout — his piquant New England face peering down over the old-fashioned black kerchief that swathed his long, thin neck. It was Emerson, the glorious transcendentalist of Concord. He stood in an easy, contemplative attitude, with his hands loosely folded in front, and his head slightly inclined. He has the queerest New England face, with thin features, prominent hatchet nose, and a smile of childlike sweetness and simplicity arching the face, and drawing deep curves down the cheek. Eyes, too, full of sparkling geniality, and yet in a moment turning cold, clear, and searching like the eyes of a god. I remember, when introduced to him, how kindly he took my hand, and with that smile still upon his face, peered deep with those calm blue eyes into mine.

When the hour arrived we went into the lecture room. Let me try to bring up the scene again. The room is crowded to the door — so crowded that many of the students have to sit on the steps leading up between the sections of concentric seats, and stand crushed three or four deep in the passages along the walls. What a sea of pale faces, and dark, thoughtful eyes!

Holmes, Emerson, and Agassiz are cheered loudly as they enter and take their seats. The Principal opens proceedings with a short prayer — the audience remaining seated. Dr. Holmes now gets up, steps forward to the high desk amidst loud cheers, puts his eye-glasses across his nose, arranges his manuscript, and without any prelude begins. The little man, in his dress coat, stands very straight, a little stiff about the neck, as if he feels that he cannot afford to lose anything of his stature. He reads with a sharp, percussive articulation, is very deliberate and formal at first, but becomes more animated as he goes on. He would even gesticulate if the desk were not so high, for you see the arm that lies on the desk beside his manuscript giving a nervous quiver at emphatic points. The subject of his lecture is the spirit in which medical students should go into their work — now as students, afterwards as practitioners. He warns them against looking on it as a mere lucrative employment. "Don't be like the man who said, 'I suppose I *must* go and earn that d —— d guinea!'" He enlivens his lecture with numerous jokes and brilliant sallies of wit, and at every point hitches up his head, looks through his glasses at his audience as he finishes his sentence, and then shuts his mouth pertly with his under lip, as if he said, "There, laugh at that!"

Emerson sits listening, with his arms folded loosely on his breast — that queer smile of his effervescing at every joke into a silent laugh, that runs up into his eyes and quivers at the corners of his eyebrows, like sunlight in the woods. Beside him sits Agassiz, leaning easily back in his chair, trifling with the thick watchguard that glitters on his capacious white waistcoat, and looking like a man who has just had dinner, and is disposed to take a pleasant view of things.

Holmes is becoming more animated. His arm is in motion now, indulging in mild movements toward the desk, as if he meant to kill a fly, but always repents and doesn't. He shows less mercy on the persons and opinions that he has occasion to criticize. He comes down sharply on "the quacks, with or without diplomas, who think that the chief end of man is to support the apothecary." He has a passing hit at Carlyle's "Shooting Niagara," and his discovery of the legitimate successor of Jesus Christ in the drill-sergeant. He has also a fling at Dr. Cumming, of London, and "his prediction that the world is coming to an end next year or next week, weather permitting, but very sure that the weather will be unpropitious."

The lecture lasted about an hour, and at its close was applauded again and again — Holmes being a great favourite with the students. I met him afterward at a dinner given to Longfellow and his literary friends, in congratulation on the completion of the poet's translation of Dante; and hoped there to enjoy one of the Autocrat's after-dinner speeches, which are said to be amongst his most brilliant performances. Longfellow, however, unlike most Americans, shrinks from any kind of public speaking himself, and Mr. Fields came round at dessert to inform us that Longfellow had declared, that if he had to make a speech he should be in torment all the evening and lose the enjoyment of his dinner. It had, therefore, been resolved that there should be no speeches: so Holmes' power as an *improvisatore* had no opportunity for exercising itself that night.

David Macrae, *The Americans at Home: Pen-and-Ink Sketches of American Men, Manners, and Institutions* (Edinburgh, 1870).

Henry James

VERENA'S GUIDED TOUR

(1886)

If Henry James could be said to have had an American home it was certainly Cambridge. Brought up in "deliberate cosmopolitanism," he did not take a formal college course but attended the Harvard Law School, beginning in 1862, and in Cambridge came under the influence of Norton and Howells. It was in Cambridge that he began his role as a spectator of life, about 1866. His novel, The Bostonians, *written in England, is among the best and most ambitious of his early books. It thoroughly satirizes the cause of Feminism and makes fun of reformers and philanthropists. Unpopular when first published because of its realistic treatment of polite*

*society, it has since received more favorable critical appraisal. In the tour
of the Harvard Yard the protagonists are Verena Tarrant (convinced disciple of the Feminist leader, Olive Chancellor) and Basil Ransom, a lank,
good-humored Mississippian who is James's satiric foil throughout this
scene.*

THEY presently reached the irregular group of heterogeneous buildings —
chapels, dormitories, libraries, halls, which, scattered among slender trees,
over a space reserved by means of a low rustic fence, rather than en-
closed (for Harvard knows nothing either of the jealousy or the dignity
of high walls and guarded gateways), constitutes the great university of
Massachusetts. The yard, or college-precinct, is traversed by a number
of straight little paths, over which, at certain hours of the day, a thousand undergraduates, with books under their arm and youth in their
step, flit from one school to another. Verena Tarrant knew her way round,
as she said to her companion; it was not the first time she had taken an
admiring visitor to see the local monuments. Basil Ransom, walking with
her from point to point, admired them all, and thought several of them
exceedingly quaint and venerable. The rectangular structures of old red
brick especially gratified his eye; the afternoon sun was yellow on their
homely faces; their windows showed a peep of flowerpots and bright-
coloured curtains; they wore an expression of scholastic quietude, and
exhaled for the young Mississippian a tradition, an antiquity. "This is the
place where I ought to have been," he said to his charming guide. "I
should have had a good time if I had been able to study here."

"Yes; I presume you feel yourself drawn to any place where ancient
prejudices are garnered up," she answered, not without archness. "I know
by the stand you take about our cause that you share the superstitions
of the old bookmen. You ought to have been at one of those really mediaeval universities that we saw on the other side, at Oxford, or Göttingen, or
Padua. You would have been in perfect sympathy with their spirit."

"Well, I don't know much about those old haunts," Ransom rejoined.
"I reckon this is good enough for me. And then it would have had the
advantage that your residence isn't far, you know."

"Oh, I guess we shouldn't have seen you much at my residence! As
you live in New York, you come, but here you wouldn't; that is always
the way." With this light philosophy Verena beguiled the transit to the
library, into which she introduced her companion with the air of a
person familiar with the sanctified spot. This edifice, a diminished copy
of the chapel at King's College, at the greater Cambridge, is a rich and
impressive institution; and as he stood there, in the bright, heated stillness, which seemed suffused with the odour of old print and old bindings,
and looked up into the high, light vaults that hung over quiet book-
laden galleries, alcoves and tables, and glazed cases where rarer

treasures gleamed more vaguely, over busts of benefactors and portraits of worthies, bowed heads of working students and the gentle creak of passing messengers — as he took possession, in a comprehensive glance, of the wealth and wisdom of the place, he felt more than ever the soreness of an opportunity missed; but he abstained from expressing it (it was too deep for that), and in a moment Verena had introduced him to a young lady, a friend of hers, who, as she explained, was working on the catalogue, and whom she had asked for on entering the library, at a desk where another young lady was occupied. Miss Catching, the first-mentioned young lady, presented herself with promptness, offered Verena a low-toned but appreciative greeting, and, after a little, undertook to explain to Ransom the mysteries of the catalogue, which consisted of a myriad little cards, disposed alphabetically in immense chests of drawers. Ransom was deeply interested, and as, with Verena, he followed Miss Catching about (she was so good as to show them the establishment in all its ramifications), he considered with attention the young lady's fair ringlets and refined, anxious expression, saying to himself that this was in the highest degree a New England type. Verena found an opportunity to mention to him that she was wrapped up in the cause, and there was a moment during which he was afraid that his companion would expose him to her as one of its traducers; but there was that in Miss Catching's manner (and in the influence of the lofty halls) which deprecated loud pleasantry, and seemed to say, moreover, that if she were treated to such a revelation she should not know under what letter to range it.

"Now there is one place where perhaps it would be indelicate to take a Mississippian," Verena said, after this episode. "I mean the great place that towers above the others — that big building with the beautiful pinnacles, which you see from every point." But Basil Ransom had heard of the great Memorial Hall; he knew what memories it enshrined, and the worst that he should have to suffer there; and the ornate, over-topping structure, which was the finest piece of architecture he had ever seen, had moreover solicited his enlarged curiosity for the last half-hour. He thought there was rather too much brick about it, but it was buttressed, cloistered, turreted, dedicated, superscribed, as he had never seen anything; though it didn't look old, it looked significant; it covered a large area, and it sprang majestic into the winter air. It was detached from the rest of the collegiate group, and stood in a grassy triangle of its own. As he approached it with Verena she suddenly stopped, to decline responsibility. "Now mind, if you don't like what's inside, it isn't my fault."

He looked at her an instant, smiling. "Is there anything against Mississippi?"

"Well, no, I don't think she is mentioned. But there is great praise of our young men in the war."

"It says they were brave, I suppose."

"Yes, it says so in Latin."

"Well, so they were — I know something about that," Basil Ransom said. "I must be brave enough to face them — it isn't the first time." And they went up the low steps and passed into the tall doors. The Memorial Hall of Harvard consists of three main divisions: one of them a theatre, for academic ceremonies; another a vast refectory, covered with a timbered roof, hung about with portraits and lighted by stained windows, like the halls of the colleges of Oxford; and the third, the most interesting, a chamber high, dim, and severe, consecrated to the sons of the university who fell in the long Civil War. Ransom and his companion wandered from one part of the building to another, and stayed their steps at several impressive points; but they lingered longest in the presence of the white, ranged tablets, each of which, in its proud, sad clearness, is inscribed with the name of a student-soldier. The effect of the place is singularly noble and solemn, and it is impossible to feel it without a lifting of the heart. It stands there for duty and honour, it speaks of sacrifice and example, seems a kind of temple to youth, manhood, generosity. Most of them were young, all were in their prime, and all of them had fallen; this simple idea hovers before the visitor and makes him read with tenderness each name and place — names often without other history, and forgotten Southern battles. For Ransom these things were not a challenge nor a taunt; they touched him with respect, with the sentiment of beauty. He was capable of being a generous foeman, and he forgot, now, the whole question of sides and parties; the simple emotion of the old fighting-time came back to him, and the monument around him seemed an embodiment of that memory; it arched over friends as well as enemies, the victims of defeat as well as the sons of triumph.

"It is very beautiful — but I think it is very dreadful!" This remark, from Verena, called him back to the present. "It's a real sin to put up such a building, just to glorify a lot of bloodshed. If it wasn't so majestic, I would have it pulled down."

"That is delightful feminine logic!" Ransom answered. "If, when women have the conduct of affairs, they fight as well as they reason, surely for them too we shall have to set up memorials."

Henry James, *The Bostonians* (London and New York, 1886).

Paul Bourget

A FEARFUL GAME

(1893)

*The novelist, poet, and critic Paul Bourget (1852–1935) toured the United
States during the year 1893–94 and recorded some of his impressions in
a series of articles for James Gordon Bennett, editor of the New York
Herald. In 1895 Bourget's material was assembled in a book called
Outre-Mer: Impressions of America. Because of his easy generalizations
and exaggeration Bourget, a member of the French Academy, was severely
criticized, but his insight into the American character is sharp, nevertheless. Bourget does not apparently entirely understand the game of football
as played in 1893, but there is no doubt that he put his finger on the bad
points of the game which caused its temporary banishment at many colleges thirteen years later. The game described by Bourget was played on
Jarvis Field, November 30, 1893, and resulted in a 26–4 victory for
Harvard.*

HAVING exaggerated his nervous and voluntary tension to the pitch of
abuse, almost to vice, it is impossible that the American should amuse
himself as we Latins do, who hardly conceive of pleasure without a
certain relaxation of the senses, mingled with softness and luxury . . .
[The Americans'] pleasures seem, in fact, to imply, like their ideas and
their labors, something unrestrained and immoderate, a very vigorous
excitement, always bordering on violence, or, rather, on roughness and
restlessness. Even in his diversions the American is too active and too
self-willed. Unlike the Latin, who amuses himself by relaxation, he
amuses himself by intensity, and this is the case whatever be the nature
of his amusements, for he has very coarse and very refined ones. But a
few sketches from nature will explain better than all the theories that
kind of nervousness, and, as it were, fitful sharpness in amusement, if we
can here use that word which is synonymous with two of the least
American things in the world, — unconstraint and repose.

The most vehement of those pleasures and the most deeply national
are those of sport. Interpret the word in its true sense, and you will find
in it nothing of the meaning which we French attach to it, who have
softened the term in adopting it, and who make it consist above all of
elegance and dexterity. For the American, "sport" has ever in it some
danger, for it does not exist without the conception of contest and
daring. Thus with yachting, which to us means pleasure cruises along
the coasts, means to him voyages around the world, braving the tempests

and the vast solitudes of the Atlantic, or else rivalries of speed in which everything is taken into consideration except human life . . .

Among the distractions of sport, none has been more fashionable for several years past than football. I was present last autumn, in the peaceful and quiet city of Cambridge, at a game between the champions of Harvard College — the "team," as they say here — and the champions of the University of Pennsylvania. I must go back in thought to my journey in Spain to recall a popular fever equal to that which throbbed along the road between Boston and the arena where the match was to take place. The electric cars followed one another at intervals of a minute, filled with passengers, who, seated or standing, or hanging on the steps, crowded, pushed, crushed one another. Although the days of November are cruelly cold under a Massachusetts sky, the place of contest, as at Rome for the gladiatorial combats, was in a sort of open-air enclosure. A stone's throw away from Memorial Hall and the other buildings of the University, wooden stands were erected. On these stands were perhaps fifteen thousand spectators, and in the immense quadrilateral hemmed in by the stands were two teams composed of eleven youths each waiting for the signal to begin.

What a tremor in that crowd, composed not of the lower classes, but of well-to-do people, and how the excitement increased as time went on! All held in their hands small, red flags and wore tufts of red flowers. Crimson is the color of the Harvard boys. Although a movement of feverish excitement ran through this crowd, it was not enough for the enthusiasts of the game. Propagators of enthusiasm, students with unbearded, deeply-lined faces, passed between the benches and still further increased the ardor of the public by uttering the war-cry of the University, the "Rah! rah! rah!" thrice repeated, which terminates in the frenzied call, "Haaar-vard." The partisans of the "Pennsy's" replied by a similar cry, and in the distance, above the palings of the enclosure, we could see clusters of other spectators, too poor to pay the entrance fee, who had climbed into the branches of the leafless trees, their faces outlined against the autumn sky with the daintiness of the pale heads in Japanese painted fans.

The signal is given and the play begins. It is a fearful game, which by itself would suffice to indicate the differences between the Anglo-Saxon and the Latin world — a game of young bull-dogs brought up to bite, to rush upon the quarry; the game of a race made for wild attack, for violent defence, for implacable conquests and desperate struggles. With their leather vests, with the Harvard sleeves of red cloth, and the Pennsylvania blue and white vests and sleeves, so soon to be torn — with the leather gaiters to protect their shins, with their great shoes and their long hair floating around their pale and flushed faces, these scholarly athletes are at once admirable and frightful to see when once the demon of contest has entered into them. At each extremity of the field is a goal, representing, at the right end one of the teams, at the left the other. The entire object is to throw an enormous leather ball, which the champion of one or the other side holds in turn. It is in waiting for this throw that all the excitement of this almost ferocious amusement is concentrated. He who holds the ball is there, bent forward, his companions and his adversaries likewise bent down around him in the attitude of beasts of prey about to spring. All of a sudden he runs to throw the ball, or else with a wildly rapid movement he hands it to another, who rushes off with it. All depends on stopping him.

The roughness with which they seize the bearer of the ball is impossible to imagine without having witnessed it. He is grasped by the middle of the body, by the head, by the legs, by the feet. He rolls over and his assailants with him, and as they fight for the ball and the two sides come to the rescue, it becomes a heap of twenty-two bodies tumbling on top of one another, like an inextricable knot of serpents with human heads. This heap writhes on the ground and tugs at itself. One sees faces, hair, backs, or legs appearing in a monstrous and agitated *mêlée*. Then this murderous knot unravels itself and the ball, thrown by the most agile, bounds away and is again followed with the same fury. It continually happens that, after one of those frenzied entanglements, one of the combatants remains on the field motionless, incapable of rising, so much has he been hit, pressed, crushed, thumped.

A doctor whose duty it is to look after the wounded arrives and examines him. You see those skilled hands shaking a foot, a leg, rubbing the sides, washing a face, sponging the blood which streams from the forehead, the eyes, the nose, the mouth. A compassionate comrade assists in the business and takes the head of the fainting champion on his knee. Sometimes the unlucky player must be carried away. More frequently, however, he recovers his senses, stretches himself, rouses up, and ends by scrambling to his feet. He makes a few steps, leaning on the friendly shoulder, and no sooner is he able to walk than the game begins afresh, and he joins in again with a rage doubled by pain and humiliation.

If the roughness of this terrible sport was for the spectators only the occasion of a nervous excitement of a few hours, the young athletes would not give themselves up to it with this enthusiasm which makes them accept the most painful, sometimes the most dangerous of trainings. A mother said to me: "He adores football. He is already captain of his eleven. I should not be anxious if he never played against any but little gentlemen, but they have a mania for playing against common people. It is in such struggles that dangerous accidents are always to be feared."

"What will you have?" replied one of the professors of Harvard. "In the frenzy of the game they deal each other some hard blows, it is true, and it is true, above all, that the heroes of matches like that of to-day are victims. The training is too intense. The nervous system cannot bear up against it. But the feats of the champions keep the game fashionable. Hence all the small boys in the remotest parts of America take up this exercise, and thus athletes are formed." He was putting into abstract form that which is the instinct of the American crowd, an instinct which does not reason and which shows itself in very strange ways. During the contest, which I have attempted to describe, I heard a distinguished and refined woman, next to whom I was seated, crying out, "Beauty!" at the sight of rushes that sent five or six boys sprawling on the ground.

No sooner are such matches as these in preparation than the portraits of the various players are in all the papers. The incidents of the game are described in detail with graphic pictures, in order that the comings and goings of the ball may be better followed. Conquerors and conquered are alike interviewed. From a celebrated periodical the other day I cut out an article signed "A Football Scientist," wherein the author sought to show that the right tactics to follow in this game were the same as those used by Napoleon. What can be added to this eulogium, when we know the peculiar position occupied by Napoleon in the imagination of the Yankees?

Paul Bourget, *Outre-Mer: Impressions of America* (New York, 1895).

George Birkbeck Hill

HOW FEW ARE THE SIGNS OF UNIVERSITY LIFE!

(1893)

George Birkbeck Norman Hill (1835–1903), Honorary Fellow of Pembroke College, Oxford, and one of the foremost Johnsonians of his time, visited Cambridge during 1893 and was so taken with Harvard University during his stay that he went home to write a book about the place. Harvard College, by an Oxonian is a rambling, largely factual account of Harvard which both describes the past and contemporary history of the college and summarizes in a pleasant fashion Harvard life of the time. Hill was attracted to Harvard from his first sight of it. In his journal he wrote of the Yard: "There is no quadrangle in Oxford more delightful on a hot summer day. Harvard surely is a College that a man can love."

OF MY first impressions of the undergraduates, I made the following record in my journal: "They are shorter and slighter than our Oxford men, with much less colour; a year or two older, I think, unless the hot climate makes them look older. I do not see so many gross, stupid faces, but, on the other hand, I have not as yet noticed any of those fresh-coloured, pleasant, innocent faces which are so attractive at Oxford." On seeing more of the men, I came to doubt whether in appearance they were older than our undergraduates. Near the end of my residence in Cambridge, I thus sum up my observations:

> How few are the signs here of university life compared with those seen in Oxford! In Oxford, a real town though it is, and not a suburban village like Cambridge, the presence of the students, nevertheless, is much more conspicuous. No one can walk about its streets and roads without noticing the large number of young men — often moving in a long stream — young men, moreover, who, as their very appearance, their dress, their manner of walking, their features show, are not in business. In the afternoon their suit of flannel makes it clear that they are bent on pleasure, or, at all events, on exercise; in the morning and evening the cap and gown indicate the student. The style, the very make of their clothes, are not those of the young business man. Their easy, confident step distinguishes them from the ordinary youth of a town. The separation of the Colleges distributes this life over the city, so that undergraduates and graduates are constantly passing along the streets from College to College, or from College to the University buildings. The Parks, the upper river, the lower river, and the Cherwell increase this diffusion. It is increased, moreover, by the Englishman's love of walking and riding.

In the American Cambridge there is very little of this open and palpable university life. The College buildings, which are numerous, are mostly in one enclosure, the Yard. Those which are not there — the more modern additions — are separated from them only by a road. The students, therefore, in going to and from lectures, do not cross the town. Outside the Yard I have never seen them moving in a stream, except on the days of some great baseball or football match, and then they have but a few yards to traverse. Beyond the immediate surroundings of the College they are scarcely noticeable. A stranger, whose walks did not lead him past the Yard, might for some time live within a quarter of a mile of the College, without discovering that he was in a University town. Boston attracts the students in large numbers, and to Boston they go, not on foot but on the tram-cars. In their dress, their general appearance, their gait, I discover little of the undergraduate. In England and Germany this clan does not hide itself. An Oxford man lets the world know that he is an Oxford man. His self-satisfaction gives an assurance, sometimes even a kind of swagger, to his whole behaviour. He walks along the High Street as if it belonged, not to the Corporation, but to himself. His apparel too oft proclaims the *man*. There is nothing of this here. The Harvard undergraduate talks of himself and his comrades as boys. He has not learnt to swagger. Probably it takes many years at a great English public school to acquire the true manner. Like the art of beating the French at Waterloo, it is best learnt on the Playing Fields of Eton. His dress, too, is much less costly and showy; for the most part it is of a dark cloth. I notice none of those waistcoats with which an Oxford man dazzles the poorer scholars of his college and startles his friends at home. The ordinary Harvard man might have stepped out of a city office or a Normal School for Teachers. He belongs to a poorer class. Clothing, moreover, is so expensive that many have to be content with one suit a year. An undergraduate who had visited Europe in the previous Long Vacation, told me that the clothes he was wearing, for which he had paid three pounds in England, in Cambridge would have cost him six. Every afternoon there are no doubt men to be seen in the dress of young athletes; but though there is the greatest possible interest taken in the yearly boat-race with Yale, and in the baseball and football matches, nevertheless, those who share in these sports are far fewer than we should find in an English university. It is, I am sure, a picked few rather than the mass of men who play. Nowhere is there such a sight as is to be seen any afternoon at Oxford on the river and in the Parks on the days when there is no great race or match. The build of the men proves, moreover, that they have not gone through that long course of rough games which has formed the active and powerful frames of the young English under-graduates. I am told, however, that during the winter half of the year, North Avenue is a training-ground for runners, who in the afternoon and evening sweep along the "sidewalks," as if the smooth pavement had been laid down for them, and not for quiet, decent Christians. A noble gymnasium, moreover, has been lately built, which is much frequented. "The fever of renown," gained not by the brain, but by the body, is spreading rapidly through the veins of young America. By its "strong contagion" Harvard has been badly caught. One of my friends, whose three sons have recently graduated, lamented to me the excessive interest they all took in the contests of athletes. How different it was when he was young! In those happy days his brother, when home from College, used to talk of books. His sons' talk was of running and jumping, of rowing, baseball, and football. The change is great, indeed, since the time when Dr. Wendell Holmes lamented the general indifference of the youth of New England to bodily exercise . . .

Harvard has not been quite free from a certain kind of affectation which is only too common in the English Universities, but which is known in America as "Harvard indifference." It was not from their forefathers that the New Englanders got this poor quality. It was never carried across the sea in the ships of the early settlers. It is the very opposite of that stubborn strength of character, and of that burning zeal which sent them to the wilderness, and their descendants, "the embattled farmers," to Concord, Lexington, and Bunker Hill. It is the contempt for all that eagerness of heart and thought and life which inspires "the young enthusiast" when first "he quits his ease for fame." "I do not love a man," said Goldsmith, "who is zealous for nothing." These lovers of indifference he would have shunned. Long indulged, it becomes ingrained in the character. It is a great maker of bad citizens. In a young man it almost always begins with affectation, and happily often dies an early death. It is killed by his nobler qualities, or by some strong influence from without.

More than sixty years ago Channing rebuked it. When the Revolution of 1830 broke out in France, he was

> astonished that the freemen of America, especially the young, should be so moderate in their expressions of joy. He went back in memory to his boyish days, when the Cambridge collegians had processions, speeches, and bonfires. Now all was still. One evening a graduate called upon him. "Well, Mr. ——," said he, "are you too so old and so wise, like the young men at Harvard, as to have no foolish enthusiasm to throw away upon the heroes of the Polytechnic School?" "Sir," answered ——, "you seem to me to be the only young man I know." "Always young for liberty, I trust," replied Dr. Channing with a bright smile and a ringing tone, as he pressed him warmly by the hand.

Thirty years had to pass, and then this Harvard indifference was swept away by the Southern revolt. In the presence of that dreadful strife, indifference would no longer have been ridiculous, it would have become hateful.

Professor Goodwin thinks that it was by "the equable pressure" of a revised system of instruction and examination that "the older enthusiasm" of the place was mainly repressed, and this indifference was encouraged. Free play was no longer given to the student's mind. He was forced to attain to mediocrity in many subjects, and was not encouraged, and was scarcely allowed to secure excellence in one or two. There had been students who had refused to cramp themselves in the narrowness of the prescribed course. Lowell read widely, and was rusticated in consequence. Motley escaped this disgrace, but not the reproach of his tutor, who one day "remonstrated with him upon the heaps of novels upon his table. 'Yes,' said Motley, 'I am reading historically, and have come to the novels of the nineteenth century. Taken in the lump, they are very hard reading.'" At the present day the author of *The Biglow Papers* and the historian of the Dutch Republic could have indulged their tastes to the full. This "Harvard indifference" cannot surely long survive the great reforms in education which have already done so much to transform the University from a mere place of teaching to a place of learning.

There is another fault for which Harvard men are reproached by their rivals and enemies. They are distinguished, it is said, by a certain priggishness, a certain consciousness too openly shown that they are not only the salt, but the superfine salt, of the earth — a priggishness and a self-consciousness which, it is said, sometimes cling to them throughout life. What Boston is to Massachusetts, what Massachusetts is to New England, what New England is to the United States, what the United States are to the Universe, that Harvard is to Boston. Among "the five points of Massachusetts decency" laid down by Wendell Phillips, to be a graduate of Harvard College holds the second place. The "old Harvard spirit" on which they prided themselves, was thought by some to be the spirit of a gentleman carried to preciseness. They are fond of telling a story of a man who had twin sons, one of whom he sent to Harvard, and the other to Yale. Before they entered College, no one, not even their father, could tell them apart; but after graduation the difference was plain. One was a Harvard gentleman, the other a Yale *tough*. Wealth and family are said to count for much at Harvard. The New Englander is as proud of his pedigree, and often with as much reason, as any English nobleman or squire. A Bachelor of Arts of Yale, who recently spent two years at Harvard, the first as a graduate-student, and the second as an instructor, — evidently a fair-minded man, — writes:

> I have lived long enough at Yale to know that Yale students are not commonly ruffians; and I have seen enough of Harvard to know that Harvard students are not as a class snobs. Yet there is a slight element of truth even in these gross caricatures; it is the difference between "Fair" Harvard and "Dear Old" Yale. The Harvard atmosphere occasionally produces "an affectioned ass," and the Yale spirit sometimes turns out an insolent rowdy.

I have been told by one familiar with the Continental Universities that, measured by their standard, the Harvard students are deficient in those graces which were so dear to Lord Chesterfield's heart. In formal politeness, in the lesser morals, the students in their behaviour towards a Professor fall short of the standard which is observed in Germany and France in their behaviour towards each other. Nevertheless, beneath this somewhat unpolished outside much real kindness lies hidden. A young Professor, who had but recently joined the University, told me that in the midst of the work of his first term he had been struck down by diphtheria. His pupils not only every day sent flowers and fruit, but begged that one of them in turns should always sleep in his house as long as the illness lasted, so that in case of sudden need there might be a swift messenger close at hand to summon the doctor. He had won their hearts, as I learnt from another source, by his courage and his devotion to his work. As soon as he knew the nature of his illness, he had sent them word that he was attacked by a dangerous malady, which would very likely carry him off; but that he hoped that they would go on with the experiments on which he had left them engaged. To such students as these might be applied Goldsmith's saying about Johnson: "He has nothing of the bear about him but the skin."

Whatever pride of wealth and birth may exist in Harvard or in Yale, no student in either of these great Universities need hang his head for honest poverty. Many of them gain their own living more or less, and gain it by bodily labour.

George Birkbeck Hill, *Harvard College by an Oxonian* (London and New York, 1894).

Rupert Brooke

BOSTON AND HARVARD

(1913)

Rupert Brooke, "young, happy, radiant, extraordinarily endowed and irresistibly attaching" as Henry James called him, wrote this commentary about the Harvard of Commencement Week for the Westminster Gazette during a tour of the United States, Canada, and the South Seas in 1913. It was published posthumously as one of fifteen sketches called Letters from America, edited by Brooke's friend, Edward Marsh, with a note on Brooke by James who first met "the charmed commentator" just before the latter won a Fellowship from King's College in 1909. Brooke died of blood poisoning on a French hospital ship to which he had been transferred while on his way with his contingent to the Dardanelles campaign.

IT IS RIGHT to leave Boston late in a summer afternoon, and by sea. Naval departure is always the better. A train snatches you, hot, dusty, and smoky, with an irritated hurry out of the back parts of a town. The last glimpse of a place you may have grown to like or love is, ignobly, interminable rows of the bedroom-windows in mean streets, a few hovels, some cinder-heaps, and a factory chimney. As like as not, you are reft from a last wave to the city's unresponsive and dingy back by the roar and suffocation of a tunnel. By sea one takes a gracefuller, more satisfactory farewell.

Boston puts on her best appearance to watch our boat go out for New York. The harbour was bright with sunlight and blue water and little white sails and there wasn't more than the faintest smell of tea. The city sat primly on her little hills, decorous, civilised, European-looking. It is homely after New York. The Boston crowd is curiously English. They have nice eighteenth-century houses there, and ivy grows on the buildings. And they are hospitable. All Americans are hospitable; but they haven't *quite* time in New York to practise the art so perfectly as the Bostonians. It is a lovely art . . . But Boston also makes you feel at home without meaning to. A delicious ancient Toryism is to be found here. "What is wrong with America," a middle-aged lady told me, "is this *Democracy*. They ought to take the votes away from these people, who don't know how to use them, and give them only to *us*, the Educated." My heart leapt the Atlantic, and was in a Cathedral or University town of South England.

Yet Boston is alive. It sits, in comfortable middle-age, on the ruins of its glory. But it is not buried beneath them. It used to lead America in Literature, Thought, Art, everything. The years have passed. It is remarkable how nearly now Boston is to New York what Munich is to Berlin. Boston and Munich were the leaders forty years ago. They can't quite make out that they aren't now. It is too incredible that Art should leave her goose-feather bed and run away to the raggle-taggle business-men. And certainly, if Berlin and New York are more "live," Boston and Munich are more themselves, less feverishly imitations of Paris. But the undisputed palm is there no more; and its absence is felt.

But I had little time to taste Boston itself. I was lured across the river to a place called Cambridge, where is the University of Harvard. Harvard is the Oxford and Cambridge of America, they claim. She has moulded the nation's leaders and uttered its ideals. Harvard, Boston, New England, it is impossible to say how much they are interwoven, and how they have influenced America. I saw Harvard in "Commencement," which is Eights Week and May Week, the festive winding-up of the year, a time of parties and of valedictions. One of the great events of Commencement, and of the year, is the Harvard-Yale baseball match. To this I went, excited at the prospect of my first sight of a "ball game," and my mind vaguely reminiscent of the indolent, decorous, upper-class crowd, the sunlit spaces, the dignified ritual, and white-flanneled grace of Lord's at the 'Varsity cricket match. The crowd was gay, and not very large. We sat in wooden stands, which were placed in the shape of a large V. As all the hitting which counts in baseball takes place well in front of the wicket, so to speak, the spectators have the game right under their noses; the striker stands in the angle of the V and plays outwards. The field was a vast place, partly stubbly grass, partly worn and patchy, like a parade-ground. Beyond it lay the river; beyond that the town of Cambridge and the University buildings. Around me were undergraduates, with their mothers and sisters. "Cambridge!" . . . but there entered to us, across the field, a troop of several hundred men, all dressed in striped shirts of the same hue and pattern, and headed by a vast banner which informed the world that they were the graduates of 1910, celebrating their triennial. In military formation they moved across the plain towards us, led by a band, ceaselessly vociferating, and raising their straw hats in unison to mark the time. There followed the class of 1907, attired as sailors; 1903, the decennial class, with some samples of their male children marching with them, and a banner inscribed "515 Others. No Race Suicide"; 1898, carefully arranged in an H-shaped formation, dancing along to their music with a slow polka-step, each with his hands on the shoulders of the man in front, and at the head of all their leader, dancing backwards in perfect time, marshalling them; 1888, middle-aged men, again with some children, and a Highland regiment playing the bagpipes.

When these had passed to the seats allotted for them, I had time to observe the players, who were practising about the ground, and I was shocked. They wear dust-coloured shirts and dingy knickerbockers, fastened under the knee, and heavy boots. They strike the English eye as being attired for football, or a gladiatorial combat, rather than a summer game. The very close-fitting caps, with large peaks, give them picturesquely the appearance of hooligans. Baseball is a good game to watch, and in outline easy to understand, as it is merely glorified rounders. A cricketer is fascinated by their rapidity and skill in catching and throwing. There is excitement in the game, but little beauty except in the long-limbed "pitcher," whose duty it is to hurl the ball rather further than the length of the cricket-pitch, as bewilderingly as possible. In his efforts to combine speed, mystery, and curve, he gets into attitudes of a very novel and fantastic, but quite obvious, beauty. M. Nijinsky would find them repay study.

One queer feature of this sport is that unoccupied members of the batting side, fielders, and even spectators, are accustomed to join in vocally. You have the spectacle of the representatives of the universities endeavoring to frustrate or unnerve their opponents, at moments of excitement, by cries of derision and mockery, or heartening their own supporters and performers with exclamations of "Now, Joe!" or "He's got them!" or "He's the boy!" At the crises in the fortunes of the game, the spectators take a collective and important part. The Athletic Committee appoints a "cheer-leader" for the occasion. Every five or ten minutes this gentleman, a big, fine figure in white, springs out from his seat at the foot of the stands, addresses the multitude through a megaphone with a "One! Two! Three!" hurls it aside, and, with a wild flinging and swinging of his body and arms, conducts ten thousand voices in the Harvard yell. That over, the game proceeds, and the cheer-leader sits quietly waiting for the next moment of peril or triumph. I shall not easily forget that figure, bright in the sunshine, conducting with his whole body, passionate, possessed by a demon, bounding in the frenzy of his inspiration from side to side, contorted, rhythmic, ecstatic. It seemed so wonderfully American, in its combination of entire wildness and entire regulation, with the whole just a trifle fantastic. Completely friendly and befriended as I was, I couldn't help feeling at those moments very alien and very, very old — even more so than after the protracted game had ended in a victory for Harvard, when the dusty plain was filled with groups and lines of men dancing in solemn harmony, and a shouting crowd, broken by occasional individuals who could find some little eminence to lead a Harvard yell from, and who conducted the bystanders, and then vanished, and the crowd swirled on again.

Different enough was the scene the next day, when all Harvard men who were up for Commencement assembled and, arranged by years, marched round the yard. Class by class they paraded, beginning with veterans of the 'fifties, down to the class of 1912. I wonder if English nerves could stand it. It seems to bring the passage of time so very presently and vividly to the mind. To see, with such emphatic regularity, one's coevals changing in figure, and diminishing in number, summer after summer! . . . Perhaps it is nobler, this deliberate viewing of one-self as part of the stream. To the spectator, certainly, the flow and transiency become apparent and poignant. In five minutes fifty years of America, of so much of America, go past one. The shape of the bodies, apart from the effects of age, the lines of the faces, the ways of wearing hair and beard and moustaches, all these change a little, decade by decade, before your eyes. And through the whole appearance runs some continuity, which is Harvard.

The orderly progression of the years was unbroken, except at one point. There was one gap, large and arresting. Though all years were represented, there seemed to be nobody in the procession between fifty and sixty. I asked a Harvard friend the reason. "The War," he said. He told me there had always been that gap. Those who were old enough to be conscious of the war had lost a big piece of their lives. With their successors a new America began. I don't know how true it is. Certainly, the dates worked out right. And I met an American on a boat who had been a child in one of the neutral States. He used to watch the regiments forming in the main street of his town, marching out, some north and some south. He said it felt as though pieces of his body were being torn in different directions. And he was only nine.

The procession filed in to an open court, to hear the speeches of the recipients of honorary degrees, and the President's annual statement. There was still, in every sense, a solemn atmosphere. The President's speech floated out into the great open space; fragments of it were blown to one's ears concerning deaths, and the spirit of the place, and a detailed account of the money given during the year. Eleven hundred thousand dollars in all — a record, or nearly a record. We roared applause. The American universities appear still to dream of the things of this world. They keep putting up the most wonderful and expensive buildings. But they do not pay their teachers well.

Yet Harvard is a spirit, a way of looking at things, austerely refined, gently moral, kindly. The perception of it grows on the foreigner. Its charm is so deliciously old in this land, so deliciously young compared with the lovely frowst of Oxford and Cambridge. You see it in temperament, the charm of simplicity and good-heartedness and culture; in the Harvard undergraduate, who is a boy, while his English contemporary is either a young man or a schoolboy, less pleasant stages; and in the old Bostonian who heard, and still hears, the lectures of Dickens and Thackeray. Class Day brings so many of that older generation together. They reveal what Harvard, what Boston, was. There is something terrifying in the completeness of their lives and their civilisation. They are like a company of dons whose studies are of a remote and finished world. But the subject of their scholarship is the Victorian age, and especially Victorian England. Hence their liveliness and certainty, greater than men can reach who are concerned with the dubieties and changes of incomplete things. Hence the wit, the stock of excellent stories, the wrinkled wisdom and mirth of the type. They are the flower of a civilisation, its ripest critics and final judges. Carlyle and Emerson are their greatest living heroes. One of them bent the kindliness and alert interest of his eighty years upon me. "So you come from Rugby," he said. "Tell me, do you know that curious creature, Matthew Arnold?" I couldn't bring myself to tell him that, even in Rugby, we had forgiven that brilliant youth his iconoclastic tendencies some time since, and that, as a matter of fact, he had died when I was eight months old.

DATE DUE

WITHDRAWN

DEMCO 38-296

Please remember that this is a library book,
and that it belongs only temporarily to each
person who uses it. Be considerate. Do
not write in this, or any, library book.